U0760145

扫描二维码获取音频资料

老外看福建

[中英对照]

【美】潘维廉 著
潘文功等 译

厦门大学出版社
XIAMEN UNIVERSITY PRESS

Have fun in Fujian!

Meet Koxinga – last defender of the Ming

Get a kick out of S.Shaolin Kung Fu

Cuddle with planet's longest snakes (10meter pythoms)

Learn how China's largest Taoist statue can help you live to be 120!

Discover why Hui'an Maidens' bare their bellies!

Stay overnight in a well-rounded Hakka earthen castle

Give traditional Zhangzhou handpuppets a hand

Play with Fujian kitty cats! (Meihua Mtn's Amoy Tigers)

Make a pilgrimage to Ninghua
(Home of the Hakka)

Marvel at ancient biological engineering on
the world's longest bridge of the Middle Ages!

Visit the Planet's last temple to
the Persian Prophet Mani

Explore 2000-year-old ruins of the
Min Kingdom (Wuyi)

Enjoy ancient wooden
covered bridges

Frolic in China's largest
waterfalls complex (9 Dragon Falls)

More Fun in Fujian!

Visit Mawei – Cradle of Chinese
(Since 200 B.C.!)

Visit the ***real*** "Water World!"

Tour Gulangyu Islet's
international architecture

Smell the roses in
Zhangzhou
"City of Flowers"

Delight in China's largest
piano museum(Gulangyu
"Isle of Music")

Discover why the
Buddha jumps the wall!

佛跳牆

Visit start of "Long March"
(and "Short April")

Visit the Carp Cemetery (locals have worshipped carp 800 years!)

Ascend a Stone-age escalator?

Zhouning Highland Tea

Let Wuyi's Wu Guangmin enlighten you on Big Red Robe--
(world's most expensive tea at over 34,000 USD per ounce!)

Or...enjoy an elegant Minnan Tea Ceremony
(and fine Anxi tea,which even we mortals can afford!)

Visit China's 1st Protestant Church(1848,in Xiamen)

Study Chinese in Xiamen Univ. China's most beautiful campus!

Learn about famous scholars like Zhuxi – founder of neoConfucianism

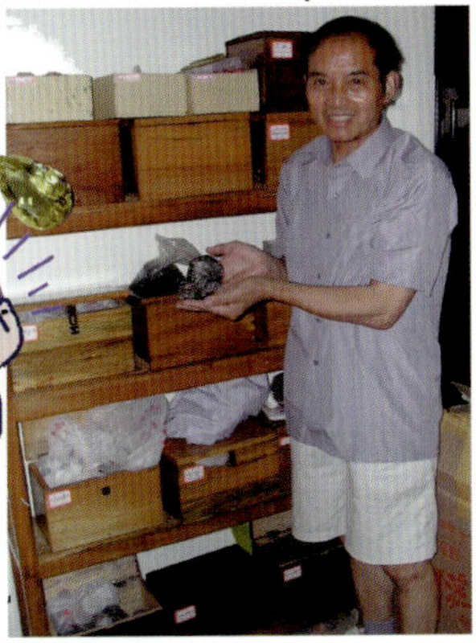

Seek your fortune in Mingxi – China's 4th largest gem bed.

Try to rouse China's largest sleeping Buddha! (Sanming's "god of xiuxi?")

Feast on Shaxian cuisine Famous throughout S.E. Asia

Find out who is pulling strings in Quanzhou – home of Chinese Mationettes

Learn how egrets battled snakes for Xiamen!

Try to find your way in Chongwu – one of China's few remaining walled cities

Spend all your money saving money in Dehua – one of China's 4 ancient porcelain capitals

Discover that Chinese ***do*** use foks!

Learn to walk on water! (Baishuiyang)

Visit "Potala Palace on the Sea"

Anxi has a "Potala Palace" as well

Learn how a Fujianese lady built ancient Mulan Dam

Discover how little Miss Mo became the sea goddess

Ponder the purposes of the "Stone Bamboo Shoot" (fertility totem)

Visit Putian's famous
S.Shaolin Kung Fu temple

Raft down 9-Bend Stream in Wuyi
(UNESCO World-Heritage Site)

Savor surrealistic scenery(Mt. Taimu)

Bed down in the Xianyou temple
where "Dream Praying" began

Would Pandas get a square
meal from Wuyi's famous
"square bamboo"?

序

福建广播影视集团新闻中心英语新闻节目邀请厦门大学管理学院潘维廉博士合作拍摄的60集中英文双语电视系列报道“老外看福建”中英文双语对照读物,在厦门大学出版社的帮助与支持下,与广大英语学习者、爱好者见面了。外语教学专家说,它是一本非常“本土”的中英对照读物,配上光盘,非常适合高一年级以上学生、大中专生以及广大外宣、外事、旅游工作者作为听说、阅读教材使用,可以帮助他们用地道的英语,自豪地在外国朋友面前宣传福建、推介福建。在此,我谨代表福建广播影视集团对这本中英文双语对照读物及其配套光盘的出版表示祝贺。

长期以来,我国对外宣传以普通话为主,对象主要是台、港、澳同胞和海外华侨、华人。在新闻,特别是广播电视新闻日益国际化的今天,要使我们的对外宣传报道与我国的国际地位相称,让世界听到中国的声音,就必须大力发展外语、特别是事实上已经成为国际语言的英语的新闻报道。福建省是我国改革开放的前沿省份,近年来,对外经贸合作与交流、交往日趋活跃。尽管目前在闽长期居住的外籍人士还不太多,但我们依然投入人力、物力、财力,在卫视东南台开设《英语新闻》节目,我们考虑得更多的是福建省的对外开放形象。

立足本地,播报福建本土新闻,《福建英语新闻》节目开播三年来较为全面地播报福建省重要的时政、经贸活动和文化生活等领域的新闻、资讯,制作了上万分钟的英语新闻节目,并把所有的英文稿件发布在网站上,供热心观众和英语学习者阅读、使用。2002—2003年,节目制作人员连续两年,冒着盛夏的酷暑,与厦门大学MBA中心的潘维廉博士合作,拍摄了中英文双语大型系列报道“老外看福建”,用外籍友好人士的视角,对外宣传福建。

今年2月,福建省广播影视集团正式挂牌成立。这是一个以广播、电视、电影、传输网络、报刊出版和互联网站宣传为主业,兼营科技开发、影视艺术、广告经营等其他相关产业的综合性新闻传媒集团。作为党和政府的重要喉舌，我们将始终坚持以宣传为中心，牢牢把握正确的舆论导向，不断提高舆论引导水平。同时，我们还将通过集团化运作，进一步促进生产要素的合理性流动，努力把福建广播影视集团建设成为国内一流水平、与国际发展同步接轨的新型传媒集团，为我省广大人民群众提供更多更好的精神食粮。

福建省广播影视集团董事长

舒　展

2004年8月

主编致辞

2001年12月1日深夜，一档10分钟的“英语新闻”节目开始在福建卫视东南台悄然亮相。细心的观众立即联想到上个世纪90年代初，福建电视台曾经播出过的一个英语专栏，每周一次20分钟的“What's New”。外语界的朋友和媒体同仁经常追问《福建英语新闻》与“What's New”的区别。我们总会耐心解释说《福建英语新闻》是新闻节目，是一档用英语宣传福建的新闻节目。虽然对英语学习者、爱好者可能有些帮助，但它绝对不是英语教学节目，也不是国际、国内大事无所不包的大杂烩。

三年来，在实际操作过程中，《福建英语新闻》节目虽然也吸引了一部分在闽工作、生活和来闽交流、访问的外籍人士，但由于受播出时间和节目内容等方面的制约，三资企业和涉外单位工作的白领员工，大中小学英语教师、学生，外经、外贸、旅游、外事等部门的翻译、导游、文秘和其他涉外人员反而成为节目的主要信息反馈来源。福州某国外驻榕机构的首席代表告诉英语新闻节目人员：以前给公司总部写报告，她每天都要先浏览福建省主要报刊、杂志，收集公司总部需要的经贸政策资讯，然后翻译成英文，最后再整理成英文报告、送回总部。现在，有了《福建英语新闻》节目，就省事多了。省外办的一位翻译说，他是通过福建电视台的网站(www.fjtv.net/tvnews/subjecteng)阅读《福建英语新闻》节目的文稿。在那里，他可以轻松地找到具有福建地方特色的新词汇和新表达方法的英文翻译，并随时用于外事接待工作中。他说，本职工作使他们比一般观众更加经常使用英语，《福建英语新闻》节目变成了他们翻译工作的好帮手。

立足本地，播报福建本土新闻，三年来《福建英语新闻》节目较为全面地播报福建省重要的时政、经贸活动和文化生活等领域的新闻、资讯，累计制作英语新闻节目一万多分钟，在网站上发布的英语新闻条数接近六千条。2002至2003年，节目人员连续两年，与厦门大学MBA中心的潘维廉博士合作，拍摄了中英文双语大型系列报道《老外看福建》(英文名称为：*Magic Fu-*

jian)60集节目，总长度超过300分钟。在厦门大学出版社的支持下，系列报道《老外看福建》的中英文双语对照电视脚本和配套的CD盘终于顺利地结集出版了。我们希望，英语学习者和使用者能够批判地吸收和利用，并且非常自豪地在您的外国朋友面前，宣传福建、推介福建，而不总是抓住老外问天气，问英语学习方法，谈国际、国内形势……

最后，应该感谢福建广播影视集团的领导、厦门大学出版社和《福建英语新闻》节目专兼职人员以及我们的合作伙伴潘维廉博士。正是大家的关心、指导和努力，使得《福建英语新闻》节目找到了正确的发展方向。因为，有了正确的方向，即将年满三周年的《福建英语新闻》节目肯定可以走得更稳、更好！

福建省广播影视集团新闻中心
王跃宏
2004年8月

编写人员

总 顾 问:舒 展

主　　编:王跃宏

副 主 编:史 青 刘 毅

英文撰稿:William N. Brown(潘维廉)

节目策划:潘文功

语言顾问:林本椿 陈小慰 王振南

责任编辑:潘文功 包东宇 尤丽云 郑 芬 王传榕

现场出镜:Dr. Bill Brown ——潘维廉

Bobby Bao——包东宇

Joyce Liu——刘银燕

Deborah Zheng——郑芬

Contents

目录

Learn English?　学英语？

Learn Fujian!　看福建！

When I was in high school in the U.S. ,our French class's top students set off in high spirits on a field trip to Paris and returned ten days later with their tail tucked between their legs. One said to me, "I aced the written exams, but I could not manage a face-to-face conversation with a Frenchman!"

Language students the world over often find that mastery of a written language does not guarantee oral proficiency because oral language skills are perfected socially, not academically. A 2nd language must be learned the same way as one's 1st language—not by burying ones nose in books but by actually speaking aloud, nonstop, to anyone who will listen! This method is simple and virtually foolproof. After all, how many children fail to learn their native tongue? But children, of course, have plenty of people to talk to. Who does the English learner in China talk to, and what do they talk about? This book, adapted from FJTV's series, *A Foreigner Looks at Fujian*, not only addresses both those problems but also explains why foreigners need you to talk to them!

How to Capture a Laowai Audience! Fujian now has Laowai aplenty, but how do you corner them? Even the friendliest foreigners can be tired of endless conversations beginning with stale questions like "Where are you from? Is America hot or cold? Do you like Chinese food? How much are you paid?"

After 16 years I've answered these so often that I've considered printing the answers on my business cards so when English learners pounce on me I can hand them the card, say "Read this!" and make a hasty escape. But there ***is*** a way to insure that Laowai flock to you rather than flee from you! Just find a topic that interests them—and one subject that China's Laowai love to discuss is China!

If you learn to chat with foreigners about your home's culture, history, cuisine, etc., you'll kill two birds with one stone. First, you'll be guaranteed a captive Laowai audience on which to hone your English. Second, you'll help the world better understand Fujian, which in my eyes is China's most fascinating province—but also a province virtually unknown to the outside world!

Unknown Fujian The foreigners' image of China typically includes Beijing's Great Wall, Xi'an's terracotta warriors, Shanghai's Bund, and Guilin's uniquely Chinese mountains, but Fujian rarely comes to mind, and they have no idea if Fujian borders Taiwan or Tibet. For example, while representing Quanzhou in the Nations in Bloom competition in Holland, the vice-mayor of Aperdoorn said, "I read your book, 'Mystic Quanzhou' . An amazing city—but where on earth is Fujian?"

It's ironic that Fujian is such a mystery to foreigners today, because for centuries this province was China's great window upon the world, and home to the country's most entrepreneurial and adventurous people.

Fujian—the Melting Pot of Asia Ancient Fujian was a great commercial and cultural crossroads, with the greatest seaport in the ancient world, rivaling Alexandria, Egypt. Marco Polo wrote of Quanzhou, from which he sailed home, "I assure you that for one shipload of pepper that goes to Alexandria or elsewhere , destined for Christendom, there come a hundred such, aye and more too, to this haven of Zaytun, for it is one of the greatest havens in the world for commerce."

"Soup's Up!"

Foreigners from all over the world not only visited Fujian but also settled down, took up permanent residence, and assumed government offices as high as the provincial level. Foreigners brought with them their philosophies and religions, making Fujian a center of just about every major world religion (in 1992, UNESCO dubbed Quanzhou the "World Museum of Religion").

Fujian's Rich Diversity Fujian also enjoys an amazing cultural diversity, thanks to its endless mountain ranges. I often joke that Fujian would be China's largest province if someone flattened it. (Fujianese say their province is "*Yishan, Yishui, Yifentian*" 1 part mountain, one part water, one part fields). The age-old isolation created by endless mountains and deep valleys has results in Fujian having more dialects than any other province in China, and many unique customs found nowhere else.

Tough Terrain, Tough People Most Overseas Chinese came from Fujian, and many who stayed behind became famous as merchants, artisans, educators, and philosophers. Fujian is the home of neoConfucianism, which shaped Asian history for centuries, and Southern Shaolin Kung Fu. Fujian was famous for all three of ancient China's 3 major exports: tea (from Anxi), porcelain (from Dehua), and silk (from Zhangzhou and Quanzhou). Quanzhou was the ancient marionette capital, and West Fujian had one of ancient China's 4 major printing centers. Fuzhou, the provincial capital, was not only the birthplace of China's maritime shipbuilding and famous for its merchants and adventurers, but also a great center of learning, and home to China's 1st public library.

Fujian has also long been famous for its biological and natural diversity. It's endless mountains and primeval forests boast rich nature reserves that are home to Amoy tigers, 33 foot pythons, panthers, leopards—all thriving in beautiful settings that include such sites as China's largest waterfalls complex (in Zhouning), and the United Nations Heritage Site of Wuyi Mountain, or the otherworldly beauty of Taimu Mountain.

It is no wonder that ancient Fujian fascinated the world, and our province is more open today than ever. But you can help open it further, and improve your English, by sharing about our beautiful home with Laowai!

Master English by Promoting Fujian! One reason the world is so ignorant about Fujian is that we have relied too much on targeting Overseas Chinese with promotional materials in Chinese. But if Fujian is to compete with Shanghai, Beijing and Guangzhou, we must begin emphasizing English for two reasons. One, as China continues to open her doors to the rest of the world, Overseas Chinese are an increasingly small percent of overseas investors. Two, many 2nd and 3rd generation Overseas Chinese don't even read Chinese (many have e-mailed me asking for English materials about their ancestral province!).

Fujian's people, as well as her government, must do their part to promote Fujian—as I learned from an Australian business person who had traded in China for 20 years before setting foot in Fujian. She said, "All Chinese cities are the same to foreign business people: airports, hotels, and factories. And Xiamen did not impress me much—until a Chinese factory worker showed me around one afternoon!" She added, "Guangzhou and Shanghai are bigger, and more convenient in some ways, but now I prefer Fujian—though I'd have never returned had it not been for that 4 hour tour."

FJTV Opens Laowai Eyes! In 2002 I was delighted when FJTV asked me to help adapt materials from my books for 63 5-minute episodes about Fujian. For weeks, we traveled around the province, filming by day and writing by night, and the programs were broadcast in Chinese and English. But my friends thought it a waste to show the programs only a few times and shelve them, so they suggested I adapt the script for a bilingual book to help Fujianese study English while learning more about their home province. I also hope this book may help foreigners learn more about Fujian, as well as learn more Mandarin!

So to Laowai and Laonei alike, enjoy your language learning—and enjoy Fujian!

Best wishes,

Bill Brown
Xiamen University MBA Center
January, 2005

Episode 1 "3 Links, 1 Family"

With friends in Taiwan, 1977

Introduction From 1976 to 1978, Dr. Bill Brown served in the U.S. Air Force in Taiwan, never dreaming that ten years later, he and his family would be living on the opposite side of the Taiwan Straits in Fujian.

In the early 1990s, Dr. Brown wrote a 24-page handbook, *Survival Guide for Foreigners in Xiamen*. He expanded the book over the years, and in the year 2000 he published *Amoy Magic*, a tour guide to Xiamen. He no longer called it a Survival Guide because life for foreigners in Xiamen is no longer survival but fun and rewarding.

At the moment, Dr. Brown is working on *Magic Fujian*, the second of his books to help foreigners and Chinese, especially the Fujianese, to better understand Fujian and rediscover the beauty of her culture and tradition.

A FJTV film crew followed Dr. Brown and recorded his discoveries, which will be presented as a TV news series both in English and in Chinese through Fujian Southeast TV. Today, we begin the series with Dr. Brown's experiences in Taiwan 26 years ago.

Dialogue – Dr. Bill's MBA Office

Bill: Hi! I'm Bill Brown, Pan Weilian in Chinese, and I've been teaching here at Xiamen University's MBA Center for 14 years. I've seen most of China, but Fujian province is the most interesting, and so I was very honored that FJTV would ask me to help introduce Fujian to you. I'm sure most of you know my friend here Bobby Bao, from FJTV.

Bobby: Laowai, Ni hao!

Bill: Laonei, Ni hao!

Bobby: Doctor Brown, how did you end up in China?

Bill: That's a long story. In 1976, when the U.S. Air force sent me to Taiwan, it was like going to another planet. But I fell in love with Taiwan from day one, and China has been in my blood ever since.

When I first went to Taiwan, I knew nothing about Chinese history and culture, or that ancient Chinese had invented almost everything. I had never seen chopsticks, never eaten Chinese food, and never met a Chinese face to face, even though they were ¼ of the world's population.

第1集　三通，一家

♪导语

1976 年到 1978 年，比尔·布朗先生在台湾的美国空军基地服役。他做梦也想不到，十年之后，他和他的家人会搬到台湾海峡对岸的福建来生活。他本人还取了个中国名字，叫作潘维廉。

20 世纪 90 年代初，潘维廉博士写了一本叫作《外国人厦门生存指南》的小册子。在以后的几年里，他将小册子的内容不断扩充。2000 年，他出版了一本厦门导游书，叫作《魅力厦门》。这本书不再叫作“生存指南”，因为潘博士觉得，老外在厦门的生活已经不仅仅是生存，而是丰富多彩，并且充满乐趣。

目前，潘维廉博士正在撰写一本叫《魅力福建》的新书。与他的上一本书一样，《魅力福建》同样是为了帮助外国人以及中国人，尤其是福建人更好地了解福建，体验福建山水人文的无穷魅力。

今年暑假，我们派出摄制组，跟随潘维廉博士的脚步，记录下了他在福建各地的种种发现。我们将把这些发现制作成中英文双语的电视系列片，通过福建东南电视台的新闻节目奉献给大家。今天，我们就先从他 26 年前踏上台湾的那段经历说起。

♪现场（潘维廉博士办公室）

潘维廉：大家好，我是比尔·布朗，中文名叫潘维廉。我在厦门大学工商管理中心教书已经 14 年了！我到过中国的大部分地方，不过我还是觉得福建是其中最吸引人的省份。福建电视台希望通过我把福建介绍给大家，我感到十分荣幸。相信大家都认识我福建电视台的朋友——主持人包东宇吧。

包东宇：老外，你好！

潘维廉：老内，你好！

包东宇：潘博士，你怎么会在中国住下来的呢？

潘维廉：说来话长。1976 年美国空军派遣我去台湾的时候，我感觉就像被派到了另一个星球。不过从我踏上台湾的第一天起，我就爱上了她，中国情结从此融入了我的血液。

♪解说

我刚到台湾的时候，对中国的历史和文化一无所知。我不知道中国发明了从草纸到圆周率到几乎所有的东西，我从未见过筷子，没吃过中餐，也从未与一个中国人见过面。虽然，算起来他们占了世界人口的将近四分之一。

I hiked and biked all over Taiwan, entranced by Mt. Ali's snowy peaks, Toroco Gorge's polished marble cliffs, Oluanpi's white sands, Sun Moon Lake's romantic valleys. I could not speak Chinese but I understood the smiles of villagers who even in the remotest mountains offered me tea, lodging, and food—even cobra venom in rice wine!

Taiwan, 1977

I loved Taiwan, but I never forgot that I was an airman, and that our rivals were only 100 miles away. But I soon learned the mainland was family, not enemy.

Dialogue – A Sign From Heaven!

Bobby: How did you come to know that the mainland and Taiwan are family?

Bill: I got a sign straight from heaven!

Bobby: Really!

On a hot summer's day in 1977, mainland propaganda leaflets dropped right onto our Air Force Base. Police warned us not to touch them, which made me only more curious. So of course I grabbed some, and hurried back to my room.

Taiwan, 1976

That night, curtains closed and lights dimmed, I spent hours looking at the photos of happy farmers and tumbling acrobats. I didn't believe any of it, but it sparked my interest in Chinese history and culture. I learned that ¾ of Taiwanese came from Southeast China, I decided that someday I'd meet the rest of the family.

When I made it to Fujian ten years later, I found Fujianese are much like Taiwanese. They share the same dialects, folk tales, arts, festivals—even unique customs like moon cake gambling. Taiwan fishing boats often anchor just off Fujian's coast, and locals joke that bread baked in Fujian is still warm when fishermen get back home to Taiwan.

A few years ago, a mainland TV film crew left some materials on Jinmen. "Oh no!" the director said. "To get it we will have to go back through Hong Kong, Taipei, Jinmen, and back again!"

A fisherman said, "Don't worry." And he rowed over that night and had relatives get it for him!

或骑单车，或轻装远足，我用双脚丈量台湾的青山绿水。我沉醉于阿里山的雪峰，太鲁阁的悬崖绝壁，鹅銮鼻的白沙，还有那日月潭浪漫的山谷。我听不懂汉语，但我读得懂人们的微笑。即使在最偏远的山区，那里的村民也留我住宿、待我以饭茶——甚至包括浸泡眼镜蛇的药酒。

虽然我喜欢台湾，但我从未忘记自己是一名空军士兵，而我们的对手就在 100 英里开外的海峡对岸。不过，我很快就发现，大陆与台湾其实不是敌人，而是一家人。

♪现场

包东宇：你是怎么知道大陆和台湾是一家人的呢？

潘维廉：我从天上得到了一个谕示！

包东宇：是吗？

♪解说

1977 年一个闷热的夏日，当大陆的传单像雪片一般飞向我所在的台湾清泉岗空军基地时，警方警告说：“任何人不准阅读，违者入狱！”而这只会让我倍感好奇。我往口袋里塞了几张传单，跑回屋里。那天晚上，我门窗紧闭花了好长时间研究传单上的图片。虽然我并不相信那些喜气洋洋的农民和动作夸张的杂技高手，不过这些传单仍然激发了我对中国历史和文化的兴趣。后来，我得知四分之三的台湾人都来自中国的东南沿海，于是我发誓有朝一日我要会会这个大家庭的其他成员。

十年之后，当我来到福建的时候，我发现福建人和台湾人是如此的相像，他们使用同样的闽南方言，拥有同样的民间传说、艺术和节日——甚至在中秋节玩会饼搏状元这样的独特习俗都是相通的。台湾渔船经常在离福建海岸不远的地方下锚。当地人开玩笑说，渔民们回到台湾后，从福建带回家的面包还是热的。

几年前，大陆的一个电视剧组从金门拍摄归来，导演突然发现有东西忘在了金门。他懊恼地说：“天哪！要把东西取回来，我们又得从香港到台北再到金门，然后再折回来！”厦门的一位渔民安慰导演说不要紧。当天晚上，这个渔民就驾了条小船，通过他在金门的亲戚把东西取了回来！

Dialogue—Xiamen's Island Ring Road

Bobby: It's very beautiful, isn't it?

Bill: Yes, it is. Xiamen and Jinmen are so close that if use binoculars you can see the soldiers over there patrolling the island. So close, and getting closer. [1]

Angling, not Wrangling. In 1998 Xiamen held a cross-straits fishing contest. It was nice to see both sides of the family angling instead of wrangling. Nowadays, tour groups can go directly between Jinmen and Xiamen. It's a pity that Taiwan and the mainland are still hampered by cross-straits barriers that hinder China's peace, prosperity and reunification. After all, both sides are family.

When our family came to Xiamen University in 1988 to study Chinese, I had a Ph.D. in management. I was surprised to learn that Xiamen University also had one of China's first MBA programs, and they needed a foreign teacher!

After 14 years teaching MBA in China, I've come to see that Chinese on both sides of the Straits have the same desire as their ancestors—peace and prosperity, for themselves and for their children. The key to this is the speedy adoption of the "San Tong"—the Three Direct Links of mail, transport and trade. This will free up cross-straits communications.

In 1992 I was honored to become Fujian's first Laowai to get permanent residence, and in 1993, Premier Li Peng gave me the Friendship Award. I shook hands with him and didn't wash my hands for 3 days! In 2001, I was also very honored to receive honorary citizen of Fujian Province.

Dialogue—in Dr. Bill's Home

Bill: I am very honored to receive these awards, but the fact remains, I am a lao wai, not a lao nei,[2] I am an American. But my Taiwan friends, they're Chinese, not by adoption, but by birth. So I hope they embrace this unique opportunity and responsibility to help China and help reunite China, and to help China achieve the prosperity and peace that it deserves.

---

[1] Getting closer: as of December, 2004, Fujianese can visit Jinmen Island as tourists (I'm not sure if that includes Fujian's foreigners as well)

[2] Laonei: Chinese call foreigners (4/5 of the globe) Laowai (老外, venerable outsider), so I return the favor with my own phrase, Laonei (老内, venerable insider)

Island Ring Rd. Sculpture

♪**现场**（厦门环岛路）———

包东宇：这里风景真不错，是吧？

潘维廉：是啊，厦门和金门离得那么近，只要有个望远镜，你就可以清楚地看见对面小岛上的台湾士兵在巡逻。真近，而且越来越近了！

♪**解说** ———

1998 年，厦门举办了海峡两岸首届钓鱼竞赛。同一大家庭的成员奋力“争鱼”而不是争吵，看了真叫人高兴。如今，旅游团已经能在金门和厦门之间往来穿梭。但可惜的是，台湾和大陆仍然被海峡间的屏障所牵制。这个屏障阻碍着中国的和平、繁荣和统一——毕竟，台海两岸都是一家人。

1988 年我和家人来到厦门大学学习中文的时候，我已经获得了管理学的博士学位。我很惊喜地发现，厦门大学是中国最早开辟 MBA 课程的高校之一，而当时他们正好需要一个外籍教师！在中国教书的 14 年间，我渐渐意识到，海峡两岸的人民和他们的祖先有着同样的渴望，那就是和平和繁荣——为了他们自己，也为了他们的子孙。而这关键就在于“三通”的早日实现——即两岸直接“通邮、通航、通商”。这样就能够让海峡两岸的人民享受自由往来的便利了。

1992 年，我有幸成为福建省第一个获得中国永久居留权的外国人。1993 年，李鹏总理向我颁发了“友谊奖”。和他握手之后我三天都舍不得洗手。2001 年，我又很荣幸地获得了“福建省荣誉公民”的称号。

♪**现场**（潘维廉博士家中）———

潘维廉：能够得到这些荣誉，我感到非常的荣幸。但我在血统上还是一个美国人，是“老外”而不是“老内”。而我在台湾的朋友们，他们生来就是中国人，并不是从什么别的地方迁徙来的。我希望他们把握天赋的机会和职责，促进中国统一，为使中国更加和平与繁荣尽一臂之力。

（节目在潘维廉次子马休的钢琴演奏中结束）

Episode 2 Tan Kah Kee – Entrepreneur & Educator

Introduction In the last episode of *Magic Fujian*, we followed Dr. Brown from Taiwan to Xiamen. Today he and Bobby Bao discover the legacy of the overseas Chinese patriot, Tan Kah Kee.

Dialogue—Tan Kah Kee Pioneer's Education

Bill: Most foreigners have heard of Sun Yat-sen, who helped create a new China. But few Westerners have heard of Tan Kah Kee's Contributions.

Bobby: What contributions do you mean?

Bill: Tan Kah Kee helped lay the foundation of a new China by reforming education. It's ironic because China led the world in education for centuries.

Many centuries ago, Chinese had a boldly democratic idea. They decided to select officials based on their ability, rather than their heredity and clout (guanxi). Anyone, whether they were a prince or a peasant, could be an official if they could pass the imperial exams. And some people never gave up. At times, grandfather, father and son competed in the same exam.

Chinese education was centuries ahead of its time. And 1,000 years ago, China had the technology and military to rule the world. Fortunately for us Westerners, China was interested only in commerce, not conquest! If China had gone to war, we barbarians would now be eating our cheeseburgers with chopsticks at McRice, instead of McDonalds!

But times changed, and China did not. By the 20th century we Laowai were dividing China into little Western colonies, and ancient China was drowning beneath a tide of opium. Some Chinese blamed Qing Dynasty corruption. Some blamed other things, like foreigners' opium. But Tan Kah Kee's concern was not the cause but the cure—which he saw as modern education.

Dialogue—by Jimei Turtle Garden

Bill: It seems strange to me that Tan Kah Kee would be a man to help modernize Chinese education.

Bobby: Why is that?

Bill: He was a businessman, not an educator. But sometimes doing a business can be a best education! I wish he were here now, so he could teach MBA for us.

Tan Kah Kee left Amoy in 1890, when he was only 17, to help his father sell rice in Singapore. When this failed, he borrowed to start a pineapple plantation and cannery. But it was the rubber trees between the pineapple rows that made him rich!

第2集　爱国侨领陈嘉庚

导语

在上一期的“老外看福建”中，我们跟随潘维廉博士从台湾来到了厦门。今天潘博士将和我们的记者包东宇一起，在厦门探寻著名爱国侨领陈嘉庚先生的足迹。

现场（厦门大学陈嘉庚雕像前）

潘维廉：外国人大都知道在中国缔造共和的孙中山先生，但却很少有人提及陈嘉庚先生为中国建设所做出的贡献。

包东宇：你指的是哪些贡献呢？

潘维廉：陈嘉庚先生通过教育改革为现代中国的发展奠定了基础。有意思的是，在此之前的千百年间，中国的教育一直领先于世界的其他国家。

解说

好几个世纪以前，中国出现了大胆的民主思想。那时候，政府官员的选拔标准就已经是任人唯贤，而不是任人唯亲、靠“关系”。无论是皇亲贵族还是平民百姓，只要通过科举考试，就有机会谋得一官半职。因此，有些人一考再考也决不轻言放弃。有时候，甚至还会出现祖孙三代同时参加科举考试的情况。

当时，中国的教育已经比其他国家领先了好几百年。事实上，早在一千年多前，中国拥有的科技和军事力量就足以统治整个世界。值得我们西方人庆幸的是，中国当时只热衷于和西方做生意，对侵略似乎并不感兴趣。假如中国当时发动战争，恐怕我们这些番鬼们如今只能在“麦当米”——而不是“麦当劳”里，用筷子吃汉堡了！

后来，时代变了，但中国却没能与时俱进。到了 19 世纪末，西方列强把中国分割成一块块的殖民地，古老的中国被淹没在了鸦片的黑潮中。为此，有些人痛斥满清政府的腐败，而其他人则抱怨诸如西方列强带来的鸦片等等。但陈嘉庚先生并没有纠缠于中国落后的原因，而是关注中国摆脱落后的出路。这条出路，他认为，就是现代教育。

现场（集美鳌园）

潘维廉：我觉得奇怪的是，帮助中国发展现代教育的，居然是像陈嘉庚这样的一个人。

包东宇：为什么这么说呢？

潘维廉：因为他是个实业家而不是教育家。不过，有时商业本身也能很好地教育人。假如他还在世就好了，那他就可以给我们讲授 MBA 课程了。

解说

1890 年，17 岁的陈嘉庚离开厦门，前往新加坡帮助父亲经营米铺。米店的生意失败之后，陈嘉庚借钱办起了菠萝种植园和罐头加工厂。但真正使他富有起来的，却是菠萝园中的橡胶树！

During World War I, he moved into shipping. During the 1930s, his businesses suffered, but Mr. Tan was still able to retire wealthy, and he spent his remaining years reforming Chinese education.

Dialogue—Japan "out-Wests" the West

Bobby: Why do you think a businessman decided to promote education?

Bill: I look at it from an MBA teacher's perspective. I think Tan kah Kee had a sense of strategy. And I think he learned from Japan's experiences…

When Western countries forced unequal treaties on Japan, the Japanese realized they could not maintain their isolation from the world, so they decided, "If you can't beat them, join them—then beat them!"

Their strategy had 3 parts: clothes, courts, and cash. They wore fine Western clothes so Westerners could not treat them as backwards people. They learned Western laws and created a constitution—forcing the West to treat them in a so-called legal way. And they really won the West's heart by spending lots of cash! They paid the British to build ships and train sailors, the French to train soldiers, and the Americans to light their streets and build railroads.

Mr. Tan Kah Kee, the great entrepreneur, never missed an opportunity. When he saw the Japanese' success, he learned from their example.

Dialogue—Mr. Tan's Chinese-Western Architecture

Bobby: Do you understand why Tan Kah Kee combined Western architecture with Chinese roofs?

Bill: Maybe he couldn't decide which one he liked best?

Bobby: No! They represent his dream of a nation with Chinese spirit and traditions grounded upon Western academics and technology.

FJTV films Xiamen Univ.'s classic architecture

在第一次世界大战期间，他又把资金投入了航运业。20 世纪 30 年代世界经济大萧条，陈嘉庚的生意遭到了重创，不过，他的个人财富并没有遭受太大的损失。此后，陈嘉庚便将自己的余生奉献给了中国的教育改革。

现场（集美鳌园内）——

包东宇：你认为陈嘉庚先生为什么会下决心发展教育呢？

潘维廉：以一个 MBA 教师的角度来看，我觉得他具有商人的谋略，而且他还借鉴了日本人的做法。

解说

当西方列强把不平等条约强加给日本的时候，日本人意识到他们不能再像以前一样闭关锁国了。他们拿定主意："要是不能打败他们，那就先加入他们，然后再打败他们！"

日本人的策略包括三个部分：服装、法庭和金钱。他们换上雅致的西服，这样西方人就不能称他们是落后的民族了；他们学习西方的法律，还制定了宪法，这样西方国家就必须以所谓的"合法方式"来对待他们；与此同时，他们还花费了许多金钱来讨好西方国家，而且果真赢得了他们的欢心。他们出资请英国人为他们打造舰船和培养水手，让法国人替他们训练士兵，还让美国人为他们安装路灯和帮他们修建铁路。

作为一个杰出的企业家，陈嘉庚先生从来都不会错过任何良机。在看到日本人的成功之后，他便开始学习他们的经验。

现场（在厦大上弦场中西合璧的建筑物旁）——

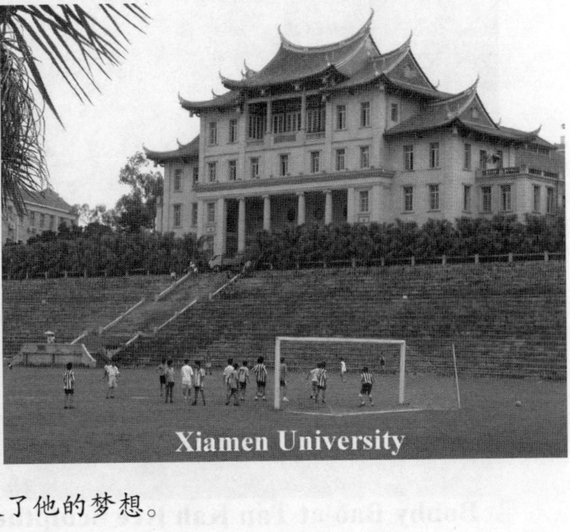

Xiamen University

包东宇：你知道陈嘉庚先生为什么把西式的建筑同中式的屋顶融合在一起吗？

潘维廉：不知道，也许他搞不清自己更喜欢哪一种吧？

包东宇：不！他希望借助西方的科学技术建设一个具有中华民族精神和传统的国家，而这些建筑就形象地代表了他的梦想。

Xiamen University—Model for the Future In the 1920s and 30s, Tan Kah Kee spent millions of dollars on colleges in Jimei, and on Xiamen University. He spent thousands of dollars monthly just on teachers' salaries alone. His vision even excited foreigners. In the 1920s, an American writer in China, Mr. Hutchinson, wrote of Xiamen University,

> "This school is entirely a Chinese institution, with no foreign teachers and no foreign connections, and right out in a small Chinese village. The course of study is being made very practical…When we think of the future days, it is one of the most encouraging things to be seen in the whole of China."

Dialogue—by Tan Kah Kee Statue

Bill: I'm very thankful that Xiamen University has Laowai today, including several hundred foreign students studying Chinese language and other subjects, over there in the Overseas Correspondence College.

Bobby: Ah, and I suppose you enjoy living on such a beautiful campus.

Bill: Of course! Xiamen University is a very important campus, and I also think it's the most beautiful campus (of course I'm totally unbiased!) ,So I would like to join all of my Chinese friends in a very hearty thank you to Mr. Tan Kah Kee for his great contributions to Chinese education. Gum Xia li! ("Thank you" in Minnan Dialect)

Bobby Bao at Tan Kah Kee Sculpture (Xiamen Univ.)

解说

在20世纪20和30年代，陈嘉庚先生拿出毕生积蓄建起了集美学村和厦门大学。他每个月还要花费数千美元为教职员工发薪水。他的远见卓识甚至使外国人都感到兴奋不已。20世纪20年代，一位旅居中国的美国作家哈钦森先生是这样描述厦门大学的：

“这完全是一所由中国人自己创办的学校，没有外国教师，也没有外国背景。它建在乡下的一个小村庄里，但学校的课程设置却非常的实用……想到它未来的发展，我们觉得这是全中国最令人鼓舞的事情之一。”

现场（厦大芙蓉湖边陈嘉庚雕像旁）

潘维廉：我觉得很幸运，因为厦门大学现在终于有老外了！而且在厦大海外教育学院，还有好几百名外国学生在学习中文和其他学科。

包东宇：我想你也一定很乐意住在这么美的校园里吧？

潘维廉：当然了。厦门大学是中国唯一一所设在经济特区的重点大学。而且，我觉得厦大拥有中国最美丽的大学校园，当然，我这么说完全没有任何私心。因此，我要和我所有的中国朋友一起，衷心地感谢陈嘉庚先生为中国教育事业所做出的巨大贡献。感谢你（闽南话）！

Tan Kah Kee's Home (Jimei)

Episode 3 Garden Island Vacation

Introduction In our last episode of *Magic Fujian*, Dr. Bill and friends explored Tan Kak Kee's legacy. Today he explains how he and his wife (Susan) got the idea of taking vacations right in their hometown of Xiamen.

Dialogue—Egret Goddess Statue

Bill: Xiamen is called "Egret Island" because a long time ago, an army of egrets defeated the snakes. And this is the Goddess of Egrets.

Bobby: She's very beautiful. Very lucky egrets!

Bill: The first time I saw a photo of her, the caption left off the "Goddess" part and just said "Egret." I had to look a long time before I saw the egret. No wonder so many Xiamen people are bird watchers!

B.B.
Egret Goddess

Xiamen's Metamorphosis[1] Xiamen is also called the "Garden Island", though we didn't think it was much of a garden back in 1988. Back then, roads were narrow and dark at night. The buses were old and unreliable. Even Yungdang Lagoon, which is so beautiful today, was very polluted. So when my wife Susan and I wanted a rest we escaped to other towns, like Zhangzhou or Quanzhou, or even Hong Kong.

Dialogue—Yungdang Lagoon

Bobby: But Xiamen is very beautiful now. What happened?

Bill: Xiamen changed—almost overnight! One day, my son Shannon said, "Xiamen is so beautiful now—like a little Hong Kong." Susan and I were always inviting people to visit our city, but we never got to enjoy the new city ourselves. So one day we said we're going to become tourists in our own town!

Susan Marie booked a couple of weekends in hotels that gave us special rates, since we were locals. We relaxed in the rooms, enjoyed the great views of the city, sampled local cuisine, and strolled the lakes and parks at night. Susan likes Yuandang Lake's dancing fountains and music, and the skyline mirrored in the river. I like the 119 traditional and modern sculptures scattered around—especially the Egret Goddess! And both of us enjoy the beach.

---

[1] Metamorphosis: change (as a caterpillar metamorphoses into a butterfly)

第 3 集　花园鹭岛好度假

导语——

在上一期的“老外看福建”中，潘维廉博士和我们的记者包东宇一同探寻了著名爱国侨领陈嘉庚先生的足迹。今天潘博士将告诉大家他和他的太太苏珊女士是如何度假的，而且度假地就选在他们住了十几年的厦门岛。

现场（白鹭洲，白鹭女神雕像旁）——

潘维廉：厦门的别称叫“鹭岛”，因为传说很久以前，一群白鹭曾在这里征服过毒蛇。看，这就是白鹭女神的雕像。

包东宇：她真是太美了。这些白鹭真是吉祥鸟。

潘维廉：是啊。我第一次看到白鹭女神的照片时，当时的标题把“女神”漏掉了，只剩下“白鹭”两个字儿。我找了半天才发现女神肩膀上的那只白鹭，难怪厦门那么多人喜欢看鸟儿！

解说——

厦门又被称作“花园之岛”。不过，我们觉得 1988 年的时候，厦门可不太像花园。那时候，街道很窄，而且一到晚上就黑乎乎的。公交车又破又旧，还老不准点。就连筼筜湖，现在是挺漂亮的，可那时候也是脏得不得了。所以，当我和我妻子苏珊想度假的时候，我们就跑到其他地方去，比如说漳州或泉州，甚至是香港。

现场（白鹭洲公园花间小道）——

包东宇：可现在的厦门真的很美。到底是怎么回事儿呢？

潘维廉：厦门变了——几乎就在一夜之间！有一天，我儿子仙侬说：“厦门现在真漂亮，就像个小香港。”

解说——

我和苏珊经常邀请别人来厦门玩儿，可我们自己对新厦门也不太了解，于是有一次我们就说：“我们要在自己居住的城市当一回游客！”

有几个周末，我和苏珊到饭店订了房间。因为是本地人，饭店还给我们打了折扣。白天，我们在房间里放松心情，一面放眼城区美景，一面品尝厦门美食，晚上，我们就到湖滨的公园里散步。苏珊喜欢白鹭洲的音乐喷泉，还有那湖面上高楼的倒影。我喜欢散布在公园各个角落的 119 座传统和现代雕塑，尤其是那座白鹭女神雕像！当然，我们俩都特别喜欢海滨的沙滩。

Island Ring Road Ten years ago, the beach road was narrow and dusty. But now Xiamen has rebuilt it into a wide and modern Island Ring Road. It is a beautiful place to ride bicycles, skate, stroll, fly a kite, have a picnic—or just to sit and read a book! But for a change of pace we often hike into the hills behind us, to the beautiful gardens.

Growing but Greening! Xiamen was awarded the title "Garden City of China" in 1997. Xiamen has 31 urban gardens, 4 forest gardens, and one botanical garden. Many residents have their own little gardens, or plants in pots on balconies. And in the year 2,000, over 100,000 volunteers helped plant 755,000 trees in Xiamen! The city has also planted 5,448 mango trees along roads. The profit from the fruit helps fund the island's greening projects.

In October, I will be part of a delegation of three to give a presentation in Germany as Xiamen competes for the Nations in Bloom Award. The competition is stiff. We wish them good luck![2]

Dialogue—Xiamen Botanical Garden

Bill: I like the 10,000 Rocks Botanical Garden better than the other gardens, but it's my favorite garden. It's not only a garden, but it's a botanical research center with over 5,000 kinds of tropical and sub-tropical plants.

Bobby: And, of course, 10,000 Rocks!

Bill: Well, 9999 now.

Chinese tourists like the ancient calligraphy, but I enjoy sites like Laughing Rock—and this beautiful concrete palm tree W.C.!

Botanical Garden

Dialogue—A Wonderful W.C.!

Bill: I am very honored to tell you that this is Xiamen's most beautiful public toilet. Do you want to tour? This is a real tree and that looks like it's made out of trees, but that is fake, not real. Concrete!

Another of my favorite parks is Zhongshan park, which has gardens, boats, and a small zoo.

Dialogue—Zhongshan (Sun Yat-sen) Park

Bill: I think that every city in China must have a Zhongshan Park and a Zhongshan Road.

Bobby: That's probably true. Zhongshan is Mandarin for Dr. Sun Yat-sen, the Father of Modern China.

---

[2] Xiamen **did** win the gold medal, beating Chicago, Hangzhou and others!

十年前，海边的这条路又窄又脏。现在，厦门市已经把这条滨海道路建成了现代化的环岛路，既宽阔又漂亮，特别适合骑车、溜冰、散步、放风筝和野餐。就算只是坐下来看本书也很惬意！不过，有时候为了换换口味儿，我们常常会到岛内的山上远足，或者到那些漂亮的花园里去体验另一种风情。

1997 年，厦门获得了“中国花园城市”的称号。现在，厦门拥有 31 座城市花园，4 座森林公园，以及一座植物园。许多居民都有自己家的小花园，或是在阳台上栽花种草。仅 2000 年一年，就有十万多名志愿者在厦门种下 755000 棵树！厦门市还在市区道路两侧栽种了 5448 棵芒果树。这些果树的收益为鹭岛的绿化提供了部分资金。

今年（2002 年）10 月，我将作为厦门代表团的三位成员之一，到德国参加一场演讲，为厦门争取“国际花园城市奖”。竞争将很激烈，让我们预祝厦门好运！

♪**现场**（厦门万石植物园）———

潘维廉：在厦门众多的公园中，我最喜欢的是万石植物园。它不仅仅是个花园，还是一个植物研究中心，里面有 5000 多种热带和亚热带植物。

包东宇：顾名思义，那儿也该有一万块石头吧？（从地上拿起一块石头）

潘维廉：那当然！不过……哈哈，现在只有 9999 块了！（从包手中拿走一块石头）

♪**解说**———

中国游客喜欢万石植物园里的古代摩崖石刻，我却喜欢像“笑石”这样的景点，还有那个水泥做的棕榈树洗手间！

♪**现场**（棕榈树公厕）———

潘维廉：很荣幸地告诉大家，这就是厦门最漂亮的公厕。去看看吧！

瞧，这是一棵真的棕榈树，而那（公厕）看起来好像也是用树干造的，不过那个是假的,是水泥做的！

♪**解说**———

厦门中山公园也是我最喜欢的公园之一，那儿有花园、游船，还有个小型动物园。

♪**现场**　（中山公园）———

潘维廉：我想，中国的每座城市里都有中山公园和中山路吧？

包东宇：有可能！孙中山就是孙逸仙博士，中山公园就是为纪念他而建造的。

Bill: Yes, Zhongshan Park has a statue to him [film statue and inscription]. The inscription by his grand daughter says, "The Great Democratic Revolutionary Pioneer of new China." Thousands of people come here to pay their respects—especially now that Zhongshan Park is free.

Bobby: "It's great that some parks are free to visitors now!"

Dr. Sun Yat-sen

Less Walls, More Green A few years back, Beijing started a "Less Walls, More Green" campaign. Solid walls around parks and institutions came down, replaced by nice iron fences. I think this kind of thing symbolizes China's new openness. And today in Xiamen, Zhongshan Park and many others are free.

Dialogue—by Gulangyu Ferry

Bobby: Not all parks are free, are they?
Bill: No! Especially on Gulangyu, they're charging liushi (60) Yuan just to climb that rock up there, Sunlight rock! But the ferry's free.
Bobby: How could it be free?
Bill: Simple. It's free going but they charge you coming back! Of course, you could always swim coming back. We could take a ferry and check it out!
Bobby: Let's go!

Tour Boat to Gulangyu

潘维廉：是啊，中山公园里有一尊他的塑像。底座上有他孙女的题字：“伟大的民主革命先驱孙中山先生。”成千上万的游人到这里来景仰他。现在，中山公园还对公众免费开放。

包东宇：现在很多公园都对游客免费开放。这真是太好了！

解说

几年前，北京搞了个“拆墙透绿”的活动，就是把公园和各单位四周的围墙都拆了，换上漂亮的铁栏杆。依我看来，这体现了中国的某种新的开放姿态。在厦门，中山公园和其他许多公园也都是免费开放的。

现场（鼓浪屿轮渡码头）

包东宇：现在有的公园还是要收费的，对吧？

潘维廉：没错，尤其是在鼓浪屿，爬那边那个日光岩一次就得花 60 元。不过，去鼓浪屿的轮渡是免费的。

包东宇：怎么可能免费呢？

潘维廉：很简单。去的时候免费，回来的时候就收费了。当然，你可以游回来。鼓浪屿这么美，游回来还是值得的。不信，我们这就搭轮渡过去瞧瞧！

包东宇：走吧！

Episode 4 Gulangyu—Piano Island

Piano Island

Introduction In the last episode of *Magic Fujian*, Dr. Bill took an Amoy vacation right in his hometown of Xiamen. Today he gets in tune with Gulangyu, China's Piano Island.

Dialogue—Bill Blows the Flute—or Cow?

Bobby: Do you know how to use it?

Bill: No idea. 我不会吹笛子，但我肯定会吹牛！[I can't blow a flute but I can definitely "blow the cow!"[1]] I think we Laowai and Laonei are alike in many ways, but also very different in some ways.

Bobby: What is one of the biggest differences between Chinese and Americans?

Bill: Well, besides the chopsticks, there's the music!

Music or Mayhem? Chinese music sounds off key to many foreigners. Songs end on odd notes. The horns are shrill, the cymbals clang, and it's hard to follow the beat on the drums! It sounds so odd to us that I used to pretend I was performing Chinese opera by banging pots and pans while singing in a high voice. My Laowai friends thought it sounded similar!

Dialogue

Bobby: So you don't like Chinese music?

Bill: I do like Chinese music now. In fact, I like traditional music from all over the world. But it took me some time to really appreciate Chinese music.

Chinese Opera—in English! Chinese opera, like Western opera, is hard to understand if you don't know the story. It helps to be able to read the words while you watch and listen. But we Laowai can't read the Chinese shown on the screens, and don't know the stories and traditions. In fact, I didn't really start appreciating Chinese opera until a Xiada Professor, Ji Yu Hua, sang one sentence of Chinese opera for me—but in English! That encouraged me to learn a few pieces myself.

Dialogue—Bill Sings Chinese Opera (Cover your ears!)

Bobby: Can you remember any now?

Bill: I've forgotten most of it. But I can still remember a little of the *Red Lantern Opera*. Something like… "Ting ba nai nai, shuo hong deng…"

---

1 Blow the cow: Chinese slang for "boast"

第 4 集 钢琴之岛鼓浪屿

导语 ———

在上一期的“老外看福建”节目中，我们看到潘维廉博士是如何在他的第二故乡厦门度假的。今天，他将带我们上一趟中国的钢琴之岛——鼓浪屿。鼓浪屿还是东西方音乐交融的地方。

现场（在乐器店里拨弄中国传统乐器）———

包东宇：你会吹笛子吗？

潘维廉：不会。我不会吹笛子，但是我肯定很会吹牛！（I can not play flute, but definitely I can brag fluently!）我觉得我们老外有很多地方跟你们“老内”很相似，但也有很多区别。

包东宇：你觉得中国人和美国人最大的区别是什么？

潘维廉：除了筷子，我想恐怕就是音乐了。

解说 ———

对许多外国人来说，中国的传统音乐听起来很古怪。歌曲常常以奇怪的音符结尾；号声尖锐刺耳，钹声咣咣乱响，鼓点让人几乎跟不上节奏。

有一回，我一边敲着盆盆罐罐，一边扯起嗓子，装模作样地唱了几句中国戏。我的那些老外朋友们说，听起来还挺像回事儿！

现场（鼓浪屿钢琴博物馆大门前）———

包东宇：这么说，你不喜欢中国音乐喽？

潘维廉：不，我现在挺喜欢中国音乐的。实际上，世界各国的传统音乐我都很喜欢。不过，我花了挺长的时间，才真正懂得欣赏中国音乐。

解说 ———

跟西方的歌剧一样，要是你不了解故事情节的话，中国的戏曲是很难看懂的。看戏时，如果旁边有台词放映就比较好懂一点。可惜我们老外看不懂银幕上的中文台词，也不了解故事情节及其文化背景。

实际上，是在厦门大学的纪玉华教授给我唱了一句中国戏之后，我才真正开始欣赏中国戏曲的。他可是用英语唱的！这使我下决心自己也要学着唱几段。

现场（钢琴博物馆外）———

包东宇：你现在还会唱吗？

潘维廉：忘得差不多了。不过我还记得《红灯记》里的几句。好像是这么唱的：“听罢奶奶，说红灯……”

Bobby: Not bad.
Bill: Thank you.
Bobby: So you really like Chinese opera?
Bill: I can't say I really like it. But I appreciate the heritage behind it. And I really appreciate the difficulty of singing it and that's why nobody asked me to sing twice! But fortunately for me, I like music and Xiamen is famous now not just for Chinese music but for Western music as well!

East Weds West Rudyard Kipling wrote, "East is East and West is West and never the twain shall meet." But he was wrong. East and West have met many times in China, especially on Gulangyu, which we call Piano Island.

Piano Islet In the 1800s, Western missionaries arrived in ancient Amoy with Bibles in one hand and pianos in the other. They must have had very big hands!

Gulangyu residents fell in love with the versatile piano. Today, Gulangyu has more pianos per capita than any other place in China, perhaps the world—one in five households! Gulangyu's Piano Museum is unique in China and the largest in Asia, and Xiamen has become an oasis of Chinese and International Music culture.

Dialogue—by Amoy Academy of Music

Bobby: But how many people actually get involved in music?
Bill: Six or seven? Just joking! Actually, quite a few. Graduates from places like Xiamen Music School have received broad claim internationally—fortunately they perform at home as well as abroad.

Rich Musical Heritage In the year 2001, Xiamen spent 716 million Yuan on cultural and musical festivities. Recitals or performances are held somewhere every week in Xiamen or on Gulangyu. But Xiamen also preserves unique Chinese musical traditions. The Xiamen Nanyin (the Southern Music) Musical Troup preserves and performs the 1,000 year old music that Chinese call "living music fossil" and "divine oriental melody."

Every May, Gulangyu Islet hosts "International Music Week." August is Xiamen's "Public Cultural Festival Month. Xiamen also hosts China's Juvenile Piano Competition and the biannual Gulangyu Piano Festival. In 2002 we host the First Gulangyu International Piano Arts Festival and the 4th International Tchaikovsky Competition for Young Musicians.

Xiamen Philharmonic Orchestra

包东宇：不错嘛！

潘维廉：谢谢!

包东宇：你现在真的挺喜欢中国戏曲，是吧?

潘维廉：嗯，还不能说十分喜欢。不过，我很欣赏中国戏曲背后的文化传统。我知道，要唱好戏需要高超的技巧。正因为这一点，别人绝对不会叫我唱两遍。作为一个音乐爱好者，我觉得挺幸运的，因为厦门不仅以中国传统音乐闻名，它在西洋音乐方面也是久负盛名。

解说

鲁得亚德·奇普林（Rudyard Kipling） 曾经写道："东方就是东方，西方就是西方，两者永远无法相融。"但是他错了。在中国，特别是在鼓浪屿这个被称作钢琴之岛的地方，就有不少东西方文化兼收并蓄的例子。

19 世纪的时候，西方传教士来到厦门，他们一手拿着圣经，一手带着钢琴。我猜，他们一定是有一双大手！

鼓浪屿上的居民很快就喜欢上了极富表现力的钢琴。现在，鼓浪屿的人均钢琴拥有量在全中国，也许在全世界都是最高的——每五个家庭就拥有一架。鼓浪屿的钢琴博物馆在全国独一无二，在亚洲也是最大的。厦门已经成为中国和国际音乐文化的一块绿洲。

现场（厦门音乐学校前）

包东宇：那么，厦门到底有多少人从事音乐呢?

潘维廉：六七个？哈哈，开玩笑，有不少。像厦门音乐学校这些院校的毕业生在国际上都受到广泛的认可。幸好他们除了出国演出，也在厦门本地表演。

解说

2001 年，厦门在文化艺术活动上就花费了 7 亿 1600 万元。在厦门岛或鼓浪屿上，每周都有钢琴音乐会或者其他演出。同时，厦门还保留着独特的国乐传统。厦门南音乐团表演的千年古乐被称为"音乐活化石"和"神圣的东方旋律"。

每年 5 月，鼓浪屿都会举办"国际音乐周"。8 月是厦门的"群众文化节"。此外，厦门还是全国青少年钢琴比赛，以及两年一届的鼓浪屿钢琴音乐节的举办地。2002 年，厦门还承办了首届鼓浪屿国际钢琴艺术节以及第四届柴可夫斯基国际青少年音乐比赛。

Episode 5 Xiamen Architecture

Introduction Yesterday, on *Magic Fujian*, Dr. Bill visited our planet's only piano island. Today he discovers that Gulangyu and Xiamen also possess a unique architectural heritage.

Dialogue—Quiet Gulangyu Streets

Bill: I love Gulangyu because it is so quiet!

Bobby: Yes, No cars, and no bicycles.

Bill: Before Xiamen outlawed car horns, I used to escape to Gulangyu Island.

Bobby: Really?

I think Gulangyu people took their tranquility too much for granted. A few times I thought of strolling around Gulangyu at midnight, ringing a bike bell, so they could taste the kind of racket we lived with on the other side of the harbor. But I never dared to because Koxinga's statue is standing guard!

A walk on Gulangyu Island is like going back in time a century, before the invention of noisy buses and cars. And Gulangyu and Xiamen's unique Chinese and Western architectures also bring back memories of an earlier, simpler era.

Xiamen's oldest buildings are, of course, Chinese. The sprawling Nanputuo Temple was built over 1,300 years ago, in 686 A.D.. Haicang's Ciji Palace was built in 1,151 to honor doctor Wu Tao. And the house of the great astronomer Su Song is 1,000 years old. Su Song invented the world's first astronomical clock, and he compiled a great medical book. But foreigners especially like Gulangyu and Xiamen's International architecture, which the city has taken great pains to preserve.

Dialogue—by Former Dutch Consulate

Bobby: So the Europeans came to Xiamen pretty early, didn't they?

Bill: The Dutch were here already 400 years ago. And after the Opium War in the 1840s, Xiamen became one of China's first five treaty ports. In fact, Gulangyu was like another country!

Gulangyu International Settlement By the 20th century, Gulangyu Islet was an international settlement, with consulates and embassies from 13 countries. The Gulangyu international settlement even had their own government council, and police force. Many foreign firms, and wealth foreigners and overseas Chinese, built mansions, hospitals and schools on Gulangyu. Xiamen and Gulangyu now have such a rich heritage of international architecture that the city has spent 76 million RMB on the Gulangyu Islet Historical Architectural Protection Plan.

第5集　厦门建筑

导语

在昨天的“老外看福建”节目中，布朗博士见识了全世界唯一的一座钢琴岛——鼓浪屿。今天他将带大家一同去领略鼓浪屿和厦门岛上独特的建筑传统。

现场（走在鼓浪屿的曲折细小的巷子里）

潘维廉：我喜欢鼓浪屿，因为这里特别清净！
包东宇：是啊，这里既没有汽车，也没有自行车。
潘维廉：厦门其他地方没有禁鸣喇叭之前，我就常常来鼓浪屿躲避对岸的喧闹。
包东宇：是吗？

解说

我觉得鼓浪屿上的居民过于把安静的生活环境当作理所当然的事情。有好几次我想半夜在鼓浪屿一边散步一边按响自行车铃，让岛上的居民体验一下对岸生活的喧嚣。可我一直都不敢这么做，因为岛上有郑成功的雕像在守卫着呢。

走在鼓浪屿上就像是回到了一个多世纪以前，回到那个吵死人的汽车还没被发明出来的时代。鼓浪屿和厦门岛上众多古老的中式和西式建筑，也能勾起人们对那个久远而淳朴的年代的回忆。

厦门最古老的建筑当然是中式的。在这些中式建筑中，有建于 1300 年前，也就是公元 686 年的南普陀寺；有公元 1151 年为纪念名医吴涛（Dr. Wu Tao）而建造的海沧青礁慈济宫；还有千年古厝天文学家苏颂（Su Song）的故居。苏颂创制了世界上第一台天文钟，他还编纂了一部伟大的医学著作。除了中式建筑以外，许多外国人还对鼓浪屿和厦门岛上那些具有异域风情的国际建筑特别感兴趣。这些建筑都是厦门市花了很大力气才保存下来的。

现场（在鼓浪屿荷兰领事馆旧址旁）

包东宇：欧洲人很早就来到了厦门，对吧？
潘维廉：早在 400 年前荷兰人就来到了这里。19 世纪 40 年代第一次鸦片战争以后，厦门成为中国最早的五个通商口岸之一。当时的鼓浪屿几乎就像是另外一个国家！

解说

到 20 世纪的时候，鼓浪屿成了一个公共租界地，岛上驻有 13 个国家的大使馆和领事馆。当时鼓浪屿上甚至有公共租界自己的议会和警察部队。许多外国公司、有钱的外国人和海外华侨在岛上建起了宅邸、医院和学校。现在，这些国际建筑成了厦门和鼓浪屿宝贵的历史遗产，因此市政府拨出 7600 万人民币的专项资金实施“鼓浪屿历史风貌建筑保护计划”。

The protected buildings include the French style Lin House, the neo-Gothic Catholic church, the neo-classical Trinity church, the geometric Art-Deco court building, the Filipino Huang Yongyuan Mansion, deng deng (Chinese for "etcetera").

Gulangyu Catholic Church

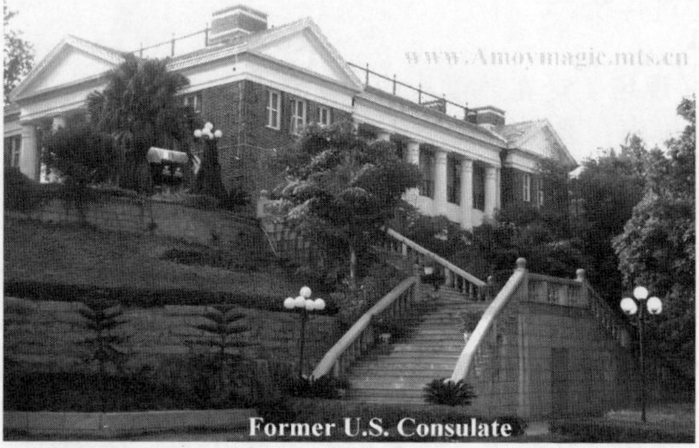

Former U.S. Consulate

Dialogue—at Corner of Zhongshan and Siming Roads

Bobby: That's a beautiful building. Is it colonial?

Bill: No—it's only 4 or 5 years old! The city tried to renovate the original building, but it was too far-gone. So they rebuilt it in the original style, from the ground up.

Bobby: Xiamen's colonial architecture is quite unique.

Bill: Yes, foreigners enjoy it. But I think the most interesting places are the places not in the tour guide—like the umbrella roads!

Corner of Siming and Zhongshan Roads

受保护的建筑有法国风格的林宅、新哥特式的鼓浪屿天主堂、新古典主义风格的三一教堂、以几何图案为装饰特色的庭院建筑以及菲律宾风格的黄永元故居，等等。

♪**现场**（中山路思明路口，大陆商厦等古典风格建筑）——

包东宇：那栋房子真漂亮，是不是殖民时代的建筑？

潘维廉：不，刚建四五年的时间。市政府本来想尽力修复原来的那座建筑，但它实在是破得没法修了，所以他们就照原先的风格重建了一座。

包东宇：厦门殖民地时期的建筑风格真是很特别。

潘维廉：是啊，外国游客很喜欢这些建筑。可我觉得厦门最有趣的地方是那些在导游手册中没有介绍的地方——比如说老城区的那些小巷子（“伞路”）！

Sea and Sky Palace

Umbrella Roads Nowadays Xiamen looks very modern, with its highways, cloverleaf interchanges, tunnels and bridges. But the narrow little roads behind the highways can take you back in time a century!

100 years ago a foreigner wrote that Xiamen's streets were so narrow you could not open an umbrella in some. Of course, maybe he just had a very big umbrella! He also said that few Amoy streets were straight. Some Chinese believed devils could follow them only in a straight line. Of course, that doesn't keep us foreign devils from exploring them! And they can lead to hidden treasure like China's oldest Protestant Church, Xinjie Church.

But I most enjoy watching people busy at life—the goldsmiths, sidewalk seamstresses, shopkeepers—or friends sipping tea and chatting.

Dialogue—Hong Bu Ren—Xiamen's Living History Book

Bill: Every time I walk down the umbrella streets, someone like Mr. Fu invites me in for tea, and talks about the old days!

Bobby: It must be interesting! Do you like the stories of old Xiamen?

Bill: I love them. And no one knows old Xiamen like the Walking History book—Mr. Hong Bu Ren.

Bobby: Walking History book? I'd like to meet such an amazing person.

Bill: OK, let's go to meet him.

While the Japanese occupied Xiamen from 1938-44, Professor Hong studied the classics in the home of Lixi , the famous scholar. Young Hong's imagination was fired by passionate debates between literati like Wang Xuan Xian, Zhong Wen Xian , and Shi Qian. But his life's course was set by Teacher Lixi's comment, "Data collection is crucial. No data, no history".

Professor Hong is now a walking history book and advisor to universities and governments. He has two apartments crammed with wall-to-wall shelves of books and notes. Lucky man! (My wife allows me only one corner, by the bed!)

Professor Hong is now writing a 500,000 word history on Xiamen. He said, "If I don't do it, who will when I'm gone?" Professor Hong is excited that scholars around the world are taking a keen interest in Xiamen's history. "Xiamen is making many foreign friends again, just like the good old days!"

♪解说——

宽阔的公路、四通八达的立交桥、便捷的隧道和桥梁，使如今的厦门看起来非常现代化。而大马路后面的条条小路却能让你领略一个世纪前厦门的模样！

100 年前有一位外国人描写说，厦门的街道是如此狭窄，在有些小巷里甚至连伞都撑不开。当然，也许因为他的伞太大了！这位外国人还写到，厦门的街道难得有一条是直的，因为据说有些中国人认为鬼跟踪人的时候只会走直线。即便如此，中国人后来还是没能阻止我们这些“洋鬼子”的到来。在这些小路上还隐藏着一些宝藏，比如中国最古老的新教教堂——新街礼拜堂。

不过，我最喜欢看的是忙碌中的人们——比如金匠、人行道边的女裁缝、小商店的店老板——或者在一起品茶聊天的朋友。

♪现场——

潘维廉：每次我在伞路上漫步的时候，总会有人像傅先生一样邀请我喝茶，向我讲述过去的时光！

包东宇：那一定很有趣！你喜欢听老厦门的故事吗？

潘维廉：啊，太喜欢了。而且没有人比洪卜仁先生更了解老厦门了，他简直就是厦门的“历史通”。

包东宇：“历史通”？我真想见见这位神奇的人物。

潘维廉：好啊，我们这就去拜访他吧！

♪解说——

1938 年到 1944 年日本占领厦门期间，洪教授在一位著名学者李禧的家中学习古典文学。像王选闲、钟文献、施乾等文人之间热烈的辩论激发了青年洪卜仁的灵感与想像力。而他恩师李禧的一句话则影响了他的一生：“史料非常重要，没有史料，就没有历史。”

现在对于政府部门和大学来说，洪教授就是一本会说话的历史书。他的两套公寓里到处都是书架，上面摆满了书籍和笔记。他运气真好！（我妻子只许我把书摆在房间靠床的一角！）

洪教授现在正在写一部 50 万字的关于厦门历史的书。他说：“如果我现在不写的话，将来我不在了，谁还能来写呢？”令洪教授感到欣慰的是，现在世界各地的许多学者都开始把关注的目光投向厦门的历史。洪教授说：“厦门像从前一样，又交上了许多外国朋友！”

Episode 6 Xiamen's Economics, and CIFIT

Introduction In today's episode of *Magic Fujian*, Dr. Bill explains how the Garden Island of Xiamen has not only preserved its environment but also enjoyed rapid economic growth, thanks in part to the E-Silk Road of the Sea, CIFIT.

Dialogue—Xiamen—Part of the Maritime Silk Road

Bill: Xiamen had long lived up to its name, "Mansion Gate", which implies the south gate to China.

Bobby: How long have foreigners been trading here?

Bill: The Dutch came here[1] about 400 years ago, and we foreign devils have been crashing the gates[2] ever since!

Quanzhou, just 70 miles north, was once the starting point of the Silk Road of the Sea. The greatest port in the world, it rivaled Alexandria in Egypt. When Marco Polo was in China, Xiamen was part of Quanzhou, and many of the giant Chinese ships anchored right here because Xiamen has one of the deepest natural harbors in the world.

A century ago, Dr. Sun Yat-sen envisioned Xiamen's Haicang as becoming an Oriental Mega-Port. Now his dream is finally coming true.

Xiamen now enjoys commercial and trade relations with over 160 countries and regions. Her GDP has averaged an annual increase of 18.4% since 1981, and the city now ranks in China's top ten in overall economic strength.

Dialogue—Xiamen's Secret to Success

Bill: You know it's pretty amazing that Xiamen has developed so rapidly while at the same time protecting its environment.

Bobby: What's the secret for Xiamen's success?

Bill: Hah! If I tell you that it won't be a secret anymore!

Bobby: Oh, please!

Bill:... Ok, I'll tell you. But don't tell anyone else!

Xiamen's 2 Advantages Xiamen has had two advantages: One is leadership. Two is CIFIT. First, the leadership.

---

1 Portuguese came shortly before the Dutch

2 Crashing the gates: forcing our way in uninvited

第 6 集　厦门经济与中国投资贸易洽谈会

导语

在今天的这期“老外看福建”当中，布朗教授将讲述厦门不仅保持了优美的环境，还取得了经济的快速发展，而这在相当程度上要归功于“电子海上丝绸之路”——“九八”中国投资贸易洽谈会。

现场

潘维廉：长久以来厦门都是名副其实的“华夏之门”，也就是中国东南沿海的门户。

包东宇：外国人在这儿从事贸易的历史有多久了？

潘维廉：大约 400 年前荷兰人来到厦门，然后我们“洋鬼子”就开始不断蜂拥而入了。

解说

厦门往北 110 多公里（70 英里）的泉州是古代海上丝绸之路的起点。她当时是世界上最大的港口之一，能与埃及的亚历山大港相媲美。马可·波罗来到中国时，厦门还隶属于泉州，当时许多大型的中国帆船就停泊在厦门，因为厦门是世界最深的天然港湾之一。

一个世纪以前，孙中山先生曾设想厦门的海沧将成为一个东方大港，现在他的梦想终于成为了现实。厦门现在与世界上 160 个国家和地区有贸易往来。从 1981 年以来，厦门的国内生产总值保持了 18.4%的年均增长率，目前厦门已经跻身中国城市综合经济实力前十强。

现场

潘维廉：厦门能在经济迅速发展的同时又保护好环境，真是了不起！

包东宇：厦门成功的秘诀是什么呢？

潘维廉：哈！如果我告诉你，那就不是秘密了。

包东宇：拜托！

潘维廉：好吧，我告诉你，但你不能告诉别人哦！

解说

厦门具有两大优势：一是管理，二是投洽会。

首先，在管理方面。

The former mayor Hong Yong Shi said many times that Xiamen did not want to follow the West's practice of pollution then solution. As much as possible, Xiamen tries to develop and modernize while protecting the environment at the same time.

Second, CIFIT. Quanzhou became such a great port 1,000 years ago because China was so vast and difficult to travel in that few foreigners went inland. So Chinese traders met Laowai on the coast. It was for this reason that the Silk Road of the Sea, which began just 70 miles north of us, was responsible for promoting trade not just in Fujian but all of China. Today, CIFIT does the same thing.

Thanks to rapid and comprehensive growth in China's infrastructure, Laowai and Laonei alike can now do business just about anywhere in the country. But even still, China is a vast country, and there is just no way that foreigners can travel the entire nation seeking just the right opportunities or partners. CIFIT provides the solution.

CIFIT is held every September 8th, in Xiamen's new state-of-the-art Xiamen International Conference and Exhibition Center. CIFIT is China's only national level event focused on attracting foreign direct investment. Representatives from every province in China, as well as from countries around the world, and many of the great multinationals, set up booths. So for Chinese and foreigners alike, it's the Wal-Mart of Investment Fairs—One Stop Shopping.

Dialogue—CIFIT's Success

Bobby: How effective has CIFIT been?

Bill: Pretty incredible I'd say. In recent years, nearly half of the foreign investment for China's small and medium foreign investment cooperation projects have come right here through CIFIT!

Bobby: That's incredible. All from one Fair!

CIFIT's past five sessions have lured 50 billion USD in foreign investment. The last CIFIT had over 50,000 participants and 9000 business guests from 97 countries and regions, representing companies like Siemens, Motorola, GE, Canon, Mitsubishi, Dell and Toshiba.

The Xiamen International Conference and Exhibition Center is five stories high, covers 150,000 sq.m, and has warehouses, catering, a 250 room hotel with a nice view of Taiwan's Jinmen Island—and most important to me, great restaurants!

CIFIT's International Forum speakers have included top Chinese leaders, as well as Nobel Prize winners, UN leaders and vice premiers of various countries.

CIFIT's website gets over 100,000 hits a month, so it's the most popular and most authoritative electronic bridge linking both domestic and overseas participants with investors.

前厦门市市长洪永世曾经多次说过，厦门不能重蹈西方“先污染后治理”的覆辙。因此，厦门在努力进行现代化建设的同时竭尽所能保护好环境。

其次就是中国投资贸易洽谈会（简称“9·8”投洽会）。泉州在一千多年前就成为著名的海港，这是因为中国那么大，旅行不便，外国人很少进入内地，于是中国商人就在沿海一带与老外打交道。正因为如此，古代海上丝绸之路虽然始于与厦门毗邻的泉州，但它不仅促进了福建，更促进了全国各地对外贸易的发展。今天，在厦门举办的投洽会正起着同样的作用。

随着中国的基础设施建设取得迅速全面的发展，如今老外和“老内”几乎可以在全国的任何一个地方做生意。但是，中国毕竟幅员辽阔，老外不可能跑遍全中国去寻找一个合适的商机或合作伙伴。投洽会正好解决了这个难题。

中国投资贸易洽谈会每年 9 月 8 日在厦门最现代的国际会展中心举行。投洽会是中国唯一以吸收外商直接投资为主的全国性国际投资促进活动。来自全国各省市区、世界各地的代表团，以及众多跨国公司的参展商在这里设立展位。因此无论对中国人还是外国人而言，投洽会都可以说是沃尔玛般“一站式购物”的投资贸易洽谈盛会。

♪现场 ———

包东宇：投洽会的效果如何？

潘维廉：应该说非常好！近几年来，中国中小型外商投资项目近一半的外资都是通过“9·8投洽会”引进的。

包东宇：真令人难以置信，居然都是从这一个洽谈会引进的！

潘维廉：没错。

♪解说 ———

过去的五届的投洽会已经为中国吸引了 500 亿美元的外商投资。2001 年举办的第五届投洽会吸引了 50,000 多名参观者，来自 97 个国家和地区的近 9,000 名客商云集厦门，其中包括来自西门子、摩托罗拉、通用电器、佳能、三菱、戴尔和东芝等世界知名公司的代表。

厦门国际会展中心共有 5 层，占地面积 15 万平方米，配备了仓储、餐饮设施和一个拥有 250 个房间的海景酒店。从酒店的房间里可以清晰地看到对岸小金门岛的美景，另外， 对我而言很重要的是这里还有一个很棒的餐厅。

投洽会上国际投资论坛的发言人包括中国政要、诺贝尔奖得主、联合国有关机构领导人和一些国家的副总理级人物。投洽会官方网站的月点击量超过 10 万次，可以说，这是联系国内外客商和投资者最权威也最便捷的电子桥梁。

Dialogue—CIFIT, the E-Silk Road of the Sea

Bill: In a real sense, CIFIT is the new Silk Road of the Sea.

Bobby: So maybe we should call it E-Silk Road!

Bill: That's a good idea. And all we have to do now to travel the E-Silk Road is to log on to I the internet at www. chinafair.org.cn And make sure you tell them Bill Brown sent you, so I get a commission!

Seriously, I think CIFIT really is the E-Silk Road—the way of the future. But to really appreciate its role, we should visit the real Silk Road—the ancient port of Quanzhou![3] I just hope Toy Ota can float!

Visit CIFIT at: www.chinafair.org.cn !

[3] Quanzhou was the starting point of the Maritime Silk Route, but Xiamen was part of Quanzhou at that time, and Xiamen has always had the deepest port—so we can say Xiamen was part of the Maritime Silk Route as well! We visit Quanzhou in a later chapter.

♪**现场**（投洽会组委会办公室，显示着贸洽会网址的电脑前）———

潘维廉：从某种意义上，投洽会是一条新的丝绸之路。

包东宇：或许我们可以称之为“电子丝绸之路”！

潘维廉：好主意！而且要踏上这条电子丝绸之路，你只需登录网站 www.chinafair.org.cn 就可以了。不过你一定要告诉他们是布朗博士介绍的，这样我就可以拿到佣金了。

♪**解说**（组委会办公室外景，开车从厦大门口出来）———

老实说，我的确觉得投洽会是一条电子丝绸之路，一条未来之路。不过要充分理解它的意义，我们还应该到古老的泉州港去，参观一下真正的海上丝绸之路的起点。我真希望我的“疯甜”车（TOY OTA）能当船驶！

Supplementary Reading One

Dethroned

I love China, but I'm sometimes thrown for a loop[1] by the most mundane things—like Chinese toilets. I was shocked when I learned they are little more than a white ceramic hole in the ground. "Where on earth do I sit?" I demanded.

"You don't sit," Susan Marie explained carefully, as if I were one of her sons, and not her husband. "You plant your feet on the raised rectangular or shoe-shaped platforms and squat."

"You're kidding!" I valiantly gave it a go—and lost face when I fell on my face.

When Sue learned that I could not squat flat footed without holding on for dear life to a wall or pipe, she demanded, "What do you mean you can't squat? I can do it. Your sons can do it. You're the only one in the world, Bill Brown, who can't squat!"

"Easy for you to claim squatter's[2] rights!" I retorted. "You were born and raised in Taiwan, and Shannon and Matthew grew up in Xiamen. But I'm American, and I can't squat!"

Alas, years of comfortably ensconcing myself upon the great ceramic, and sometimes cushioned, thrones[3] of America have rendered my body too inflexible for flat-footed squatting, no matter how desperate the situation. While Barbie, Ken, and G.I. Joe[4] may be fully bendable, I am not.

Ironically, Chinese are the ones who invented the sit-down flush toilet that I so long for, though I must confess that the squat versions are indeed more practical and durable. Not much can go wrong with a ceramic hole, and there are no lids or seat rings to clean or fix (because seat rings often break when unenlightened souls squat atop the Western sit-down toilets in China's western restaurants). But practicality notwithstanding, I still miss the days of sitting pretty[5] upon the throne while browsing the newspaper or Reader's Digest (or, nowadays, Common Talk!).

---

1 Thrown for a loop: confused or dismayed

2 Squatter: a person who illegally settles (squats) on land (as we squat on Chinese toilets)

3 Throne: Americans refer to Western toilets as "the throne"

4 Barbie, Ken and G.I. Joe: popular children's dolls that are fully jointed and bendable

5 Sitting pretty: successful, or comfortable

补充读物（一）

事后诸葛：没有“宝座”的日子里

我喜欢中国。但有时候，我也会为尘世间最为平凡的东西困扰不已。比如说，中国的厕所。中国的厕所经常是在地面上挖个坑，然后再铺上洁白的陶瓷便器。“这厕所，我怎么上?”我问道。

“当然不能坐在茅坑上。你要蹲在凸出的矩形或鞋型位置上。”我太太苏珊·玛丽耐心地向我解释道。那情形好像我是她儿子，不是她丈夫。

“你不是在开玩笑吧！”我勇敢地试了一下，面子全丢。

蹲厕所的时候，我拼命地扶住墙壁或者水管。苏珊听说后，嘲笑道：“厕所你蹲不了？这是什么回事？我蹲得了。你的两个儿子也都会蹲。你却蹲不了。老公，你可真是举世无双呀！”

“你们当然没有问题！你自己在台湾出生、长大，我们的儿子在厦门长大。我呢？我是美国人，当然不会蹲茅坑了！”

唉！在美国，无论形势有多紧迫，我们一直都是舒舒服服地坐在巨大的陶瓷便器上出恭。有时候还有软垫。这样的美式“宝座”叫我如何吃得消中国的蹲式茅坑。腿脚早就不灵了。芭比娃娃、凯恩和 G·I·乔之类的洋娃娃腿脚也许还可以弯曲。我却弯不来。

有趣的是，中国是最早发明令我向往很久的座式冲水马桶的国家。当然，必须承认，蹲式厕所的确更加实用和耐用。蹲式厕所只有一个陶瓷坑洞，没有盖子、坐垫，当然坏不了，也用不着清洗和修理。不论怎么说，刚到厦门时，我还是挺怀念坐在“宝座”上的日子：一边用厕，一边浏览报纸或《读者文摘》（现在改看《厦门日报》周末英语版——Common Talk 了！）。

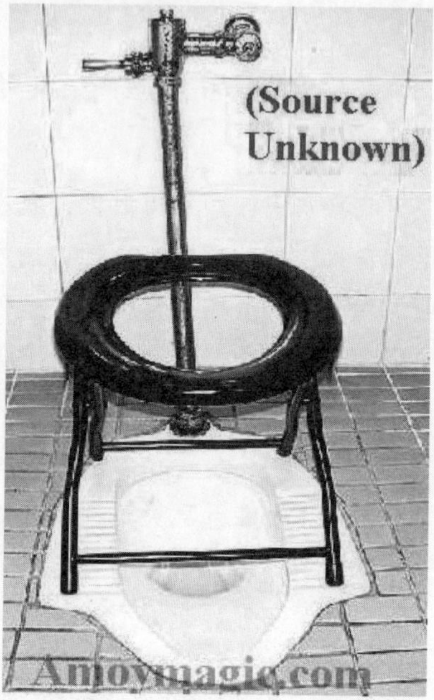

Fortunately, while Chinese ceramic holes are still the norm, toilet paper has improved immensely. Not surprisingly, Chinese invented toilet paper as well as toilets. Almost 1,000 years ago, imperial households employed small squares of perfumed paper upon their royal rears. Even commoners used recycled paper—though one scholar firmly opposed using paper with poetry upon it. But when I came to Xiamen in 1988, I was hard pressed to believe that toilet paper (TP) was a Chinese invention. Xiamen TP felt like recycled sandpaper, and it was months before our tender bourgeois bottoms could cope.

Happily for those of us with acute hindsight, Xiamen firms now put out quality TP, and it turns out that foreign bourgeois buttocks weren't the only ones ready for pampering. Chinese also prize the new TPs, many of which have fragrances, and delicate prints. An American lady in Quanzhou told me her favorite brand is "Mind Act Upon Mind," which boasts, "For soft and comfortable life you can really feel good."

But for life to be soft and comfortable for me, I need an American sit-down toilet, because Susan Marie's disdain notwithstanding, I still can't squat.

尽管中国蹲式厕所风采依旧，但中国的卫生纸质量已经有很大的改进。纸是中国人发明的。一千多年前，中国的皇室就开始使用带香水味的方形手纸。一般平民百姓也用上了再生纸。当然，读书人是不用带字的手纸的。1988 年当我刚到厦门的时候，听说手纸是中国人发明的，我实在不敢相信。因为当时厦门的手纸简直就像砂纸，我那资产阶级嫩臀好几个月后才慢慢适应过来。

如今，厦门已经可以生产高质量的卫生纸。卫生纸也不再是专供老外的资产阶级嫩臀使用。卫生纸的新产品不仅芬芳宜人，而且印工精致。中国人还给它们评奖呢。住在泉州的一位美国同胞告诉我，她最喜欢的品牌是“心相印”。它的广告词写道：“柔软舒适好心情。”

不过，对我来说，不管苏珊怎么想，舒适柔软的生活就是需要美式的座式便器，因为茅坑，我还是蹲不来！

Episode 7 Fabled Quanzhou—the Great Melting Pot

Introduction In the last episode of *Magic Fujian*, Dr. Bill explained how Xiamen, and much of China, has grown because of the CIFIT, the new Electronic Silk Road of the Sea. But today he takes us to the city that was the starting point of the real Silk Road of the Sea, the ancient port and melting pot of the planet—Quanzhou.

Dialogue—How Bill Beat Columbus!

Bill: Columbus is famous for discovering America, but actually he was looking for a shortcut to Quanzhou, and he ended up in Cuba! Until he died he thought he had reached India or some of the outlying Chinese islands. So Columbus never did make it to Quanzhou, but I've been there several times!

Bobby: Okay, but you didn't have to travel halfway around the world to get there. Our drive from Xiamen to Quanzhou takes only 90 minutes.

Bill: Well, that's true. And fortunately, both the roads and the driving have improved over recent years.

Just over a century ago, a Laowai named Mr. G. Phillips wrote that the trip just between Fuzhou and Quanzhou took five days! Mr. Phillips said,

> "The road from Fuzhou to Quanzhou, which also takes five days to travel over, is bleak and barren, lying chiefly along the sea-coast, and in winter a most uncomfortable journey..."

Nowadays it takes not five days but two hours! Foreign travelers in China have never had it so easy! If exotic Quanzhou was hard to get to 100 years ago, imagine what it must have been like almost 700 years ago when Ibn Battuta, the great Arab adventurer, showed up in the world's greatest port. Historians like Henry Yule estimate that the great Arab adventurer, Ibn Battuta, traveled over 75,000 miles in his lifetime. But even Battuta was absolutely astonished when he saw Quanzhou. Batutta wrote, "The harbour of Zaytun is one of the greatest in the world. I am wrong; it is the greatest! I saw in it about a hundred large junks; as for small junks, they could not be counted for multitude…"

Dialogue—Exotic Zaytun

Bobby: Why do you call Quanzhou "Zaytun?"

Bill: "Zaytun" was the Arab name for Quanzhou. And it's also the word from which we get the English word 'satin,' because at that time Quanzhou exported a lot of different kinds cloth and silk.

Bobby: Do you know what "Zaytun" meant?

Bill: Well, the Arab word Zaytun looks like the Arab word for "olive", and "olive" has long been the symbol of peace. It's very appropriate, because Quanzhou has long been a center of peace and prosperity—at least over 1,300 years ago it was.

第 7 集 传奇泉州——中外文化的大熔炉

导语

在上一期的"老外看福建"里，布朗博士解释了厦门以及中国的许多地方，是如何借助中国投资贸易洽谈会这个新的电子海上丝绸之路，而加快发展的。今天他将把我们带到真正的海上丝绸之路的起点去看一看，这就是古老的港口城市以及世界文化的大熔炉——泉州。

现场

潘维廉：哥伦布因为发现美洲大陆而闻名，但他当时其实是在寻找前往泉州的捷径，结果却到了古巴。直到死，他还认为他到的是印度或者中国近海的某些岛屿。哥伦布最终还是没能到达马可·波罗笔下的传奇城市刺桐，而我却已经到那儿好几次啦！

包东宇：得了吧，你又不必像哥伦布那样航行半个地球。我们开车从厦门到泉州只花了 90 分钟的时间。

潘维廉：没错，没错。并且幸运的是，近几年不仅路好走了，我的车技也提高了。

解说

就在一个世纪之前，一位名叫 G·菲利普的老外还写到，仅仅是福州与泉州之间的旅程就需要花费五天的时间。菲利普先生说："从福州到泉州五天的路程中，道路荒凉贫瘠，大多沿海岸而行，到了冬天旅途最为艰难。"

现在，从福州到泉州完全不必五天那么久，只要两个小时就够了。外国旅游者大概想不到这段路已经变得如此快捷。

如果说风情万种的泉州在 100 年前还是难以企及的话，那么想象一下，在 700 年前，当伟大的阿拉伯冒险家伊本·贝图塔出现在这个世界上最了不起的港口时，那该是怎样的一番情景。

根据亨利·玉尔等历史学家的估计，伊本·贝图塔一生的行程超过 75,000 英里（约 12 万公里）。但即使是贝图塔这样见多识广的冒险家来到泉州时也大为震惊。贝图塔写道："刺桐港是世界上最伟大的港口之一。不，它就是最伟大的。我在这里看到了上百艘巨大的帆船；至于小船，则是数不胜数。"

现场

包东宇：为什么你称泉州为"刺桐"呢？

潘维廉：这是泉州的阿拉伯语名字。英语中的"绸缎"一词就是从这个名字中得来的，因为当时泉州出口了大量的丝绸。

包东宇：那么"刺桐"本来的意思是什么呢？

潘维廉：其实"刺桐"在阿拉伯语中是"橄榄枝"的同音词。橄榄枝一直是和平的象征。而实际上刺桐城早在 1300 年前，就已经是一个和平而繁荣的城市了。

With 12 fine harbors, Quanzhou was already an important port by the 5th century, but it really took off after 1087, when the Emperor decided foreign ships could pass customs in Quanzhou rather than Guangzhou.

Quanzhou exported agricultural products, as well as timber, steel, and Fujian's famous Dehua porcelain. Quanzhou and Zhangzhou silk was said to surpass even than that of Hangzhou and Suzhou, the silk capitals of China. Ibn Battuta, wrote,

> "Silk is very plentiful among them [Chinese]...For that reason it is so common to be worn by even the very poorest there. Were it not for the merchants it would have no value at all..."

By the 10th century A.D., bustling Quanzhou had three concentric city walls. By 1230, the outer wall was ten miles long, and enclosed even the foreigner's living area. Tens of thousands of foreigners, of every known religion, lived and worked in harmony with the Chinese in this great melting pot. They even intermarried. But the Mongol conquerors always remained afraid of the Chinese—especially the Fujianese, who sailed everywhere and feared nothing. The ancient historian Su Shi wrote, "Only the crafty merchants of Fujian dare to travel to North Korea... Men such as Xu Jian of Quanzhou are legion."

The Mongols tried to keep the Chinese in check by appointing Laowai to high government positions, even at the Provincial level, and foreigners had great trade contacts abroad. At one time a single Arab accounted for fully ¼ of China's external revenue!

Foreign relations and trade declined during the late Ming Dynasty. But today, foreigners and Chinese alike are rediscovering just how vast an impact Quanzhou had on the ancient world.

Dialogue—Quanzhou Maritime Museum

Bill: Quanzhou has so many fascinating attractions it's hard to know where to start!

Bobby: What do you find most fascinating about Quanzhou?

Bill: Well, Quanzhou 1,300 years ago was already a bustling international seaport, but UNESCO has also designated Quanzhou a World Museum of Religion because at one time it had just about every major religion in the world! Whichever you want to look at, the Maritime Museum is the good place to start.

Quanzhou Maritime Museum

解说

有着 12 个天然良港的泉州在公元 5 世纪就已经是一个重要的口岸了。而它真正的腾飞是在 1087 年以后，当时的皇帝宣布外国船只可以改从泉州而不只是广州通关。

泉州当时主要出口农产品，以及木材、钢铁和福建著名的德化瓷器。据说当时泉州和漳州的丝绸甚至胜过中国丝绸之都苏杭两地的丝绸。伊本·贝图塔写道："中国丝绸遍地……因此在那里即便是十分穷苦的人也普遍能穿丝绸。假如不是用于通商的话，它根本就不值钱……"

到公元 10 世纪，热闹非凡的泉州已经拥有三重城墙。在 1230 年的时候，外城的城墙有 16 公里长，城内甚至划出了外国人的居住区。上万名信仰各种不同宗教的外国人在这个大熔炉当中，与当地的中国人和睦相处，共同生活和工作。他们甚至联姻通婚。但是元朝统治者始终对汉人保持警惕——尤其是四处航海，天不怕、地不怕的福建人。古历史学家苏轼曾经写道："只有福建的商人才敢于远行高丽……像泉州人徐戬这样的男子为数众多。"蒙古人试图用任命老外为政府高官的办法控制汉人，甚至是省一级的官员。而且外国人与海外有许多贸易往来，曾经有一个阿拉伯人上交的税款足足占了当时中国整个外税收入的四分之一。

明朝末年中国的外交关系走向下坡，对外贸易也逐渐衰落。而在今天，外国人和中国人正一起重新探寻泉州对古代世界所产生的深远影响。

现场

潘维廉：泉州有这么多吸引人的地方，真不知道我们该从哪儿说起。

包东宇：你觉得泉州最令人着迷的是什么呢？

潘维廉：嗯，这可真是个艰难的选择！泉州早在 1,300 多年前就是中国最繁忙的海港之一。不过联合国教科文组织还授予泉州"世界宗教博物馆"的称号，因为它一度几乎包容了世界上所有主要的宗教。无论从哪个方面来看，泉州世界一流的海上交通史博物馆都是我们开始这次泉州之行的最好地点。

Episode 8 Quanzhou—Master of the Sea

Introduction In today's Episode of Magic Fujian we follow Dr. Bill and friends to the ancient city that in Marco Polo's day was called Zaytun.

Tourists always want to visit Beijing and the Great Wall, or Xi'an's Terra Cotta Warriors, or Guilin. But only now are foreigners and Chinese alike starting to rediscover the ancient glory of Quanzhou, the starting point of the Silk Road of the Sea! Quanzhou has more historical sites than any place in China but Beijing and Xi'an!

Dialogue—Quanzhou Maritime Museum

Bill: It's the Fujianese that have always been China's greatest seafarers and adventurers, so in a way we could say that Fujian is the home of the world's seafaring.

Bobby: How can you say that? Lots of countries went to sea!

Bill: That's true, what most foreigners don't know was that it was Chinese ships and Chinese inventions that made long distance sea travel both possible, and safe.

A Loud Silence About Chinese Seafaring English reference books, including the authoritative Encyclopedia Britannica, have almost nothing on China's role in the development of seafaring. Under the heading Ship, it shows ancient Greek and Middle Eastern vessels, and European ships, but nothing about Chinese ships. It shows the "Prussen" and says it was the, "Only five-masted, full-rigged ship ever built." It never mentioned that some ancient Chinese treasure ships had 11 masts!

Here's a drawing of one of Columbus' ships, but imagine if Columbus had come across Zhenghe's 440 foot flagship! Here's a drawing of how the two would have compared. Britannica has only one small note, referring to the volume on boats. And the boats section only talks about one-masted sampans.

Westerners, and even Chinese, know too little about China's great maritime accomplishments—what they built and what they invented, and where they traveled. This maritime museum, with its many exhibits and Chinese and English captions, is a real eye opener. First, we'll look at the development of Chinese shipbuilding, and then we'll discover the exploits of Zhenghe, Chinese greatest Admiral.

第 8 集 大海的主人

导语

在今天的“老外看福建”节目中，我们将跟随布朗博士和他的朋友们的脚步，一起到在马可·波罗时代被称为“刺桐”的古城——泉州去看一看。

解说

游客们一直都热中于逛北京游长城，到西安看兵马俑，或者去欣赏桂林山水。只是到了最近，老外和中国人自己才开始重新发掘古代海上丝绸之路的起点——泉州光辉灿烂的历史。除了北京和西安之外，可以说泉州拥有的文物古迹比全国其他任何地方都多。

现场（泉州海上交通史博物馆前）

潘维廉：中国最出色的海员和冒险者很多都出自福建，因此在一定程度上我们可以说福建是世界航海之乡。

包东宇：怎么能这么说呢？世界上好多国家都有人航海啊！

潘维廉：你说的没错，不过大多数外国人都不知道，其实是中国的造船技术和中国发明的航海设备使远洋航海既可行，又安全。

解说

英文的工具书，甚至包括权威的大英百科全书上面，对中国在世界航海发展史上的地位都几乎没有什么介绍。在船舶的词条下面，既有古希腊和中东的船，也有欧洲的船，但就是没有介绍中国的船。

大英百科全书上介绍了“普鲁森”号（Preussen），并说它是“迄今唯一一艘五桅、满帆的帆船”。而书上根本没有提到有些中国古代帆船甚至拥有 11 根桅杆！

这儿有一张哥伦布帆船的图画，不过请想象一下，如果哥伦布的船遇上了郑和长达 440 英尺的旗舰那将会是什么情景！

这张图画恰好展示了两艘帆船对比的情况。

大英百科全书中关于船舶容量的内容只有短短的一小段。而在介绍舟船的章节中，也只是提到了中国的单桅小舢板。

现场（海交馆大堂）

潘维廉：西方人，甚至连中国人自己，对中国在航海方面取得的伟大成就都是了解得少之又少。他们不知道中国的航海发明，也不清楚中国人远航的历史。而这个海上交通史博物馆中数量众多的展品都带有中英文说明文字，实在是让人大开眼界。

首先，我们一起来看看中国舟船发展的历史，然后再去探寻中国最伟大的航海家郑和的英勇事迹。

Evolution of Chinese Watercraft The Maritime museum shows the development of watercraft from simple rafts to dugout canoes and dragons boats. This drawing shows that Chinese had dragon boat races over 2,000 years ago!

The pictures above the door prove Chinese visited South America long ago. Some Chinese and South American pottery are identical, and at least one ancient piece used a Chinese character!

In this chamber we see all kinds of craft, many still used today, including strange crafts like the Tibetan's yak skin coracle, and goatskin rafts—some of which used 700 inflated goatskins! That would really get someone's goat![1]

Judging from this model of Zhenghe's flagship, the ship was like a city upon the sea. It probably had everything but karaoke!

I liked the crooked bow boat, though I'm not sure why it was crooked. Maybe it was for sailing crooked rivers! And over here are the houseboats. A century ago, almost every foreign family and many wealthy Chinese in Fuzhou, Hangzhou, Shanghai and Canton spend hot summers cruising the rivers on their houseboats. I wouldn't mind having one in Xiamen.

Dialogue—Innovative Chinese Shipbuilding

Bill: This is one of my favor wings in the museum, because it not only shows a lot of different kinds of Chinese ships, but also has models of how they were made.

Bobby: That should be interesting—I hope some day we can see people making real wooden ships.

Bill: Maybe, but until then, maybe we can make do with the models, and I especially like this one.

Museum Ship Models This one you can see clearly the specialized water-tight compartments that Chinese developed probably a thousand years ago, I don't know how long, but westerners didn't start using them until the 19th century, and you see here these , ingenious rubbers, the balanced rudder, and this keel, there were special keels for oceans, for rivers, for different type of conditions—you know, rough seas, smooth seas. It's amazing, but what I really like is the sails. You know, a lot of people think that these sails are very old-fashioned like you see the junks in Hong Kong, they're old fashioned, exotic, but actually they're very ingenious. And in western countries, they're starting—they're studying Chinese sails and learning to use them, because they found out they are very stable, heavy seas, they sort of just apparently adjust themselves. I'm not a seaman, I don't know, but it's pretty amazing.

I also like the dioramas of shipbuilders, and fishing villages.

[1] Get someone's goat: anger or annoy someone

♪解说 ———

泉州海交馆中展示了水上交通工具的发展历程，从木排、独木舟到龙舟应有尽有。有一幅图片显示，中国早在两千多年前就有龙舟赛了！

展厅门框上的这些照片证明，中国人很早就到过南美洲。有些在南美洲出土的陶器跟中国陶器非常相似，至少其中有一块古陶残片上面有中文字！

在这个展厅里我们可以看到各种各样的舟船工具，有不少现在还在使用，其中包括一些模样奇特的交通工具，比如说羊皮筏子和西藏的牦牛皮小舟。有些羊皮筏居然用了 700 张吹得鼓鼓的山羊皮！我猜想那个吹羊皮的人一定也是气鼓鼓的！

从这个船模来看，郑和的旗舰几乎就像一座海上的城市。大概上面除了卡拉 OK 以外什么都不缺。

我很喜欢这条弯弯的小船，虽然我并不清楚它为什么这么弯。我想大概是为了在弯弯的小河里行驶吧！

这边还有画舫。100 年前，在福州、杭州、上海和广东这些地方，几乎每一个外国人家庭和中国的有钱人家都会坐着自家的画舫在河上消夏避暑。我也想在厦门弄上一艘。

♪现场（进入东侧展厅）———

潘维廉：这是海交馆里我最喜欢的展厅之一，因为里面不仅展示了许多各种各样的中国舟船，还有演示造船过程的模型。

包东宇：那一定非常有趣，我希望有一天我们能亲眼看到真正的打造木船的过程。

潘维廉：有可能哦！也许，到那个时候，我们只要用这些模型就足够了。我特别喜欢这一个……你看，早在哥伦布时代之前中国人就发明了这种带有密封隔舱的船。西方人直到 19 世纪才开始采用这种技术。中国人还造出了灵巧的船舵，以及适合在海中或是河中航行的龙骨，这令航行非常平稳，适合在风高浪急、风平浪静等各种不同的气候条件下使用。实在叫人称奇。不过，我最喜欢的还是这种船帆。许多人认为，它有点土，就像你在香港还可以看到的那种，虽然样式有点老旧，但还是很奇特，实在富有创造性。现在，在西方国家，人们正在研究中国的船帆及其使用方法，因为他们发现，中国的船帆稳定性很好，特别在风高浪急的时候，这种船帆显然能够自我调节。虽然我不是海员，也不是非常内行，不过你看，这种船帆实在令人称奇。

♪解说 ———

我也很喜欢那些造船工匠和渔村的缩微模型。

One of China's greatest inventions was the compass, invented thousands of years ago. Europeans started using the compass about 500 years ago but they didn't really understand it. Some captains refused to let sailors eat onions because they were afraid onions would take away the compass power!

The endless styles of Chinese ships each had different uses. But the most impressive are the ancient warships. And this paddlewheel ship was sheer genius!

Ancient Paddlewheel Battleship

Dialogue—Ancient Chinese Seapower

Bill: Do you know the ancient Chinese invented land mines, water mines, crossbows and cannons?

Bobby: Wow! And with their unsinkable ships, they could have ruled the world.

Bill: It was a good thing for us barbarians that they didn't want to rule the world. The ancient Chinese weren't conquerors, they were traders and adventurers, like the great Admiral Zhenghe. In fact, nowadays, even the Westerners are getting interested in his exploits!

2000-year-old Battleships

中国最伟大的发明创造中，有一项是几千年前发明的罗盘（指南针）。欧洲人大约在 500 年前开始学会使用罗盘，不过他们知其然却不知其所以然。有些船长甚至拒绝让水手们吃洋葱，因为他们害怕洋葱会令罗盘失效。

中国船的花样数不胜数，每一种都有独特的功用。不过还是古代的战船最醒目。像这种用明轮推进的船绝对是天才的创造！

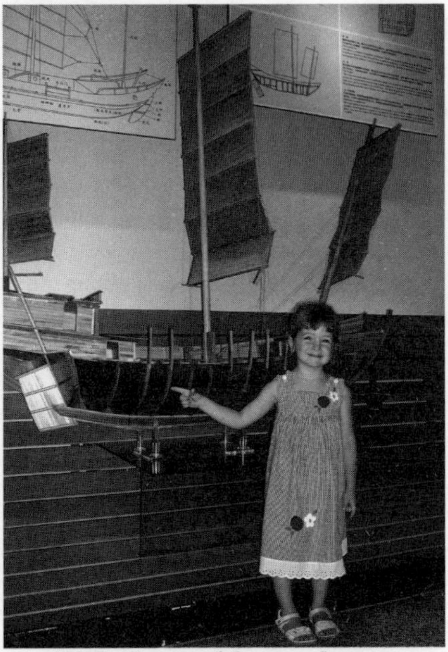

Little Laowai learn about Chinese shipbuilding

♪**现场**（走向展馆内郑和的蜡像）———

潘维廉：你知道吗，是古代中国人发明了火炮、弩弓，还有地雷和水雷？

包东宇：哇，那么再加上无敌战船，他们岂不是可以征服全世界！

潘维廉：这么看我们番佬还挺走运的，因为中国人并不想统治全世界。他们不是征服者，却是商人和探险家，就像伟大的航海家郑和一样。实际上，西方国家现在也开始关注他当年取得的丰功伟绩。

Ancient Hi-tech "Stealth Junk"

Episode 9 The Great Admiral Zhenghe

Introduction In our last episode of Magic Fujian, Dr. Bill said that the ancient Chinese were great seamen. Today he introduces us to the most daring of ancient admirals, Zhenghe.

Dialogue—Zhenghe Discovered America?

Bobby: The Western media has been talking a lot about Zhenghe lately.

Bill: I think that's because some experts in England have been studying old maps and claimed that Zhenghe discovered America before Columbus did.

Bobby: Do you believe it's true?

Bill: I don't know. It could be, during his 28-year career he went to just about every other place on the planet.

Columbus' adventures pale beside those of Admiral Zhenghe. During his 28-year career, he commanded at least 317 ships and 37,000 men. He sailed from Korea to Antarctica, and even around the southern tip of Africa into the Atlantic Ocean. And it's quite possible that part of his fleet sailed to South America. But in his youth he did not seem a likely candidate to become one of history's greatest adventurers—he was a eunuch!

Zhenghe's ancestors included the King of Bukhara, which is now southern Uzbekistan, and the governor of Yunnan, the last Mongol holdout against the Ming. But the Ming armies brought Yunnan to its knees in 1381. Zhenghe became a scholar, and turned out to be adept in languages and philosophy. He was hired by the prince who overthrew the emperor, and then Zhenghe was appointed Admiral.

Zhenghe's nine masted flagship was 440 feet long—1 ½ time the length of a football field, and just about the length of Noah's Ark![1] Thanks to Chinese innovations like watertight compartments, new sails, and central rudders, and undefeatable weaponry, seafaring was relatively safe, and during his seven voyages Zhenghe sailed most of the known world, and some that wasn't known. His excellent navigational charts remained unsurpassed for centuries.

Dialogue—Zhenghe, Man of Peace—Usually!

Bobby: I wonder what people thought when Zhenghe showed up on their shores with his vast fleet of giant ships?

Bill: Personally, I'd have been terrified. I think back then, giant ships like this showing up would be like a flying saucer today landing on the White House lawn!

Bobby: Did Zhenghe's navy ever attack any nations?

Bill: As far as I know, all 7 journeys were peaceful—except for one incident.

---

[1] Noah's Ark: from the Biblical story of the great global flood; Genesis, chapters 6-9

第9集　大航海家郑和

导语——

在上一期的“老外看福建”节目中，潘维廉博士说中国人在古代就是出色的航海者，今天他就要为我们介绍一位伟大的古代航海家——郑和。

现场（海交馆郑和蜡像）——

包东宇：最近西方媒体经常有关于郑和的报道。

潘维廉：我想这大概是因为英国的一些专家一直在研究古代地图。他们声称，郑和的船队可能比哥伦布早半个多世纪就到过南美洲了。

包东宇：你觉得会不会真是这样？

潘维廉：我不知道。不过很有可能，因为郑和在他 28 年的航海生涯中几乎走遍了大半个地球。

解说——

哥伦布的探险经历如果和伟大的航海家郑和比起来会显得黯然失色。在郑和远航的 28 年中，他统领过至少 317 艘船和 37000 多人。他的舰队到过的地方北至朝鲜半岛，向南接近南极洲，甚至可能曾经越过非洲南端的好望角进入了大西洋。郑和船队中有一部分船只很可能到过南美洲。不过郑和年轻时并不像是个会成为历史上最伟大的探险家的人选——因为他是个太监！

郑和的家族祖上曾经有布哈拉的国王，布哈拉现在在中亚乌兹别克斯坦南部；还有元朝抵抗明朝的最后根据地云南的首领。郑和最终成了一个学者，而且尤其擅长于语言和哲学。他为燕王朱棣所用，朱棣从建文帝朱允手中夺取帝位后，郑和被任命为皇家舰队的统领。

郑和的那艘九桅旗舰长达 440 英尺（约 140 多米）几乎相当于一个半足球场，也就是跟诺亚方舟差不多长吧！正是得益于中国人发明的密封隔水舱、平面帆、中央方向舵和精良的武器这些东西，远洋航海才变得比较安全易行。郑和七次下西洋，到过当时为人所知的大部分地方，同时还发现了不少新地方。他在国际航海史上的成就几百年都没有人能够超越。

现场——

包东宇：我真想知道当郑和庞大的舰队出现在海岸边人们的眼前时，他们会是怎样的一种感受。

潘维廉：如果是我，一定会被惊呆。当时的人们看到一支由那么多大船组成的舰队肯定非常惊诧，就好比现代人突然看见飞碟降落在白宫南草坪上一样。

包东宇：郑和的舰队有没有攻击过什么地方？

潘维廉：据我所知，他的远航都很和平，只有一次遇上了点儿麻烦。

Zhenghe's first voyage, in 1405, included 62 ships and 27,800 men. Yet in spite of the vast size of this Chinese armada, and its formidable weapons, Zhenghe had only peaceful intentions. He visited South Vietnam, Thailand, Western Malaysia, Java, India, and Sri Lanka, and returned home to China in 1407. But during the second journey, in 1409, the King of Ceylon was not terribly hospitable. Zhenghe simply dethroned him and brought him back to China. He seemed very matter of fact about it!

Quanzhou still has a Sri Lankan Prince's home, beside the Ashab Mosque. A Quanzhou native told me, in all solemnity, that the Sri Lankan prince's female descendants all have natural holes in their earlobes.

Zhenghe visited Western Indonesia on his third voyage, and went as far as Egypt and Mecca on his fourth. Zhenghe returned from his seventh and final voyage in 1433 with a cargo that included, amongst other things, giraffes and zebras. But the Emperor was slowly coming to the same conclusion as dozens of Emperors before and after him—that China was pretty much self-sufficient. Zhenghe died soon after, and international trade was never again the same.

Dialogue—an Excavated Song Dynasty Ship

Bill: Zhenghe's accomplished so much, he almost seems like a legend! He seemed determined to sail to the ends of the earth and back—not once but seven times.

Bobby: I can't imagine what it must have been like to sail so far back in those days.

Bill: I can't either. But this unearthed Song Dynasty ship in the museum here gives us a small taste of what it must have been like.

In 1974, locals discovered the ancient hull of a 24.2 meter long, 9 meter wide Song Dynasty ship near Houzhu harbor. The ship had 13 separate watertight compartments, and many features not found on western ships until the middle of the 15th century. In February 1991, a UNESCO delegation investigated a wealth of archaeological artifacts and determined that Quanzhou's Jiuri Mountain was indeed the beginning of Marco Polo's fabled Silk Road of the Sea. There is even an inscription now, in Chinese and English, commemorating the UNESCO delegation's visit.

Quanzhou—Holy Land of Asia! Nowadays, Westerners are learning about Zhenghe, and the Silk Road of the Sea—but many don't know that not only did traders from all over the world converge in the great port of Zaytun, but they also brought with them their own philosophies, beliefs and religions. So Zaytun was not only the Alexandria of Asia but also, in a sense, the Holy Land of Asia! The city hosted almost every religion known to man. It's no wonder that UNESCO has also called the city, "A World Museum of Religion." And at least one of those Western religions is now found nowhere in the world but Quanzhou!

♪解说

郑和在 1405 年第一次远航的时候，率领了 62 艘“宝船”和 27800 多人。虽然这支中国舰队规模庞大并且配备了精良的武器，郑和远航的目的却是和平的。他访问了占城（今越南南部）、泰国、苏门达腊（今马来西亚西部）、爪哇、印度和锡兰（今斯里兰卡），于 1407 年回国。不过郑和 1409 年第二次下西洋的时候，锡兰国王对他挺不客气的，于是郑和就把他赶下台带回了中国，看起来郑和对这事还挺慎重的。

泉州现在还保存着一处锡兰王子的故居，就在清净寺旁边。一个泉州当地人挺严肃地告诉我说，那位锡兰王子后裔中的女子，耳垂上都带有天生的耳孔。

郑和第三次下西洋的时候到了印度尼西亚西部，第四次则远航到埃及和麦加。1433 年，郑和第七次也是最后一次远航归国的时候，他带回的大量物资中甚至包括长颈鹿和斑马。不过明朝皇帝（明成祖朱棣）最终还是像其他帝王一样，觉得中国完全可以自给自足。郑和回国以后很快就去世了，从此国际贸易也是风光不再。

♪现场（开元寺古船陈列馆）

潘维廉：哇，郑和的功勋简直就是一部传奇。他好像一心要找到天尽头然后再回头——并且不止一次而是七次！

包东宇：我几乎不敢想象当年人们怎么能够航行那么远。

潘维廉：我也是。不过，后来出土的这艘宋代古船遗骸上面，我们多少还能感受到一点当年的情形。

♪解说

1974 年，这艘长 24.2 米，宽 9 米的宋代古船在泉州后渚港附近被发现。这艘船有 13 个密封防水隔离舱，还具有许多直到 15 世纪中叶才在西方船舶上出现的其他特征。1991 年 2 月，联合国教科文组织的一个代表团对泉州丰富的文物古迹进行了考察，他们最后确认泉州九日山就是马可·波罗所说的海上丝绸之路的起点。现在九日山的岩壁上还用中英文刻有联合国教科文组织代表团访问的纪念文字。

现在，越来越多的西方人开始认识到郑和和古代的海上丝绸之路。不过许多人只知道来自世界各地的商人曾经汇聚在刺桐港，并不了解他们也带来了各种各样的哲学思想、信仰以及宗教。因此，刺桐不仅仅是亚洲的亚历山大港，在某种意义上更是亚洲的宗教圣地！泉州城几乎包容了所有的宗教派别，无怪乎联合国教科文组织会把泉州命名为“世界宗教博物馆”。至少，其中有一种源于西方的宗教如今世上只有在泉州还能找得到。

Episode10 Quanzhou, the Holy Land of Ancient Asia

1000-yr-old Ashab Mosque
www.Amoymagic.mts.cn

Introduction In today's episode, Dr. Bill explains why he calls the ancient port of Quanzhou the Holy Land of Ancient Asia.

People from all over the world met in Quanzhou because it was the starting point of the Silk Road of the Sea. Of course, when they met they also shared and adopted each others ideas, philosophies and religions. So it's no surprise that Quanzhou was not only one of the greatest ports of ancient times, but also a great center of religion. In a way, it was the Holy Land of Asia, because it had representatives of every major religion on the planet! It's no wonder that UNESCO has designated Quanzhou as a World Museum of Religion. In addition to local religions, Quanzhou had one of the world's oldest Muslim communities, with at least 7 mosques, as well as Nestorian Churches, Franciscan churches and cathedrals, and places of worship for Hindus and Jews, as well as other minor religions.

Tomorrow, we'll look at the foreign religions—but today we'll start with Confucianism, Taoism—and Buddhism's oldest temple in Fujian.

Dialogue—Jiuri Hill, Start of Maritime Silk Road

Bobby: This little temple is Fujian's oldest Buddhist temple?

Bill: That's right. Yanfu temple was built here, at the base of Jiuri Mountain in 288 AD. And on the peak is the Stone Buddha Pavilion, which is 300 years older than the old Stone Saint, the Taoist Stone Saint.

Quanzhou officials used to gather here on Jiuri Hill twice a year because this was the official starting point of the Silk Road of the Sea.

A UNESCO delegation visited Jiuri Hill, and left an inscription written in both English and Chinese. So in a way I suppose this is a holy place for Buddhists and businessmen alike. It's also a quite beautiful place. One stone has the characters "Qiji", which means people are so moved by Jiuri Mountain's beauty that they want to stay forever.

These characters "Qiji" mean people are so moved by Jiuri Mountain's beauty that they want to stay here forever.

Dialogue—Jiuri Mountain Men

Bill: You know, maybe the mountain really does make people want to stay here all their life.

Bobby: Why is that?

Bill: The Monk Wudeng stayed in this cave here for 44 years!

Bobby: You're kidding!

Bill: No, I'm not! And the pavilion on the top of the mountain was built in honor of the poet Chenxu. He lived on top of the mountain for 23 years—I wouldn't want to live here.

第 10 集 泉州，古代亚洲的圣地

导语

在今天的“老外看福建”节目里，潘维廉博士将向大家解释为什么他要称赞泉州为古代亚洲的圣地。

解说

来自世界各地的人们会聚泉州，因为泉州是古代海上丝绸之路的起点。当人们聚在一起的时候，他们会很自然地交流并接受彼此的思想观念和宗教信仰。因此不难理解为什么泉州当时不仅仅是一座东方大港，还是各种宗教信仰交汇的地方。可以说，泉州是古代亚洲的一处宗教圣地，因为这里几乎汇集了世界上所有主要的宗教派别。难怪联合国教科文组织会将泉州命名为“世界宗教博物馆”。除了当地固有的佛教、道教等宗教以外，泉州还有世界上最古老的穆斯林族群，并且曾经拥有至少七座伊斯兰教清真寺。此外，基督教长老会、天主教圣芳济会都在泉州设立了教会和大教堂。同时泉州还拥有印度教和犹太教的礼拜场所，以及其他的一些小教派。

现场（九日山延福寺）

潘维廉：明天我们会说到外国宗教。今天，我们先从儒教、道教，还有福建最早的佛教寺庙说起。

包东宇：这座小庙就是福建最早的佛教寺院吗？

潘维廉：没错。这座延福寺在公元 288 年时就建在了九日山的山脚下。山顶上还有一个石佛厅，里面的那尊石佛比清源山上的道教老君岩还早 300 年。

解说

古代时泉州的地方官员每年要在九日山上举行两次祈风仪式，因为这里是海上丝绸之路的“官方”起点。联合国教科文组织的代表团参观九日山后，留下了一处用中英文两种语言书写的纪念石刻。

我想，无论对于佛教徒还是商人来说，九日山都是个朝圣的好地方，而且这里的风景也挺不错。九日山上有一块石头，上面刻着“奇迹”两个字，意思是说九日山上的景色实在太美了，让人想在这里呆上一辈子。

现场（九日山上无等洞、秦系亭等）

潘维廉：依我看，九日山可能真的让人想在这里呆上一辈子。

包东宇：这是为什么？

潘维廉：你看，无等和尚就在这个小洞里呆了 44 年！

包东宇：你不是开玩笑吧！

潘维廉：这是真的！山顶上那座亭子是为了纪念唐代诗人秦系而建造的。他就在那里住了 23 年。不过，我可不愿意住在这里。

Bobby: I can't see how anyone could stay on one hill for so long.

Bill: Evidently Chinese, only Chinese, have the heart for it. There was an Indian monk that came here, in fact he was the one that cut out this Chinese chessboard here 1700 years ago, but he only last here two years, and he went back home.

Kaiyuan Temple Miraculous Mulberry Tree One of Fujian's greatest religious centers is Quanzhou's Kaiyuan Temple, which was built during the Tang Dynasty in 686. Legend claims that a monk asked a rich man to donate land for the monastery. The landowner told the monk, "Only if this mulberry tree sprouts lotus flowers within 3 days." To his dismay, it did. He handed over the land, and eventually Kaiyuan temple boasted over 4.500 acres of land, and by 1285 A.D. had 120 affiliated schools. Friar Odoric wrote that Kaiyuan had 3,000 monks and 11,000 idols!

Kaiyuan's Miraculous Mulberry Tree

Kaiyuan Temple covers 30,000 square meters and the main hall is supported by 100 stone columns, hence its nickname, Hundred Pillar Hall. Each pillar is carved in a unique design, and on the crossbeams are carved 24 winged singers and dancers, resembling angels in Catholic churches. Kaiyuan also has a library with over 37,000 volumes of Buddhist scriptures, a Buddhist Museum, a maritime museum, the 1400 year old Mulberry—Lotus tree—and two pagodas that may have given birth to China's version of the monkey king legend!

Dialogue—Fujian, Home of the Monkey King?

Bill: Did you know that some people claim the Monkey King legend came right here from Quanzhou?

Bobby: No, I've not heard that. But Monkey King isn't a religion.

Bill: That's true. But he's a folk hero, and many people worship him. And because these two stone pagodas had carvings of a Monkey King-like character long before Journey to the West was written in the 16th century, some people say the Monkey King came right here from Quanzhou, of course, probably it originated in India long ago.

包东宇：我想不出怎么有人能在一座山上住那么久。

潘维廉：很显然，只有中国人才有这种耐心。从前有个叫拘那罗陀（中文名真谛）的印度和尚来这里住过。他就是 1700 年前刻出这个棋盘的那个人。他只在九日山上住了两年就回家去了。

解说——

泉州开元寺是福建最有名的佛教寺院之一，开元寺始建于唐朝垂拱二年，也就是公元 686 年。相传有一个和尚请求一位财主把他的桑园捐出来建寺庙。财主对和尚说："如果这些桑树能够在三天之内开出莲花来我就捐园建庙。"结果，桑树真的开出了白莲花，财主也只好捐出了土地。后来开元寺的面积曾经一度达到 4500 多英亩，到了公元 1285 年，开元寺已经拥有 120 个附属禅院。14 世纪的圣方济会修士弗莱尔·奥多里克（Friar Odoric）曾描述说，开元寺拥有 3000 名僧人和 11000 尊佛像！

目前，开元寺的占地面积有 78000 平方米。主体建筑大雄宝殿由近百根石柱支撑，所以人们又称它为"百柱殿"。殿内的石柱雕刻图案独特，大殿的斗拱间有 24 尊手持乐器的"飞天"，看上去好像基督教的天使。开元寺的藏经阁内存有 37000 多册佛经。寺内还有一家佛教博物馆、一个古船陈列馆和一株近 1400 年的桑莲古树。开元寺内的东西双塔还可能是中国版"美猴王"传说的发源地。

现场（双塔）——

潘维廉：你知道吗，有些人说美猴王的传说最早来自于泉州？

包东宇：我没有听说过，不过美猴王并不是什么宗教信仰啊。

潘维廉：话虽不错，但他是民间传说中的英雄，现在还有人对他顶礼膜拜呢。这两座石塔上有的人物雕刻看上去很像美猴王，而且这些雕刻比 16 世纪写出的《西游记》还要早几百年，因此有人说美猴王的故事可能起源于泉州。当然，也有可能是很早以前从印度传进来的。

Monkey King
(Quanzhou Pagoda)

Twin Pagodas These twin pagodas were first built of wood (the East in 679, the West in 916), then later rebuilt in brick, and in the early 13th century reconstructed in stone. The East pagoda is 48 meters high, while the west one is 44 meters high. Each tower has 16 large relief carvings, and more than 40 smaller relief carvings on the pedestals.

Pondering the Pagoda

Old Stone Saint To the north of Quanzhou lies one of Taoism's most sacred sites: Mt. Qingyuan. Taoist alchemists in Ziji Hall labored from the mid seventh century to find the elixir of eternal life. Evidently they failed, because their mortality rate was the same as ours: 100%.

Tourists visit the mountain today to enjoy the rocks, forests, springs, and the Song Dynasty 5.55 meter statue of Lao Zi, the founder of Taoism.

Dialogue—The Stone Saint Gets Rubbed the Wrong Way[1]

Bobby: Did you know this is the largest Taoist sculpture in China?

Bill: No, I didn't know that. But I do know that in 1989, when I first came to see this, the locals told me that if you rubbed his nose you lived to be 120, and if you rubbed his eyes you'd live to be 160! So many people were rubbing him that they had to fence him off.

Bobby: Oh, maybe too many people were rubbing him the wrong way!

Bill: Yeah, I think so.

Quanzhou is holy for Buddhist, Taoists and Confucians. It also competes with Putian and Fuqing for being home to Southern Shaolin Kungfu. But Quanzhou is especially famous for not only hosting but even financing half a dozen foreign religions!

---

[1] Rub the wrong way: annoy or anger someone

解说——

开元寺的双塔最初都是木质结构，东塔镇国塔始建于 679 年，西塔仁寿塔始建于 916 年。后来双塔都改建为砖塔，13 世纪上半叶又先后被改建为石塔。东塔高 48 米，西塔高 44 米。两座塔的塔身上各有 16 幅大型浮雕，塔座上还有 40 多幅比较小的浮雕。

位于泉州北郊的清源山是一处道教圣地。紫矾殿中的道教术士从 7 世纪中叶的时候就开始寻求长生不老的灵丹妙药，很显然他们没有成功，因为他们的死亡率跟我们是一样的——百分之百。

现在游人们到清源山来欣赏这里的奇松怪石、飞瀑流泉和那座高 5.63 米的宋代老君造像。这位老君就是道教的创始人老子。

现场（老君岩前）——

包东宇：你知道吗，这是中国现存最大的宋代道教石刻？

潘维廉：不知道。不过 1989 年我第一次来看他老人家的时候，当地人告诉我说，如果摸到他的鼻子，你就能活到 120 岁；如果摸到他的眼睛，你就能活到 160 岁！后来因太多人爬上去摸，管理人员只好用栅栏把他隔开了。

包东宇：哦，可能是很多人摸错了地方，惹他老人家生气了吧！

解说——

泉州是佛教、道教和儒教的圣地。同时还跟莆田和福清一样，号称自己是南少林功夫的发祥地。不过泉州同样以包容并支持了五六种外来宗教的发展而闻名于世。

Episode 11 Quanzhou, the Holy Land of Foreign Religions

Introduction In yesterday's episode of Magic Fujian, Dr. Bill explained why UNESCO selected Quanzhou as a World Museum of Religion. Today, he looks at the foreign religions that came in upon the Silk Road of the Sea.

From Mohammed to Quanzhou? Quanzhou not only has one of the oldest Buddhist temples in China but also one of the oldest Muslim Communities as well. Legends claim that Mohammed sent four disciples to China, and two of them came to Quanzhou. The two Muslim saints' tombs are on a hill called Spirit Hill, because it supposedly glowed at night.

Dialogue—Wind Moving Stone

Bobby: Do you think the tombs are genuine?

Bill: I don't know. But archaeologists say some of these stones are from the Tang Dynasty, so that would put it about the right period. By the way—have you ever seen that Wind Moving Stone over there?

Bobby: Yes, I heard Dongshan island also has one.

Bill: Yes, well the local Muslims say that this one is a miraculous gift from Allah! Want to try it?

Bobby: All right.

Ashab Mosque At one time Quanzhou had at least 7 mosques, but only the Ashab mosque remains today. It was built in 1009 A.D., and modeled after a beautiful mosque in Damascus. The white dome above the Fengtian Altar collapsed during the 1607 earthquake, but the 20 meter high vaulted entrance and four walls remain, and Quanzhou's Muslims plan to restore the mosque to its former glory. Today, it is considered one of China's ten most important historic sites.

Dialogue–The Museum's Ancient Gravestones

Bobby: Look! Some of these gravestones are written in both Chinese and Arabic!

Bill: Yeah, and if you look close, you can see that the Arabic was kind of square, like Chinese characters! So you can see that the Arabs and the Chinese had a lot of influence on each other.

Nestorian Tombstone

第11集 泉州，外国宗教圣地

♪导语

在昨天的“老外看福建”节目中，潘维廉博士解释了为什么联合国教科文组织会把泉州命名为“世界宗教博物馆”。今天，他将为我们介绍通过海上丝绸之路涌入泉州的外来宗教。

♪解说

泉州不仅仅拥有中国历史最悠久的汉传佛教寺院之一，同时也有中国最古老的穆斯林族群之一。相传唐代时穆罕默德派遣四个门徒来华，其中有两个在泉州传教。这两位穆斯林先贤的墓葬所在地叫作灵山，因为据说这座山晚上能闪现灵光。

♪现场（看伊斯兰教圣墓和风动石）

包东宇：你说这灵山圣墓真会是穆斯林先贤的墓葬吗？

潘维廉：我也说不准。不过，根据考古学家的考证，这里的一些石刻确实是唐朝的。因此，两者在时间上基本吻合。对了，你看到那边的风动石了吗？

包东宇：看到了。我听说东山岛上也有一块。

潘维廉：没错。当地的穆斯林说，这块风动石是真主安拉恩赐的神奇礼物。想不想去推推看？

包东宇：好啊！

♪解说

泉州历史上曾经有七座伊斯兰教清真寺，不过，保存至今的只有清净寺（阿拉伯名叫“艾苏哈卜大寺”）。清净寺始建于公元 1009 年，是仿照大马士革一座漂亮的清真寺建造的。清净寺奉天坛（礼拜大殿）的白色圆顶在 1607 年的大地震中被震塌，不过 20 米高的门楼和大殿的四壁依旧保存完好，具有极高的历史价值。泉州的穆斯林正准备重修清净寺，让它再现当年的辉煌。目前，清净寺已被列为中国十大名寺之一。

♪现场（海交馆古代宗教石刻）

包东宇：看，有些墓碑的碑文有中文和阿拉伯文两种文字！

潘维廉：对，而且凑近看的话你就会发现，有些阿拉伯文字看上去方方正正，就像中文字一样！所以说阿拉伯人和中国人在许多方面是相互影响的。

Hundreds of Ancient Artifacts Workers have recovered over 150 Islamic stones used to refurbish city walls and gates during the late 14th and 15th centuries. The Maritime Museum's collection includes 138 Islamic fragments, as well as 133 Hindu, 44 Christian, and one Manichean. One tombstone was of the son of the Persian prime minister killed in 1312.

The ancient Arabs have tens of thousands of descendants in Quanzhou. Just Baiqi Island alone has over 10,000 Arab descendants surnamed Guo.

Researchers discovered that 1,000 or so Xunpu people, in a tiny fishing village just south of Quanzhou, are descendants of an Arab official of the Yuan Dynasty (1271-1368).

Dialogue—Imperial Sponsorship of Foreign Religions

Bill: Quanzhou had so many religions back at that time because even then China was the biggest market. The Nestorians and the Catholics competed with each otherand both of them competed with the Muslims.

Bobby: What did the Emperor think of all this religions competition?

Bill: He pretty much left them to themselves. In fact, Andrew of Perugia said that the Emperor even financed foreign religions!

Bobby: But who was Andrew of Perugia?

Bill: Andrew of Perugia was the 3rd Catholic Bishop of Zaytun. I've read so much about him that I was pretty excited to see his headstone! Of course now I wonder where he rests his head.

Bishop Andrew wrote that the Emperor granted the Franciscans a living allowance like the one he gave to foreign princes, orators, warriors, artists, entertainers, and poor people. This allowance was so generous that they used it towards building their churches, convents, and a cathedral. In fact, he said that the Emperor's grants, called Alafas, were larger than the annual budget of many European kingdoms!

In January, 1326, right here in Quanzhou, Bishop Andrew wrote,

"Even I who am here in China can hardly believe the things I hear…It is a fact that in this vast empire there are people of every nation under heaven, and every sect, and everyone may live freely according to their own belief."

The Manichaean Religion of Persia Quanzhou did indeed have followers of just about every religion there was. But one of the most unusual religions began over 1700 years ago in Persia, and today is found only here in Quanzhou!

Carving of Persian Mani

解说——

建筑工人们曾经在工地挖掘出 150 多块伊斯兰教石刻。这些石刻在 14 世纪末、15 世纪初的时候曾被用作翻修泉州城墙和城门的石料。现在，泉州海上交通史博物馆保存着 138 块伊斯兰教墓石，133 块印度教雕刻，以及 44 块基督教石刻和一块摩尼教石刻。其中有一块墓碑是纪念一位波斯首相之子的，他死于 1312 年。

Vishnu Statue in Quanzhou

古代阿拉伯人在泉州的后裔数以万计，仅在白岐岛，就有 1 万多名郭姓的阿拉伯人后裔。

研究者还发现，在泉州南部一个叫作浔浦的小渔村，这里的大约 1000 名村民都是元代（1271-1368）一位阿拉伯官员的后裔。

现场（海交馆宗教石刻）——

潘维廉：泉州当时拥有那么多的宗教派别，这是因为当时中国是一个巨大的市场。长老会跟天主教相互竞争，而两者又都在跟伊斯兰教竞争。

包东宇：那么，当时的中国皇帝是怎么看待这种宗教竞争的呢？

潘维廉：他基本上是放手让他们自己管理。其实根据佩鲁贾·安德鲁书中的记载，皇帝甚至还资助过外来宗教的发展！

包东宇：佩鲁贾·安德鲁又是谁呢？

潘维廉：安德鲁是天主教在泉州的第三任主教。我读过不少关于他的东西，现在能看见他的墓石真的很高兴，只可惜见不到他本人。

解说——

安德鲁主教在书中写道，皇帝拨给圣芳济会的修道者一笔生活津贴，跟外国王子、演说家、武士、艺术家、演员和穷人一视同仁。这笔津贴相当可观，他们就把它用来修建教堂、修道院和一座大教堂。他说，其实皇帝拨发的津贴甚至比欧洲有些王国一年的预算还要多！

1326 年 1 月，安德鲁主教在泉州写道：“就算是身处中国的我也很难相信我听到的这些事情……这个庞大的帝国容纳了天下所有的民族和所有的教派，所有的人都能遵循各自的信仰自由地生活在这里，而这一切都是实情。”

泉州的确曾经拥有世界上几乎任何一种宗教的追随者。还有一种 1700 多年前起源于波斯的独特教派，如今只有在泉州还能找到它的踪影。

Dialogue—Use the Force!

Bill: The prophet Mani lived in Persia over 1700 years ago, and he taught that all religions had some grain of truth in them. He said the whole universe was just a battle between Good and Evil, Light and Dark.

Bobby: Wow. Sounds kind of like the Star Wars movies!

Bill: Yeah! Use the force, Luke!

Even the great Western philosopher St. Augustine followed the Mani religion for ten years, until the Catholic church came down on it heavily.

Eventually Mani's disciples went abroad to escape persecution, and one reached Quanzhou in 694 A.D. He is buried on Mt. Qingyuan, site of the Old Stone Saint.

Chinese called Mani's faith the "Religion of Light, which gave it trouble in the end. The word for light was "Ming"—same as the Dynasty, so the Emperor outlawed it.

The Cao'an Nunnery, built in 1148 on Huabiao Mountain, is the last remaining place on earth where Mani is worshipped, and the sculpture of Mani, with his distinctive dreadlocks and aura, is now the emblem of the International Manichaeist Research Society.

Dialogue—Jewish Artifact?

Bobby: It looks like Quanzhou was a religious buffet—something for everyone!

Bill: It sure was. Archaeologists have uncovered over 300 Hindu fragments of Hindu stones, so it's very likely that Quanzhou even had a Hindu temple. In just last year, archaeologists uncovered this stone. This could be the first archaeological proof of the ancient Jewish settlement. It has here what looks like a star of David that has been worn over the years. And on the other side they think there could have been a Jewish candleholder. So UNESCO was right on target when they said Quanzhou was a World Museum of Religion.

Ancient "Star of David?"
(unearthed in Quanzhou)

♪**现场**（华表山摩尼教草庵）———

潘维廉：先知摩尼是 1700 多年前生活在波斯的一位异人。他声称任何一种宗教都蕴含了某种真理。他说，整个宇宙就是善与恶、光明与黑暗之间的一场较量。

包东宇：哇，听起来有点像电影星球大战！

潘维廉：是啊。使出你的力量吧，卢克！

♪**解说**———

伟大的西方哲学家圣·奥古斯丁曾做过十年摩尼教的信徒。后来天主教的势力迅速膨胀，摩尼的弟子纷纷逃向海外以躲避迫害。其中，有一个弟子在公元 694 年到达了泉州。他死后就被葬在清源山上。

中国人把摩尼教叫作“明教”。结果后来犯了忌讳，因为“明教”的“明”跟“明朝”的“明”是同一个字，于是明朝皇帝就把明教给取缔了。

始建于 1148 年的摩尼教草庵坐落在晋江罗山镇的华表山上，是世界上仅存的摩尼教遗址。草庵内供奉的摩尼光佛坐像散发披肩，背后毫光四射，现在成了国际摩尼教研究会的标志。

Planet's Last Manichean Temple

♪**现场**（天后宫寻找石刻）———

包东宇：泉州就好像一个宗教集市，什么教派都找得到！

潘维廉：没错。考古学家已经发现了 300 多处零散的印度教石刻，因此泉州很可能有过一个印度教寺院。就在去年，考古人员发现了这块石刻，上面这个图案看上去很像犹太教的大卫之星，虽然年代久远，有些模糊。他们还怀疑，石头的另一面有个图案是犹太教的烛台。这很可能就是古代犹太人曾经定居泉州的物证。所以说，把泉州称作“世界宗教博物馆”是再合适不过了。

Episode 12 Quanzhou Culture

Introduction In the last few episodes of Magic Fujian, Dr. Bill showed how Quanzhou was an ancient center of world trade and religion. Today he explains how this affected local culture.

Fujianese, especially those from the great ancient ports of Fuzhou and Quanzhou, have always been the bold adventurers and merchants of ancient China. And bold people live life boldly.

Quanzhou's Jubao (Treasure) Street It's hard to believe that this quiet street was once perhaps the center of the world's greatest trade in jewels and gold, and as an ancient Chinese wrote, "Throughout the market are precious gems, and the amusements of song and dance are intoxicating; it is enough to make most anyone dead drunk."

Ancient Quanzhou still intoxicates people even today, though not so much with its wild international trade as its festive atmosphere 365 days a year—especially at night, when the lamps are lit, lights are slung through trees, and ancient temples and pavilions are outlined in neon. The performers are on the street corners, and markets are abuzz with buyers and sellers.

Sherbert Bikes Even bicycles reflect Quanzhou people's fun loving spirit. People all over China pedal bicycles but Quanzhou people pedal what Sue and I call "Sherbet bikes—"bikes with plastic wheels in ice cream colors that look good enough to eat. Sue and I like seeing how many flavors of ice cream we find—lemon, lime, vanilla, and cherry.

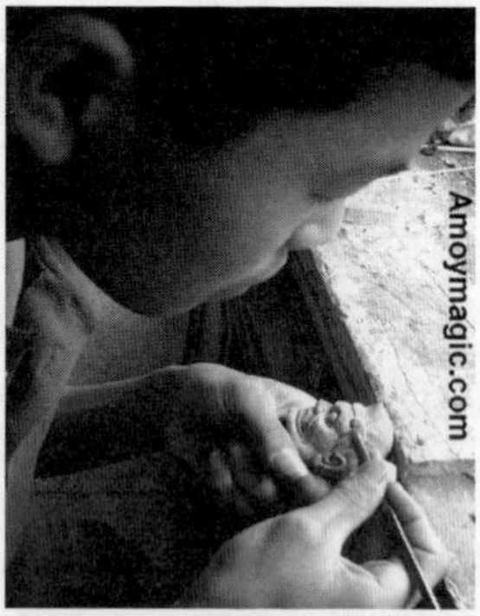

Dialogue—Quanzhou Marionette Museum

Bill: Bobby, did you know that Quanzhou was once the marionette capital of China?

Bobby: Yes, Quanzhou's puppets are famous all over the world.

Bill: But have you ever seen one made?

Bobby: No, I haven't. Do people still make them by hand?

Bill: Yes, they do—but it's a vanishing art.

Bringing a Puppet to Life When Gepetto made Pinocchio, he wanted a real boy. In the hands of a master, Chinese puppets come to life! They can even bend down and pick up something from the floor with their hands! And they all began with a block of camphor wood. It is shaped until ready to paint, and then given several coats. Mass production puppet heads can be made in only 3 days or so, but a true master may spend 2 to 4 weeks, and the quality is worlds apart—even to my undiscerning eye. And the costumes are a work of art in themselves. The detail on these costumes is incredible. It's no wonder that puppets can cost so much.

第 12 集 泉州文化

导语

在前几期的“老外看福建”节目中，潘维廉博士向我们讲述了古代泉州曾经是一个世界贸易和宗教的中心。今天，他将为我们介绍泉州独特的文化传统。

解说

福建人，尤其是生活在福州和泉州这样的著名港口的福建人，一直都是中国古代最无畏的冒险者和商人。而无畏者的生活也往往是豪迈不羁的。

很难想象眼前这条平和的街道（聚宝路）可能曾经是世界上最繁忙的金银珠宝集散地。正如中国一位古人所写得那样：“集市上满眼珍宝，欢畅的歌舞令人迷醉，足以让任何人在此醉生梦死。”

古老的泉州今天同样令人着迷，虽说国际贸易不如从前那么繁荣，但城里一年到头都好像沉浸在节庆气氛中。特别是在晚上，路灯亮了起来，街边的树上挂满彩灯，古老的寺庙和亭台在霓虹灯的勾勒下流光溢彩。民间艺人在街角演唱，集市里则是熙熙攘攘。

甚至连自行车都能折射出泉州人对激情生活的追求。全中国的人都骑自行车，不过只有泉州人特别爱骑这种“雪糕单车”——这些自行车的塑料轮圈带有各种可爱的雪糕般的颜色，于是我和我妻子苏珊就把它们叫作“雪糕单车”。我们时常在街头数看到了多少种口味的自行车——有柠檬的、宜母子的、香草的和樱桃的。

现场（在木偶博物馆表演木偶）

潘维廉：包，你知道泉州曾经是中国的木偶之都吗？
包东宇：没错，泉州木偶在世界上都很有名。
潘维廉：那么你看见过木偶是怎么生产出来的吗？
包东宇：没有。现在还需要用手工制作吗？
潘维廉：要，不过现在手工制作木偶的工艺已经快失传了。

解说

当木雕艺人吉派托刻出匹诺曹的时候，他想要的是一个真正的小男孩。而在中国工艺大师的手中，木偶真的被赋予了生命，它们甚至可以弯下腰，用自己的手从地上捡起东西来！要知道，它们最初不过是一块樟木而已。木偶头在雕刻成形之后，漆上油彩，再穿上几件衣裳，就成了一个完整的木偶。批量生产的木偶头只要三天左右就可以完成，而一个真正的精品则需要耗费两到四个星期的时间，它们的品质可以说是天差地别，就连我这种外行都能看得出来。木偶服装的设计制作其本身就是一种艺术，服装图案之精细令人咋舌，也难怪这些木偶要卖得那么贵了。

Dialogue—Vanishing Craft

Bobby: Why did you say earlier that puppet making is a vanishing art?

Bill: Oh, there's only a few dozen people in Quanzhou that make puppets now—and perhaps only 10 to 20 master craftsmen that make the real high quality ones. The problem is that most young people nowadays aren't patient enough to spend 10 to 15 years it takes to master the art, and it doesn't pay that much anyway.

Quanzhou, the center of puppet culture, is afraid the craft will die out. So as early as kindergarten and primary schools, they teach children about puppetry and if they show an interest, they may select them to attend the arts primary school, where they are taught to work with puppets.

Huang Shaolong, director of the Quanzhou marionette troupe, which has over 700 plays dating back 400 years, once said that puppet making "isn't for the faint-hearted, as it requires dedication, commitment, and endless hours of practice."

Some puppets have four heads on one puppet, with four mouths and eight eyes, and all can move. One finger controls head and all those other things. I can see why it's not for the faint-hearted!

Dialogue—Quanzhou Night Life

Bill: The best thing about Quanzhou is the nightlife.

Bobby: How is it different from other cities?

Bill: Well, it is like Lantern Festival every night of the year—they have the lights and the music. For example, every night on the major intersections, I think they have performances of traditional arts like this Nanyin Opera!

Bobby: Very interesting!

Strolling Downtown Zhongshan Road My wife and I also enjoy just walking about town, watching the deaf artists perform quick caricatures, or listening to street side performers. The sights and sounds are rounded off by the smells. Nothing beats the aroma from the sweet potato man's barrel, or the Muslim's shish-ke-bab. A lady selling barbequed duck and pork had a long line in front of her stall. I figured she must be good. I was surprised when she absolutely refused any money. "First time for free!" she said. Her daughter helps her barbeque until 3 AM—but she likes the life, and meeting people.

现场（木偶作坊）——

包东宇：先前你为什么要说木偶制作的工艺快要失传了呢？

潘维廉：是这样的，现在泉州只有几十个人还在制作木偶，而且能做出高水准的木偶的大师级艺人只剩下十来个了。问题是现在大多数年轻人都没那个耐心花上十几年来学习木偶雕刻的技艺，况且干这行也挣不了很多钱。

解说——

作为中国的木偶艺术之乡，泉州十分珍视这份宝贵的文化遗产。因此泉州在幼儿园和小学中就开展了木偶戏知识的教育。如果学生对木偶兴趣浓厚，他们可以被选入艺术小学，在那里他们可以更深入地学习木偶制作的技术。

泉州木偶剧团能够表演400年来积累下来的700多出木偶戏。剧团团长黄少龙曾经说过，身子弱的人不适合演木偶戏，因为干这行需要奉献精神，需要专注和长年累月的艰苦训练。

有一些木偶头上面有四个小头，每个头上都有嘴巴和眼睛，这四张嘴巴八只眼睛都能活动。而这种木偶头的所有活动全靠一根手指来操纵，难怪身子弱的人干不了这一行！

现场（观看南音表演）——

潘维廉：我最喜欢泉州的夜生活了。

包东宇：泉州的夜晚和其他地方有什么不同吗？

潘维廉：哦，这里一年365天，每天晚上都像元宵节，到处都是彩灯和音乐。在市区一些主要路口旁的空地上，每天晚上都会有传统曲艺的表演，比如我们正在听的南音。

包东宇：嗯，挺有意思的！

解说——

我和我太太很喜欢在泉州城里到处逛，看聋艺人给人画速写，或者听卖唱的在街头表演。不过，百闻不如一见，百见不如一尝，烤红薯和烤肉串的香味绝对让人无法抗拒。

有一回，我看见一位大姐的烤肉摊前面围满了人。我猜她的手艺肯定很不错，就凑了上去。没想到她居然不收我的钱，还说："初次光临免费！"她和她女儿每天要做到凌晨三点，不过她说，她喜欢这种生活，还能认识不少人。

Staying Cool in Quanzhou Maybe that sums up Quanzhou's culture—it's cool—especially on a very hot summer's day, in the Water Park. Quanzhou's people have always enjoyed work and play and life, today perhaps more than ever as the city prospers and grows.

A Quanzhou City website website said that the city hopes its "reinvigorated culture and the openness of the heart and mind of its people will continue to rouse their thoughts, spread their field of vision, and enhance their spirits in order to live up to a proud past as well as the expectations of the current age.

The June 28th issue of Strait City Daily had an article entitled, "Quanzhou Plans the 'Silk Road of the Air.'" For Quanzhou, the best is yet to come.

Quanzhou's Water World

我想，泉州文化就是这样的赏心悦目，就像炎炎夏日里徜徉在泉州游乐园水上世界一样令人舒心畅快。泉州人一向是工作休闲两不误，而且随着这座城市的日益繁荣，泉州人也越来越会享受生活。

有一家泉州的网站曾经说，泉州将以其开阔的胸襟和勃勃的生机，激励人们继续开拓、奋进，建设一个无愧于辉煌过去的新泉州。

今年(2002 年)6 月 28 日，《海峡都市报》刊登了一篇名为《泉州要开辟一条“空中丝绸之路”》的文章。对泉州来说，好日子还在后头呢。

Episode 13 The Walled City of Chongwu

Introduction Join us on today's episode of Magic Fujian as Xiamen University's Dr. Bill takes us to Chongwu, one of China's few remaining walled cities, and home not only to Fujian's celebrated Hui'an maidens but also to one of the most unique temples in all of China!

Walled City of Chongwu

In ancient times, cities around the world were walled, and only a century ago China had hundreds of walled cities scattered around the country. Even Xiamen was walled until the 20s and 30s, when the walls were destroyed to allow the downtown area to expand more easily.

Today, Chongwu is one of the few remaining walled cities in China. The walls were built in 1384, and are 2.5 kilometres long and 7 meters high. Over 1600 battlements allowed locals' to safely fend off Japanese pirates, Chinese pirates, and foreign barbarians like myself!

Dialogue—Walled City of Chongwu

Bill: The biggest attraction here is that garden over there with 500 statues—but personally, I prefer the walled city itself!

Bobby: Why do you like it?

Bill: It's because when you go through these ancient gates here, it's like going back in time! Inside, it's peaceful, quiet. I love it!

I usually enter the gate by Xin Hua Nan Street. It is such a maze inside that I've considered tying a piece of string to the gate and my belt so I can find my way back out again! But the walled city is small, so if you go in one direction long enough you're bound to come out upon the wall, a gate, and freedom.

I enjoy the Chen family's beautiful old home with its carved stone, wooden paneling, and courtyard. The last time I visited, their son was making a batch of Chongwu's famous fish balls. I took a batch home and fried them up. Heavenly!

第 13 集　崇武古城

导语

欢迎收看系列报道“老外看福建”。今天，厦门大学的潘维廉博士将带我们去看看崇武古城。崇武古城是中国为数不多保存完好的古城。那里不仅有远近闻名的惠安女，还有中国大陆最独特的一座庙宇。

解说

远古时代，世界各地都喜欢用高墙围城。100 多年前，中国各地完好地保存着数百座古城墙。厦门的城墙一直保留到上个世纪二三十年代。后来，由于城区拓展，厦门的城墙才被拆除。

崇武古城是中国为数不多的保存较为完整的古城之一。古城的城墙建于 1384 年，长 2.5 公里，高 7 米。城墙上设有 1600 多个城堞，用于抵御日本倭寇、中国海盗和像我这样的番鬼。

Granny Chen whips up fine fish rolls!

现场

潘维廉：崇武最著名的旅游景点是拥有 500 多座雕塑的石雕园。不过，我个人更喜欢围墙内的古城。

包东宇：你为什么更喜欢古城?

潘维廉：因为走进古城门，就像走进历史。里面很平静、祥和。我特别喜欢。

解说

我一般是从新华南街进入古城。古城像一座迷宫，要想进城不迷路，必须带上一根绳子，一头绑在城门，一头系在腰间。还好，崇武古城不大。进城后，沿着一个方向往前走，你一定会找到城墙、城门和出路。

我喜欢古城陈家漂亮的古宅以及古宅里的石雕、庭院和木板饰面。上次造访时，陈家的儿子正在制作崇武鱼丸。我买了些回家，用油炸着吃。味道好极了！

At the "T" intersection we go right until we reach the wall, and then walk along it to the lighthouse. This offers the best view in town of the walled city, and of the curved beach. Hui'an is famous for its dozens of miles of fine beaches.

I love the exotic walled city of Chongwu—it's narrow streets, and ancient homes. But Chongwu also has one of the most unique temples in China!

Dialogue—The PLA Temple

Bill: Can you imagine a temple where they play revolutionary songs instead of Buddhist chants, and they worship 27 PLA soldiers?

Bobby: Well, it sounds pretty unusual.

Bill: It's one of a kind. I'll show it to you!

Bobby: Ok.

PLA Temple

Ms. Zhenghen

When the temple's founder, Ms. Zhengen, was only 12 years old, her family moved to Chongwu from Singapore. On September 17th, 1949, Taiwan planes attacked while she was on the beach. 24 PLA soldiers died to save the girl, and ever since Zhenghen has burned incense and offerings to show her gratitude and respect. And with two million Yuan in donations she began this temple in 1991. She had a hard time getting approval at first. But gradually they came to understand that her intent was merely to help people understand the sacrifices that these soldiers, and others, have made not only for her but for all Chinese in New China. And today, people from all over come to pay their respects to the martyred PLA soldiers.

But people also come from all over China to see the exotic Hui'an maidens!

进城后，我们在丁字路口右转，一直走到城墙。然后沿着城墙，找到了灯塔。灯塔是俯看崇武古城和弧型沙滩的最佳位置。惠安细白、金黄的沙滩延绵数十英里，远近闻名。

我喜欢崇武古城狭窄的街巷，古老的民宅以及古城里异乎寻常的情调。崇武古城附近还有一座中国独一无二的解放军战士庙。

♪现场

潘维廉：你能想像得到，寺庙不放佛教音乐，却播革命歌曲，里面还供奉着 27 名解放军战士？

包东宇：嗯，听上去有点特别。

潘维廉：没错，我们一起去看看。

♪解说

崇武 27 解放军战士庙是一位名叫曾恨的老太太筹集资金兴建的。曾恨 12 岁的时候，举家从新加坡迁回福建崇武。1949 年 9 月 17 日，曾恨在海滩上游玩，台湾军机来袭。为了救曾恨，24 名解放军战士光荣牺牲。从那以后，曾恨烧香供祭，以示她的感激和敬重之情。1991 年，曾恨募集 200 万元，开始建造 27 解放军战士庙。起初，申请建庙遇到了一些困难，但后来有关部门逐渐地意识到，建庙是为了让后人更好地了解解放军战士为曾恨和新中国所作出的巨大牺牲。如今，各地游客纷至沓来，在这座庙里向解放军战士致意。当然，中国各地的游客来到崇武，另一个目的就是亲眼目睹惠安女的迷人风采。

Well supplied--forever!

Episode 14 Hui'an Stonemasons & Maidens

Introduction In today's episode of Magic Fujian, Xiamen University's Dr. Bill meets Hui'an's legendary stonemasons and exotic Hui'an maidens.

I love Chongwu's ancient walls and narrow winding streets. But as in most of China, the real attraction is not the place but the people—especially the Hui'an maidens' traditional costumes, although few young girls bother with them nowadays.

Dialogue—Bare Bellied Maidens

Bobby: What makes Hui'an maidens so interesting?

Bill: It's mainly their unique costumes and their marriage customs.

Bobby: Yeah, I've noticed they cover their heads and leave their bellies bare!

Bill: Yes, locals call that feudalistic head and the democratic belly!

A Chongwu girl told me that in the Minnan dialect, "belly" is 'bazai,' which sounds like Mandarin's 'facai,'—to prosper. But blouses are also short for a practical reason—so they stay dry when girls bend over in the sea.

Each color is symbolic. Blouses are blue, like the sea and sky. Bamboo hats are yellow, like Hui'an's miles of golden beaches. The baggy trousers are black like fishing nets, and creased to represent waves. Scarves are often flowery, but when white they represent clouds. Young Hui'an girls often have over 100 scarves, which they use not only to protect their faces from sun and wind but also to make their round girlish faces look longer and prettier. Older women often have over 300 colorful scarves, which they think help them recover their youthful appearance.

The elegantly costumed Hui'an maids may look dainty but they're tough as nails! I often see them in construction sites, carrying baskets of stone or sand that I can barely lift, much less carry! So when they tell me not to photograph them—I obey!

第14集　惠安石雕与惠安女

导语

系列报道“老外看福建”今天向您介绍福建的惠安石雕和惠安女，一起跟厦门大学的潘维廉博士去看看。

解说

我喜欢崇武的古城墙和古城内狭窄弯曲的街巷。不过，跟中国其他大多数地方一样，崇武真正的魅力不在于古城，而是古城里的人。惠安女的传统服饰特别迷人，尽管年轻姑娘现在感觉穿起来有些麻烦。

现场

包东宇：你说，惠安女怎么会这样迷人呢？
潘维廉：我看，主要是她们独特的服饰和婚俗。
包东宇：我注意到，惠安女把头遮得严严实实地，肚子却露在外面。
潘维廉：没错！当地人说，这叫作“封建头，民主肚”。

解说

一位崇武姑娘告诉我，闽南话“肚脐”跟汉语的“发财”谐音。惠安女的上衣较短，很实用，出海弯腰时不会沾湿。

惠安女服饰上的每一种颜色都有象征意义。上衣是蓝色的，象征大海和天空。竹笠是黄色的，象征惠安延绵的金色沙滩。宽松的裤子是黑色的，象征渔网；裤子上的皱褶象征海浪。花头巾五颜六色，其中白色象征白云。年轻的惠安女拥有上百条的花头巾。她们戴头巾是为了防风防晒，同时也使自己圆滚滚的脸蛋变得更加修长、好看。年纪较大的惠安女头巾更多，色彩更丰富，穿戴的目的也许在于恢复自己的青春美貌。

穿上漂亮服饰的惠安女举止优雅，娇美俊俏。她们还能够吃苦耐劳，意志特别坚强。我经常在建筑工地上看到惠安女的身影。她们挑的沙石，我连提都提不动！她们不让我拍照，我只好遵命。

Dialogue—Fear of Photos

Bill: Do you know why Hui'an girls don't like to have their photos taken?

Bobby: Maybe they're shy?

Bill: Could be! But last time, a Hui'an girl told me that the old ladies especially don't like their photos taken, because they think that takes away part of their life!

Bobby: I've heard people in other countries believe that, but I didn't know Chinese did.

Hui'an girls have some very unique marriage customs!

Unmarried girls wear embroidered cloth belts, and after marriage their husbands give them a silver belt weighing from 1 ½ pounds to 6 ½ pounds, which they wear over their cloth belt. I was told that's a kind of marital insurance—husbands don't dare divorce because their wealth is around their wife's waist!

It used to be that in Chongwu, a man could spend the night with his wife only three nights a year, on holidays, until the girl had a child. Actually, this practice was common in many areas of old China, but it has pretty much died out. Nowadays, most Chongwu maidens don't follow this marriage custom either.

Locals say that centuries ago, a Hui'an maiden refused to marry a rich man so he bound her and forced her to tie the knot.

Ever since, the Hui'an maidens' costumes have had designs on the sleeves to represent the girls bonds.

Dialogue—1700 Years of Stonework

Bill: In addition to its beautiful Hui'an maidens, Hui'an is known all over Asia for its stonework.

Bobby: How long have Hui'an people been carving stone?

Bill: As far as I know, at least 1700 years!

Father 'n Son

Mr. Lin's stone tomb in Hui'an's Tuling village was carved in 304 A.D. Mr. Lin was an imperial representative from the Central Plains, and probably brought the stone carvers with him.

Hui'an stone masons produce everything from deities to garden bridges and lanterns. Even flat-roofed Hui'an homes are stone. And one of the newest arts is copying photographs onto stone! It's fascinating to watch them at work.

现场

潘维廉：你知道惠安女不喜欢拍照的原因吗？
包东宇：也许是害羞吧？
潘维廉：嗯，有可能。不过，一位惠安女告诉我，上年纪的惠安女尤其不喜欢拍照，因为她们担心拍照会缩短寿命。
包东宇：我只听说过国外有些地方的人是这样想，但我不知道中国人也有这种说法。

解说

惠安女的婚俗很奇特。未婚姑娘佩戴绣花的布腰带。婚后，丈夫会给她们打造一条银腰带，戴在布腰带上。银腰带的重量从 1.5 磅到 6.5 磅不等。有人告诉我，这是婚姻的某种保证，因为家庭的财富集中在妻子腰间，丈夫就不敢轻提离婚。

在过去，崇武男人每年只能在逢年过节的时候与妻子同居三天。直到生下小孩，妻子才能住进夫家。实际上，这种陋习在旧中国是很常见的，现在几乎灭绝了。崇武也不例外。

当地人告诉我，数百年前，有一位惠安姑娘不想嫁给有钱人。这个有钱人把这位姑娘绑回来，强迫她结婚。此后，惠安女的衣袖上就多了一些图案，象征少女的婚约。

现场

潘维廉：除了美丽的惠安女，惠安石雕也闻名亚洲。
包东宇：惠安石雕的历史有多长？
潘维廉：据我所知，至少 1700 年。

解说

在惠安涂岭，有一座林氏石墓，建于公元前 304 年。作为中原皇室的钦差，林公南下时也许带来了一批能工巧匠。

惠安的石雕作品包罗万象，从女神像到廊桥宫灯等。而最新的雕刻工艺当属影雕！看着这些惠安姑娘把画像雕刻在石头上，真有趣。

Forest of Statues The best introduction to Hui'an stonework is Chongwu's seaside park, with its over 500 stone statues. They include 108 famous ancient Chinese generals, and statues from the novel "Dream of Red Mansions." But foreigners need a good guide to explain them. [Bill smacks a bull] Many people smack this black bull, claiming it gives them good fortune.

Dialogue—Filial Piety

Bobby: Do you know the meaning of these statues?

Bill: I don't know. I guess something about Confucius?

Bobby: Good guess. They represent 24 Confucian stories about children caring for parents.

Bill: Oh, I know! Like the story of the guy who let mosquitoes bite him so they won't bite his parents. And there's also the story of the guy who uses his warm body to thaw out a frozen river, so he can get his sick mother a fish.

Bobby: Would you do such a good deed for your parents?

Bill: No! I'd rather buy them a mosquito net, or a fish sandwich from MacDonald's!

Breastfeeding Mom

The black and white cats represent Deng Xiao Ping's pragmatic saying, "It doesn't matter if a cat is white or black, as long as it catches mice!"

I also liked the Maitreya (Milofu). But when I told a tourist Maitreya resembled a Disney dwarf, the man protested, "No way! This is better than Disney!"

Dialogue—Earth Art

Bill: Do you see the carvings on the shore, there?

Bobby: Yes, I thought it is natural formation!

Bill: It's almost natural, but not quite! There's a professor from Zhejiang, who, with a few strokes, transforms these rocks into sculptures. They look so natural that they fit right into the environment.

I joked to a student once that China had more funerals than any country. He said, "That's not true! We have great medical care!" I soothed him with, "It's not a matter of medicine but mathematics. Biggest population, remember?"

Chongwu sure has its share of funerals. The last time here I was caught behind a funeral procession that lasted forever. And we encountered a funeral today, but this one ended on a happier note because a procession for a new bride followed close behind!

Dialogue—Weddings and Funerals

Bill: Busy day in Chongwu— a wedding and a funeral! I've been here a dozen times, and I see something new each time.

Bobby: I like it too—especially the Hui'an girls.

Bill: Well, you're still single. Maybe I can introduce you to one.

Bobby: No, thanks!

当然，最能展示惠安雕刻的地方当属崇武的石雕园。这里有500多尊的石头雕像，从梁山泊的108 条好汉到《红楼梦》里的众多人物。不过，要让老外看懂这些石雕，必须要有一位好导游。

人们喜欢抚摸这座黑牛雕像。他们认为，摸黑牛会带来好运气。

♪现场——

包东宇：你知道这些石雕背后的故事吗？
潘维廉：不知道。不过，我想应该与孔夫子有关。
包东宇：没错。是有关孔子二十四孝的故事。
潘维廉：噢。我想起来了。这座石雕讲的是孝子让蚊子叮咬，以防蚊子叮咬父母。另外这座石雕说的是，孝子用自己的体温破冰钓鱼，孝敬病床上的母亲。
包东宇：你也会这样孝敬父母亲吗？
潘维廉：不会这样做。不过，我会给父母买张蚊帐，或一份麦香鱼汉堡。

♪解说——

石雕园内还有一只白猫和一只黑猫的雕像，象征着一代伟人邓小平所说的：不管黑猫、白猫，会捉老鼠就是好猫。我也喜欢弥勒佛的雕像。有一次，我告诉园里的游客说，弥勒佛有点像迪士尼乐园的小矮人。他说：“不可能。弥勒佛比迪士尼的小矮人强多了！”

♪现场——

潘维廉：你看到海滩上那些雕刻了吗？
包东宇：看到了，我还以为是天然的呢。
潘维廉：那些岩石是天然的，雕刻是浙江的一位教授凿凿砍砍，花了不少精力创作的。这些雕刻与周边的环境溶为一体，简直是巧夺天工。

♪解说——

有一回，我跟学生开玩笑说，中国的葬礼比世界上其他国家多。他马上抗议道：“不对！我们国家现在的医疗保健条件好多了。”我安慰他说，“这跟医术无关，而是算术问题。别忘了，中国人口有多少！”崇武也不例外。上一次到崇武，我的车子被堵在一支长长的送葬队伍后面。这一回，在古城里，我们又碰上一场葬礼。送葬人群走过之后，紧跟着一个迎亲队伍，给这场悲伤的葬礼增添了一些愉快的音符。

♪现场——

潘维廉：今天在崇武，够忙的吧？一场葬礼，一场婚礼。我来过十几趟崇武，每次都有新发现。
包东宇：崇武给我印象很深，特别是惠安女。
潘维廉：你还没有结婚，有机会。要不要我给介绍一个？
包东宇：谢谢，免了。

Supplementary Reading Two

Half the Sky —Get a Baomu

"A woman is like a teabag—only in hot water[1] do you realize how strong she is."
Nancy Reagan

After seven years in Los Angeles, life in China seemed to proceed at a snail's pace. But even so, we had little free time, because our everyday chores took all day—until we hired a baomu (housekeeper/cook).

Unless you have a baomu, the head of the house, or her husband, must spend hours each morning haggling over every onion, carrot, head of cabbage, or block of tofu with merchants who point to enigmatic[2] scratches on bamboo scales that haven't changed in 5,016[3] years, and proclaim that 4 eggs weigh a pound and a half. And once back home, the cleaning, chopping, cooking and dishwashing takes hours. No wonder that a baomu is a top priority for even poor professors.

We eventually heeded our colleagues' urges to hire a baomu. Our first candidate was a grandmother who crossed our threshold and crossed my wife[4] in one fell[5] swoop by instructing Susan on the errors of her ways in cooking, cleaning, studying, and raising kids.

She did not last a week. Our next time around we tried our hand with students, who were thrilled at getting paid for learning English (which is what they interpreted their job to be). Xiao Hong and Melanie did little but read our English books and watch TV.

At long last a Chinese professor suggested, "Why not hire a baomu from the countryside? They are honest, hard-working, dependable, and cheap."

"Cheap" went straight to my heart, and the next day we met Lixi, a cook's wife, never imagining that froward[6], silent soul would become like family.

It was an oppressively hot and muggy October day, but Lixi sported her entire wardrobe: long johns[7] and striped naval undershirt beneath cotton pants and long-sleeved shirt; over that, a vintage, frayed exercise suit, topped off with a ratty[8] gray sweater buttoned to the neck, and olive drab canvas regulation army tennis-shoes that were probably handed down from the Long March (or the Short April[9]).

---

1 In hot water: in trouble

2 Enigmatic: puzzling (we foreigners don't understand the scales' markings)

3 5016 years: I was told China has 5,000 years of history but that was in 1988, so it's now 5016 years

4 Crossed my wife: angered my wife

5 Fell: cruel, sinister, evil

6 Froward: stubborn, obstinate

7 Long Johns: long-sleeved winter undergarments

8 Ratty: dilapidated, shabby

9 Short April: March is long, with 31 days; April is short, with only 30 days.

补充读物（二）

半 边 天

——雇个保姆吧!

Half the Sky

女人就像袋泡茶，只有放在热水里才显示出她的能量。

——南希·里根

在洛杉矶呆了七年之后，忽然觉得在中国的生活慢得就像蜗牛。但即便如此，每天的杂务还是占去了我们大部分的时间。直到雇了保姆，情况才有所改变。

家里要是没有保姆，一家之主，或是她的丈夫，打一早起就得为了每一根洋葱、萝卜、白菜，抑或是一块豆腐，和小贩们吵个不停。当你还在对他们手里的那柄 5015 年未曾变过的杆秤纳闷时，四个鸡蛋怎么就重四磅多。待回到家，洗、切、煮，还有最后的刷碗，又得花几小时。因此，即使对穷教授来说，雇个保姆也算得上是重中之重。

最终，我们响应了同事的劝告，雇了个保姆。我们的第一个保姆是位祖母级的，一进家门就劈头盖脸地数落起苏姗，说她在煮菜、清洁、学习以及看护小孩等等方面犯了这样那样的错误。

“祖母”最后只干了一个礼拜。我们决定试用学生保姆，一听既能学英语，又能拿工钱，别提有多高兴。于是，小红和 Melanie 在我家就只顾读书看电视，别的好像什么也没干。

过了很久，一位中国教授建议：“为什么不从乡下找一个保姆呢？他们诚实可靠，手脚勤快，价格也便宜。”

“便宜”一下子打动了我的心。于是，第二天，我们就见到了李西，一名厨师的妻子，但不曾想到就是这位既固执又寡言的老婆子后来竟成了我家不可或缺的一员。

那是一个闷热的十月天，但李西依然全副武装：一条棉布裤，裤脚还露出半截的贴身棉毛裤；条纹贴身内衣外穿着长袖衬衫；衬衫外叠着一件古老、磨损的运动衫，外头又罩着一件破旧的灰色毛衣，纽扣一直扣到脖子；脚蹬一双泛黄帆布解放鞋，像是经历了二万五千里长征的洗礼。

Lixi contemplated her navel while her husband, wise to the "honest, hardworking peasant" lore, extolled her virtues. The few times I addressed Lixi directly, she peered furtively through thick, disheveled bangs, then resumed picking her frayed cuffs with calloused fingers.

"Can she speak?" I inquired.

"Not Mandarin, just the Minnan dialect," her husband confessed, "But she's smart. Just show her what to do."

"Can she cook?"

"No, but I'll teach her."

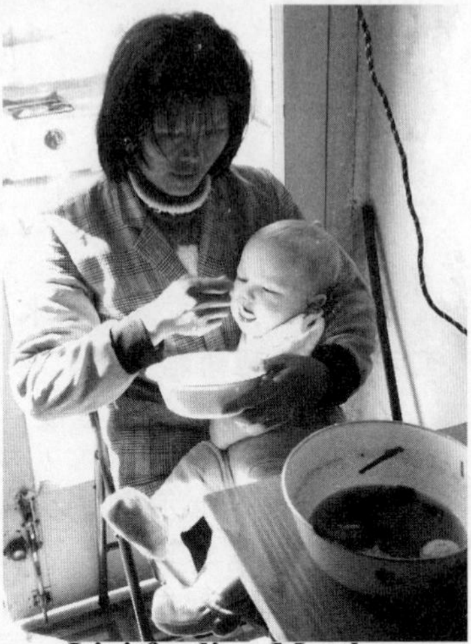

Lixi feeding Matthew

I suspected this sullen apparition was incapable of motion, either physically or mentally, but just as I sought to tactfully end the interview--she moved. Matthew was edging towards the doorway and the dangerous street beyond, and Lixi flew to her feet, snatched him to her breast with practiced swoop, and face aglow, bustled him off to his room. Then she retreated to her chair, donned her practiced frown, and picked at her frayed cuffs.

Inspired, her husband cried, "She's great with children."

Enough said. Sue hired her on the spot—to my immediate regret.

If the way to a man's heart is through his stomach, Lixi ought never to have landed a man. No wok wizard[10], she was more of an alchemist than a cook. She transmuted the choicest slices of fish into blackened slabs of charcoal, and fresh vegetables, baptized in oil and pickled in salt, became mush

And how to communicate with her? Her Mandarin was worse than ours, and she could not read. Even sign language failed. I suggested to Sue that we dismiss her, but Lixi's desperation defused my anger, and I consoled myself that man does not live by rice alone[11].

Though incommunicado with us, Lixi was telepathic with tots—especially Matthew, whom she bore on her back from dawn to dusk. But no wonder she understood children: she had four of her own before begging the doctor to tie things off down below.

Mark Twain wrote, "There was never yet an uninteresting life. Such a thing is an impossibility. Inside of the dullest exterior there is a drama, a comedy, and a tragedy." Twain must have meant Lixi, whose plebeian[12] dust jacket does no justice to her contents.

---

[10] Wok wizard: expert with wok (rounded Chinese cooking pan)

[11] Rice alone: a play on Jesus' saying, "Man does not live by bread alone" (the Bible, Matthew 4:4)

[12] Plebeian: unrefined or coarse; common person

李西的丈夫不停地在吹她的优点：老实、勤劳…… 只有她低着头站在一旁。我几乎很少直接称呼李西，但每当此时，她也只是透过浓密、凌乱的刘海偷偷瞥上我一眼，而后又用她那双长满老茧的手扯捏着磨损的衣袖口。

“她会说话吗？”我问到。

“不会讲普通话，就会闽南话，”她的丈夫承认，“不过，她不笨。只要教她怎么做就行了。”

“那么她会烧饭吗？”

“还不会，我来教。”

Auntie Lixi and Matthew

我开始怀疑这个迟钝的灵魂是否还能作出任何反应。但当我正想得体地结束面试的当儿，她突然动了起来。我那宝贝儿子马修不知什么时候挪到了门口，眼看就要溜到危险的大街，只见李西一下子飞了过去，一把抓住抱在胸口，硬是给揣回了房间，她的脸也一下子涨的通红。接下来，李西又坐回椅子，皱上眉头，又开始扯捏起磨损的衣袖口。

也许是受了启发，李西的丈夫突然喊到，“她挺会带孩子。”

这就够了。苏珊二话没说就点了头，全然不顾我的感受。

如果说征服一个男人必先征服他的胃口，那么李西一辈子也别想得到男人。李西与其说是厨师，还不如说是巫师。上好的鱼片到了她手里结果成了黑木炭，新鲜蔬菜在油里泡过之后，再用盐一搅拌，最后变成一团糊。

更成问题的是如何与她交流。她的普通话比我们的还差，而且还不会阅读。即使用手势也无济于事。我向苏珊暗示不如炒了算了，但李西的执著平息了我的愤怒。我只有自我安慰，其实男人靠的不仅仅是米饭。

尽管和我们很少言语，李西却是带孩子的好手。尤其是马太，她总是从早背到晚。其实这也不奇怪：她前后生了四个孩子，最后才央求医生干脆一刀了事。

马克·吐温曾经写到：

“生活从来就不会乏味。乏味是不可能的。 在无聊的外表之下，总隐藏着一出戏，要么是喜剧，要么是悲剧。”

莫非马克·吐温先生讲的就是李西。她那平庸粗俗的外衣掩盖了她丰富的内涵。

Lixi raised four children single-handedly by working the fields until her staunch Buddhist family drove her from home after she became a Christian. She trekked over the mountains to Xiamen and became a day laborer, lugging baskets of granite slung across her brawny shoulders. After two years in the school of hard rocks[13], she graduated and became our brawny baomu, lugging towheads with heads lighter but harder than the granite she was used to hauling around.

Lixi applied her diehard spirit to becoming a capable member of our household. She learned Mandarin and, to my chagrin, taught herself to read some of the characters that still eluded me. She even taught herself to cook both Chinese and Western food. By watching Susan she learned how to whip up a pizza, sandwiches, burgers and fries, Irish stew. Even Chinese guests begged for her recipes.

After Lixi had been with us for two years, we moved her four children to Xiamen to help educate them and to fatten them up a bit, for they were skin and bone. Her oldest son eventually took up computers, her sister opened a small shop, and Lixi used her limited income to help those even poorer than herself, both in Xiamen and back home in Anxi, proving that investments in the poor reap compound interest.

"Give and it shall be given…"[14]

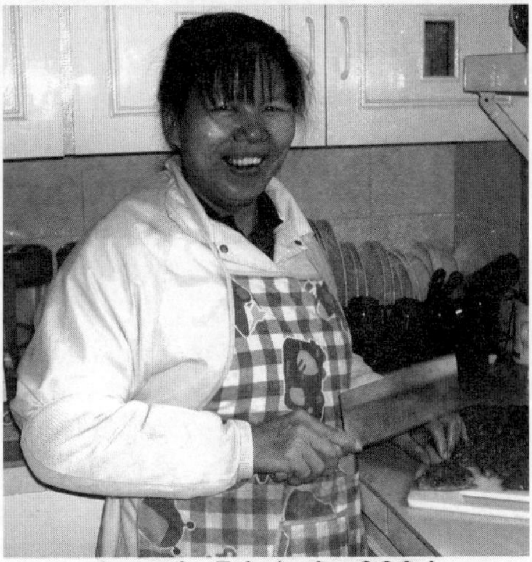

Auntie Lixie in 2004

Chairman Mao claimed, "Women hold up half the sky," but I think that was an understatement. Chinese women, even with hands bound by lack of education, hold up a lot more than half. Hire a baomu!

---

[13] School of hard rocks: a play on the phrase "School of hard knocks" (learning from adversity)

[14] "Give and it shall be given to you": Christ's saying in the Bible, Luke 6:38

此前，李西一直在田里劳作，一手带着四个孩子。直到有一天成了基督徒，她那虔诚的佛门之家把她赶了出来。之后，她只身翻过大山来到厦门，先是干搬运花岗岩的苦力。两年后，她从岩石学校毕了业，成了我家保姆。这回拉的虽不是沉重的花岗石，但技术要求却要高得多。

李西尽心尽力地在努力融入我家。她开始学习普通话，又自学起我至今仍云里雾里的汉字，甚至还学做起中西餐。通过观察，她学会了如何做比萨、三明治和汉堡，又学会了炸薯条和炖爱尔兰煲。就连来我家的中国客人也纷纷索要她的食谱。

两年后，我们帮忙把她的四个孩子接到了厦门并让他们上学，也让他们从又黑又瘦中解脱出来。后来她的大儿子干上了计算机的活，她的妹妹也在厦门开了一家小店。而李西则用她微薄的收入去救济那些比她更困难的人。

帮助别人的人理应得到别人的帮助……

毛主席曾经说过，“妇女能顶半边天”，于我这还过于保守。中国妇女，尽管受缺乏教育的束缚，但撑起的远远大于半边天。

雇个保姆吧!

Episode 15 Zhangzhou—"Land of Plenty"

Introduction In today's episode we follow Dr. Bill to Fujian's largest plain, the "Land of Plenty," and the ancient trading port of Zhangzhou.

Dialogue—9 Dragon River

Bill: Did you know that many foreigners argue that the ancient port of Zaytun was here in Zhangzhou, not Quanzhou?

Bobby: Do you think it was Zhangzhou?

Bill: No, I don't. But in fact this is a great ancient port, and foreigners have written about the place for centuries.

Ancient Silk Center Ancient Zaytun was the Silk Road of the Sea, but much of the finest silk came not from Hangzhou but right here in Fujian—particularly Quanzhou and Zhangzhou.

In 1888, George Philips wrote,

"Zhangzhou in the Middle Ages was the seat of a great silk manufacturer, and the production of its looms, such as gauzes, satins and velvets, were said to exceed in beauty those of Suzhou and Hangzhou."

In 1889, another Laowai, Reverend McGowan, wrote,

"The people of Zhangzhou were proud and haughty. They were prosperous and well-to-do… They were proud, too, because of the exquisite silks and satin stuffs they could produce. Their looms were famous, and their designs were rare, and beautifully executed."

Today, Zhangzhou silk still fetches a high price in international markets. I was told that in Hong Kong it can go for over $100 USD a meter! And today Zhangzhou is well known for its textile industry.

Zhangzhou was a beautiful city, with great walls, gates and arches right up until a century ago. Mcgowan might have thought the Zhangzhou people to be proud and haughty, but he also wrote, "Zhangzhou…is one of the most beautiful that I have ever seen in China."

Mcgowan said the entire city was covered with a canopy of trees and flowers, so that from above it looked like a forest. Zhangzhou's shaded streets were crowded with traders from all over the world buying not just Zhangzhou's fine silks but products from all over China. Zhangzhou was like an early version of CIFIT!

Dialogue—Flat Land and Dragons

Bill: I love bananas. Last time I was in Zhangzhou, I bought a bunch, big bunch, had two mice inside. My cat loves them.

第15集　漳州——“富庶之地”

导语

在今天这一集的“老外看福建”节目里，我们将跟随潘维廉博士去看看福建最大的平原，同时也是“富庶之地”和古代贸易港口的城市——漳州。

现场

潘维廉：你知道吗？许多外国人认为古代的港口刺桐实际上是在漳州，而不是泉州。

包东宇：你认为是在漳州吗？

潘维廉：我不这么认为。但是漳州的确是一个了不起的古代港口，几个世纪以来西方人都有提及。

解说

古代刺桐是海上丝绸之路的起点，但是大部分质地优良的丝绸不是出自杭州，而是出自福建——尤其是泉州和漳州。

乔治·菲利普斯在1888年写到：“中世纪的漳州是大丝绸商的聚集地。织布机生产出来的薄纱、缎子和天鹅绒，据说比苏州和杭州产的还要美。”

1889年，还有一个名叫麦高文的牧师写到：“漳州人洋洋自得，小康有余。他们为自己能够生产出精致的丝绸和缎原料而感到自豪。他们的织布机很出名，设计独到，制作精美。”

今天漳州丝绸在国际市场上仍然卖很高的价钱。我听说在香港1米的漳州丝绸要卖到100多美元。今天，漳州的纺织业也很发达。

漳州直到一个世纪之前还是一座有城墙、城门和拱门的美丽城市。麦高文也许认为漳州人有点洋洋自得了，但是他也写到：“漳州是我在中国见到的最美丽的城市之一。”

麦高文说城市遍布鲜花和树木，因此从高处俯瞰，整个城市像是一座森林。在漳州绿树成荫的街道上挤满了来自世界各地的商人。他们来买的不只是漳州质地优良的丝绸，还有来自中国各地的产品。漳州就像是中国投资贸易洽谈会的早期版本！

现场

潘维廉：我喜欢香蕉，上次我在漳州买了一大串香蕉，里面还躲了两只老鼠，我家的猫咪可高兴坏了。

Bobby: Why did Zhangzhou become such a great city?

Bill: Geography, I suppose. This is the biggest piece of flat land in Fujian, the biggest plain.

Bobby: Flat plain?

Bill: It also helps to have nine dragons, I suppose.

9 Dragon River Zhangzhou straddles the Nine Dragon River. It was named Nine Dragon River because long ago someone saw nine dragons playing in it. And thanks to the Nine Dragons, droughts in Zhangzhou are almost unknown. That's why it has the nickname of "land of plenty," and was settled so long ago.

The Minyue people came to Zhangzhou about 5,000 years ago, and it became an imperial prefecture in 686—the same year Quanzhou's magical mulberry tree produced lotus flowers and Kaiyuan Temple was built!

Dialogue—Zhangzhou Narcissus

Bobby: Zhangzhou is famous for its flowers, isn't it?

Bill: Yes. Locals have raised and sold flowers for hundreds of years, here.

Bobby: As far as I know, Zhangzhou's bonsai trees, narcissus and other flowers are quite popular in international market.

Bill: Laonei like them, too.

In 1889, Macgowan wrote, "The Chinese have a passionate love for trees and flowers, and consequently every householder had planted some kind of a tree in his courtyard…" Today, Zhangzhou is still famous for its flowers. Hundreds of vendors sell every kind of plant imaginable—and some that I can't imagine. For example—look at that giant cactus.

Dialogue—Colossal Cactus!

Bill: My students argued that this was real. I argued that it was impossible for any cactus to grow this large.

Bobby: So is it real or fake?

Bill: I won't tell you! And if viewers want to know they'll have to come and find out themselves!

100 Flower Village The heart of Zhangzhou horticulture must be the 100 Flower Village, which is about 2.5 km south of Zhangzhou. These villagers have been raising and selling flowers ever since the Ming Dynasty! Zhude, the great marshal/generalissimo, was awed by the variety of plants when he visited in 1963. Today, they claim to have over 20,000 kinds of flowers. I wonder who on earth had time to count them all?

包东宇：为什么漳州当时能够成为这样一个大城市呢？

潘维廉：我想是由于地理位置的关系。漳州是福建省最开阔的一块平地，或者说平原。

包东宇：平原？

潘维廉：我想这里说不定还卧着九条龙呢。

♪解说——

九龙江贯穿了整个漳州市。九龙江之所以得名据说是因为很久以前有人看到有九条龙在江中嬉戏。多亏了这九龙江，漳州几乎没有过关于干旱的历史记载。这就是为什么漳州有着“富庶之地”的美誉，并且很早就有人在这片土地上休养生息的原因。

早在大约5000年前，古闽越人就来到了漳州，公元686年朝廷批准建置漳州郡——就在同一年，漳州传说中的桑树奇迹般地开出了莲花，开元寺也随之建立了起来！

♪现场——

包东宇：漳州的花也很出名，不是吗？

潘维廉：没错。当地人种花、卖花已经有几百年的历史了。

包东宇：据我所知，漳州的盆景，水仙，还有其他一些花卉在国际市场上十分热销。

潘维廉：嗯，老内也很喜欢它们。

♪解说——

麦高文在1889年曾经写道：“中国人对花草树木有着强烈的爱好，因此每个家庭都在自己的后花园里种一些树……”

如今漳州仍然因为它的花卉而出名。许许多多的花商出售你能想象出来的各种花卉——有些我是想象不出啦。就好像——那株巨大的仙人掌。

♪现场——

潘维廉：我的学生坚持认为这仙人掌是真的。我对他们说任何仙人掌都不可能长到这么大。

包东宇：那么它到底是真的还是假的呢？

潘维廉：我不告诉你！假如观众想知道的话，他们就得自己过来寻找答案。

♪解说——

漳州园艺的心脏地带一定是漳州往南大约2.5公里处的百花村了。这里的村民从明朝起就开始种花、卖花了。1963年，朱德元帅到这里参观的时候，就大为惊讶，这里的植物品种竟然这么丰富。现在的百花村号称有两万多种的花卉。我真不知道究竟是谁去花时间算出来的。

Episode 16 Changtai, Xiamen's Backyard

Introduction On today's Magic Fujian, Dr. Bill visits Xiamen's beautiful backyard, Changtai.

Dialogue—Raindrops and Frogs

Bill: Hah, this Changtai brochure says that average annual raindrop[1] in Changtai is 1.5 meters!

Bobby: Wow. A 1.5 meter rain drop could drown you!

Bill: Hah! I think so. There's more! It also says that Changtai is without frogs[2] 328 days a year!

Bobby: frogs?

Bill: Frogs, so that explains why there's no frog on the menu!

Bobby: It should be frost!

Bill: Frost? Like snowman?

Changing Changtai About 1995 I waded down this river when they were considering building a river rafting resort. I'd have never imagined that it would become China's national kayak training center!

I should not have been surprised. Changtai people have always had vision. And today, their vision is to modernize and prosper while at the same time protecting their beautiful environment.

It's hard to believe that only a decade ago, this pristine river was a dark, smelly channel for local factories' pollutants. But Changtai's young magistrate, like Xiamen's mayor, said, "We must avoid the "West's "pollution then solution" approach.

The decrepit buildings by the river were razed, and replaced by a park. A big challenge was dealing with wastes from Changtai's 30,000 dairy cows! Now they have a closed-cycle recycling system. Cow urine provides methane for cooking and lightning, and manure provides fertilizer for fruit and mushrooms. Mr. Yang closed polluting factories and set strict standards. He also stopped the quarrying that was scarring the scenic mountains that have inspired over 1,000 years of poets.

Dialogue—Perfect Climate for Farming

Bill: Changtai was first settled during the Stone Age, and then later the She people came here.

Bobby: What attracted so many people to Changtai?

Bill: Maybe it was 328 days a year with no frogs?

Bobby: Frogs?

Bill: Ok, just joking. Actually, believe it or not, it was the weather.

---

1 Raindrop: typographical error. "Raindrop" should have been "rainfall"

2 Frogs: another typographical error. "Frog" should have been "frost"

第16集　长泰，厦门的后花园

导语

在今天这一集的“老外看福建”节目中，潘威廉博士将带领我们游览厦门风景如画的后花园——长泰。

现场

潘维廉：哈！这本介绍长泰的小册子说，长泰每年的雨珠有1.5米！
包东宇：哇！1.5米的雨点可以淹死一个人了！
潘维廉：哈！我想也是。那册子上甚至还说在长泰每年有328天见不到青蛙！
包东宇：青蛙？
潘维廉：对，是青蛙。难怪菜单上没有青蛙这道菜！
包东宇：他们把“霜”误写成青蛙了。
潘维廉：是霜？还是像雪人？

解说

1995年左右，当我经过这条河的时候，他们正在考虑建设一个竹筏渡河的项目，我怎么也没想到这里居然能成为中国国家队皮筏训练中心！

我本不该这么惊讶。长泰人一向是很有远见的。今天，他们正打算在保护好优美环境的同时繁荣长泰，实现现代化。

很难相信10年前，这条纯净的小河还是一条被当地工厂污染了的肮脏的臭水沟。但是年轻的长泰地方官员，和厦门市长一样，曾经说“我们必须避免走西方先污染后解决”这样的老路。

河边的老房子拆除了，取而代之的是一座公园。

怎样处置长泰三万头奶牛的排泄物曾经是个非常棘手的问题。现在，他们建起了一个密闭的循环系统。奶牛的尿液转化成沼气供煮饭照明使用，粪便则用作水果和蘑菇的肥料。

杨先生关闭了污染性的工厂并制定了严格的规章制度。

他还禁止了将风景宜人的山川弄得伤痕斑驳的采石业，而这风景宜人的山川一千多年来给多少诗人带来了灵感。

现场

潘维廉：长泰早在石器时代就有人居住，后来畲族人迁徙到这里。
包东宇：是什么吸引了这么多的人来长泰居住呢？
潘维廉：也许是因为328天都见不到青蛙吧。
包东宇：青蛙？
潘维廉：开玩笑啦。事实上信不信由你，正是天气的缘故。

Bobby: This weather?[3]
Bill: Yeah, no accounting for taste.

Changtai was a paradise for early farmers. The mild climate allows three harvests a year of grains, vegetables, and some of China's best fruits. Changtai became a county in AD 955, and the Han from the central plains brought their culture, technology, and arts. Wenchangge Pagoda was built over 1,000 years ago, in the Tang Dynasty.

Prof. Gongjie

Dialogue—Wenchange Pagoda
Bill: Look at the pagoda over there.
Bobby: Do you want to go see it?
Bill: No way!
Bobby: Why no way?
Bill: Well, one, because it has been struck by lightning twice, it's been burned down, it's fallen down! The only way I'm going to look at it is from a safe distance!
Bobby: What about this distance?
Bill: Maybe this is too close.

Dialogue—On a Mountain Road in Changtai
Bill: Experts used to say that in Fujian there are four kinds of architecture, but in Changtai they've discovered a fifth!
Bobby: What kind is that?
Bill: They found the Stone Fortress (shibao). It's not very easy to find!

I'd have never learned about many of Changtai's historical sites without the help of Xiamen Museum's curator, Mr. Gongjie (龚洁) He showed me the Mountain Goat Stone Fortress Shanchong hamlet (山重村). It's so remote that this area still has rare pangolins, ancient tortoises, wolves, mountain goats, wild board—and plenty of snakes! They also have a 700 year old tree that is 15 meters around the base.

Dialogue—Up a Tree[4]
Bill: The locals say this is the biggest tree in Fujian, do you believe that?
Bobby: I don't know. What do you think?
Bill: I don't know. But it's pretty big. I'll show you a secret. You can go inside. Maybe someday I'll live here.
Bobby: Amazing!
Bill: It's pretty good, huh? We'll climb up here.

---

[3] It poured rain the entire time we filmed in Changtai, and we were soaked

[4] Up a tree: euphemism for "in trouble" (as if one climbed a tree to escape a wild animal)

包东宇：像今天这样的天气？
潘维廉：不,关键是你自己怎么看。

解说

对于早期农民来说，长泰就跟天堂一般。温和的气候让长泰人每年都能收获三季的稻谷、蔬菜，和中国一些最好的水果。公元955年，长泰建郡。汉人从中原带来了他们的文化、技术和艺术。文昌阁建立于一千多年前的唐朝。

现场

潘维廉：你看文昌阁耸立在那边呢。
包东宇：你想去看看吗?
潘维廉：不想。
包东宇：为什么不想?
潘维廉：它两次遭雷击，一次被烧毁，还倒塌了一次。我宁愿站在一个安全的地方欣赏它。
包东宇：这位置怎么样?
潘维廉：还是近了点。

现场

潘维廉：据专家考察，福建有四种建筑的样式，但他们在长泰发现了第五种!
包东宇：那是什么呢?
潘维廉：石堡。这是很难找到的。

解说

要不是厦门博物馆馆长龚洁先生的帮忙，我不可能知道这么多的长泰历史遗迹。他带着我参观山洋楼古堡山重村。

古老的山村依然可见珍惜的穿山甲、古龟、狼、山羊，以及成千上万的蛇！这里还有一棵700年的老树，荫蔽了直径达15米的一片地。

现场

潘维廉：当地人说，这是福建最大的树，你相信吗?
包东宇：我不清楚，你认为呢?
潘维廉：我也不知道，但这树的确很大。我发现一个秘密，你可以钻到树洞里面，说不定哪一天我会住这儿呢。
包东宇：实在很奇特!
潘维廉：感觉不错吧?我们继续往上爬!

The Mountain Goat Stone Fortress was built in 1623 as a defense against Japanese pirates, who attacked ShanChong on October 16th, 1580. Over 1,000 locals formed the Prosperous Peace Army (Fu'anjun, 副安军), which battled the Japanese for over a century. The walls are 1.6 meters thick at the base, 90 centimeters at the top, and 6 meters high (they were originally 3 stories high). The holes in the wall were used for cannon that shot jagged bits of metal.

The family that lives here welcomed me like the prodigal son[5] returned home. Of course, the first words the granny said were, "M 'dei!" Have some tea. Our English word for tea comes from the Minnan word, 'dei.'

Almost everything in the house, from cradle to furniture, is handmade. The wooden farm implements, darkened with age, look like museum exhibits. Their design probably hasn't changed in 1,000 years, but why reinvent the wheel? They do the job!

Lindun Town Our next stop is Lindun Town (林敦). It's right across that mountain, but there's no direct road so we have to go around. Too bad we don't have Yugong to move the mountain for us!

Dialogue—the Opium Baron's Manor

Bill: I think we need a horse. Feel like I'm riding a horse.

Bobby: that's a long drive to see such a small town. What's so special about Lindun?

Bill: Well, there are several things about Lindun. But I especially like the ancient city walls, and the Opium baron's house.

Bobby: They grow opium in Lindun?

Bill: No, not now! But they did before liberation!

Locals call this 180 year old stone mansion the Big Intersection Building (Dalukou Bldg., 大路口楼) because by Lindun standards this is a good sized road.

Lintianding (林天定), a Xiamen tobacco king, built this place to last. One of the granite blocks is 6.1 meters long, 60 cm wide, and 26 cm thick. The tall wooden columns are thicker than telephone poles, and mounted on granite globes. The clay roof tiles are still intact, though coated in rich green mold.

---

5 Prodigal son: wasteful son (from Jesus parable about the son who returned home after wasting his entire inheritance, yet was still welcomed by his father; Bible, Luke 15:11-32)

解说

1580 年 10 月 16 日，倭寇攻打山重。为了抵御倭寇，这里的人民于 1623 年建成了山洋楼石堡。一千多名当地居民组建起“福安军”，和倭寇对抗了一百多年。

墙的底部厚 1.6 米，顶部 0.9 米，高 6 米（最初有 3 层楼高）。大炮架在墙上的洞里，射出来的是一些自制的疙疙瘩瘩的炮弹。

住在这儿的一家子接待了我，就像是欢迎在外漂流的浪子回家一样。当然啦，老奶奶的第一句话就是：“M ‘dei!”喝口茶。英语中关于茶的词就是来自闽南语的“dei”字。

屋里所有的东西，无论是摇篮还是家具，都是手工制造的。那些木制的农具，由于年代久远而呈黑色，跟博物馆的展品似的。它们的款式极有可能经千年不变，但我们为什么又要重新发明轮子呢？他们已经发明了！

我们的下一站是林敦寨。它就在山的那一边，可惜没有径直的道路直达，我们只有绕道。要是有愚公帮我们移山就好了。

现场

潘维廉：我想我们需要一匹马，我们这会儿好像在马背上颠簸。

包东宇：来看这么一个小寨，我们可是走了很长的一段路啊。林敦寨究竟有什么特别之处呢？

潘维廉：可多了——但最特别的当数古城墙，和鸦片大王的房子了。

包东宇：他们在林敦种植鸦片？

潘维廉：不是现在。解放前的事了。

解说

Opium Baron's Manor　B.B.

当地人称这座有着 180 年历史的石头公寓为大路口楼是因为，照林敦标准，这是一条相当规模的道路了。厦门烟王林天定建这地方是要让它万古永存的。其中一块花岗石长 6.1 米，宽 60 厘米，厚 26 厘米。这些支撑在球形花岗石上、高高的木头柱子比电线杆还粗。尽管被厚厚的青苔所覆盖了，屋顶上黏土制成的瓦片依然完整。

Only 60 years ago, these hillsides were blanketed in opium poppies, and this house was an opium processing center. They must have thought the building was pretty secure—look at the size of the lock! But the opium baron was finally executed in 1940.

I had been to Lindun 4 times but had no idea some ancient walls remained intact. (林敦古城) The six meter high town walls were built to keep out Japanese pirates. And oddly enough, there was a wall down the middle too! I was told the village had two factions who were at each other's throats—except when they united to fight the Japanese!

A military leader used to live in the 350 year old house at the top of the steps. Along the wall here are the places that used to hold the cannon.

Outside the southern gate is a small shrine to a little porcelain local god. He's smaller than the incense sticks and mineral water they offer him, but he's grinning so he must be happy!

Dialogue—Sue lips[6] Over Kayaks

Bill: I think I've been to Changtai now a dozen times at least.

Bobby: Really? What do you like best here?

Bill: I don't know. But my wife and boys really flipped over the 2 ½ hour kayak ride.

Bobby: Have you ever been up a creek without a paddle?[7]

Bill: Only since I met you.

Sue Flips Out!

Changtai has hosted the International Kayaking championship, the First National Kayak championship, and China's 9th National athletics championship inMany international teams have practiced here, including groups from Germany, America, the U.K., Brazil, Japan, Indonesia, Thailand, Russia, Belize, and France. The center has a hotel, a conference center, and a very nice restaurant—and they used to have giant tortoises roaming around the floor!

Dialogue—Talking Turtle[8]

Bill: Those tortoises were this big. They were giant. I asked: Did you eat them? He said, "Of course not! They're over 100 years old. We'd never eat anything that old!"

Bobby: But where are they now?

Bill: They say they turned them loose. I was hoping to see them.

---

6 Flipped over: became very excited about

7 Up a creek without a paddle: in trouble, with no means of escape

8 Talking turtle: a play on the phrase "Talk turkey" (talk business)

就在60年前，这里的山坡上还种满了罂粟花，而这房子就是鸦片加工中心。他们一定是认为这座房子非常的安全——你看这锁！但这鸦片大王终于在1940年被正法了。

我曾四次来访林敦，却从未想到过有一些古城墙还能保持完整。这六米高的城墙是建来防御倭寇的。奇怪的是，在寨的中央还有一面墙！据说寨里存在着相互敌对的两部分势力——直到为打击倭寇才联合起来。

一位军官一直居住在台阶最高层处有着350年历史的老房里。沿着城墙，这里是放置大炮的地方。

南门外有一间小神坛，供着一小尊陶瓷塑的土地神。虽然说他比人们供奉给他的棒香和矿泉水瓶都要小，但你看他在笑，他一定很幸福！

♪现场 ——

潘维廉：我来长泰不止十来次了。
包东宇：是吗？你最喜欢这里的什么呢？
潘维廉：我不清楚。但我的妻子和孩子的确是花了两个小时半的时间泛舟于马洋溪上。
包东宇：你有没有试过不用桨也能逆溪而上？
潘维廉：遇见你以后就可以了吧。

♪解说 ——

长泰曾主办过国际皮筏锦标赛、第一届全国皮筏锦标赛，以及中国第九届运动会的皮筏赛。许多国际上的运动队曾经在这里练习过，包括来自德国、美国、英国、巴西、日本、印度尼西亚、泰国、俄罗斯、洪都拉斯和法国的队伍。中心设有旅舍、会议中心，以及一个非常漂亮的餐馆——以前餐馆里还有巨龟在地板上漫爬。

♪现场 ——

潘维廉：那些龟有这么大，大极了！我问龟的主人：“你们有吃龟的习惯吗？”对方回答：“当然没有啦。它们都不止一百岁了。我们从不吃那么长寿的动物。”
包东宇：但它们现在都在哪里？
潘维廉：他们说，都放生了。当时，我真想再见到它们。

Bobby: They don't eat old turtles, so what do they eat?

Bill: Well, there's plenty of wild veggies and there's all kinds of wild animals—but you're not going to find any frogs. And you know why. Because the 328 days of no frogs here, a brochure said, and also very big raindrops. So cheers to old turtles! Ganbei!

Matthew, Shannon and turtles

Changtai
Xiamen's Beautiful Backyard

Changtai is a beautiful place, rich in culture, history, and resources. It's no wonder that the Ming Dynasty official Tang Tai missed his hometown so much that he resigned his high post, returned to Changtai, and donated all his properties to build educational institutions. I would not mind a place here myself—at least for the summers! But then again, I might also like to spend the summer on Fujian's Hawaii, Dongshan Island…

包东宇：他们既然不吃长寿龟，那他们吃什么呢？

潘维廉：这里有很多野菜和各种野生动物——但你找不到青蛙，你知道原因的，因为正如当地一本小册子所说的，这里一年有328天没有青蛙，而且有硕大的雨滴。向长寿龟干杯！

♪解说 ———

长泰是一个美丽的地方，文化、历史和资源都蕴含丰富。难怪明朝时候，长泰籍官员唐泰因为十分思念家乡，终于辞官回家，把他毕生的财力都投入到学堂建设。我自己本身并不介意住在这么一个地方——至少可以避暑。

但话说回来了，我也很乐意在福建的夏威夷——东山岛度过夏天。

They're *my* bananas!

Episode 17 Dongshan Island, Fujian's Hawaii

Introduction In today's episode of Magic Fujian, we join Dr. Bill as he tours Dongshan Island, Fujian's Hawaii.

Dialogue

Dongshan Island's Endless Beaches

Bill: Dongshan is so beautiful that I can see why some people call it Fujian's Hawaii. But it's not as much fun if you don't know where to go or what to do.

Bobby: So how did you come to know the island so well?

Bill: That's a piece of cake. I was holding a class, and mentioned to my students that I'd like to go to Dongshan Island, and it turned out one of my students was from this island. So six of them brought me down here for the weekend.

Bobby: Did you enjoy that?

Bill:Oh, I had a blast. I mean this is his home. He knew every place, showed me all these places I'd never find my own.

On the road to Dongshan Island I passed Yunxiao Town, which has a unique claim to fame! For 500 years the locals have criticized politics with tongue twisters and poems in the local Minnan dialect. One story tells of a man lighting a gigantic firecracker. Everyone covered their ears and ran away, but instead of exploding it just fizzled out. The moral? Some people who talk the loudest do the least.

Tenfu Tea This large Tenfu tea depot is popular with travelers, but most of them don't even notice the beautiful site to the east—the rows of overlapping ranges of the peculiarly shaped mountains that only China can produce. China really does look like the old paintings!

Changtai Seafood Americans eat to live but Chinese live to eat, and since Dongshan is famous for sea food we headed straight to a restaurant.

Dialogue—a Dongshan Restaurant Looking at an octopus]

Bill: My students said six is better, another one said, no, no, it' s eight! Another one said 'summer' or 'winter'.

Bobby: Only have eight.

Bill: I don't know. I don't know anything about this stuff. It's not very happy, is it?

第17集　东山岛，福建的夏威夷

导语

在今天这一集的“老外看福建”里，让我们跟随潘维廉博士一起去游览福建的夏威夷——东山岛。

现场

潘维廉：东山岛太美了，我可以想象得出为什么人们把它叫作福建的夏威夷。但是如果你不知道去哪儿和去做什么，那么就没有太大的乐趣了。

包东宇：那么你怎么会这么了解这座岛屿的呢？

潘维廉：这个简单。有一次，我在上课时告诉我的学生，我很想到东山岛玩一番，巧的是有一个学生就来自东山岛。结果，六个学生带我一起去了东山过周末。

包东宇：玩得开心吗？

潘维廉：玩得痛快极了.我那个学生的家就在东山，他对那里的一切很熟悉，并带我游览了那些靠我自己永远无法找到的地方。

解说

在去东山岛的路上，我们经过了云霄镇。这个城镇之所以出名，原因很独特。500年来，当地人通过闽南话的绕口令和诗歌来针砭时弊。有一个故事是这样说的。有一个人点着了一个很大的鞭炮。每个人都捂住了耳朵跑开了，但是鞭炮却没有响，最后熄灭了。至于故事的寓意呢，就是有些人说话响亮，做得却最少。

这座规模较大的天福茶庄深受旅游者的欢迎。但是他们中间的许多人没有注意到东面优美的风景——山峦层层叠叠，形状独特，只有在中国才看得到。中国真得就像是一幅山水画。

美国人为了活着而吃，中国为了吃而活着。东山的海鲜很有些名气，所以我们直接就进了一家饭店。

现场

潘维廉：我的学生说，六只脚的章鱼好吃，另一个学生就争辩道，不不，八只脚的才好吃呢。还有的争论冬天的螃蟹是不是比夏天的好吃啦。

包东宇：章鱼只有八只脚呢。

潘维廉：不清楚，我不管这些，讨论这些挺无趣的，不是吗？

Sowing Seaweed

Dongshan's white shore slopes so gradually that you can walk out hundreds of meters—almost to the mythical site of the last Ming Emperor's sunken palace. Locals say that the very day the Mongols killed the last Ming Emperor on Hainan Island, his Dongshan palace sank into the sea. A black stone rose in its stead, and you can supposedly see it at low tide—though my student had never seen it.

Locals are very imaginative! They say that robbers were executed on the beach, and now when typhoons approach, you can see the robbers' ghosts running up and down the shore, sabers drawn.

Most of these people make their living from the sea, and burn offerings to gain local gods' protection. Seaweed grown on underwater frames is a common local crop. It takes ten days to harvest the seaweed.

I was surprised to learn that part of the seaweed processing is done with a plain old washing machine!

Dialogue—a Mischievous Minister

Bill: You know this man was so mischievous that his father put him on an island by himself so he would study!

Bobby: But he was a great man! He was the last prime minister of the Ming Dynasty.

Bill: Well, then I guess putting him on a desert island worked. I'll have to try it on my own two boys, or maybe I can even try on these two girls here! How about this girl?

Donshan's #1 site is the ancient Copper Mountain Castle and the beautiful gardens of Guandian Temple. It's hard to believe this narrow road was once the main street!

Tiger's Mouth Cave A tiger once dwelt in this cave, which is called Jade Drip in Tiger's Mouth Cave." My students say the water is very sweet.

Dialogue—by Wind Rocking Stone

Bill: So this is Dongshan island's famous wind rocking stone. But I could not get it move.

Bobby: I think we should use our feet?

Bill: Ok, go for it! On the count of three! One, two, three!

Bill: Well, maybe we should find some German sailors?

Bobby: Why German sailors?

Bill: Because Xiamen had a wind rocking stone until 1908 and then some German sailors rocked and rolled it right down the hillside. Maybe that's how rock 'n roll started! What's this calligraphy here…?

♪解说 ——

东山的白色海岸坡度很缓，以至于你可以朝着大海走出几百米远——几乎可以到达传说中明朝最后一个皇帝沉没的宫殿。当地人说，就在元兵在海南岛杀死明朝最后一个皇帝的那一天，他在东山的宫殿沉入了大海。在宫殿沉入的地方冒出了一块黑色的岩石，据说在潮退的时候你就可以看到它——虽然我的学生从来也没有见到过。

[捡起一块黑石头]或许这就是那黑色岩石的一部分吧。

当地人真是富有想象力！他们说以前的人在海滩上处死强盗。现在每当台风来临的时候，你就会看到强盗的鬼魂手持大刀，沿着海岸来回奔跑。

这里许多人靠海谋生。他们焚烧祭品来求得神灵的保佑。

生长在水下木框架上的海带是当地普遍种植的一种作物。收获海带需要十天的时间。

我很惊讶地听说处理海带的部分工序要通过一台普通的老式洗衣机来完成！

♪现场 ——

潘维廉：这尊雕塑有一个故事，这个人小时候太淘气了，他的父亲就把他孤零零地扔到一座岛屿上，让他好好学习。

包东宇：但是他是一个伟人！是明朝的最后一位丞相。

潘维廉：那么我猜把他关在那座岛上一定发挥作用了。我得在我两个儿子身上试试看！或者我也可以在这两个小女孩身上试试，这个女孩怎么样？

♪解说 ——

东山的头号景点是铜山古城和关帝庙美丽的花园。真是难以相信这条狭窄的道路曾经是主要的街道！

曾经有一只老虎穴居在这个山洞里。人们把山洞叫作虎口玉滴穴。我的学生说这里的水很甜。

这个花园太棒了。我特别喜欢这些奇怪的雨伞形状的树。

♪现场 ——

潘维廉：这就是东山有名的风动石，可是我却没有办法推动它。

包东宇：也许我们要用上脚才行？

潘维廉：好吧，来！一起数数，一、二、三！

潘维廉：嗯，也许我们需要找几个德国的水手来？

包东宇：为什么是德国的水手？

潘维廉：因为厦门原来也有个风动石，后来德国的水手在1908年把石头摇滚下山，也许这就是摇滚的由来吧。这些石刻是什么意思？

This cracked boulder has a unique story. The brass plaque below says that on May 31st, 1992, at 3:32 P.M, the rock cracked, smoke came out like a stone monkey, and an 80 pound python emerged.

I could believe the python part; snakes are a dime a dozen in Fujian. But what on earth does a stone monkey of smoke look like?

Museum of Widows Our last stop on Dongshan—and the most sobering one—was the museum commemorating the hundreds of women whose husbands were kidnapped by Chiang Kaishek's army when it fled to Taiwan.

Nearly the entire male population of some villages vanished. Most of the women never remarried, though the husbands in Taiwan invariably found new wives. Decades later, some returned to Dongshan Island to visit their former families, and even brought their new wives and children.

Dialogue—Widow's Museum

Bobby: It's hard to believe that the world ignored such barbarities.

Bill: I think too few people knew about it. Hopefully the world is small enough today such barbarities can not go unnoticed—or conveniently ignored.

On the way home I stopped at a Petro China to refuel. Four girls greeted me and gave me four oranges, some shoe polish, and a Chinese calendar.

"Wow!" I said. "It used to be just tissue paper or mineral water!" She looked surprised, hurried off, and returned with a box of tissue and some mineral water!

I wonder what else I could have asked for?

解说

这块裂开的石头有一段很独特的历史。旁边的牌匾记载着在 1992 年 5 月 31 号下午 3 点 32 分石头开裂了。冒出来的烟雾形状像是一只石猴，然后一条 80 磅重的蟒蛇窜了出来。

我相信会有蟒蛇，因为蛇在福建比一角钱的硬币还要多。但是究竟烟雾做的石猴会是什么样子呢？

我们在东山的最后一站，同时也是最令人清醒的一站是寡妇村博物馆。这个博物馆的建立是为了纪念几百名妇女。他们的丈夫被溃逃的蒋介石军队拉去了台湾。一些村庄几乎所有的男子都不见了踪影。大多数的妇女都没有再嫁，而她们在台湾的丈夫大多找了新的妻子。几十年过去了，一些人回到东山看望他们以前的家庭，有的甚至带来了他们续娶的妻子和儿女。

现场

包东宇：真是难以相信这个世界曾经忽略了这样残忍而不人道的罪行。

潘威廉：我想很少有人知道这件事，所幸现在世界变小了，这样的事不会再不为人所知——或者说，不会这么容易被忽略。

解说

在回家的路上，我在一家中国石油加油站停车加油。四个身穿绿色迷你裙的女孩向我致意，还给了我四个橘子、一些擦鞋剂还有一个中国日历。

Christmas is a gas!

“哇！”我说：“以前不过是面巾纸或者矿泉水！”她惊讶地看着我，然后跑开了，回来的时候竟然给我带来了一盒纸巾和几瓶矿泉水！

我真不知道我还能再向她要些什么。

Episode 18 Koxinga—Liberator of Taiwan

Introduction In today's episode of Magic Fujian, Dr. Brown visits the ancestral hometown of Koxinga, one of China's greatest heroes.

Koxinga Guards Xiamen Harbor

Dialogue—Koxinga Tackles[1] Typhoons?

Bill: Zhengchenggong is Xiamen people's great hero. In fact, they even believe that he protects the island from typhoons.

Bobby: So Xiamen never has typhoons?

Bill: No, in Oct. 1999, the typhoon nearly wiped us out. The Chinese friend told me Zhengchenggong was out of town.

Chinese value filial piety perhaps above all other virtues. Confucian tales give examples of children sacrificing themselves for their parents. One youth thawed a frozen lake with his own body so he could get his sick mother a fish. Another let mosquitoes bite him so they would not bite his parents. A Chinese friend asked me if I was that kind of son and I said, "No way. I'd buy them a mosquito net!"

Koxinga, the great patriot, defied his own father when he fought the invading Manchu. Yet in spite of his breach of filial piety, Chinese the world over admire him as a hero. So do the Japanese. 19th century plays about Koxinga were as popular in Japan as Shakespeare's plays were in England. Japanese admired his courage and loyalty. And besides, Koxinga was born in Japan.

Dialogue—Made in Japan Chinese Hero!

Bill: Did you know Koxinga was born in Japan?

Bobby: No, I don't. But Koxinga was Chinese, not Japanese.

Bill: You're right, Bobby—but only half right. His father was Chinese, but his mother was Japanese.

Bobby: Really!

Legend claims that lights shone in the heavens the night Koxinga's Japanese mother gave birth to him in Japan. At age seven he moved to China to study. Koxinga was a distinguished scholar but like his father he took up piracy. But unlike his father, Koxinga had strong principles, and refused to betray the doomed Ming Dynasty.

---

[1] Tackles: handles, manages, subdues, overcomes

第18集　民族英雄郑成功

导语

在今天的"老外看福建"节目里，潘维廉博士将参观中国的民族英雄郑成功的家乡。郑成功从荷兰侵略者手中收复了台湾。他的军队曾经以鼓浪屿为根据地，厦门人说，郑成功现在还是厦门的守护者。

现场（鼓浪屿上远眺郑成功塑像）

潘维廉：郑成功是厦门人民心目中的大英雄。他们甚至相信郑成功能够使厦门岛免受台风的侵袭。

包东宇：这么说，厦门从来不刮台风喽？

潘维廉：倒也不是。1999 年 10 月，一场台风几乎把我们厦门掀翻。一位中国朋友告诉我说，郑成功刚好不在城里！

解说

中国有句俗话：百善孝为先。儒家二十四孝的故事就是子女为父母尽孝道的生动范例。其中有一个故事是说，一位年轻人用体温在湖上融出一个冰窟窿，来为他生病的母亲捕一条鱼。另一个故事说到，一个青年用自己的身体来吸引蚊子，这样他的父母就可以免受蚊虫的叮咬。一个中国朋友问我会不会做那样的孝子。我说："没门儿。我会给他们买顶蚊帐！"

伟大的爱国者郑成功在抵抗清兵南下的时候，和他的亲生父亲闹翻了。虽然郑成功的做法有悖孝道，不过，全世界的华人还是把他当作英雄来敬仰。日本人也一样。19 世纪时，有关郑成功的戏剧在日本非常流行，跟当时莎士比亚的戏剧在英国的受欢迎程度不相上下。日本人敬佩郑成功的忠诚和勇气。此外，日本还是郑成功的出生地。

现场（南安郑成功祠）

潘维廉：你知道吗，郑成功是在日本出生的？

包东宇：不知道。不过，郑成功是中国人而不是日本人啊。

潘维廉：你说的对，但是不全对。郑成功的父亲是中国人，但他的母亲是日本人。

包东宇：是吗？

解说

据说，郑成功的日本母亲生他的那个晚上，天上有一道耀眼的亮光。郑成功七岁的时候回到中国上学。虽然他学识渊博，但他还是像父亲一样当了海盗。跟他父亲不同的是，郑成功很讲原则，也不肯背叛衰亡的明朝。

The Ming Dynasty appealed to Koxinga's father, Zheng Zhilong, for help against the Manchu. Zheng not only refused, but he routed the Ming fleet and seized Amoy in 1627. Other Fujian families refused to serve Zheng because he was not a leader but an opportunist. Zheng responded by betraying his fellow Fujianese. The Ming rewarded him with a new Ming military rank, fleets, and soldiers, and put the arch pirate Zheng Zhilong in charge of suppressing piracy! Of course, this pretty much gave him a monopoly on most foreign trade.

Dialogue

Bobby: So Koxinga's father really was just an opportunist!

Bill: He was—but his opportunities narrowed considerably when his own son turned against him.

Bobby: What moved Koxinga to break with centuries of Confucian tradition and oppose his father?

Bill: I think the last straw was when his father betrayed the Ming Prince in Fuzhou and that led to the suicide of his Japanese mother.

Once he was certain the Ming would fall, Zheng Zhilong betrayed the Ming Prince in Fuzhou. The Manchu seized Fujian, and Koxing's mother happened to be in Amoy when they took the island. Manchu soldiers raped her, and in humiliation she plunged a samurai sword into her belly and leapt from Xiamen's city wall.

This was the last straw for Koxinga. Generals everywhere were surrendering without even a fight, but not Koxinga. The Manchu tried to buy him off. Even Koxinga's father wrote imploring letters from Beijing, where he had been given a minor position under virtual house arrest—the Manchu knew better than to trust a traitor.

Dialogue

Bobby: Koxinga must have been furious with his father.

Bill: He was furious. And though Confucius is famous for saying, "The angry man is never right," on one occasion when he got angry himself, he explained to his disciples, "Well, this is a different occasion!"

For Koxinga, Confucian filial piety and scholarly detachment were a thing of the past. He responded to his father's letters by burning his hard-won scholarly robes in a Confucian temple like the one we're standing in now. And after denouncing his father as a traitor, he declared war on the Manchu.

In 1658, with 100,000 troops and 1,000 ships, Koxinga fought his way up the Yangtze River to the very gates of Nanjing. Land fighting wasn't his expertise, but the Manchu made a big mistake when their 800 ships chased him out to sea—where he was undefeatable. Koxinga destroyed the Manchu fleet, and sent 4,000 Manchu prisoners back to Beijing—minus their ears and noses.

当时的明朝朝廷请求郑成功的父亲郑芝龙帮助抵抗满清军队。郑芝龙不但拒绝了朝廷的请求，还在1627年指引清军的舰队夺取了厦门。福建的其他官员拒绝为郑芝龙效命，因为他见风使舵是个机会主义者，不配当大家的首领。郑芝龙最终还是背叛了福建的父老乡亲。作为回报，清廷给郑芝龙重授了军职，还拨给他战船和士兵，并且让这个海盗头子负责清剿海盗！当然，这也在很大程度上给了他垄断对外贸易的权力。

现场（郑成功碑林）———

包东宇：这么说，郑成功的父亲确实是个机会主义者！

潘维廉：没错。不过，当他的亲生儿子站出来反对他的时候，他就没那么多机会了。

包东宇：是什么让郑成功冲破千年的传统礼教来对抗他父亲的呢？

潘维廉：他父亲背叛了在福州的明朝太子，并导致郑成功的日本母亲自杀身亡。我想，可能就是这个最后的打击，迫使郑成功和他的父亲决裂。

解说 ———

当郑芝龙确信明朝将要灭亡的时候，他就背叛了在福州的明朝太子。清军随后攻占了福建。当清军攻克厦门的时候，郑成功的母亲正好就在岛上。清兵凌辱了她，屈辱之下，她剖腹自尽并从厦门的城墙上跳了下去。

母亲的死让郑成功忍无可忍。当时，各地的将领都纷纷不战而降，只有郑成功拒不投降。清军想用金钱收买他。甚至连他在北京的父亲都写信来劝降。当时，郑芝龙得到了一个低微的官职，而实际上则是被软禁了起来——满人也不愿重用一个叛徒。

现场（泉州孔庙孔子像前）———

包东宇：郑成功一定对他父亲的所作所为很愤怒。

潘维廉：他的确很愤怒。虽然孔夫子说过“怒者无常”，但是，有一次孔子自己生气的时候，就对弟子解释说：“这次的情况不同。”

解说 ———

对此刻的郑成功来说，儒家的孝道和学者的超然都已经是明日黄花了。他把自己辛苦得来的学者青衣在一座文庙里付之一炬，以此作为对父亲劝降书的回应。在宣告父亲为叛徒之后，郑成功正式向清军宣战。

1658年，郑成功率领十万大军和上千艘战船从长江口逆流而上，一直攻打到南京城下。郑成功并不善于陆战，但清军的800条战船追到海里时，他们才发现自己犯了多么大的错误，因为，郑成功在海上几乎是所向无敌。郑成功击溃了清军水师，并且将4000名割去耳鼻的清兵俘虏送回了北京。

From the heights of Gulangyu Islet's Sunlight Rock, overlooking the island on which his mother had committed suicide, Koxinga drilled his fleets and trained marines so tough that only those who could lift and carry a 600 pound stone qualified as "Tiger Guards." His soldiers wore iron aprons and iron masks, and wielded bows and arrows painted green.

On April 30th, 1691, Koxinga's armada of 300 ships and 25,000 marines sailed to Taiwan. The Dutch surrendered nine months later, and Koxinga let them leave with their personal possessions.

I said "Leather" Apron!

Dr. Bill as Dutch Governor

Dialogue—Bill Surrenders to Koxinga!

Bill: I was really impressed with the way Koxinga treated the defeated Dutch—especially after I played the last Dutch governor of Taiwan in a TV mini series.[2] I had to surrender to the great man!

Bobby: Hah! So Koxinga took over control of Taiwan from you?

Bill: Yeah, he did—in a way. Unfortunately not for very long. He set up an efficient administration, and he invited other fellow Fujianese to settle the island with him. But he died within a year.

Koxinga's father was beheaded, and to cripple Koxinga's army the Manchu depopulated the entire coast of China, from Shandong in the North to Guangdong in the South. Millions of ordinary Chinese' lives were uprooted, and hundreds of thousands went abroad, but wherever they put down roots, they never forgot they were Chinese—and they never forgot their debt to Koxinga.

---

[2] I asked a Shanghai director why I always play the bad egg in Chinese TV series (like Tan Kah Kee, Lin Zexu, deng deng). She replied, "Yang guizi meiyou hao dan!" "No foreign devils were good eggs!")

从鼓浪屿日光岩上，可以居高临下俯瞰对面的厦门岛，郑成功的母亲就是在那里自杀身亡的。郑成功据守鼓浪屿，严格操练他的水师。谁能扛起600磅重的石头才有资格入选他的“老虎营”。郑成功的士兵都是金盔铁甲，操着漆成绿色的弓箭。

1691年4月30日，郑成功率领300艘战船和25000名水师将士假道澎湖进攻台湾。九个月后，侵占台湾的荷兰殖民者向郑成功投降。郑成功让他们带上私人财物离开了中国。

♪**现场**（崇武古城城墙上）———

潘维廉：郑成功对待战败的荷兰人的方式令人钦佩，特别是我在一部电视剧中扮演了向郑成功投降的荷兰最后一任台湾总督之后，印象就更加深刻！

包东宇：哈！你是说郑成功从你的手里解放了台湾？

潘维廉：可以这么说。不过，遗憾的是时间并不长。郑成功在台湾岛上建立了有力的政权，并且邀请更多的福建同乡迁往台湾开发宝岛。可惜他几个月后就去世了。

♪**解说** ———

郑成功的父亲后来被砍了头。为了孤立郑氏的势力，清政府还在中国沿海实行海禁。北至山东、南至广东的广大沿海地区，数百万平民被迫离乡背井迁往内地，还有成千上万的人逃往海外。不过，无论在哪里扎根，他们都不会忘记自己是中国人，也不会忘记郑成功的功绩。

Gate to Koxinga's Fort

Episode 19 Introduction to Ningde

Mt. Taimu Hoodoo's

Introduction Welcome to today's episode of Magic Fujian, as we join Xiamen University's Dr. Bill and his friend Joyce Liu in Ningde, which was once the cultural and economic center of Fujian, and perhaps even the birthplace of South China civilization.

Dialogue—Fei Luan Tunnel

Bill: Do you see that tunnel ahead?

Joyce: Yes, it's the Feiluanling Tunnel. What about it?

Bill: New highways, and tunnels like the Feiluanling Tunnel, 3180 meters long, these will help Ningde resume its role as a commercial and cultural center in China.

Joyce: Oh, was Ningde very important in the ancient times?

Bill: It sure was. Back when most of the travel was by water, Ningde's Xiapu was the center an area stretching from Zhejiang's Wenzhou all the way south to Putian. The lack of roads has hurt Ningde in recent decades, but that is changing now.

Joyce: Oh, I see.

A new Ningde highway

The Feiluan tunnel, new roads, and marvels like the Qiaotou Po Bridge have cut off at least half a day of driving. Nowadays it is easier than ever for Laowai and Laonei alike to appreciate the natural and cultural wonders of northeastern Fujian, which has almost 2,000 years of recorded history.

Huotong Mtn. is considered the birthplace of south China civilization, and the Ming Emperor Yongle designated it, "Number One Mountain Under Heaven." Ningde was home to the Song Dynasty poet Lu You, and the philosopher Zhu Xi.

Japanese also revere Ningde because it was here that Kukai, the founder of Japanese Esoteric Buddhism, was rescued from a shipwreck when he arrived in China seeking the Buddhist scriptures.

第 19 集 认识宁德

导语

欢迎收看系列报道“老外看福建”。今天，厦门大学 MBA 中心的潘维廉博士和主持人刘银燕将带领我们走进宁德，深入了解闽东作为福建经济文化重镇的辉煌历史。此外，闽东还是中国南方文明的发祥地之一。

现场

潘维廉：你看到前面的隧道了吗？

刘银燕：看到了。是飞鸾岭隧道。有什么特别的地方吗？

潘维廉：新建的高速公路，加上全长 3180 米的飞鸾岭隧道，可以帮助宁德重振福建商业、文化中心的雄风。

刘银燕：是吗？宁德以前很重要吗？

潘维廉：很重要。在过去，出行大多靠水路。宁德霞浦是很重要的区域中心。它北控浙江温州，向南一直管到福建莆田。在过去的几十年里，宁德的公路交通一直未能得到改善。宁德深受其害。现在，情况有了很大的改观。

刘银燕：噢，是真的吗？

Ancient Ningde Calligraphy

解说

飞鸾岭隧道，新修建的高速公路以及诸如桥头堡、古老的大桥公路等奇迹，使福州前往宁德的车程至少节约了半天。闽东拥有近 2000 年的人类史。现在，宁德市的交通条件得到了很大的改善。国内、外游客前往闽东观赏美景、探寻文化也方便多了。

宁德霍童是中国南方文明的发祥地之一。明朝永乐皇帝钦赐宁德霍童山为“天下第一山”。宋代诗人陆游、理学家朱熹都曾经在宁德居住过。

日本佛教创始人空海法师前来中国取经时，遇上海难，被霞浦的渔民救起。因此，日本人对闽东人心存感激。

Dialogue—Unique Ningde

Bill: When I first came to Ningde a year ago, I knew nothing about this place, but it has become one of my favorite corners of Fujian.

Joyce: Because of the history and culture?

Bill: Well, besides that, but also the natural beauty of Taimu mountain, and the Nine Dragon Falls, which is China's largest waterfall complex. And in Baishuiyang, even a mortal like myself can walk on water!

Joyce: I don't believe you can walk on water!

Bill: Well, in a few days, I'll show you how it's done! But first, I'll take you to Sandu'ao and show you why Ningde once was the biggest commercial and cultural center of Fujian.

Ningde was a commercial and cultural hub in ancient days because most travel was by water and Ningde had 1/3 of Fujian's coastline—878 kilometers. It also has 344 islands and islets.

Sandu'ao, the world's deepest ice-free harbor, was home to businesses from a dozen Western countries until Japanese bombers razed it to the ground twice during the 1930s. We'll visit Sandu'ao's Spanish architecture and fascinating floating fishing villages tomorrow.

And speaking of tomorrow—Ningde has great hopes for the future!

For now at least, Ningde may look like many other Chinese towns, with its narrow, tree-lined streets, and vendors selling everything from local pottery to tropical flowers. Teashops are a dime a dozen because Ningde produces more tea than anywhere else in Fujian. In a few days we'll visit a couple of young tea entrepreneurs in Zhouning. Ningde is also famous for seafood, with over 600 kinds of marine animals, including prawns, and razor clams. And it has our planet's last spawning ground for the prized yellow croakers, which we feasted on during lunch.

Dialogue

Bill: Ningde's officials are betting that this city will once again become an economic powerhouse.

Joyce: But Ningde is so remote!

Bill: It is, for now. But soon, this new freeway will connect Fuzhou in the south with Zhejiang Province in the north.

Joyce: Well, that should put this ancient city back in the limelight!

Elevated highways already cross Ningde city, suspended high above miles of mud flats on which have been staked out vast tracts for future development of streets and government offices, exhibition centers, industrial complexes, and entertainment and tourist resorts. The 5,000 seat stadium has already been completed!

♪现场——

潘维廉：去年，我第一次来的时候，对宁德并不了解。现在，宁德变成了我在福建最喜欢的地方之一。
刘银燕：是因为历史，还是因为文化？
潘维廉：嗯，两者兼而有之。还有太姥山的自然景观，周宁的九龙祭瀑布可以说是中国最大的瀑布群。在屏南的白水洋，像我这样的凡人还可以在水上走呢！
刘银燕：水上行走？我不信！
潘维廉：那好，再过几天，我走给你瞧瞧。现在，我们还是先去三都澳，探寻宁德作为福建省重要的商业、文化中心的历史。

♪解说——

宁德拥有大小岛屿 344 座，海岸线 878 公里，约占福建的三分之一。在过去，出行大多走水路。因此，宁德成了福建重要的商贸、文化中心。宁德的三都澳拥有世界上最深的不冻港。在 20 世纪 30 年代日本轰炸机把三都澳夷为平地之前，这个港口常驻着西方十多个国家的商业机构。明天，我们将走访三都澳的西班牙建筑和迷人的海上渔村。

谈起宁德的明天，可以说是前途无量。跟中国其他城镇一样，宁德城区街道狭窄，绿树成荫。街边商贩贩卖无所不卖，从陶瓷器皿到热带花卉。茶叶店遍地开花，因为宁德的茶叶产量比福建省任何一个地方都多。再过几天，我们还将走访周宁的一对制茶小夫妻。宁德的海鲜名气很大，有 600 多种的海产品，包括对虾和竹蛏。此外，宁德还是珍稀黄花鱼在地球上的唯一产卵地。今天中午，我们将尝一尝大黄花鱼的味道。

♪现场——

潘维廉：宁德市的官员认为闽东将再次成为经济强市。
刘银燕：可是，宁德这么偏远！
潘维廉：现在是有点偏。不过，高速公路建成之后，闽东将与南面的福州和北边的浙江温州连成一片。
刘银燕：是吗？这样的话，古老的闽东会再次吸引世人的眼光。

♪解说——

闽东的高速公路已经修到了宁德市区。高架桥跨过城郊数十里的农田，直奔山野。当地政府为城市的发展预留了大片的土地，用于兴建新的街区、办公大楼、展览中心、工业区和旅游度假村。其中，一座能够容纳 5000 名观众的体育馆已经完工。

Officials gave me the book, "Ningde Tomorrow," showed me the model of the future city, and then gave me a bird's eye view of the future city from the heights of Pagoda Hill, and its Song dynasty pagoda.

I suggested they photograph Ningde's spectacular view at least once a year for posterity. I explained that visitors to Xiamen, which now resembles a small Hong Kong, cannot believe that 14 years ago the island had only one skyscraper! Likewise, a decade from now, Ningde will bear little resemblance to the vast tract of mud and marsh it is today.

Beautiful beaches and mountains

Dialogue

Bill: To be frank, at first I thought Ningde's officials were setting their sights a bit high.

Joyce: Do you still think Ningde is building castles in the clouds?

Bill: Not at all! In fact, Ningde is already proving to be a potent player in China's development.

Ningde already has 7 commercial docks capable of handling 1,000-ton class vessels. And exports total over 100 million USD annually. But most impressive to me is that locals' incomes have soared to over 4000 Yuan annually in towns, and 2000 Yuan annually in rural areas. That, after all, is what development is about, and I look forward to when Ningde again becomes a major player in world trade. Especially Sandu'ao, which we will visit tomorrow!

B.B.

宁德市的领导送我一本《明日宁德》画册，并向我展示了城市发展规划。他们带我上塔山，从宋代古塔鸟瞰宁德市区。我建议他们每年拍摄一次宁德市区，以备后用。我解释说，厦门现在像一个“小香港”，而14年前，厦门全岛只有一栋高楼。因此，可以预见，10年后宁德城区会变得难以辨认，城郊的农田、水塘也将不复存在。

Ningde's famous seafood

♪现场 ———

潘维廉：说句实话，我当初以为宁德市政府把目标定得太高了。

刘银燕：你现在还认为，宁德人是在建造“空中阁楼”吗？

潘维廉：不！事实将证明，宁德会成为中国经济发展最有潜力的地区之一。

Cameraman Libiao learns FJTV's driver is a chef! (Ningde)

♪解说 ———

宁德市目前已拥有七座千吨级商业码头，年出口值超过 1 亿美元。闽东城镇居民年均收入超过 4000 元，农民收入 2000 元。这些数据给我的印象最深。这就是发展带来的好处。我期待着有朝一日，宁德再次成为中国对外贸易的重要窗口。特别是对明天即将访问的三都澳，我寄以厚望。

Episode 20 Sandu'ao, the World's Deepest Ice-free Harbor

Introduction Welcome to today's episode of Magic Fujian, in which Xiamen University's Dr. Bill and his friend Joyce Liu discover the world's deepest ice-free harbor—which also harbors a real-life water world!

FJTV Cameraman on Floating Village

Dialogue

Bill: Have you heard about Kevin Kostner's movie Water World?

Joyce: Yes, it is about a future society that lives entirely on water.

Bill: Well, that future society is already here—in Fujian at Sandu'ao!

Joyce: Really? I'd like to see such a place.

Bill: Ok! I hope you can swim!

Joyce: Like a fish?

Bill: Probably like a bird!

Fujianese have always been at home on water—whether inland or at sea, but fishermen in Sandu'ao have taken it to an extreme, building entire villages upon the sea! Sandu'ao is famous for its seaweed and shellfish, and it's yellow croakers.

While the vast bay looks like open ocean, it is in fact almost entirely landlocked, so the floating villages usually lay calmly on waters that resemble an endless expanse of smooth jade. And Sandu'ao is not only the world's deepest ice-free harbor but also, I've been told, getting deeper every year.

Sandu'ao began trade with foreign nations over 1,000 years ago, back in the Tang Dynasty. In 1694, the Sandu'ao administered nine ports, and the port was opened to foreign ships in 1897. By the 1930s, the island was home to at least 20 foreign companies from Britain, the U.S., Germany, Russia, Japan, Holland, Sweden, Spain, and Portugal. But ancient Sandu'ao's glory ended overnight when Japanese bombers razed the island to the ground twice, leaving only a few small buildings—including a magnificent Spanish Catholic stone Church and an American nunnery, which we will visit later.

Our speedboat was powered by a Yamaha 150 horsepower outboard motor, but I was fascinated by the gasoline motors on the small fishing boats. They looked like they had been welded together by hand. I never cease to marvel at Chinese ingenuity!

第 20 集　深水良港三都澳

导语

欢迎收看系列报道“老外看福建”。厦门大学的潘维廉教授和主持人刘银燕今天要带我们去看的是世界上最深的不冻港——三都澳。在三都澳，你还会看到港湾里货真价实的水上世界。

现场

潘维廉：你有没有听说过凯文·考斯特勒的电影《水上世界》？

刘银燕：听说过。这部电影讲的是完全建在水上的未来世界。

潘维廉：嗯！这种未来世界在福建的三都澳已经变为现实。

刘银燕：真的吗？我倒想去看看。

潘维廉：行。只要你会游泳。

刘银燕：像条鱼？

潘维廉：也许更像鸟！

解说

无论在内河，还是在外海，福建人简直如履平地，无拘无束，无所顾忌。在三都澳，渔民们把这种水上生存能力发挥到了极点。他们把整个村庄建在海上。三都澳以盛产黄花鱼、海带和贝类海产而著名。港区三面环山，水面宽阔，颇像大海。海上渔村就这样宁静地横卧在三都澳的港湾里，像一片无垠的光滑玉石。当地百姓告诉我，三都澳是世界上最深的不冻港，海水每年还在不断地刷深三都港。

早在 1000 多年前的唐朝，三都澳就开始与外国通商贸易。1694 年，三都澳管辖九个港口。1897 年，三都澳被迫对外国轮船开放。到了 1930 年，三都澳岛上常驻着近二十家来自英、美、德、俄、日、荷兰、瑞典、西班牙和葡萄牙等国的外国公司。日本战机的两次轰炸把三都岛夷为平地，三都澳的辉煌顿时变成了历史。如今，岛上像样的建筑所剩无几。其中，有我们即将参观的一座石结构西班牙天主教堂和一座美国修道院。

坐上快艇，我发现，挂在船尾的雅马哈马达功率高达 150 马力。不过，小渔船上的汽油发动机着实令人着迷。这些汽油发动机乍一看像是用人工捆扎起来的。我不禁为中国人的心灵手巧、聪明才智而感到惊奇。

Dialogue—the Real Water World

Bill: I've heard that some of the fishermen in these floating fishing villages never set foot on dry land!

Joyce: Yes, that could be true. They even have their own police and medical services.

Bill: It's amazing. Floating stores, floating houses, floating restaurants, floating gas stations. And when they call the police, they come up in speedboats!

Joyce: That's what they call "110".

Bill: "110". Yes, the one said that they are faster here than on land.

Mile after mile, villages float upon sturdy platforms fabricated from bamboo and wood wired to barrels or blocks of styrofoam. Fishermen get around in craft ranging from crude wooden crafts to fine fiberglass boats. Some boats look almost handmade but they suffice, given the placid waters of the bay. Except perhaps during typhoons like Toraji, which in August 2001 devastated Taiwan and caused some $20 million in damage.

At times like that I would think people would prefer dry land. Though on the other hand, at least floating villages don't get flooded out!

Joyce and I visited one of the floating villages and were, of course, greeted with, "Come in and have some tea!" The little home was a lot more comfortable inside than I'd expected it to be, and the farmers told me that their small water farm yielded tens of thousands of yellow croakers annually.

Dialogue

Bill: I heard that Sandu'ao's Dragon Eye fruit is really good!

Joyce: I don't know about that. But I know that Ningde is famous for its seafood.

Bill: Really? Well, we Americans say the best way to a man's heart is through his stomach, and it's just about lunchtime—so why don't we go try the seafood out!

Joyce: Ok, if you buy!

Bill: Ok, I'll buy—but you pay!

Joyce: Okay, I'll pay, but with your money.

Bill: Somehow this is not working out like I expected.

Sandu'ao has a marvelous variety of shellfish, and shrimp the size of small lobsters. We feasted on fish, and I was told that the tender green seaweed was cultivated on a seaweed farm that was over 160 acres.

现场

潘维廉：听说海上渔村的一些渔民从不上岸。
刘银燕：是吗？有可能！他们在海上可以叫到警察和医生。
潘维廉：实在不可思议！（海上渔村）有店铺、房屋、客栈、餐馆和加水站等等。需要警察和医生的时候，他们就会坐快艇赶来。
刘银燕：这就是他们所说的“海上110”。
潘维廉：没错！“海上110”。这里的人都说，“海上110”来得比陆地上的更快。

解说

海上渔村漂浮在坚固的平台上，绵延数里。这些平台是用竹竿、木头和塑胶桶以及泡沫块堆扎起来的。海上渔民的交通工具从粗制滥造的小木筏到精工细作的玻璃钢船，无奇不有。一些船看上去几乎是手工制作。在三都澳，港湾里风平浪静，用这种船就可以四处转悠。当然，千万别碰上像去年5月的“桃芝”台风。那场台风横扫台湾全岛，造成了大约两亿美元的损失。

碰上那种气候，渔民们也许会更喜欢上岸。当然，台风暴雨的时候，住在海上渔村，倒不用担心岸上的洪灾！

我们拜访了三都澳港湾里的一座海上渔村。村民们热情地邀请我们进屋喝茶、做客。走进矮小的海上渔屋，里面的条件比我们想象的更加舒适。村民们还告诉我，这座海上渔村每年产出成千上万吨的黄花鱼。

现场

潘维廉：听说三都澳的龙眼很好吃。
刘银燕：这个，我不太了解。我只知道宁德的海鲜很出名。
潘维廉：真的吗？嗯，我们美国人常说，要想赢得男人的心，就得管好他的胃。该是吃午饭的时候了，我们去试试宁德的海鲜,怎么样？
刘银燕：没问题，只要你买单。
潘维廉：行，我买单，你付钱。
刘银燕：行，我付钱，用你的钱买单。
潘维廉：咦,这我倒没想到。

解说

三都澳贝类海产种类繁多，大对虾简直赛过小龙虾。当天中午,我们以鱼做饭。我们还要了一种口感嫩滑的绿色海藻。当地渔民告诉我，这种海藻是由附近的一个海上农场种植的，这个农场面积超过160英亩。吃过甜点——当地龙眼，我们继续上路，沿着山坡，寻访天主教堂。

After a dessert of local Dragon Eye fruit, we continued our tour up the hill to visit the Catholic Church.

But the hill was too steep to handle a foreigner and Libiao, FJTV's gentle giant of a cameraman. The three-wheeled motorcycle taxi flipped backwards.

The distraught driver said, "Are you okay? I've never had this happen before!"

I laughed heartily. "It's my first time too, but there's a first time for everything. Don't worry!" My only regret was I didn't get a photo.

Above many of the doors were paper drawings of odd symbols, which I learned were Buddhist or Taoist. I also saw at least half a dozen Catholic crosses on doors of households that probably attend the stone Catholic church on the hilltop.

The Catholic stone church, with its distinctive Spanish architecture, is said to be the best preserved old church in Fujian Province. Unfortunately, we weren't allowed to take photos inside, so we headed for the old American nunnery behind it.

The old nunnery is now called Tianlao Yuan— "Heaven's Garden for the Elderly." Some of these nuns have been here sixty years! One gave us a tour of the rooms and courtyard. A dozen elderly ladies were praying in a small chapel that had paintings and crosses around the walls, and a large crucifix in front. The praying sounded like Buddhist chants to me, and when we retraced our steps down the hill we heard similar chanting in other homes. But I'd be praying too if I'd gone through what those people have.

Inside the former American nunnery

Sandu'ao has yet to recover fully from the devastation of the Japanese bombings in the 1930s. While Sandu'ao's population was 30,000 in the 1940s, it is only 20,000 today. And life is not easy for the islanders, but you could not tell it from the hearty laughter and smiles of the people I met. For their sake, I hope Ningde achieves her ambitious development goals.

♪现场

潘维廉：听说海上渔村的一些渔民从不上岸。
刘银燕：是吗？有可能！他们在海上可以叫到警察和医生。
潘维廉：实在不可思议！（海上渔村）有店铺、房屋、客栈、餐馆和加水站等等。需要警察和医生的时候，他们就会坐快艇赶来。
刘银燕：这就是他们所说的“海上 110”。
潘维廉：没错！“海上 110”。这里的人都说，“海上 110”来得比陆地上的更快。

♪解说

海上渔村漂浮在坚固的平台上，绵延数里。这些平台是用竹竿、木头和塑胶桶以及泡沫块堆扎起来的。海上渔民的交通工具从粗制滥造的小木筏到精工细作的玻璃钢船，无奇不有。一些船看上去几乎是手工制作。在三都澳，港湾里风平浪静，用这种船就可以四处转悠。当然，千万别碰上像去年 5 月的“桃芝”台风。那场台风横扫台湾全岛，造成了大约两亿美元的损失。

碰上那种气候，渔民们也许会更喜欢上岸。当然，台风暴雨的时候，住在海上渔村，倒不用担心岸上的洪灾！

我们拜访了三都澳港湾里的一座海上渔村。村民们热情地邀请我们进屋喝茶、做客。走进矮小的海上渔屋，里面的条件比我们想象的更加舒适。村民们还告诉我，这座海上渔村每年产出成千上万吨的黄花鱼。

♪现场

潘维廉：听说三都澳的龙眼很好吃。
刘银燕：这个，我不太了解。我只知道宁德的海鲜很出名。
潘维廉：真的吗？嗯，我们美国人常说，要想赢得男人的心，就得管好他的胃。该是吃午饭的时候了，我们去试试宁德的海鲜,怎么样？
刘银燕：没问题，只要你买单。
潘维廉：行，我买单，你付钱。
刘银燕：行，我付钱，用你的钱买单。
潘维廉：咦,这我倒没想到。

♪解说

三都澳贝类海产种类繁多，大对虾简直赛过小龙虾。当天中午,我们以鱼做饭。我们还要了一种口感嫩滑的绿色海藻。当地渔民告诉我，这种海藻是由附近的一个海上农场种植的，这个农场面积超过 160 英亩。吃过甜点——当地龙眼，我们继续上路，沿着山坡，寻访天主教堂。

After a dessert of local Dragon Eye fruit, we continued our tour up the hill to visit the Catholic Church.

But the hill was too steep to handle a foreigner and Libiao, FJTV's gentle giant of a cameraman. The three-wheeled motorcycle taxi flipped backwards.

The distraught driver said, "Are you okay? I've never had this happen before!"

I laughed heartily. "It's my first time too, but there's a first time for everything. Don't worry!" My only regret was I didn't get a photo.

Above many of the doors were paper drawings of odd symbols, which I learned were Buddhist or Taoist. I also saw at least half a dozen Catholic crosses on doors of households that probably attend the stone Catholic church on the hilltop.

The Catholic stone church, with its distinctive Spanish architecture, is said to be the best preserved old church in Fujian Province. Unfortunately, we weren't allowed to take photos inside, so we headed for the old American nunnery behind it.

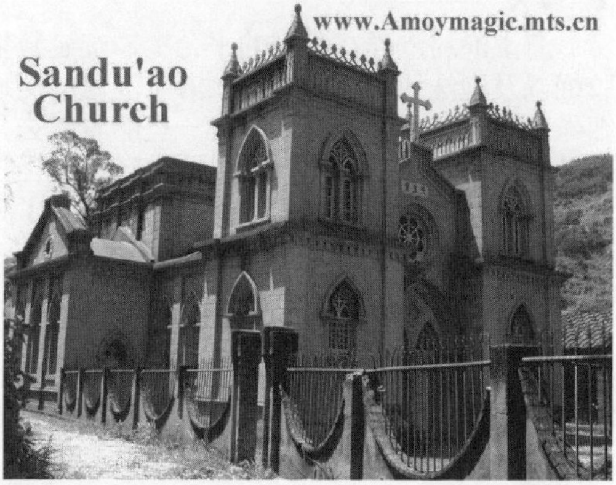

The old nunnery is now called Tianlao Yuan— "Heaven's Garden for the Elderly." Some of these nuns have been here sixty years! One gave us a tour of the rooms and courtyard. A dozen elderly ladies were praying in a small chapel that had paintings and crosses around the walls, and a large crucifix in front. The praying sounded like Buddhist chants to me, and when we retraced our steps down the hill we heard similar chanting in other homes. But I'd be praying too if I'd gone through what those people have.

Inside the former American nunnery

Sandu'ao has yet to recover fully from the devastation of the Japanese bombings in the 1930s. While Sandu'ao's population was 30,000 in the 1940s, it is only 20,000 today. And life is not easy for the islanders, but you could not tell it from the hearty laughter and smiles of the people I met. For their sake, I hope Ningde achieves her ambitious development goals.

上山的坡度太大，三轮摩托拉不动我这个老外和大块头的摄像李飚。我们翻车了。

摩托车主被吓坏了。他不停地问：“没事吧？以前都不会这样。”

我开心地笑道：“破天荒，第一次。凡是总要有个第一。别担心。我很遗憾没能及时拍张照片。”

三都岛上人家的门上贴着许多奇形怪状的图案。有人告诉我，那是道教或佛教的象征。我还看到有五六户人家门上挂着天主教的十字架。他们也许是山上天主教堂的信徒。

石结构的天主教教堂是一座典型的西班牙建筑。据说，这是福建省保存最完好的教堂。由于未能获准入内拍摄，我们只好去拜访教堂后面的美国修道院。

古老的修道院现在是一座养老院，改名叫“天老园”。一些修女在院里一住就是 60 年！她们带我们参观了天老园的庭院和房舍。我看到， 10 多位上了年纪的老太太在园内的一个小教堂里祈祷。小教堂的墙壁上贴满各种宗教绘画和十字架，前面还有耶稣受难的十字架画像。

对我来说，祈祷声听起来很像佛教徒在颂经。当我们顺着原路返回时，我还听到从普通百姓家里传出的祷告声。假如跟她们一样历尽沧桑，我想，我也会这样祈祷的。

三都澳要彻底地从上个世纪30年代的废墟堆中恢复过来还需要等上一些时日。19世纪 40 年代，三都澳人口多达三万。目前，只有两万人左右。对岛上居民来说，生活是艰辛的。但从我们所接触的岛民脸上，你看不出这种艰辛。他们笑得很开心、甜美。告别岛民，我衷心地祝愿宁德的雄伟目标能够早日实现。

Old American Nunnery

Episode 21 Xiapu, a Holy Place for Japanese

Introduction In today's episode of Magic Fujian, Xiamen University's Dr. Bill, and his friend Joyce Liu, explore the historical and natural beauty of an area treasured not only by Chinese but Japanese as well—Northeast Fujian's Xiapu!

The sign said Xiapu was only 52 km to the East, so I thought we had only an hour or so to go. Little did I know!

The tar road was as smooth as a black snake's belly, but it wound so tightly through the mountains that I was surprised it didn't tie itself in knots. Still, it was a beautiful view, with fields of grapes below and tea terraces above.

Just as I felt I was in the very middle of nowhere, I saw old houses painted red, with "Robust!" in big white letters. The Robust buildings remind me of the "See Rock City!" painted on roof barns all over the southeastern United States.

Dialogue—Japanese Holy Place

Kukai's Temple

Joyce: Xiapu seems so remote now, but wasn't it very important at one time?

Bill: Yes, it was. Xiapu was the administrative center of a region that reached from Wenzhou in Zhejiang Province to the north to Putian in the south.

Joyce: Well what happened?

Bill: The development of roads and the decline of sea commerce didn't help much, and then the Japanese bombed Xiapu which was a kind of ironic because Xiapu was a holy land for the Japanese!

Joyce: A holy place?

Bill: Yes.

Two or three times a year, Japanese make pilgrimages to a temple just a ten minute drive north of Xiapu. This temple was built in honor of Kukai, who lived from 774 to 835 AD. He traveled to China in search of the esoteric Buddhist scriptures in 804. Locals rescued and cared for him when he was shipwrecked off Xiapu. He went on to the capital of China, and returned to Japan in 806 with 451 volumes of Buddhist works, and founded Japan's esoteric Buddhism sect.

第21集　圣地霞浦

导语

在今天的这集“老外看福建”中，厦门大学的潘维廉博士和主持人刘银燕探访了闽东一块被中国人所珍爱，同时也为日本人所尊崇的一块热土，那就是历史底蕴丰厚，自然风光旖旎的霞浦县。

解说

路标上说，宁德市往东52公里就是霞浦了。因此，我想我们只需在路上行驶差不多一个小时就可到达那里，后来的事实真是出乎我的意料。

光滑的柏油路像乌黑发亮的蛇肚皮一样，蜿蜒在层峦叠嶂之间。通往霞浦的这条盘山公路紧紧缠绕在重山中，看不到任何接点，简直可以说是天衣无缝。道路两侧一派田园风光：山脚下是绿盈盈的葡萄园，山坡上是一排排的茶树。正当我沉醉于这迷人风光时，眼前忽然一亮，白色的“乐百士”标志镶嵌在刷得猩红的墙壁上，格外抢眼，一下子闯入我的视野，这光景同遍布美国东南部的刷有“观岩城 See Rock City”字样的粮仓如出一辙。

现场

刘银燕：霞浦现在看起来比较偏远，以前它是不是曾经辉煌过？

潘维廉：没错。霞浦曾经是北抵浙江温州，南达福建莆田这一大片区域的行政中心。

刘银燕：那么，后来到底发生了什么呢？

潘维廉：公路不够四通八达，海上商业逐渐衰落，这使霞浦不断走下坡路。后来日本人又轰炸了霞浦，这事说来挺可笑的，因为霞浦还是日本人崇拜的一块圣地呢！

刘银燕：日本人崇拜的圣地？

潘维廉：没错。

解说

日本人每年会向霞浦县城北边的一座寺庙朝拜两三次，这座寺庙是为了纪念日本的空海法师而建的。空海法师生于公元774年，公元835年圆寂。30岁那年，空海法师远渡重洋来到中国求取佛教密宗的经文。当他乘坐的船只航行到霞浦海域时，船只失事了。霞浦人把空海法师从海上救回来并精心照顾他。养好身体后，空海法师沿陆路前往唐朝都城长安，继续他的取经之旅。空海法师32岁那年，也就是公元806年，他携带着451卷经书满载而归，在日本创建了佛教的密宗。

Dialogue

Bill: This temple obviously means a lot to the Japanese .They spent 430,000 Yuan just on that wooden statue of Kukai.

Joyce: Oh, really, and what about this piece?

Bill: These are two embroidered Japanese mandalas. And they came from Japan in 1994. They cost 210,000 Yuan each.

Joyce: And how about the light?

Bill: The light, that's a gold-plated copper chandelier. This one light costs 210,000 Yuan.

Joyce: Too expensive!

Legends claim Kukai performed many miracles, like creating springs in draught-stricken villages. And he did give the peasants water, in a way. The dam to Shikoku's largest reservoir, which covers 3,600 hectares, was destroyed by a flood in 818. After repeated failures to repair it, Kukai was called in to direct its reconstruction because he was a native of the area. Legends say his rapid success where others had failed was due to magic. In fact, it was the result of his great rapport with the common people, who trusted and loved the man who had abandoned his well off lifestyle to become an ascetic monk.

Kukai temple was built on the seashore, near the site of Kukai's shipwreck, but the area has silted in over the years so now it's in the middle of a field. So while Japanese delegations visit the temple, they also worship on the nearby beach, and some even take home small bags of sand as souvenirs.

After visiting Kukai's temple, we headed north on a road so bumpy that locals call it a rubber road.

It's quite a challenge to build highways in mountainous Fujian. I've often said that Fujian would be the biggest province in China if somewhat flattened it. But since we can't flatten Fujian, the government is shrinking the distances by spending billions of Yuan on new highways, bridges and tunnels that will soon give easy access to every corner of our province—including the banyans and bamboo raft rides just north of Xiapu.

现场

潘维廉：空海寺在日本人心中的分量很重，仅仅这樽用檀木雕刻成的空海法师塑像，日本人就花了43万元人民币。

刘银燕：噢，那挂在墙壁上的这是什么？

潘维廉：这是刺绣品曼陀罗，共有两幅，1994年从日本带过来的，每幅价值高达29万元人民币。

刘银燕：那么顶上这盏吊灯呢？

潘维廉：这盏吊灯是用铜打造而成的，外层还镀了黄金，价值高达21万元人民币。

刘银燕：真是太昂贵了！

解说

相传空海法师创下了很多奇迹，比如他曾经使干旱的村庄冒出潺潺的泉水，他给农民带来了贵如油的水。据史料记载，日本四国岛最大的水库方圆600公顷，它的大坝在公元818年的时候被洪水冲垮。在其他人屡建屡败的情况下，空海法师被指派来重建大坝，空海法师很快就建好了大坝。人们把这次奇迹归功于空海法师的法术。实际上，他的成功源自于他同普通大众血浓于水的亲密感情。对这位抛弃锦衣玉食的苦行僧，人们信任他，爱戴他。

空海寺原本建在靠近船只失事的海滩上，但年复一年，淤泥不断蚕食沙滩。因此，现在空海寺周围是一片田野。每年日本代表团前往霞浦空海寺进香时，他们一定会到附近的沙滩上朝拜，有的人甚至还会带上一把沙子回家，作为纪念。

拜访空海寺之后，我们继续向北行进。一路上车子颠簸不已，当地人戏称，这是一条橡皮做成的路。

福建到处是山，在崇山峻岭中修筑高速公路的确是很大的挑战。我经常开玩笑说，如果把每个山头摊平的话，福建将会是中国面积最大的省份。当然，我们是凡人，不具备这种神力，所幸的是，为缩短距离，政府正投入巨额资金，修建福建的高速公路网。不久，这些公路网将延伸到福建省的每一个角落——包括我们将要游览的霞浦北部美丽的榕树林和可以漂流竹排的杨家溪。

Episode 22 Yangjiaxi Bamboo Raft Rides

Lead In On Today's Episode of Magic Fujian, Xiamen University's Dr. Bill and Joyce Liu send us down the river in Xiapu.

Xiapu is famous for seafood and beaches, but just north is also a secluded river with bamboo rafting, and a forest of ancient trees. While I love the bamboo rafts and banyans, the highlight this time around was the children, and Mr. Chen, the 70 year old ferryman. Especially his pipe!

Puff, the Magic Ferryman

Puff the Magic Ferryman![1] Mr. Chen still works the river every day, and between ferrying people he puffs on his bamboo water pipe. For every puff he had to fill the pipe with a pinch of green tobacco, and light it, but he was rewarded each time with a cloud of smoke even a dragon would have envied. And though I detest cigarettes, his tobacco smoke had a pleasing aroma, like my dad's old cherry pipe tobacco. After chatting with Mr. Chen I headed off to the beautiful banyan trees, which have now been made into a park.

Dialogue—Monkeys or hams?

Bill: These children are incurable hams[2]. They're just like monkeys, the way they climb these trees.

Joyce: "But they are very photogenic."[3]

Bill: Yes, I told the people here that they have very beautiful children. They said that's because we have good air, clean water, and good soil. I said it sounds more like you're growing crops than kids!

[Bill climbs the tree too]. Bill: "Do you want to come up?"

Joyce: I dare not!

After the trees we strolled up the winding path through the forests to the bamboo river rafting site. My last time here, our guide, Miss Li, who kept a megaphone stuck in my ear even though she was close enough to whisper, told me, "This became a 2nd class scenic area in August of '98."

"Glad to hear it," I said. "But I hope the rafts are 1st class because my swimming is not!"

---

1 Puff: the dragon in the song "Puff the Magic Dragon." The ferryman smokes like Puff.

2 Ham: an actor who overacts or exaggerates; a show-off

3 Photogenic: good subject for photography; they look good in photographs

第22集 杨家溪竹筏漂流

导语

系列报道“老外看福建”今天播出的是，厦门大学潘维廉博士和主持人刘银燕带领我们到霞浦杨家溪漂流的故事，一起来看看。

解说

霞浦的海鲜和沙滩远近闻名，但你可知道，在霞浦北部还有一条远离尘嚣的杨家溪。溪面的竹排和溪边茂盛的老榕树令我迷恋不已，而这次霞浦之行最令我难忘的当数这里的孩子，以及抽着水烟的七十多岁的老艄公老陈。

尽管年事已高，老陈依然每天在溪上摆渡，在摆渡的间隙，他总会忙里偷闲，悠悠地吸上几口水烟。要抽上这种自制的水烟，他得先往竹制的烟筒里装进一小撮纯天然烟丝，然后他就可以美美地坐在那儿吞云吐雾了。从老陈嘴里出来的那股烟雾婀娜多姿，像小青龙似的。平常我挺怕闻烟味的，但老陈的水烟芳香宜人，味道很像父亲用老式的樱桃木烟管抽的那种。跟老陈闲聊完后，我起身前往迷人的榕树林，那地方现在已开发成公园了。

现场

潘维廉：这些孩子真是古怪精灵，他们爬树的样子真像猴子。

刘银燕：你看，他们还特别上镜头呢。

潘维廉：是啊！我对当地人讲，他们的孩子真可爱，很漂亮。他们就说：“这是因为我们这里的空气、水土好，很养人。”我说，听上去怎么觉得他们养孩子就跟种庄稼一样。

潘维廉(爬上树问)：你也想爬上来吗？

刘银燕：我不敢。

解说

穿过一片枫树林中弯弯曲曲的鹅卵石小径，我们来到了杨家溪的竹排渡口。上次我到这儿来的时候，导游李小姐跟我近在咫尺，近得简直可以交头接耳，但她还是高举大喇叭，冲着我的耳朵大声介绍说：“1998 年 8 月的时候，杨家溪被评为二级风景区。”我说：“很高兴听到这消息，但我希望这竹排是一流的，因为我的游泳水平是末流的。”

And last visit I'd been told the river was pure enough to drink, though it looked muddy to me. "That's because of a recent typhoon," Miss Li had said, her megaphone stuck in my ear."

I guess I could have pretended it was coffee.

Locals totally ignored the picturesque waterfall, probably because there was no story behind it. But I liked it. The sound reminded me of our Xiamen University apartment's toilet, which never stops running, year round.

One of the islands is full of butterflies in August, and when Mandarin ducks flock in around December.

After the river rafting we walked back to the parking lot through forests so neatly kept that they reminded me of the orderly German forests, where one might expect birds to chirp like Black Forest cuckoo clocks—on the hour, sharp. The forest was peaceful but not at all quiet. The cicadas were noisier than a Cantonese restaurant at lunchtime. Still, I could have spent a week in this beautiful valley if we had not been so pressed for time.

Dialogue

Bill: Ah, this is such a nice trip. I could spend days in this place!

Joyce: So could I. After living in the city it's so nice to hear nothing but cicadas and crickets!

Bill: Fortunately, we have a nice treat tomorrow.

Joyce: Oh? What is that?

Bill: Tomorrow we climb one of China's most beautiful mountains—the legendary Taimu Shan!

Joyce: Oh, I can't wait.

人们告诉我，杨家溪的水很纯净，可以直接饮用。但上次我见到它有点浑浊，李小姐依然把大喇叭贴着我的耳根解释说："那是因为最近的一次台风暴雨造成的。"我当时在想，可以姑且把这溪水当作咖啡吧。

看起来当地人对这美丽的瀑布熟视无睹，这也许是因为没有关于这瀑布的典故吧。但我很喜欢它，哗哗的水声，很像厦门大学公寓里的水房传出来的。

杨家溪还有一个小岛，每年 8 月总能引来无数的蝴蝶。12 月份还有成群的鸳鸯聚集到这里。

从竹排到停车场，中间要穿过一片枫树林，这片枫树林是那样整齐，让我联想到在德国西南部见到的山林，在那片林子里，布谷鸟像报时钟一样，准时地尖声鸣叫。杨家溪的这片枫林很宁静，但绝不寂静，蝉儿在枝头叫得欢，吵闹劲儿绝不亚于正午时分的广东餐馆。要不是行程很紧，我真想在这多呆上一个星期！

现场

潘维廉：多么惬意的一次旅行啊，我真想在这多呆上几天！

刘银燕：我也是。在城里呆久了，到这样一个只能听到知了和蟋蟀鸣叫声的地方，真是一种享受。

潘维廉：明天还有美景等着我们去游览呢。

刘银燕：哦？是什么景致呢？

潘维廉：明天，我们将爬上名闻遐迩的太姥山！

刘银燕：是吗，我都快等不及了。

Episode 23 Taimu Mountain: Nature and Religion

Mt. Taimu's Surrealistic Beauty

Introduction In today's episode of Magic Fujian, Xiamen University's Dr. Bill shares with us a mountain top experience on mystical Taimu Mountain.

Dialogue--Taimu Park

Bill: Taimu Mountain is not only surrealistically beautiful but also one of Fujian's greatest cultural treasures.

Joyce: Yes, it is beautiful, but what does it have to do with Chinese culture?

Bill: For one thing, it has 36 temples, including one to Mani, that's the religion started in Persia about 1700 years ago!

Joyce: You're not going to make me tour all 36 temples, are you?

Bill: Of course not! Only 35. I was just kidding. I'll introduce you to a few of the key ones. But the temples can wait until tomorrow. Today, I want to show you why Taimu Mountain is becoming one of China's most favorite nature resorts.

Joyce: Sounds good to me. Lead the way, Professor Pan!

Bill: After you.

Over 10,000 people last year climbed Taimu Mountain on Labor Day, but the day of labor is well worth the climb—if you consider hiking stone steps a climb.

Over the past 5,000 years or so, Chinese have built steps up virtually every hill and mountain in the country. I suspect that even the Chinese side of Mount Everest has stone steps—and probably a vendor at the peak selling mineral water, roasted watermelon seeds, and bottles of oxygen!

The Taimu scenic and preservation area sprawls over 9,200 square kilometers. According to Taimu's Ancient Annals, it was once inhabited by the Taoist god Rong Chengzi, and during the Han Dynasty, Wang Lie wrote that Taimu was named after a young maiden who grew orchids and later became a fairy godmother. If it reminds you a bit of Cinderella, don't be surprised. The Cinderella story came from China. Of course, so did just about everything else!

第 23 集　太姥山：自然美景与宗教文化

Former Manichean Shrine

导语

在今天的“老外看福建”中，厦门大学的潘维廉博士和主持人刘银燕将同我们一起分享他们攀爬神奇的太姥山的经历。

现场

潘维廉：太姥山不仅美不胜收，而且还是福建最了不起的文化宝库之一。

刘银燕：它的美跟中国文化有什么关联呢？

潘维廉：太姥山有 36 座寺庙，其中有一座是摩尼教的，摩尼教 1700 年以前起源于波斯！

刘银燕：今天你没准备让我对这 36 座寺庙一一拜访过去吧？

潘维廉：当然不，我们只准备去看其中的 35 座。哈哈！跟你开玩笑！我只想带你参观几个主要的寺庙。今天，你将会感受到为什么太姥山越来越成为中国最受欢迎的旅游胜地之一。

刘银燕：听起来蛮诱人的，前头带路吧，潘教授！

潘维廉：女士优先！

解说

Tang Dynasty Temple atop Taimu

太姥山风景保护区绵延 9200 平方公里。据说，太姥山上曾经居住着道教的容成子。至于太姥山的名称，则来自一位种植兰花的少女，那位少女后来得道成仙了。也许你会说这个典故跟西方灰姑娘的故事有着异曲同工之妙，您说对了，中西方之间其实很早就有很多共通之处，而且西方的很多东西都源于中国。

Thread of Sky

Dialogue—36 Temples, 360 Scenic Spots!

Joyce: You said that Taimu has 36 temples, but I've also read it has 360 scenic spots!

Bill: Well, it's no wonder that an ancient Chinese wrote, "No Taimu rocks are common; they are the work of god. And they change with the mist and with your imagination—like that stone couple there."

Joyce: Then its no wonder the locals have named so many rocks and hills.

Bill: Yeah!

Some popular sites include Bare-Bellied Maitreya, Gods Sawing a Plate, Golden Tortoise Climbing the Cliffside, Crook-mouthed Toad, Cow's Backside, and Rock for Seeing God. But the most popular is probably "The Stone Couple." I told the guide, "I suppose the lower rock is the henpecked husband?"

I was joking, but the guide said, "The lower rock is the man, but he is not henpecked. "He has humbly lowered himself because he is a model husband."

I wondered if my guide had ever been married!

Tight Fit!

Dialogue—A Seat for the Sages

Joyce: "Local legend says that if you sit in this 1100 year old stone chair you'll go to heaven in 300 years!"

Bill: "Really? But where will I be in the interim?"

Joyce: "I guess we'll both find out someday!"

Bill: Well, I'll try anything once.

[Bill squeezes into stone chair]

Joyce: "Do you feel the vibrations? It's a natural massage chair."

Bill: "No vibrations yet. Maybe foreigners have different vibration in their bottoms. I don't know. I'll try it again after 300 years."

I think every Chinese mountain resort claims a 'thread of sky,' from which sandwiched tourists can view the heavens. But even CCTV has filmed this narrow crevice in Taimu Shan.

Our guide said the boulders wedged precariously in the crack above us were the '7 Stars' that had fallen from the heavens. I sincerely hoped they waited until we had passed before they finished falling.

I was just thinking Taimu's cracks and crevices were endless when our guide said, "There are only 100 or so. It takes 28 days to see all of them."

By that point I was ready just to watch them on a VCD.

♪现场

刘银燕：你说太姥山有36座寺庙，我还听说这儿有360处景点哩！

潘维廉：我一点都不觉得奇怪，一首中国的古诗称："太姥无俗石，个个似神工；随人意所识，万象在胸中。"是啊，太姥山的每一块石头都不平凡，它们是上帝的杰作。这里的云雾瞬息万变，被云雾笼罩的石头也随之姿态万千，就像那个夫妻峰。

刘银燕：哦，原来如此！难怪当地人给那么多的岩石和山峰都起了名字。

潘维廉：没错！

♪解说

太姥山的很多景点都是大家所熟知的，比如九鲤朝天、仙人锯板、金龟爬壁、二佛讲经，但最出名的也许要数夫妻峰了。

我对导游小姐说："夫妻峰中居于低处的丈夫肯定是个妻管严。"我其实只不过是开玩笑而已，导游小姐却当真地争辩道："这位丈夫甘拜下方，他才是真正的男子汉呢，并不是怕老婆，他谦卑地使自己矮一截，因为他是模范丈夫。"

我很想知道导游是否已为人妻了。

♪现场

刘银燕：当地的传说提到，要是谁能够坐进这张已有1100年历史的石椅，300年后他就会进入天堂。

潘维廉：真的？那真是太棒了。上天堂之前我会在哪儿呢？

刘银燕：我想我们总有一天会知道的！

潘维廉：我还是先来试试这张石凳再说吧。

刘银燕：你感到全身震颤吗?这可是天然的按摩椅哟。

潘维廉：还没感觉到呢！也许老外身体的振波跟老内的不一样。

♪解说

似乎中国的名山都有"一线天"，但太姥山的"一线天"连中央电视台都拍过呢。

导游告诉我们，峭壁夹缝中的这些大石头摇摇欲坠，它们是从天上掉下的"北斗七星"，我在心里祈祷，先打住吧，"北斗七星"，等我们走过去后才掉下来吧。

Dialogue—Miraculous Blue Creek

Bill: Does this water look special to you?

Joyce: I don't think so.

Bill: I don't think so either, but here's a strange story. The last time I was here, the guide said, "Up in the mountains , there's a little place where you squeeze through a narrow rock and came out on a bridge, and a creek just like this, and he said, for 1,000 years every morning at exact 9 o'clock, the water turns blue.

Joyce: Really? Amazing! Incredible.

Bill: He also said, if you take white cloth and dip in it, and take it out, it will be blue for 2 or 3 seconds. He said it's the only place in the world.

Joyce: Oh?

Bill: I don't believe it.

Joyce: You can dye your clothes in the water?

Bill: Yeah, for 2 or 3 seconds? I think he was pulling my leg. But he said, "No, I've seen it ! And another lady said, "Yes, I've seen it. Only 9 o'clock. 1,000 years! "I said, "Then how did people 1,000 years ago know when it's exactly 9 o'clock?" They said, "I don't know."

Joyce: I don't know.

Dialogue

Bill: You have to admit Taimu Mountain is as beautiful as I said it was, and with 36 temples, it's also one of the country's biggest cultural treasures.

Joyce: You promised I would not have to tour all 36 temples—at least in one day!

Bill: Don't worry! Today only the main ones. I'll leave the rest of them for the next time.

Joyce: Who says there will be a next time?

Bill: I do! Nobody comes to Taimu Mountain only once! And today we'll begin with Guoxing Temple.

Joyce: Up to you![1]

Ancient Guoxing Temple Quanzhou's Kaiyuan Temple boasts 100 pillars, but Taimu's ancient Guoxing Temple originally had 360 stone posts! Over the centuries they've been scavenged to build walls, sidewalks, and even the bridge over the creek.

Shards of Tang, Song and Ming Dynasty tile lie scattered about in the dirt, and only over the past year have archaeologists begun to unearth the historical treasures that lay a meter or more beneath the earth.

---

[1] Up to you: it's your decision

现场

潘维廉：你看这溪水跟其他地方的水有什么不同？
刘银燕：跟别的地方的水没什么两样呀！
潘维廉：我也这么认为，但关于这水，有个神奇的传说。上次我来这儿时，导游介绍说，在山上，侧身挤过石缝，路过一座小桥，你会看到有一条小溪。他说，溪水每天上午准9点会变成蓝色，千百年来一直如此。
刘银燕：溪水变成蓝色？太奇怪了，真的有点不可思议！
潘维廉：你觉得当真有这回事吗？
刘银燕：真是令人难以想象。
潘维廉：导游还说，如果你拿一块白布浸在那溪水里，拿出布后只消两三秒钟，白布就会变蓝。他说，这种奇妙的现象世上绝无仅有，只在蓝溪出现。
刘银燕：哦？
潘维廉：我不相信！
刘银燕：这么说，你可以在小溪里染衣服了？
潘维廉：是的，不过只有两三秒的时间。我想他肯定是在跟我开玩笑。他却说，不，我亲眼见过！另外一位女士也说，没错，我也见过，准九点，已经一千年了。我问他们，一千年前，人们是怎么确定九点整的呢？他们都说，不知道！
刘银燕：我也不知道！
潘维廉：太姥山的确很美，我没骗你吧！太姥山上有36座寺庙，因此，太姥山还是中国最大的文化宝库之一呢。
刘银燕：你说过不准备在一天中游览完这36座寺庙的。
潘维廉：别担心！今天咱们只拜访最主要的寺庙，没到过的寺庙留待下次拜访吧。
刘银燕：还有下次吗？
潘维廉：下次我一定再来，很多人不止一次游览太姥山。今天，我们要拜访的是国兴寺。
刘银燕：好吧，听你的！

解说

上次我到太姥山时，一个满脸带笑的和尚肩挑两筐豆腐，从后面赶上了我，我惊奇地问他："你上山还可以挑那么重的东西呀！"他答道："如果不带任何东西的话，我早都走到前头去了。今天我只挑了50斤，平常我要捎带 100 斤豆腐上山。"和尚发自内心的笑容驱走了我的倦意，我加快步伐，紧紧跟上他。和尚来自霞浦，在太姥山上已经呆了三年。我不明白，日复一日地挑豆腐，他依然能够保持乐观的心态。但此时此刻，当我和太姥山寺庙中的和尚一起用膳时，我很感谢他为我们带上来的豆腐。

泉州的开元寺有100根柱子，而太姥山历史悠久的国兴寺最早时曾拥有360根摩天石柱。经历几个世纪的沧桑后，部分石柱已被挪作他用，墙壁、道路，甚至溪面的小桥都可以见到它们的身影。在国兴寺的泥地下，散落着唐朝、宋朝、明朝的残砖碎瓦，对这些埋在地下一米多深的文化宝藏，直到去年，才由考古专家着手揭开它们神秘的面纱。

I suspect the iron fenced 1,000-year-old Iron Tree (Tieshu, 铁树) has seen a lot in its day.

The Buddhist priest in Guoxing temple told me that swastikas like the one on the Buddha's chest have been used in China for 2,545 Over 2,300 years ago, Chinese astronomers painted the swastika on silk to symbolize comet tails. The swastika probably came from India with Buddhism 2500 years ago, but it has also been found in ancient cultures all over the world, from North and South America to Israel.

During the Tang Dynasty, Emperor Tai Cong forbade printing the swastika on silk, but on the 7th day of the 7th lunar month, Chinese sought good luck by collecting spiders in the hope they would weave swastikas in the webs over fruit.

Dialogue—Vendors on Everest!

Stone Age Escalator

Bill: In China, climbing mountains is going up steps. Even Mount Everest probably has steps in China, on the Chinese side.

Joyce: Have you ever been to the Everest?

Bill: I've been close. Probably even the Chinese side of Everest has steps. And on the top of Mount Everest, there's probably a Chinese man selling water melon seeds, Kuang Quan Shui [mineral water] and oxygen bottles.

Joyce: That shows Chinese people are very intelligent.

Bill: And enterprising.

Joyce: Yeah! Enterprising, exactly.

Like many temples elsewhere, Taimu's temples offer not only excellent vegetarian fare but also lodging for hikers and pilgrims. One of my friends even spent his honeymoon on Taimu's peak. The meals include everything from sauteed greens fresh from the temple's garden to wild veggies, eggplant, noodles, and the vegetarian artificial snails that seem to be the rage in temples nowadays.

Guoxing temple's dining hall was full of monks, ranging from teenage novices to men in their 80s. The abbot and the leader of the younger monks donned their official robes for me, and young and old alike were excited to see the photos I'd taken of them with my digital camera.

On my last trip to Taimu I saw a gate built in the year 2,543. "That's over 500 years in the future," I protested. But my guide explained, "That's the Buddhist year of 2,543. Or 1999 for you nonBuddhists."

"Ah ha!" I thought. "Now I can tell people I was born in the year 2,500!"

Taimu's peak also had a 1,000 year old Manichaeist shrine, which unfortunately we didn't have time to visit this time around. It's mind boggling to think that 1,000 years ago, disciples of a Persian prophet found this mountain, much less built a little temple on it. It just goes to show how much Taimu Mountain has stirred the imaginations of centuries of people who appreciate its unique beauty.

这些用铁篱笆围起来的千年铁树，肯定见证了国兴寺的风风雨雨。国兴寺的僧人告诉我，像大雄宝殿这尊菩萨胸前的“万”字，在中国已有2545年的历史了。2300年前，中国天文学家把“万”字画在丝绸上，用来表示彗星。“万”字也许是两千五百多年前随同印度佛教一起传入中国的，在世界其他古文明发祥地也能见到“万”字，甚至连南北美洲、以色列都有“万”字的踪影。

唐朝的唐太宗下令禁止把“万”字印在丝绸上，但每年农历七月初七，中国人把很多蜘蛛放在果园里，希望蜘蛛能在网上结出“万”字，给他们带来好运道。

现场

潘维廉：这是做什么用的呢？我曾说过，在中国，爬山往往就是爬石阶，我猜想，哪怕是世界最高峰的珠穆朗玛峰，在中国境内的一侧也很可能砌有石阶。

刘银燕：你到过珠穆朗玛峰吗？

潘维廉：我曾经离珠穆朗玛峰很近，也许中国境内的珠穆朗玛峰真的砌有石阶，而且在石阶尽头的峰顶，说不定还有小商贩在那儿叫卖矿泉水、瓜子、氧气瓶什么的。

刘银燕：这说明中国人很聪明。

潘维廉：中国人还很勤奋。

刘银燕：对，勤奋，的确是这样。

解说

同其他地方的寺庙一样，在太姥山的寺庙里，旅行者和香客不仅可以品尝一流的素菜，而且可以在那儿投宿。我的一个朋友甚至在太姥山上度蜜月哩。庙里的素食除了刚从寺庙菜园子里采下来的鲜嫩的蔬菜，还有野菜、茄子、面条，而用素菜做成的人造田螺目前在很多寺庙里极为流行。

在国兴寺餐厅用膳的和尚很多，有的只是刚出家的十几岁的小和尚，有的已经是80多岁的老和尚了。庙里的住持和年轻的主事和尚披上袈裟让我拍照，看着朝夕相处的这两位和尚出现在我的数码相机中，旁边的和尚们感到特别新奇、激动。

上次我到太姥山时，看到一扇注明建于2543年的门，那可是500多年以后的事情啊——我提出疑义。导游解释说：“这是佛教的纪元，对于非佛教徒来讲，就是1999年。”“啊哈！”我暗自得意：“那我可以告诉人们我出生于2500年啰！”

太姥山顶还有一座距今千年的摩尼教神殿，可惜这回我们没来得及亲临观赏。传说中，波斯先知的信徒在1000年前发现了太姥山，并在此建了这座神殿，这件事未免让人惊奇不已，但这一传说恰恰也说明了，太姥山以其独特的美，激起了一代又一代人多么丰富的想像。

Episode 24 Naturally Air-conditioned Zhouning

Introduction Join us today on Magic Fujian as Xiamen University's Dr. Bill explores Zhouning, which at 888 meters elevation is Fujian's highest city.

Dialogue—Carp, Kung Fu & Kids

Joyce: Bill, have you ever heard of Zhouning?

Bill: Of course! It's one of my favorite places in Fujian.

Joyce: That's what I heard. But why do you like it so much?

Bill: Well, carp, kung fu, and kids!

Joyce: Right. I think you should try to show me rather than explain it.

Bill: Ok, let's go. It's just over the mountains!

Joyce: Right.

Zhouning is the next best thing to heaven on hot summer days. It's called the "Natural Air Conditioned City" because it is 88 meters high. Zhouning also has China's largest group of waterfalls, the Nine Dragon Falls, and a fascinating little village where for 800 years people have worshipped carp, and buried the dead fish in their own cemetery.

Two stone lions guard the bridge to Zhouning City, which is also called "Lion City" because two mountains supposedly resemble lions. I don't see the resemblance, but the residents are certainly lionhearted. Men in their 60s still spend 60 to 90 minutes a day practicing Southern Shaolin Kung Fu on each other!

Remote Zhouning is poorer than Fu'An to the east, and the roads reflect that. But if "Millionaires' row is any indication, all that Zhouning needs to catch up with their rich neighbors is time!

Dialogue—Millionaire's Row

Joyce: Why do they call this area millionaires' row?

Bill: Well, it's because of all the new apartment buildings. Look at these!

Joyce: Did the government build them?

Bill: No, they were all built by local successful entrepreneurs.

Joyce: Really?

Bill: They never dreamed of any places like this five years ago.

Joyce: That could be.

第24集 天然空调城周宁

导语

在今天的“老外看福建”中，厦门大学的潘维廉博士和主持人刘银燕将探索福建地势最高的山城，那就是海拔888米的周宁县。

现场

刘银燕：比尔，听说过周宁这个地方没有？
潘维廉：怎么会不知道周宁呢！这可是我在福建最喜欢的地方之一。
刘银燕：我也知道周宁很不错，但你为什么这么喜欢它呢？
潘维廉：周宁的鲤鱼、功夫和孩子，都很吸引我。
刘银燕：好吧，我想你最好带我去实地看看，总比在这纸上谈兵强。
潘维廉：那我们就走吧！翻过几座山头就到了。

解说

炎炎夏日，除了天堂，周宁可以说是天底下不可多得的避暑胜地了。周宁海拔888米，气候凉爽宜人，因此有“天然空调城”的美称。周宁除了有声势浩大的瀑布群“九龙漈”，还有一处迷人的鲤鱼村。800多年以来，鲤鱼村的人们崇拜鲤鱼，对死去的鲤鱼，村民们会把它们安葬在鲤鱼冢里。

两头石狮子雄踞在通往周宁城关的桥头。周宁被称为“狮城”，据说是因为那儿有两座山特别像狮子的缘故。我看不出有什么山像狮子，倒是当地居民像狮子一样勇猛，60多岁的老大爷每天会花上一个多钟头练习南少林武功。

比起东边的福安，偏远的周宁相对不是那么富裕，这一点从道路的路况就可以看出来。不过，只要假以一定时日，周宁人很快就能赶上他们富裕的邻居。

现场

刘银燕：农民新村是什么？
潘维廉：那是新建的豪华公寓群。
刘银燕：是政府投资兴建的吗？
潘维廉：不，是勤劳致富的企业主盖的。
刘银燕：是真的吗？
潘维廉：5年前，他们做梦都想不到能盖这样的高楼。
刘银燕：有可能！

Zhouning folk are born entrepreneurs. Fully 30,000 of the 190,000 population work elsewhere. Over 20,000 work in the Shanghai Pudong area alone. A Zhouning government leader told me, "We Zhouning people are capable, skilled, and know how to use our heads. We saw Pudong's potential before almost anyone."

The ink was still wet[1] on Pudong's development plans when Zhouning people flocked to Shanghai and got a toehold, and then a foothold, and then invited their family and friends to join them. And the money has flowed back into new homes in their ancestral hometown's Millionaire Row.

My friend said, "Alas, they're all too busy getting rich to live here!"

But one enterprising couple that does live at home in Zhouning is the 24 and 25 year old who started one of Mindong's most unique tea factories.

Dialogue—Young Tea Entrepreneurs

Joyce: It's pretty amazing what they've accomplished so quickly.

Bill: Yes, especially considering when they started out they knew nothing about tea except how to drown tea leaves in boiling water!

Joyce: How could they be so successful if they knew nothing about the business?

Bill: Lots of motivation—and learning from others!

Tea Entrepreneurs

This enterprising young couple decided to bring tea production into the 21st century. They sought the advice of different universities' experts, and imported advanced Taiwanese tea technology. Today, research students now flock to Zhouning to study their firm!

In the year 2,000, they received two national awards, including the prestigious Beijing 2000 Top Research Gold Award.

Their highland green tea is prized nationwide, especially up north in Harbin and Beijing. The young manager told me, "Our tea is the best because of the high altitude, clean air, and pure water."

"That's the same recipe people give me for pretty girls!" I said.

He responded, "Then there must be something to it!"

Whether in the construction business in Shanghai, or making tea right at home, Zhouning Folk are entrepreneurs, and on the cutting edge. And you can see their prosperity in their new homes, and shiny sedans—many which have Shanghai license plates. But Zhouning's highlanders also have a strong respect for the past and tradition—as we discovered when we visited the only village in China where carp are king!

---

[1] Ink was still wet: very new

解说

周宁人天生就是企业家，19 万人口中就有 3 万人在外地工作，而仅仅在上海浦东，就有 2 万多周宁人在那儿闯世界。一位当地官员自豪地对我说："我们周宁人真是精明能干，知道如何运用我们的脑子，比如，我们比别人抢先一步，看到了上海浦东的商机。"

浦东的发展蓝图墨迹未干的时候，周宁人就已经蜂拥到上海，并站稳了脚跟，等到闯出了一点名堂后，他们就介绍亲戚朋友加入他们的队伍。他们赚回的钞票源源不断地汇入家乡，成就了今天的农民新村。

我的朋友说："这些富人忙于挣钱，根本顾不上住在农民新村了！"

但有一对创业的夫妇的确住在周宁，他们只有二十四五岁，在周宁创办了一家颇具特色的茶厂。

现场

刘银燕：他们在这么短的时间内就创下家业，真是难以想像。

潘维廉：是啊，想想看，他们白手起家的时候，除了知道如何泡茶，他们对茶叶几乎一无所知！

刘银燕：如果当初他们对经营之道一窍不通，怎么可能这么成功呢？

潘维廉：那得归功于他们强烈的进取心，以及善于向他人求教。

解说

周宁盛产茶叶，因此，这对雄心壮志的年轻夫妇决心把制茶工业带入 21 世纪，他们向大学的专家们讨教，引进台湾的制茶工艺。现在，很多大学生纷纷到他们的茶厂参观考察。

在 2000 年，他们荣获两项国家级大奖，其中一项是具有权威的 2000 年北京高新成果研究金奖。

他们的高山绿茶享誉全国，在北方的哈尔滨和北京尤其受欢迎。年轻的老板告诉我，他们的茶是最好的，因为周宁地势很高，空气清新，水质纯净。我跟他讲，这个诀窍同人们告诉我美女是怎样长成的一模一样，他应道，也许真有什么特殊的成分在里面。

不论是在上海的建筑市场闯荡也好，或者在家乡制茶，周宁人都不愧是走在前头的企业家。崭新的楼房，亮闪闪的挂着上海牌照的小轿车，都折射出他们的富裕。而且，在高山上的周宁人还特别尊重传统文化——这一点我们在参观鲤鱼村的时候充分感受到了，这个村是中国唯一一处把鲤鱼敬为神鱼的村落。

Episode 25 Zhouning Carp Village

Introduction On today's episode of Magic Fujian, Xiamen University's Dr. Bill and his friend Joyce Liu visit the Carp Village that is home to carp worshippers and barehanded tiger killers!

A Zhouning brochure reads, "Zhouning is a place with the fine spirit of the universe...the carp stream arouses great joy for all men and carps."

I'm not sure about all men, but the carp must be happy because they are not only free from fear of fishermen but are worshipped, fed, and buried in their own cemetery when they die!

Dialogue—Fishy[1] Food

Joyce: What are those girls selling?

Bill: These are sesame biscuits, the holy carps' favorite food. You want to try one?

Joyce: I'm not eating fish food!

Bill: Suit yourself. I'll try one! How much?

Joyce: You want all of them?…How does it taste?

Bill: It's OK! Try one bite.

The giant pair of trees is 1,050 years old and called the Husband-Wife trees. Their branches are lovingly intertwined. Centuries before environmentalism became popular, Chinese respected ancient trees. Today it's not uncommon for highways to make abrupt detours around 1000 year old banyans. And most ancient trees are numbered and protected by the state. The male Fuqi tree, for instance, is #0903.

Dialogue—Cremated Carp

Bill: Do you know what that mound is?

Joyce: It looks like some kind of religious thing.

Bill: This is a cemetery for the carp. When they die they bury the fish here!

Joyce: Why don't they eat them?

Bill: They never eat carp in this village. They have worshipped them for 800 years!

Joyce: 800 years!

Bill : I'll show you where they put them.

---

1 Fishy: suspicious; odor or taste resembling fish

第 25 集　周宁鲤鱼村

导语

在今天的“老外看福建”中，厦门大学的潘维廉博士和主持人刘银燕抵达周宁鲤鱼村，这个村庄不仅有崇拜鲤鱼的乡亲，还曾经出现过赤手空拳打死老虎的英雄。

解说

一本有关周宁的小册子这样描述：“周宁是个最能体现博爱精神的地方，对于男人和鲤鱼来讲，那里的鲤鱼溪无异于一处乐园。”

我不晓得鲤鱼溪能给男人带来怎样的欢乐，但对鲤鱼来说，有幸在鲤鱼溪里成长确实是它们的福祉。鲤鱼溪里的鲤鱼非但可以摆脱被人捕捞的厄运，相反，它们还受到当地人的敬仰，人们精心喂养它们，而当鱼儿停止呼吸时，人们会像对待同类一样，把它们安葬在水泥冢里。

现场

刘银燕：这些小女孩在卖什么呀？
潘维廉：她们卖的是芝麻饼，这些神鱼最喜欢吃这饼了，想不想尝一下？
刘银燕：我才不吃鱼食呢！
潘维廉：随你，很多人吃这饼呢！

解说

这两棵树已经有 1050 岁了，人们叫它们“夫妻树”，你看，它们相偎相依，树枝相互交织在一起。

几个世纪前当环保意识还没盛行时，中国人就已经开始尊崇古树了，所以，今天我们经常轻易就有机会环抱千年古榕。很多古树名木往往被国家编号并保护起来，比如“夫妻树”中代表丈夫的这棵树，编号就是 0903。

现场

潘维廉：你能猜出“夫妻树”后面隆起的水泥墩是什么吗？
刘银燕：看起来像是与宗教有关的东西。
潘维廉：那是鲤鱼冢，鲤鱼溪里的鲤鱼死后就葬在那里面。
刘银燕：为什么人们不把鱼吃掉呢？
潘维廉：这里的村民从来不吃鲤鱼，实际上，他们崇拜鲤鱼的传统已经延续了 800 多年！
刘银燕：800 多年！
潘维廉：来，我告诉你，他们是怎样对待鲤鱼的。

Bill: No, no, no, not here!
Joyce: They worship here, you know.
Joyce: Wow. Of course! Bill: It's not the way I would cook one.
Joyce: You wouldn't cook them?

There are several stories explaining why carp are venerated here, but the basic theme is that when the people saw dead carp floating in the stream, they knew bad people upstream had poisoned the river. So the death of the carp saved their lives, and they have venerated carp ever since. It is a crime even to catch carp, much less eat them, and in the past violators were beaten within an inch of their lives!

The temple just past the Husband Wife trees is dedicated to an ancient who used his bare hands to destroy a tiger.

Dialogue—Tiger Killer Temple

Joyce: Who's this temple to?
Bill: A long time ago, there was a tiger that was terrorizing the neighbourhood. He liked eating Chinese—not the food, but the people. So a local man killed the tiger with his bare hands.
Joyce: Wow! How did he do that?
Bill: Probably Kungfu! Joyce: Then he must be a Kungfu expert!
Bill: I think there are a lot of Kungfu experts here.

To this day, villagers pray to him for prosperity and protection. Of course, many Zhouning people still practice Southern Shaolin Kungfu, and could probably take on a tiger. The temple walls have old paintings depicting scenes from the Chinese Classics "Three Kingdoms" and "Journey to the West" (the Monkey King story). Paintings in the top row are originals; those beneath are recent copies.

I was told the Tiger Killer has 36 temples and between 100 and 200 thousand worshippers. Right after every Chinese New Year, the Tiger Killers idol is taken from the main temple and paraded through his hometown, and I suppose all the tigers take to the hills.

Dialogue—Ancient Leftie[2]

Bill: You know they have these stone steles all over China. This one here is dear to my heart.
Joyce: What's so special about it?
Bill: You know, Chinese are always telling me that I can't write Chinese properly because I'm left handed—but this stele was engraved by a left-handed Chinese calligrapher!
Joyce: Really! We Chinese usually say that left-handed people are smarter.
Bill: Well, at least we're smart enough to let you right-handed people think so!
Joyce: Probably!

[2] Leftie: left-handed person

刘银燕：哇！
潘维廉：别紧张，我不会这样煮鱼的。
刘银燕：你不会煮了它们？
潘维廉：不，不，在这里，我不敢！
刘银燕：要知道，这可是他们崇拜鲤鱼的地方！

解说

有关鲤鱼溪的鲤鱼受到人们崇敬的典故有好几种，其中最广泛流传的一种说法是，当乡亲们发现溪中漂浮着鲤鱼的尸体时，他们由此可以判断，有坏人在溪的上游投了毒。鲤鱼用生命的代价使村民幸免于难，从此，村民就非常敬重鲤鱼，不用说以鲤鱼为食，哪怕有人胆敢捕鱼，也是一种罪过，以前就曾发生过违规者受到惩罚的事情。

“夫妻树”旁边的这座寺庙供奉着一位很久以前赤手空拳制服老虎的英雄。

现场

刘银燕：这座庙供奉谁呢？
潘维廉：很久以前，有一只老虎四处为患。它喜欢吃的不是中餐，而是大活人！结果，当地一位村民赤手空拳打死了这只老虎。
刘银燕：哇，赤手空拳怎么打死老虎？
潘维廉：他用的也许是工夫！
刘银燕：这么说来，他是一位工夫大师。
潘维廉：我想，这里的工夫大师多着呢。

解说

直到今天，村民们还向他祈求兴旺发达，平安如意。当然啦，时至今日，许多周宁人依然在练习南少林武功，他们的武功兴许对付得了老虎咧。寺庙的两侧墙壁上有很多古画，这些画描绘的都是《三国演义》和《西游记》里的故事。上边的那排画是原版，底下的这排则是最近按原样描摹上去的。

我听说在周宁，纪念打虎英雄的寺庙多达36座，信众多达十多万人。每逢春节，打虎英雄的神像会被抬出寺庙，在他的家乡巡游，我想，那时候山上的老虎肯定吓得全都躲起来了。

现场

潘维廉：古老的大理石碑遍布中国，但对眼前这块石碑，我感到特别贴心。
刘银燕：这石碑有什么特别之处吗？
潘维廉：人们常告诉我，我写不来汉字也许是因为我是个左撇子，但想不到这石碑上的字居然是一个左撇子的中国人写的！
刘银燕：中国人通常认为左撇子比较聪明。
潘维廉：嗯，至少我们左撇子已经聪明到让你们右撇子这样认为。
刘银燕：可能吧。

The temple just past the steles has statues of the goddess Guanyin and the Monkey King. Zhouning seems fascinated by the Monkey King, which is fine with me because I was born in the year of the monkey myself.

Dialogue—Spearing Nightmares

Bill: You see those tiny bows and arrows. You know what they're for?

Joyce: Maybe for hunting tiny tigers?

Bill: Good guess! But you're a tiny bit off. They are for spearing nightmares!

Joyce: Spearing nightmares. Oh…

Bill: Do you have any?

Joyce: No.

Legend has it that if a small bow is placed by a child's bed overnight, and then hung from this tree, it acts somewhat like an American Indian dream catcher, except it spears nightmares rather than catches them.

The bow and arrow are fastened to the protected tree number 903, which is over 1500 years old. The temple is shaped like a ship, and the ancient tree is the mast. So why a ship in the mountains? I was told that years ago, a man sleeping under tree #903 fell asleep and dreamed he was aboard a treasure ship full of gold. Naturally, upon awakening he asked everyone to revere this tree. He collected money to build a temple and his family indeed prospered.

Dialogue

Joyce: Local legends and fish worshipping are quite unusual.

Bill: They really are. But I find the local people are even more interesting.

Joyce: Have you met many of them?

Bill: A few—like the Kung Fu fighting Zhengs, and Granny Xu. She has bound feet, and she gave me a pair of her little tiny slippers.

Joyce: Oh, did she made them herself?

Bill: Yes, she did. Would you like to meet her?

Joyce: Yeah, sure.

Bill: OK. We'll go there after we've run out of bread.[3]

---

[3] Run out of bread: after we've used up the bread we're feeding the carp

解说

石碑旁边的这座寺庙供奉着观音和美猴王的塑像，周宁人好像对美猴王情有独钟，这对我来说也是件好事，因为我是属猴的。

现场

潘维廉：看，树上的这些弓箭，你知道它们是做什么用的吗？
刘银燕：也许是用来打小老虎的吧？
潘维廉：猜得不错，但你还是有点跑题，它们是用来驱赶噩梦的。
刘银燕：驱赶噩梦的？哦！
潘维廉：你有没有碰上噩梦？
刘银燕：没有。

解说

Ship-shape Temple

传说中，如果把这种小弓箭放在小孩的床头一宿，然后把它挂在这棵树上，噩梦就会被赶走。这有点像美国印第安人的捕梦器，只不过前者是射死梦魇，后者是擒拿。

这些小弓箭紧紧地附在这被保护起来的0905号树上，这棵树历经1500年的风雨依旧生机盎然。这座祠堂的造型像一艘船，而这棵古树则像船的桅杆。为什么船只却坐落在山间呢？原来多年以前，有个人在这棵0905号树下打盹的时候睡了过去，他梦见自己上了一条载满黄金的宝船。梦醒时他吩咐人们要善待这棵树，他自己则凑了一笔钱，在这个地方建了一座船形房子，说来也怪，从此他家果真兴旺发达起来了。

现场

刘银燕：当地这些美丽的传说以及对鲤鱼的崇拜特别与众不同。
潘维廉：没错，但是当地人本身更有意思。
刘银燕：你跟当地人打过交道吗？
潘维廉：我认识几个当地人，比如会武术的郑姓村民，小脚女人徐奶奶，徐奶奶还送给我一双她为自己的小脚缝制的迷你绣花鞋呢。
刘银燕：是她们自己做的吗？
潘维廉：是的,他们自己做。想见见她们吗？
刘银燕：当然想！
潘维廉：面包用完，我们就去。

Episode 26 Zhouning Granny Xu and Kung Fu Fighters

Introduction In today's episode of Magic Fujian, Xiamen University's Dr. Bill and his friend Joyce Liu meet several of the Carp Village's Southern Shaolin Kung Fu fighters, and grannies whose feet were bound decades ago, but whose hopes for their children are now boundless.

Boundfeet meets Bigfoot!

Bound Feet, Bound Bodies I have read much about foot binding but never expected to meet someone with bound feet. Many foreigners have condemned the practice, of course, but at least one European praised it! Domingo Navarrete, a Spanish Dominican friar who arrived in China in 1659, wrote that it was good for keeping females at home and would benefit men the world over if the practice spread.

I prefer feet like my wife Susan Marie's. They may be big but at least she won't get blown over in a storm!

For a thousand years, Chinese bound women's feet tightly in swaths of cloth to produce a tiny 3 to 4 inch stump that would fit in the "Lotus slipper." Foreigners of course criticized the practice as inhumane, and they were right. But ironically, Westerners bound not women's feet but their entire bodies!

Dialogue—Corsets Go To Waist

Joyce: When did the Westerners ever bind women's bodies?

Bill: Have you ever seen a corset?

Joyce: Yes, the Western women wore them to look fashionable and slim.

Bill: Yes, that's true. But let me show what corsets did to women's bodies. That's a corset. Women wore them from the hips all the way up to the arms. Bind them to get that small waist. And this is what they look. Is that beautiful to you?

Joyce: I think its beautiful.

Bill: It looks beautiful, but this is what it did to their bodies. This is a normal woman. And then to get that slim shape, she wore that corset, and look what it did! It squeezed her ribs, her inner organs, her heart, everything! So that it hurt her bodies. They couldn't breath, they couldn't walk, they couldn't lift their arms. It was a terrible thing to do to women.

Joyce: Just for fashion—

Bill: Just for fashion.

Joyce: For fashion, you have to pay a lot of things.

Bill: For fashion, yeah. I mean, footbinding was bad, but I think this was just as bad.

第26集　周宁的小脚女人和武术世家

导语

在今天的“老外看福建”中，厦门大学的潘维廉博士和主持人刘银燕将见识鲤鱼村的南少林武功，以及几十年前就束缚住双脚的老奶奶；当然啦，老奶奶对后辈的希望则是不受束缚的。

解说

我听说过缠足，但从未想到会亲身遇上绑小脚的女人。当然，很多外国人谴责缠足这一陋习，唯有一位欧洲人例外，他就是西班牙的天主教化缘修士多明戈。多明戈于1659年来到中国，他认为缠足可以使女人足不出户，如果这种做法被广为提倡的话，世界上的男人将会受益无穷。

我更喜欢像我妻子苏珊那样的大脚，这种脚大是大，但在暴风雨中你可以站稳脚跟，不用担心人被刮倒。千年以来，中国人用长长的裹脚布把女人的脚绑得小到只有3～4寸那么长，俗称“三寸金莲”。外国人谴责这种行为不人道，这当然有道理，然而可笑的是，西方人不是对女人缠足，而是绑住了她们的身体。

现场

刘银燕：西方人从什么时候开始束缚女人的身体？

潘维廉：你见过紧身褡吗？

刘银燕：见过，西方女人穿紧身褡，看起来既苗条又时髦。

潘维廉：没错，但我们来看看紧身褡对身体的伤害吧。那就是紧身褡，女人们穿着这玩意儿时整个腰部都被紧紧裹着，以此来塑造纤细的腰身。这就是她们的蜂腰，你觉得漂亮吗？

刘银燕：我觉得挺漂亮的。

潘维廉：看上去是很美，但紧身褡对身体的伤害可不小。这是个身材标准的女人，她穿上紧身褡后就变得这么苗条，看看是怎么回事！紧身褡挤压她的肋骨、内部器官、心脏！女人们的身体就是被这样摧残的。她们呼吸困难，步履蹒跚，甚至不能抬高手臂。这真是一件可怕的事情。

刘银燕：仅仅为了赶时髦吗？

潘维廉：仅仅为了赶时髦。

刘银燕：为赶时髦就得付出很大的代价。

潘维廉：对，时髦的代价。我的意思是，缠足很不人道，但束身也同样不人道。

刘银燕：和缠足没什么差别。

潘维廉：我也这么认为。

刘银燕：甚至比缠足有过之而无不及。

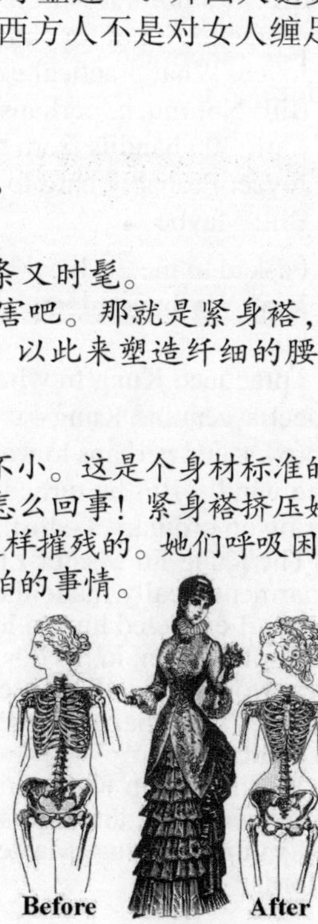

Joyce: As bad as the footbinding.
Bill: I think so.
Joyce: Even worse than the footbinding.

Footbinding was finally abolished only after Liberation in 1949—to late to help Granny Xu. She still hobbles about on 4 inch stubs. It's been a hard life, but she smiles readily, and says life is better than ever. She said that until the 1980s, she never had meat or veggies, or even rice. They ate nothing but sweet potatoes, 3 times a day, cooked in dozens of ways. Nowadays, Granny Xu has to make her own shoes, because store bought Lotus slippers are hard to find—but she never fears going to bed hungry again, so she doesn't complain. She's a tough lady—just as tough in her own way as the grandpas who practice their kung fu over an hour each day!

The Carp Village's youth have largely left home to seek their fortune, leaving grandparents to till the fields-but they can handle it, thanks in part to bodies toughened by hours of practicing Southern Shaolin Kung fu.

Dialogue—Highland Kung Fu Fighters

Joyce: I didn't know that Zhouning was known for its Kung fu fighters.
Bill: It's not known for it, exactly. But many of the locals practice it not for show but for practical purposes!
Joyce: What practical use is Kung fu nowadays?
Bill: Not much, perhaps. But before Liberation they fought off 300 bandits from the north barehanded!
Joyce: Probably bare foot too.
Bill: Maybe.

I asked to meet a local Kung Fu master and the village head said, "No problem! We have plenty! They are all masters of our special Zheng Wushu."

I practiced Kung fu when I was in Taiwan, and I was excited to have the chance to meet a genuine Kung Fu master! I expected him to have long white hair, bushy eyebrows, and perhaps to walk 6 inches off the ground, robes swathing and swooshing in the wind. But he turned out to be a plain fellow in his 50s, with a crew cut and wearing an ordinary T-shirt.

The Kung Fu Master Zheng kicked and whirled and punched the air so fast that his garments really made the whooshing and snapping sounds one hears in Kung Fu movies. I expected him to leap onto a roof any moment.

Another man, in his 60s, demonstrated his Kung Fu Fork fighting after fixing the heavy wooden handle. He'd broken it over his equally elderly neighbor during practice. "That happens pretty often," he said. Fortunately, this Kung Fu fighter is also a doctor.

South Shaolin Kung Fu is not practiced as widely now that there are no longer bandits, warlords, and tigers who like Chinese takeout. I regret the decline of the art. But I'm thankful that Master Zheng and Granny Xu no longer need fear hunger, or warlords.

解说

缠足这一陋习直到1949年才得以彻底清除，只可惜徐奶奶生不逢时，没能赶上这一好时机，现在她依旧靠那双4寸长的小脚颤巍巍地走路。徐奶奶的日子过得很清苦，但她脸上时常挂着笑容，她说，比起过去的苦日子，现在总算是熬出头了。80年代以前，她从不知道肉、蔬菜、米饭是啥滋味，一日三餐净吃地瓜，实在吃腻了就变着花样吃地瓜。现在，徐奶奶要穿鞋子的话就得自个儿缝制，因为商店里买不到尺寸那么小的绣花鞋。不过，她再也不用饿着肚皮睡觉了，因此她也很知足，并不抱怨什么。徐奶奶真是一个坚强的女性——她的坚韧丝毫不逊色于每天拿出一个多小时习武的老大爷。

鲤鱼村的青壮小伙儿大多到外面闯世界去了，留下一些老大爷在家耕地，您可用不着替他们担心，这些老大爷完全揽得起这档子农活，因为他们每天练习南少林武功，身板硬朗着呢。

现场

刘银燕：我不知道周宁的武功还挺有名的。

潘维廉：确切地说，周宁的武功并没有达到声名远扬的地步，但人们习武主要是出于实用的考虑而不是为了炫耀。

刘银燕：但如今习武有什么用处呢？

潘维廉：也许不大顶事，但解放前当地村民曾经赤手空拳赶跑一支多达300人的土匪帮。

解说

我很想见见村子里会武功的师傅，村长满足了我的要求，他说："没问题，我们村会武功的人可多着呢，他们都是郑氏武功的师傅。"

我在台湾的时候练过武功，很兴奋能在鲤鱼村遇上真正会武功的师傅。在我的想像中，师傅应该是鹤发童颜、须眉霜染，能够在离地6英寸的高度用轻功飞走，走的时候裹挟着的长袍在风中嗖嗖作响。然而出现在我面前的师傅很平常，他50开外，剪平头，着一件普通的T恤。

这位会武功的郑师傅拳打脚踢，速度极快，空气中不时发出呼呼声，这场景很像电影里出现的镜头，我真希望他能仗着轻功跃上屋顶。

另一位60多岁的郑师傅在我们面前舞弄了一番刀叉，这刀叉的柄在他同一位年龄相仿的邻居过招时，给弄断了，他告诉我这种事经常发生。这位郑师傅除了会武功，还会替人疗伤呢。

土匪和军阀早已不存在，老虎也为数不多，因此，现在练习南少林武功的人越来越少了，我很遗憾这门传统国术渐渐没落。但同时我又很欣慰，郑师傅和徐奶奶他们不再饱受饥饿之苦和军阀的骚扰。

Episode 27 Nine Dragon Falls and Baishuiyang

Introduction Today on Magic Fujian, Dr. Bill and his friend Joyce fall for China's largest waterfall complex, Zhouning's Nine Dragon Falls, and in Baishuiyang Dr. Bill teaches Joyce how to walk on water!

China is an ancient nation, and yet even today people are making spectacular discoveries in remote areas of China—like the Tibetan canyon that is even larger than America's Grand Canyon. But our own Fujian province has hidden surprises as well.

In 1978, a wood gatherer in Zhouning stumbled upon the largest waterfalls complex in China, the Nine Dragon Falls. He told the village elders about it—and the rest is history!

Dialogue—9 Dragon Falls

Joyce: If 9 Dragon Falls is so remote, how can we get there?

Bill: It's not a problem nowadays. The 12km road is paved all the way. But it's a pretty winding road!

Joyce: What road in Fujian isn't winding?

Bill: That's true enough.

We visited 9 Dragon Falls early in the morning to avoid the afternoon storms. The complex of Falls was spectacular—1000 meters long, and 300 meters from top to bottom. The largest falls drops 46.7 meters, and in heavy rains can reach a width of 83 meters—wider than China's largest single falls, Huang Guoshu—though I suspect my #2 son Matthew might argue about that.

Dialogue—Huang Guoshu Versus Niagara Falls!

Bill: I sometimes wonder if my sons are American or Chinese.

Joyce: For sure they look American!

Bill: Yes, but last time I was in the States, I took my boys to see New York's Niagara Falls, and Matthew, while we were looking at it, he said, "China's Huang Guoshu is bigger that Niagara Falls!" I said "No way! Niagara falls is a lot bigger than Huang Guoshu!"

Joyce: And how did Matthew react to that?"

Bill: He thought about it for a moment, then he said triumphantly, "Well, Huang Guo Shu is prettier!"

Joyce: Too bad he's not here to see the Nine Dragon Falls!

Bill: Next time.

第 27 集　九龙漈瀑布与白水洋

导语

系列报道“老外看福建”今天向您介绍厦门大学潘维廉博士和主持人刘银燕是怎样迷上中国的最大瀑布群——福建周宁的九龙漈瀑布的。在屏南的白水洋，他们还试了一回水上行走。

解说

中国历史悠久。直到现在，人们还不断地在她的偏远地区发现各种各样的奇特景观。譬如，根据最新发现，西藏的雅鲁藏布江大峡谷比美国科罗拉多大峡谷还大。我们福建也隐藏着许多人间奇迹。

1978 年，周宁县的一位樵夫无意中发现了中国最大的瀑布群——九龙漈瀑布，并报告给村里的长者。从此，翻开了九龙漈瀑布为世人所逐渐了解、认识的历史。

现场

刘银燕：九龙漈瀑布那么偏远，我们怎么去？

潘维廉：现在去九龙漈瀑布倒不成问题。那条路（离县城）12 公里，全铺了水泥，只不过七拐八弯的。

刘银燕：福建哪条路不是弯的？

潘维廉：的确如此。

解说

为了避开午后的阵雨，我们一大早就驱车前往九龙漈瀑布。这个瀑布群绵延 1000 多米，上下落差 300 米，场面十分壮观。最大的瀑布落差 46.7 米。下大雨的时候，瀑布宽度可达 83 米，比中国最大的单层瀑布——贵州黄果树瀑布还要宽。不过，我想，我二儿子马修的看法可能不同。

现场

潘维廉：有时候，我真弄不懂，我那两个儿子到底属于中国人还是美国人。

刘银燕：从外表看，他们当然是美国人！

潘维廉：没错！不过，上次回美国的时候，我带他们去看纽约的尼亚加拉大瀑布。我们在观赏瀑布的时候，二儿子马修说：“中国的黄果树瀑布比尼亚加拉瀑布大。”“不可能！”我告诉他，“尼亚加拉比黄果树瀑布大多了。”

刘银燕：马修怎么反应呢？

潘维廉：他想了一会儿，然后兴高采烈地说：“黄果树瀑布更漂亮”。

刘银燕：可惜他今天没来，不能亲眼看看九龙漈瀑布。

潘维廉：下回带他来吧！

At the first fork we took a right and descended to the bottom for an inspiring view of the largest waterfall. The 16m wide by 14 m deep pool to the right was called the "Eye of the Dragon," and I think it was looking right at me.

The sign warned, "Danger, Slippery, Don't Go Past This Sign!" The rocks are slippery, so we posed for photos from a safe distance.

By the third falls I was hot and sweaty, in spite of the trees shading the past. I suggested watching the rest of the Falls on video, but my guide said, "The best are yet to come!"

"But there are only so many ways that water can fall," I said. But she persuaded me to persevere—and the final view, "Dragon's Mouth," made the entire trip worthwhile!

Dialogue—Pretty, but Powerful [looking at rails destroyed by falls]

Bill: Be careful.

Joyce: What happened to these iron pipes?

Bill: Believe it or not, in 1998 when they had a big flood here, the water was so powerful, it washed these concrete filled iron pipes right out!

Joyce: I don't want to tour the falls when they're falling that heavily!

New Falls Discovered! Back in town a city leader exclaimed, "I head that today a tenth falls was discovered—a saltwater falls!"

"Where?" I asked.

"It was the sweat off Professor Pan's forehead!"

Amidst hearty laughter we shook hands, and said goodbye to our Zhouning friends, and headed west and south to Baishuiyang, home of Mandarin Ducks, Rhesus monkeys—and the marvelous lake where even mortals like myself can walk on water!

Dialogue—Walking on Water!

Bill walks on water!

Bill: You know, Joyce, I have to tell you this, I am a humble man, so I don't usually walk on water in front of people—but today I'm going to show you how it's done.

Joyce: I don't believe you can walk on water!

Bill: You think so? I'll prove it! Watch this! Ready? Come and join me!

Joyce: I can't walk on water.

Bill: Why not? The whole lake is only this deep! Come on. Walk! Qigong! Use Qigong! Ahh! My pants! My mother warned me about that. I've got to go back and roll my pants up.

解说

在第一个分叉路口，我们右转，到峡谷底部观看大瀑布壮观的景象。右边16米宽、14米深的水塘被称为“龙眼”。走在峡谷里，我老觉得“龙眼”在盯着我看！告示牌上写着：“路滑、危险，请勿靠前！”峡谷里的岩石很滑。为安全起见，拍照时，我们只好站在稍远一点的地方。

到第三级瀑布时，尽管密树遮阳，我们依然浑身冒汗。我建议回头找录像带看看九龙漈的其他瀑布，但向导说：“最好看的还在前头呢。”

我说：“尽管流法不同，瀑布总归是瀑布嘛”。导游劝我坚持一下。终于，我们看到了九龙漈最精彩的龙嘴。真是不枉此行！

现场

潘维廉：小心！

刘银燕：这些铁栏杆怎么啦？

潘维廉：信不信由你，1998年发洪水的时候，瀑布水流湍急，把这些注满水泥的铁栏杆冲垮了。

刘银燕：当瀑布水势迅猛时，我才不想到这玩呢。

解说

回到县城，县里的一位领导说：“听说九龙漈今天发现了第十级瀑布，是个盐水瀑布！”我追问说：“在哪里？”“在潘教授的额头上！”大笑之后，我们与周宁的朋友握手道别。驱车西行，然后再转南向，我们一路直奔白水洋。白水洋是鸳鸯和猕猴的栖息地。还有神奇的湖水，就连我这样的凡人都可以在水上行走！

现场

潘维廉：小刘，我告诉你，我这人挺谦虚的，通常不愿意在外人面前显露“水上行走”的功夫，不过，今天我倒想让你看看“水上行走”是怎么回事。

刘银燕：我不相信你会在水上行走！

潘维廉：你不信？让我来走给你看吧！看这里，准备好了吗，我们一起来！

刘银燕：我不会在水上行走。

潘维廉：为什么走不来？白水洋的水只有这么深。来，走吧！气功！用上气功！啊！我的裤子！我妈曾提醒我当心裤子。我得先把裤管卷起来。

Baishuiyang is one of Fujian's 7 national level scenic spots. This unique 40,000 sq. m. lake rests upon one massive flat rock, which is only a few inches below water. It was unreal seeing a peasant, baskets balanced on his shoulder, walking on the water in the middle of the lake. Baishuiyang is host to athletic competitions. It even had bicycle and truck races on the lake.

We crossed the lake wearing socks sold to us by the park headquarters. The socks helped keep us from slipping. The smooth rocks and strong current acted like a natural massage and my feet tingled afterwards for a good half an hour.

Like Nine Dragon Falls, this strange lake was opened only recently—1983. Before then, the only people that knew about it were those in the villages perched on the cliffs above. Locals call them the "Wall-Mounted Red Lantern Villages" (Denglong Guabi Cheng). They were built on cliffs as protection against bandits and warlords, but nowadays most have relocated to the valley floor.

This valley is the winter home for Mandarin Ducks, but it's hard to catch a glimpse of them. CCTV spent a week trying to film them, but every time the cameras rolled the mandarins ducked.

Baishuiyang is also China's largest preserve for Rhesus monkeys, and locals claim that the Monkey King lived in one of the caves further upstream in a vast scenic area that is still under development.

Walking on water works up an appetite, so we feasted on local mountain delicacies—golden mushrooms, bitter melons, and noodles made from the Yin Yang gourd, which require 8 steps to make them edible. We also enjoyed fish. 18 flavors in a fish head!" I was told. "Brains, lips, eyeballs, gills, cheeks—all have different flavors, and you as guest get to savor each of them." I'd have preferred a simple fish sandwich —extra tomatoes and no mayonnaise.

Dialogue

Bill: Well, Joyce, you must feel quite honored to tour Fujian with someone like me who can walk on water!

Joyce: Heh, don't forget—I walked on water too!

Bill: Ahh… but can you fly?

Joyce: Of course not. Can you?

Bill: No. But if I could I'd spend rest of my days flying low over Fujian's mountains and valleys and exploring its beautiful places. Since you can't fly though, and I can't fly, we'll rely on these endless winding roads!

An old Zhouning road!

Joyce: I think the next stop should be back to Fuzhou where we can live and enjoy the cozy life there.

Bill: OK!

解说

白水洋是福建省七个国家级风景名胜之一。近 4 万平方米的水面底下是一块平坦光滑的大岩石，水深不过几英寸。我们在白水洋拍摄时，恰好碰上当地农民肩挑重担，涉水缓行。白水洋曾经举办过一场水上运动会。他们还在水上举行自行车赛和卡车赛呢！

我们在公园的入口处买了些袜子。穿上袜子，在白水洋戏水，可以防滑。走在白水洋光滑的岩石上、湍急的水流里，真像是做脚底按摩，让我的脚板舒坦了半个多小时。

跟九龙漈瀑布一样，白水洋这块奇特的水面也是到了 1983 年才开始对外开放的。在此之前，只有栖身山崖的当地村民知道白水洋的存在。为了抵御土匪和军阀，当地村民把村子建在悬崖上，“灯笼挂壁村”因此得名。如今，那里的村民大多搬迁到了谷底地区。

白水洋峡谷还是鸳鸯的越冬地。不过，要看到这些鸳鸯实在困难。中央电视台的摄像记者曾在这里守候七天。每次开机拍摄，鸳鸯们便躲得无影无踪。白水洋还是中国最大的猕猴保护区之一。当地人说，美猴王孙悟空曾经在鸳鸯溪上游的一个山洞里住过。那一大片的风景区目前还在开发中。

水上行走之后，胃口大开。于是，我们美美地饱餐了一顿山中美味，有金针菇、苦瓜，以及需要经过八道工序才能吃的魔芋粉条。我们还吃了鱼。“鱼头十八味”，人们告诉我，“鱼脑、鱼唇、鱼眼和鱼鳃，每个部位味道都不一样。作为客人，你应当逐一品尝。”当然，我宁可吃一份简单的麦香鱼，外加一些番茄酱，而不是蛋黄酱。

现场

潘维廉：小刘，和我这个会在水上行走的人周游福建，你感到很荣幸吧？

刘银燕：嘿！别忘了——我也会在水上行走！

潘维廉：啊——但你会飞吗？

刘银燕：当然不会。你会吗？

潘维廉：不会。要是能飞，这下半辈子我真想飞越福建的山谷，探索美丽的风光。既然你我都不会飞，我们只好走弯弯曲曲、绵延不绝的山路。

Baishuiyang Cabins

刘银燕：下一站我们该回福州，享受温馨的生活了吧？

潘维廉：好咧！

Supplementary Reading Three

Pew Perils

Xiamen church pews are packed on Easter and Christmas, when even the Buddhists enjoy the choirs' special music. Get there half an hour early for a good seat. At Christmas especially, the time will pass quickly as you listen to recordings of such classic holiday hymns as Silent Night, The First Noel, Frosty the Snowman and Jingle Bells (They fit right in with the "Santa Bless You" Christmas cards sold in book stores.).

Do get there early! Otherwise, Laowai-loving ushers will oust some 90 year old granny from her front row pew so the foreign friend can see the service better, and so everyone else can see the foreign friend better. Of course, you can always gallantly refuse the granny's seat and perch on a red plastic stool on the front porch. But then you're a sitting duck[1] for that sect which believes 'speaking in tongues' means mastering English. They'll grab a stool and pull it up beside you and spend the entire hour, nonstop, practicing English. I've actually had prayers go like this:

"Our Father who art in –"
"—What country are you from?"
"Thy kingdom come, thy will be –"
"—Where do you work?"
"Give us this day our –"
"—How much money do you make?"
"And lead us not into temptation…"
…like murder!

Chinese Communion For 2000 years, Christians have 'broken bread'[2] together during Communion. Well, some have. But what about those who don't have bread to break?

When we first came to Xiamen, Christians celebrated communion with little squares of noodles. I liked the chewy texture, and the Chinese wine did more for you than the grape juice we sip back home (though I learned why communion cups are so tiny; enough of that wine and you're in the spirits,[3] not in the Spirit).

Alas, Xiamen has modernized, and that includes churches. Now they use the round, flat imported bona fide communion wafers that look and taste like Styrofoam. Granted, they look nice, with the little cross stamped on them. It would be tough stamping crosses on wet noodles. Still, I kind of miss the noodles.

---

[1] Sitting duck: easy target (it's easier to shoot a sitting duck than a flying duck)

[2] Broken bread: taken communion (in remembrance of Jesus' last meal, Bible, Matthew 26:26)

[3] In the spirits: drinking "spirits" (alcohol), versus being "in the "Spirit" (God's spirit)

补充读物(三)

长椅上的冒险

每逢复活节或圣诞节，厦门教堂里的长椅总是挤满了人。这时，连佛教徒都来享受唱诗班独特的音乐。提早半个小时到达，才能找个好位子。特别是在圣诞节，听着那些经典的圣诞歌曲录音，比如《平安夜》、《圣诞佳音》、《白白的雪人》、《铃儿响叮当》，你会觉得时间过得特别快。其实，这些歌曲在书店卖的“圣诞老人保佑你”的圣诞卡里就能听到。

千万记得一定要早点儿到！要不然的话，崇洋媚外的引座员会把 90 多岁的老太太从前排长椅上赶走，让外国朋友们能更清楚地看到宗教仪式，同时也让其他人也能更清楚地看到老外。当然你也可以每次都献殷勤地拒绝老太太的位子，自己搬把红色塑料凳坐在前廊下。这时，你可就成了人家的猎物了。有些人认为，掌握英语就要“多说”。他们会抓张凳子坐到你边上，滔滔不绝地跟你练上个把钟头的英语。有一次我作的祈祷是这样的：“上帝在……”

“……你是哪国人？”

“你的来世将会是……”

“……你在哪儿上班？”

“今天请赐给我们……”

“……你每个月挣多少？”

“且不使我们受诱惑。”

实在要命！

中国式圣餐

2000 多年来，基督徒进圣餐的时候都要分食面包。当然，有些人有面包，那么那些没有面包的人怎么办？

我们一家刚来厦门时，这里的基督徒在圣餐的时候吃的是小块的面条。我喜欢这面条耐嚼的感觉，而且这里的白酒比我们在美国老家喝的葡萄汁够味儿。不过，我也明白了圣餐的酒杯为什么这么小。因为，如果这酒喝多了，你就不是心怀神灵，而是心神不宁了。

啊，厦门变得现代化了，连教堂也不例外。他们现在用的是进口的圆圆扁扁的圣饼。不过，无论它的外观还是味道都有点像塑料泡沫。话说回来，如果要在那些小块的湿面上印十字的话恐怕不太容易。所以，我还是挺想念那种面条的。

Laowai 3rd Degree[4] In 1990, an American complained, "I'm tired of nosy Chinese! They ask me almost non-stop, 'Going to work?' 'Coming home?' 'Going shopping?' 'Eaten yet?'"

I looked about furtively,[5] then whispered, "Do you know why they ask Laowai so many questions?"

He looked surprised, and whispered back, "No. Why?"

"Because they're Communists, and they have to report on us."

"Really?" His eyes widened as paranoia took a toehold.

"Not really!" I said, laughing. "That's just how Chinese greet one another!"

A Westerners' greeting usually a simple and non-invasive "Hello" or "Good Morning" or "Nice weather today!" But Chinese are seldom content with "Ni Hao" (How are you?) or "Zao Shang Hao" (Good morning). Rather, they ask what you are doing. And unlike Americans, who don't expect an honest answer to "How are you?" Chinese do expect an answer.

I've never asked anyone how much money they make. I don't even know my own sister's salary. But Chinese have no qualms homing in[6] on a strange Laowai and firing off in rapid order the Laowai 3rd Degree:

1) "Hello, what is your name?" 2) "Where are you from?"
3) "Is it cold in America?" 4) "Where do you work?"
5) "How much do you earn?" 6) "Will you teach me English?"

It's culture, not nosiness. But with 1.3 billion Laonei pitted against a handful of Laowai, it gets to you sometimes.

Laowai Radar I was standing armpit to sweaty armpit on a hot bus when it screeched to a halt to let on a youth. He still had one foot in the door when his Laowai Radar picked me out of the crowd. With an ear to ear grin and eyes nailed to me as if I were the Holy Grail[7] (or the Worshipful Wok), and wormed his way towards me, the Laowai 3rd Degree on the tip of his tongue. As he sidled up under my arm and opened his mouth I preempted him with, "I'm Pan Wei Lian from America, which is like China. Hot in the south, cold in the north. I work in Xiamen University, and earn enough to pay taxes but not enough to avoid them. Have I missed anything?"

So much for Sino-American friendship. His jaw dropped, he slunk away, I felt like a cad[8], and I have regretted it ever since.

---

4 3rd Degree: physical or mental torture used to force prisoners to confess

5 Furtively: carefully, secretly (as if I were afraid Chinese would hear our conversation)

6 Homing in: to be guided in, as if a bomb or missile homing in on its target; moving towards a goal

7 Holy Grail: the legendary cup which Christ supposedly used during his last meal; said to possess miraculous powers, this cup was the object of many medieval crusades

8 Cad: a person without principles

拷问老外

1990年，有个美国人向我抱怨说：“我快被中国人烦死了！他们老是不断地问我‘上班啊？’‘回家啊？’‘上街去吗’‘吃了吗？’”

我偷偷环顾四周，然后小声说：“你知道他们为什么要问老外这么多问题吗？”

他吃了一惊，也悄悄对我说：“不知道。为什么？”

“因为他们是共产党员，必须要向上面报告我们的一举一动。”

“真的？”他的眼睛瞪得比铜铃还大。

“不是真的！”我大笑起来。“中国人就是这么打招呼的！”

西方人通常用简单而又无冒犯性的话互相问好，比如“你好”，“早上好”或者“今天天气不错”之类的话。但中国人不是这样，他们经常觉得只说“你好”、“早上好”还不够，他们宁可问你在做什么。美国人一般并不希望得到“你好吗”的真实答案，不过中国人可不一样，他们真的想知道确切答案。

我从来没问过别人每个月挣多少钱。我甚至连自己亲姐妹的工资是多少都不清楚。不过中国人往往很容易跟老外自来熟，并且会用极快的速度“拷问老外”：

（1）“你好，你叫什么名字？” （2）“你从哪里来？”
（3）“在美国冷吗？” （4）“你在哪儿工作？”
（5）“你能挣多少钱？” （6）“你能教我英语吗？”

这就是文化差异，并不是爱管闲事。不管怎么说，屈指可数的老外身处13亿老内中间，你难免会碰到几次这样的情形。

老外雷达

有一回，我跟别人摩肩接踵站在燥热的公交车厢里，突然一个急刹车，上来一个年轻人。他前脚刚踏进车门，老外雷达就从人群中锁定了我。他咧嘴一笑，两眼把我盯得死死的，就好像我是一座圣杯。他从人群中挤出一条缝，拷问老外的话就要脱口而出。就在他挨到我身边开口正要说话的时候我抢先一步说：“我叫潘维廉，从美国来。美国跟中国差不多，南方炎热，北方凉爽。我在厦门大学工作，赚的钱足够交税但不够逃税。还有什么没说的吗？”

中美友谊到此为止。他把下巴合上，闪到了一边。我觉得自己就像个无赖，立刻就后悔了。

The Solution! Nowadays I just answer the questions, with a smile. But I have a solution! Make life easier for Laowai and Laonei alike by just printing the answers to the Laowai 3rd Degree on the back of your business cards, and keep a stack at all times. But bear in mind that even though Chinese have no qualms in asking "personal" questions, they also have no aversion to answering them. In a way, their candor is refreshing, and we Laowai could learn from it.

But not in Church, please.

解决之道

现在我是有问必答，还面带微笑。不过，我还有个解决的办法！为了让老外和老内都活得轻松一点，你可以把拷问老外的问题的答案印在名片背面，并且随时带上一叠。尽管如此，中国人对“个人问题”几乎无所顾忌，他们也不介意回答这些问题。说起来，他们的坦白挺好的，我们老外也可以从中学到一些东西。

不过拜托，千万别在教堂问我！

Episode 28 Fujian Bridges

Introduction Join us today as Xiamen University's Dr. Bill, Bobby Bao, and Joyce Liu discover how ancient Fujianese mastered rivers as well as seas.

Dialogue—Building Bridges

Bill: I think the ancient Chinese bridges are absolutely fascinating!

Joyce: Because of the architecture, or engineering?

Bill: Well, partly that. But mainly because it helps us understand how ancient Chinese in Fujian traveled and communicated, and how they mastered the rivers as easily as they did the seas!

Joyce: Yes, I think in fact every bridge has its own characteristics.

Bill: That's true. I showed some of these bridges to Bobby Bao. And I think maybe now you and I should visit some of them. How about that?

Joyce: OK. Great.

Chinese have been as innovative with rivers as they have with seafaring. They invented the segmented arch bridge in 700 AD. Ingenious canal locks made possible the 1,000 mile Grand Canal. And some of the greatest marvels have been built right here in Fujian.

Zhangzhou's ancient Jiangdong Bridge had 15 spans. One stone alone was over 23meter long, 1.7 meters wide, and weighed 200 tons. It's incredible they could have lifted it into place. During the Song Dynasty, Quanzhou built at least 110 bridges, including the remarkable Anping Bridge and Luoyang Bridge.

Anping Bridge

Dialogue—Anping Bridge

Bobby: It's a hot day, isn't it?

Bill: Oh, yes. I probably lost ten pounds today!

Bobby: Ah, good shade!

Bill: Feels good. Maybe just wait here? Did you know Anping bridge—Peace Bridge in English—was the longeest bridge in the world in the Middle Ages?

Bobby: Yes, I did. And it's still the longest stone bridge in China today. It is 2,251 meters long.

Bill: I can believe it in a hot day like this. You know, Anping Bridge was built between 1138 and 1151 AD.□ But I still find Luoyang Bridge more interesting, even though it is shorter.

第 28 集　福建的桥

导语

厦门大学的潘维廉博士，和我们的记者包东宇、刘银燕一起，发现古往今来的福建人民不但能够征服大海，同样能够驾驭江河。在今天的“老外看福建”节目中，我们就一同去看看福建各地多姿多彩的桥梁建筑。

现场

潘维廉：中国的桥真是太神奇了！

刘银燕：是因为中国桥梁的建筑造型精美，还是因为它们的设计和建造工艺高超？

潘维廉：这是部分原因。主要是因为它们有助于我们了解古代的福建人民是怎样出行和交往，怎样像轻易地征服大海那样征服河流的。

刘银燕：我觉得实际上每座桥都各具特色。

潘维廉：没错，我跟包东宇一起看过一些这样的桥。你现在也跟我一起去观赏一些桥梁，怎么样？

刘银燕：好主意！

解说

中国人的创新精神不但体现在航海上，也充分体现在桥梁建造上。他们在公元 700 年就发明了弧形拱桥。具有独创性的运河水闸使得长达上千英里的大运河的开通成为可能。而一些最伟大的建筑奇迹就出现在福建。

漳州的江东古桥有 15 个桥洞。桥上单是一块条石就有 23.7 米长，1.7 米宽，重达 200 吨。真难以想象当时人们是怎样搬运这么大的石头的。

宋朝年间，泉州至少建了 110 座桥，其中就有著名的安平桥和洛阳桥。

现场

包东宇：今天真热啊！

潘维廉：是啊。恐怕我今天快掉了十磅肉！

包东宇：啊，这地方凉快！

潘维廉：嗯，这地方真不错。要不就在这歇会儿？你知道吗，“安平”在英语里是“Peace(和平安宁)”的意思。在中世纪，安平桥是世界上最长的桥梁。

包东宇：这我知道。现在安平桥仍然是中国最长的石桥，全长有2251米。

潘维廉：这么大热天,我不信不行。对了，我听说安平桥建于公元1138年到1151年之间。不过,我还是觉得，比它早近百年的洛阳桥虽然短些，但是更有意思。

Ancient Biological Engineers! Luoyang Bridge was built in 1059 AD, almost 100 years earlier than Anping Bridge. And it may have been one of the planet's first uses of biological engineering!

Luoyang bridge withstands the tremendous tides because of the innovative pillars. They are pointed like ships' prows so the current flows around them. Chinese describe the pillars as "1,000 Ships Launching." Very poetic—though mathematically a little off!

Iron butterfly shaped wedges held the stones together, but the most brilliant idea was using live oysters between the stones so their secretions would cement the granite blocks together—a kind of natural super glue! Of course, biological engineering was not new to Chinese. Long ago, Chinese farmers used citrus ants to eat the insects attacking their orange trees!

Dialogue—Moving Mountains

Bill: Did you know the Quanzhou government in 1993 spent over 1 million USD to reconstruct this bridge?

Bobby: 1 Million Dollars?! Why so much?

Bill: That's what I asked and the guy told me. He said, "Look at these stones. Some of them are over 10 meters long." He said, "You have to dig out half a mountain nowadays to get a ten meter stone!"

The bridge has many pagodas and statues. These were supposed to protect the bridge from typhoons, but they didn't keep the Japanese from stealing the Pusa's moonstone, which supposedly glowed at night and guided mariners into shore.

Fujian's ancient bridges were not only functional but works of art. Yet the new bridges, like Xiamen's Haicang Suspension bridge, have their own kind of beauty.

Dialogue—Haicang Suspension Bridge

Bill: Xiamen's Haicang Bridge was opened on Dec. 30th in 1999. It's a little over 5,900 meters long, was the first three span suspension bridge in Asia, and cost almost 2.9 billion yuan.

Bobby: Wow, that's a lot of money to spend on one bridge!

Bill: Yeah, but it sure beats swimming. And now that both sides, Xiamen Island and Haicang, are connected together, both sides are developing much more rapidly than before.

Haicang Bridge is a work of art—especially at night when illuminated like strands of electric pearls connecting Xiamen Island and the Haicang area, which Dr. Sun Yat-Sen had such high hopes for—and which are now coming through, thanks to one of China's greatest bridges.

解说

跨海石桥洛阳桥建成于公元1059年，比安平桥几乎早了100年。它可能还是地球上应用生物工程技术的最早范例之一。

洛阳桥首创的船形桥墩能够承受海潮的猛烈冲击。这些桥墩的两端像船头一样尖尖的，水流就从两侧流过。中国人把这些桥墩形容为“千舟下水”，虽然在数量上夸张了点，但形容得极有诗意。

此外，桥墩上的蝶形铁锲可以把石头固定在一起。不过，最高明的创意是让活牡蛎在石头之间生长，这样，牡蛎的分泌物就像一种天然的强力胶水一样，把桥基上的花岗岩牢牢地粘合在一起。当然，中国人对生物工程并不陌生。很早以前，中国农民就懂得利用柑橘蚂蚁来消灭危害橘树的害虫。

现场

潘维廉：你知道吗，1993年，泉州市政府花了100万美元重修这座桥？

包东宇：100万美元？！为什么要花这么多钱？

潘维廉：我也是这么问的。泉州市政府的一位工作人员说：“你看桥上的这些条石，有的有十多米长。”他告诉我，“现在要想得到十米长的花岗岩石料，非得挖开半座山不可。”

解说

洛阳桥上有许多宝塔和雕像，据说是用来保护桥不受台风袭击的。传说这尊菩萨雕像上原来镶了颗夜明珠，晚上夜明珠发出的光亮能指引出海的水手上岸，不过在抗日战争时这颗夜明珠被日本人偷走了。

福建的古桥不但注重功能性，同时还具有很高的艺术性。而福建的现代桥梁，比如厦门的海沧大桥，也有它们独特的魅力。

现场

潘维廉：厦门海沧大桥是1999年12月30日开通的。这座大桥全长5900多米，是亚洲第一座特大型三跨悬索桥，总造价约29亿元。

包东宇：哇，这可是一笔相当庞大的资金！

潘维廉：那是，但有座桥可以走，总比只能游过去好吧。现在由于厦门岛和海沧开发区连在了一起，两边都比以前发展得快多了。

解说

海沧大桥真是一件艺术品，尤其是在晚上，桥上亮起灯光，就好像一串串发光的珍珠，把厦门岛和海沧开发区连接起来。孙中山先生当年曾经对海沧的发展寄予厚望，有了这座大桥，他的愿望正在一步步成为现实。

Dialogue—Haicang Bridge Museum

Bobby: I had no idea that China had such a rich heritage in bridge building.

Bill: I'm thankful that the Haicang Bridge museum here in Xiamen let us enjoy that tradition without having to travel all over the country. I think they have displays of every kind of Chinese bridge imaginable .

Bobby: Look! Zhangzhou's Jiang Dong bridge.

I like the Museum, but nothing beats visiting bridges firsthand—like the 700 year old wooden covered bridge in Pingnan, where Joyce and I also ran across a traditional wedding, with the bride's carriage loaded onto a tractor bed!

Dialogue—Wooden Covered Bridges

Joyce: Between Zhouning and Pingnan, we saw at least half a dozen covered wooden bridges, some of them even three stories high.

Bill: Yeah, and some of the covered bridges were new.

Joyce: Yeah, I've even read that the Mainland hopes to build a bridge to Taiwan someday!

Bill: Well, that's the best kind of bridge. A bridge of friendship between family. And I think that's one of the things China is doing best nowadays—building bridges of friendship!

Haicang Bridge

♪**现场**

包东宇：不看不知道，真想不到中国在桥梁建筑上有这么丰富的遗产。

潘维廉：是啊，真要感谢海沧桥梁博物馆，让我们有机会不必周游全中国就能欣赏到如此丰富的桥梁文化。我看这里几乎展示了每一种你能想到的中国桥梁。

♪**解说**

我喜欢海沧桥梁博物馆，但是在博物馆里看怎么也比不上亲自上桥参观。像屏南县的这座有 700 年历史的木质廊桥就不可不看。在桥上，我们还碰巧遇上一场传统婚礼，新娘的花轿就架在一辆拖拉机上。

♪**现场**

刘银燕：单是在周宁和屏南之间，我们就至少见到六座木质廊桥，其中一些有三层高。

潘维廉：是啊，有些廊桥还很新呢。

刘银燕：我在报纸上看到，大陆希望，有一天能建造一座直通台湾的跨海大桥。

潘维廉：如果建成的话，那一定是世上最好的桥，可以说是同胞之间的友谊桥。目前中国正在做很多这样的事情，就是在人们之间架设友谊的桥梁。

Covered bridge near Baishuiyang

Episode 29 Fuzhou, the Banyan City

Introduction Welcome to today's episode of Magic Fujian, in which Xiamen University's Dr. Bill and his friend Joyce Liu begin their exploration of Fuzhou, the cradle of Chinese shipbuilding and seamanship, and home of some of China's most adventurous people.

Fuzhou—Ancient Adventurers and Academics Fuzhou, the capital of Fujian province, has long fascinated Laowai. Almost 700 years, the Franciscan Friar Odoric said the city of Fuzhou "is a might fine one, and stands upon the sea." And 150 years ago, magnificent Yankee tea clippers like the Cutty Sark made history in their races between Fuzhou and England. Today, Fuzhou is a modern city of 6.4 million people inhabiting 12,000 square miles. And over the past 2200 years, Fuzhou folk have shaped Chinese academics and trade like few other people.

Dialogue—Fiery Fuzhou Folk

Joyce: Fuzhou has been inhabited for 2200 years?

Bill: Actually, Neolithic age people settled here 7,000 years ago. But the first city walls weren't built until 202 B.C., when King Wuzhu made Fuzhou the capital of the Minyue Kingdom. By the Tang Dynasty, the fiery Fuzhou folk had already made Fuzhou an international trading port.

Neolithic Fuzhounese (Ancient Anorexic?)

Joyce: Why do you say Fuzhou people are fiery people?

Bill: Because they have always been very adventurerous, fearless people but they always maintain a strong sense of balance as well.

Joyce: Like you, right?

Bill: I said balance, not imbalance!

Fuzhou people epitomize the Chinese ideal of moderation—the Golden Mean. Though Tang Dynasty Fuzhou was an economic powerhouse, her entrepreneurs balanced commerce with culture and education. The great Tang Dynasty Poet, Han Yu, said Fuzhou's cultural level equaled that of China' s capital, Chang ' An. Fuzhou had several nationally famous academies, as well as China's first public library. Fuzhou was home to some of China's greatest shipbuilders, merchants, poets, philosophers, and patriots like Lin Zexu.

Even today Fuzhou is called the "hometown of academicians. The China Academy of Sciences and the China Academy of Engineering have elected 56 academicians from Fuzhou—more than any other city in China. Fuzhou is also home to at least 850,000 Overseas Chinese. They may have taken their enterprising spirit abroad, but their hearts are still in their ancient home, and many have returned to live here and invest in the city's development.

第29集　榕城福州

导语

欢迎收看今天这一集的“老外看福建”，让我们跟随厦门大学的潘维廉博士和他的朋友刘银燕开始今天的福州之旅。这里是中国造船业和船舶驾驶技术的摇篮，中国历史上几位敢做敢为的有识之士也出自这里。

解说

福州作为福建的省会城市，一直深深地吸引着老外们。700 多年前，圣芳济会的修道士奥多里克曾经这样描述福州：“是个优美的城市，屹立于大海之上。” 150 年前，像“卡蒂·沙克”号这样伟大的新英格兰运茶船在福州和英国之间穿行竞赛，并永垂史册。

今天，福州是一个占地 1.2 万平方英里并拥有 640 万人口的现代城市。在过去的 2200 年中，很少有哪个地方的人像福州人这样培养了自己的学者并形成自己的贸易。

现场

刘银燕：福州已经有 2200 年的历史了？

潘维廉：事实上，大约 7000 年前新石器时代人类就开始在这儿定居了。但第一道城墙直到公元前 202 年闽越王无诸在福州建都时才建造。到了唐朝，富有激情的福州人已经将这个城市变成了一个国际贸易港口。

刘银燕：为什么说福州人富有激情呢？

潘维廉：因为他们一直是无所畏惧、富有进取心——同时又能保持极好的平衡，不走极端。

刘银燕：就像你一样，对吗？

潘维廉：我说的是平衡，不是失衡！

解说

福州人体现了中国节制的理念，也就是中庸之道。虽然在唐朝时期福州经济发达，但是当地的商人在发展经济的同时也同样重视文化和教育的发展。唐朝大诗人韩愈曾经称赞说，福州的文化水准可以和京都长安相媲美。福州拥有多个全国著名的学府和中国最早的公共图书馆，巢经塔。福州还孕育了许多中国伟大的造船家、商人、诗人、哲学家以及像林则徐一样的民族英雄。甚至在今天福州还被称为“院士之乡”。中国科学院和中国工程院的院士中有56名来自福州——这是在中国其他城市所没有的！福州还是85万华侨的故乡。他们也许已经将进取精神带到了海外，但是他们的心仍然牵挂故乡，许多人已经回来定居并投资办厂，致力于福州的发展。

Dialogue—Home of Heroes

Bill: You know, I think it's Fuzhou folks' fearless pioneering spirit that explains maybe why Fuzhou has been the capital of China through 5 different Kingdoms, and also the home to various heroes like Lin Zexu, who tried to stop the opium trade.

Joyce: But Fuzhou has been important in modern times as well. You see the film. That's about China's 1911 revolution and the mountain is the Yushan Mountain. In 1933, Fuzhou was considered by many people as the "Revolutionary Capital of China."

Bill: That's true. And I also heard that at one time Fujian declared its own revolutionary government. Even Marco Polo wrote that the invading Mongols had their hands full when they were trying to deal with Fuzhou people!

Marco Polo wrote:

> "Now this city of Fuzhou is the key of the kingdom which is called Chonka...and subject to the Great Khan. And a large garrison is maintained there by that prince to keep the kingdom in peace and subjection. For the city is one which is apt to revolt on very slight provocation...."

Fuzhou people revolted on many occasions—when the Mongols invaded, when foreigners forced their way in with opium, and when foreign nations began partitioning China a century ago. Today, the Fuzhou people are still rebelling, but today the rebellion is against the poverty that has enslaved too many for too long. Few cities in China have enjoyed such dramatic growth, and its fruits are benefiting many people, from entrepreneurs to peasants.

Dialogue—Fuzhou City Museum

Bill: So far, Fuzhou doesn't have much English material that help foreigners understand the city. But this new Fuzhou city museum which is opened in January 2000 was a good step in the right direction.

Joyce: But are the exhibits in both Chinese and English?

Bill: Unfortunately, no. I hope it will take the lead of Quanzhou's excellent maritime museum and put exhibits in both Chinese and English. But in the meantime, maybe they can get some good English speaking tour guides here..

Joyce: You seem pretty fascinated with Fuzhou. But what interests you the most?

Bill: Food!

Joyce: Food?

Bill: Well, actually there are many things. But I think Fuzhou has made its great contribution to China and even the world through its shipbuilding. So I think maybe our next stop should be the great cradle of shipbuilding-- Mawei!

Joyce: Okay, let's ship out!

♪现场

潘维廉：福州人无所畏惧的创业精神也许清楚地说明了为什么这个城市可以在五个不同朝代中都作为中国的国都，以及为什么会是林则徐这样极力制止鸦片贸易的英雄的故乡。

刘银燕：福州在现代也一直发挥着重要作用。1933 年福州被许多人认为是“中国革命之都”。

潘维廉：没错。我听说福建还真的曾经建立过自己的政府！就连马可·波罗都曾经写道：入侵的元兵为对付福州人忙得不可开交！

♪解说

马可·波罗写到：“如今福州这个城市是通往 Chonka 王国的要冲……这个王国最终臣服于大汗。由王子率领的一支庞大的卫戍军队驻扎在这里以维持王国的和平与稳定。因为那是一个极易因为轻微的煽动就引起争战的国度……”

福州人民在许多时候都曾经站起来反抗过——当元兵入侵的时候，当外国人携带着鸦片强行入侵的时候，当一个世纪之前外国势力瓜分中国的时候。今天福州人民仍然在作斗争，不过现在是和已经束缚了许多人很长时间的贫困作斗争。在中国，很少有哪些城市能够像福州这样处于快速增长之中，它所取得的成果使得从企业家到农民的许多人受益。

♪现场

潘维廉：能够帮助外国人鉴赏福州神奇历史的英文资料很少，但是创立于 1999 年 1 月的福州市博物馆，向着正确的方向迈了一大步。

刘银燕：那些展览品用中英文双语说明的吗？

潘维廉：很遗憾，不是！我希望这个博物馆能像泉州的海上交通博物馆一样把展出的物品用中英文加以解释。不过老外也可以在这里请一个会说英文的导游。

刘银燕：你看起来对福州相当着迷嘛。不过到底是什么最让你感兴趣呢？

潘维廉：这很难说！或许是美食吧！但是福州在航海方面的贡献对中国乃至全世界都有着重大的影响——所以接下来我们要去的地方应该是附近的马尾，它是中国造船业的摇篮。

刘银燕：好的，让我们出发吧。

Episode 30 Mawei, the Cradle of Chinese Seamanship

Introduction Welcome to today's episode of Magic Fujian, as Xiamen University's Dr. Bill, and Joyce Liu, explore Mawei, the cradle of Chinese seamanship and site of the Sino-French Naval Battle

A century ago, few places excited the West as much as Pagoda Anchorage, which is what they called the ancient port of Mawei. They called it this because of the Southern Song Dynasty Falling Star Pagoda, built by Lady Liu Qiniang. This seven story, 31.5m octagonal granite pagoda has been a mariner's landmark for centuries.

Dialogue—the China Pagoda

Joyce: You know, Bill! This pagoda can be seen from so far away that in the Ming Dynasty Admiral Zhenghe used it in his navigational charts.

Bill: Really? Europeans used it too. Do you know what Europeans called this Pagoda?

Joyce: No, what did they call it?

Bill: China Pagoda!

Joyce: China Pagoda! Very imaginative, weren't they?!

Bill: Yeah, I think so.

Dialogue

Bill: On May 30th, 1866, 3 magnificent tea clippers, their vast sails billowing, raced out of Fuzhou's Pagoda Anchorage .

Joyce :Ah, this is China Pagoda.

Bill: They were racing to London. And on September 6, the Taiping beat the Ariel by 30 minutes.

Joyce: Is this the Ariel?

Bill: That's the Ariel. 30 minutes after all time! And the Serica was only a few hours behind! They had not seen each other for 3 months and 15,700 miles!

Joyce: That's amazing.

Bill: So amazing, so close.

The "China Pagoda"

This race, more than perhaps anything else, fired up the world's imagination about China, Fuzhou, and Pagoda Anchorage—which unknown to most Westerners was the cradle of Chinese shipbuilding 2,000 years ago. And many Chinese innovations were adopted and improved upon much later by Western shipbuilders. But Mawei ships had to be good or they'd have never survived the Mighty Min River.

第30集　马尾——中国船舶驾驶技术的摇篮

导语

欢迎收看“老外看福建”，在这一集里，我们将跟随厦门大学的潘维廉博士和主持人刘银燕一起游览马尾——这个中国船舶驾驶技术的摇篮，同时也是中法海战的遗址。

解说

一个世纪以前，很少有地方能像马尾港这样让西方人感兴趣。当时他们把马尾港称之为宝塔港，因为在马尾港矗立着一座宝塔——罗星塔，相传为南宋柳七娘所建。这座七层八角，高31.5米的花岗岩宝塔几个世纪以来一直是指引水手们的陆地标志。

现场

刘银燕：这座塔在很远的地方就能够看到，所以航海家郑和把它画进了他的航海图当中。
潘维廉：欧洲人也把它标进了地图中。你知道明朝的时候，欧洲人把罗星塔叫作什么吗？
刘银燕：不知道，叫什么？
潘维廉：中国塔！
刘银燕：中国塔！真够有想像力的，对吧？
潘维廉：对，我也这么认为。
潘维廉：1866年5月30日，三艘了不起的运茶帆船，劈波斩浪，从福州的马尾港飞速驶出。
刘银燕：啊，这就是中国塔。

The Ariel

潘维廉：这些船以竞赛方式飞速驶向伦敦。9月6日，三艘船中的“太平号”首先到达伦敦，比第二名的“羚羊号”快了30分钟。
刘银燕：这是“羚羊号”吗？
潘维廉：没错，而第三名的“思瑞克号”仅仅落后几个小时。这三艘船在3个月共15700海里的航行中从未相遇过。
刘银燕：真神奇呀！
潘维廉：是很神奇。

解说

这次竞赛，比其他任何事情，都更能勾起整个世界对中国、福州乃至马尾港的向往。而在当时，大部分的西方人都不知道马尾港在2000年前就是中国造船业的摇篮。直到很久以后中国的许多发明才被西方的造船专家所采用和改进。不过马尾造的船质量一定很好，否则它们不可能在湍急的闽江中穿行无阻。

Dialogue—the Mighty Min River

Joyce: Well, Dr. Bill, the Min River doesn't really look that mighty to me!

Bill: Still waters run deep, Joyce! The Min river might look calm, but it actually carries more water than the mighty Yangtze River.

Joyce :Oh, really?

Bill: Yeah, a lot of western and Chinese ships have gone to a watery grave here.

Mean Men on a Min River

Joyce: Really? Then maybe we should not walk so close to the edge!

Bill: Can you swim?

Joyce: Sorry, I can't.

Bill: I can't either.

Between Pagoda Anchorage and the sea, the mighty Min surged through a narrow gorge that was so tight the old salts joked about monkeys jumping from one cliff to another and getting their tails caught in the rigging. The Min river was unforgiving. The Oriental sank in 1853, and the Vision in 1857.

Fuzhou folk, of course, must have figured that if they could survive the Min River they could survive anything, so for almost 2,000 years Fuzhou people had been exploring and trading abroad.

Mawei was the logistics base from which Zhenghe sailed throughout the known world, and around the end of 1431, before his last voyage, the great Admiral Zhenghe himself erected a tablet near the mouth of the Min, in what is now called Changle.

Dialogue—French Bombard Fuzhou

After French bombardment

Joyce: Mawei has played an important role in the last two centuries as well.

Bill: That's true. In the late 19th century, Pagoda Anchorage was China's biggest shipbuilding center. China's first iron ship and first water plane were built here.

Joyce: And Mawei was also the home of China's modern navy.

Bill: That's true, but it was also the site of China's big naval disaster.

Joyce: You mean the Sino-French War?

Bill: Yeah.

Chinese gave the giant rocks outside Mawei names like, "Double Turtle Guarding the Door," "Five Tigers Defending the Gate," and "Warrior's Leg." But turtles and tigers could not handle the French, who on a sleepy Saturday morning in August 1884, destroyed the Chinese fleet.

现场

刘银燕：嗯，潘博士，闽江看上去并不那么湍急啊。

潘维廉：静水深流，银燕！闽江看起来很平静，但是它的水流量要比长江都来得多，而且已经有许多的中国以及外国船只在这里葬身鱼腹！

刘银燕：真的吗？那也许我们不应该走得离水边这么近！

潘维廉：你会游泳吗？

刘银燕：我不会。

潘维廉：我也不会。

解说

在马尾港和海洋之间，湍急的闽江奔涌地穿过一个窄小的山峡，它是那样的狭窄，以至于老水手们开玩笑说，就连猴子从这边悬崖跳到对岸的悬崖，尾巴都会被船上的缆绳给勾住。闽江是无情的。1853年东方号在这里沉没，1857年梦幻号也在这里沉没。

当然了，福州人肯定认为如果他们能够征服闽江，他们就能够征服一切。所以2000多年以来福州人一直在海外探险、经商。

马尾是郑和航行所有当时已知的世界各地的出发港和后勤基地。大约在1431年末，在开始他的最后一次航海之前，伟大的航海家郑和亲自在闽江口，也就是现在的长乐，竖起了一座石碑。

现场

刘银燕：马尾在过去的两个世纪里也起到了很重要的作用。

潘维廉：没错。在19世纪晚期，宝塔港也即马尾港是中国最大的造船中心。中国第一艘铁船和第一艘水上飞机就是在这里建造的。

刘银燕：另外，马尾还是中国现代海军的故乡。

潘维廉：是的，但它也是中国最大的海难遗址。

刘银燕：你是指——中法战争？

潘维廉：对。

解说

中国人给马尾港外的那些巨石取了名字，像“双龟守门”、“五虎护关”，还有“金刚腿什么的。但是乌龟和老虎抵挡不住法国人。在1884年8月一个静寂的星期六清晨，法国人摧毁了中国的舰队。

China opposed France's invasion of Vietnam, and its advances into South China, so France responded with an attack on the great Fuzhou shipyard. The French commander warned foreign consulates and the Chinese the day before, but international law required at least 30 days notice. The Chinese requested one more day to prepare, but the French refused and attacked. Seven hundred Chinese seamen now lie in a mass grave beside the Memorial Hall of Majiang River Naval Battle.

Originally built as The Hall of Loyalty in 1884, the memorial hall has an extensive display of artifacts, documents and photos, as well as the martyr memorial and the mausoleum.

H. Shelley Brand, who arrived in Mawei 3 years later, wrote,

"It was only three years before this that the French Bombardment had occurred, and there were still evidences of it in the battered forts and derelicts at Pagoda Anchorage. Also to be seen were the graves of the large number of Chinese who lost their lives in that one-sided battle."

The Sino-French Naval Battle was but one of many humiliations that eventually led to revolt not just of Fuzhou folk but to all of China, and eventually to Liberation in 1949 and the ousting of Laowai like myself.

Dialogue

Joyce: Well, you Laowai are back in Fuzhou again now.

Bill: Yes, and it's a good thing, because now I can enjoy one of my favorite things.

Joyce: And what's that?

Bill: Fuzhou Food! What would you like to eat?

Joyce: What about the Buddha Jumps the Wall?

Bill : Well, I have to sell my first-born son to pay for it! But OK, you make the reservation.

Famous Fuzhou Snack (but what's she looking at?)

由于中国反对法国入侵越南以及越过中国南部边界，法国对伟大的福州造船厂发动了攻击。法国司令官仅仅提前一天给外国的领事馆和中国人发出战事警告，但是当时的国际公约规定至少需要提前 30 天。中国人要求再多给一天的时间予以准备，但是法国人拒绝了，实施了进攻。700 名中国的海军将士如今长眠在马江海战纪念馆内的陵园里。

马江海战纪念馆原名昭忠祠，最早建于1884年。如今馆内陈列着许多手工制品、档案以及照片，馆内还有烈士纪念碑和陵墓。

Mawei Martyrs Memorial

在中法海战发生三年后来到马尾的雪莉·伯朗特（H. Shelley Brand）写道：“离现在仅仅三年以前，法国人炮轰了这里。战争的痕迹在马尾四处可见，到处是弹痕累累的碉堡和战争的弃物。还可以看见数量惊人的华人的坟墓，他们都在那个一边倒的战争中被夺去了生命。”

中法海战仅仅是许许多多耻辱中的一个。这些屈辱逐渐引起了福州人乃至全中国人的反抗，并最终在 1949 年获得了解放，驱逐了像我这样的老外。

现场

刘银燕：嗯，你们老外现在又回到福州了。

潘维廉：是的，这可是件好事。因为现在我可以享受我最喜欢的东西了。

刘银燕：是什么？

潘维廉：福州菜！你最喜欢吃哪道菜？

刘银燕：“佛跳墙”怎么样？

潘维廉：那我得把大儿子卖了才埋得起单！不过，没关系，点菜吧。

Supplementary Reading Four

McChina (麦中国)

A Hong Kong McDonalds' TV advertisement boasted, "It's not a place, it's an experience." And it's a quite a common experience nowadays. Hong Kong has dozens of McDonalds, including 8 of the world's 10 most profitable outlets, and Xiamen is close on its heels.

Hundreds of cheeseless Laowai were thrilled to hear that Uncle Ronald[1] was coming to Xiamen during the Mid-Autumn Festival. Cheeseburgers and mooncakes! But the grand opening was postponed until Christmas, then New Year, then Chinese New Year. We finally figured it was like the Second Coming[2]—no man knows the day nor the hour. Though it turned out that local bigwigs[3] knew both. On the long awaited opening day, we raced to the Zhongshan Rd. McDonalds and were stopped at the door by two guards. Invitation only.

Forget McDonalds! But two weeks later, Sue and I were strolling down Zhongshan Rd. on our weekly date, and it was hard to ignore the bright paper posters and menus plastered on the giant plate glass windows. We succumbed, ordered burgers and fries, and were told, "Electricity's out. Nothing but drinks." (To the vast delight of Muslim shish-ka-bob vendors whose charcoal braziers were planted right on McDonald's doorstep).

Sue ordered a coke and I a coffee, and I contemplated devouring the photo of a cheeseburger on the colorful paper place mat.

After our liquid feast I sought out the bathroom, which as expected was spotless. Or I think it was. With no lights, windows, or power, it was pitch dark. I hope I found the urinal and not the sink.

We finally landed[4] our Big Macs a week later. I still prefer Lin Duck House's 5 Yuan pork rice special, but McDs is a nice break from routine – and has the hottest (and cheapest) coffee in town.

Cheeseburger, Hold the Cheese Better than eating burgers is watching others eat them (in China, at least!). I've seen folks use two soda straws as makeshift chopsticks to eat burgers piece by piece. Speaking of straws, I cringe at the memory of the granny who tried sipping her boiling hot tea through a plastic straw. I can still hear her blood curdling scream.

---

1 Uncle Roland: the McDonald's clown

2 Second Coming: the future return of Christ (in the Bible Christ said no one knows the day or hour of his return; Matthew 24:36)

3 Bigwig: important person or official (important Europeans used to wear big powdered wigs; Hong Kong judges still do!)

4 Landed: obtained, caught (as in "He landed a fish").

补充读物（四）

麦中国

香港麦当劳的一则电视广告宣称：“这不是个去处，这是全新的体验。”现在，这种体验太平常了。香港有数十家的麦当劳快餐厅，其中有八家已经挤进了全球麦当劳赢利十强。跟他们相比，厦门麦当劳已经步步逼近了。

若干年前，当数百位没奶酪吃的老外听说中秋节麦当劳要进驻厦门，都欢欣鼓舞。芝士汉堡和月饼！然而盛大的开幕式一直往后拖，拖过了圣诞节，然后元旦，然后中国农历新年。我们最后认定恐怕这是遥遥无期了——没人知道是什么时候，虽然后来证实本地的大人物知道确切的时间。终于等到了开业那天，我们冲向中山路的麦当劳，却被门卫拦在门外。非请勿进。

忘了麦当劳吧！两周后，在我们每周铁定的约会时间，我和苏珊沿着中山路闲逛。麦当劳落地玻璃窗上张贴的海报和菜单太醒目了，我们抵挡不住诱惑，进去要了汉堡和薯条。店里的伙计却说：“因为停电，我们只能提供饮料。”我相信，麦当劳边上用炭火槽烤羊肉串的穆斯林小贩们当时肯定欣喜若狂！

苏珊要了杯可乐，我要了杯咖啡。然后，我若有所思地紧盯着五颜六色的垫纸上各种芝士汉堡的照片看。

喝完饮料后，我找到了洗手间。一尘不染，我想应该是洗手间。里面没有灯光，没有窗户，也没有电，一片漆黑。我希望，我找到的是小便池而不是水池。

一周后，我们终于买到了巨无霸。不过，我还是喜欢林家鸭庄五块钱的排骨饭。但是，偶尔吃吃麦当劳换换口味也不错。在那里，还可以喝到全市最热、同时也是最便宜的咖啡。

♪芝士汉堡，夹住奶酪 ———

看人吃汉堡比自己吃汉堡感觉还好！在厦门，我曾经看过本地人用两根吸管当筷子，夹着汉堡吃。提到吸管，我一想起那件事就后怕。当时，有位老太太用塑料吸管喝滚烫的热茶。她那尖叫声足以令血液凝固，至今仍然在我耳边回响。我当时想，这下完了。

I'm sure that was the last straw.[5] Had she been in America, she could have sued McDonald's[6] and retired her entire extended family for life, and soda straws, which are too small for warnings, would now come equipped with instruction manuals.

Thanks to street-side Ronald McDonald performances and weekly offerings of "Collect Them All!" plastic burger men, fry folk, and plastic Snoopy dolls, Xiamen may become like Japan, where children think Big Macs are as indigenous as sushi. But Ronald McDonald is no longer the only player on the field.[7] At Xiada, the demilitarized zone[8] between McDonalds and KFC is only 100 meters or so. Several times I've seen the Chinese Ronald McDonald (who looks more like a Japanese Opera star) wooing kiddies away from KFC's magician.

Burgers and pizza and fried chicken are nice for a break—but one of the nicest aspects of life in China is Chinese food. For ½ the price of a Big Mac, I can have Lin Duck's[9] Pork Special—rice, vegetables, tea egg and meat. But mom and pop[10] shops are having a tough time holding out against Uncle Ronald. With golden arches around every corner, the day may come when Xiamen tourists can find nothing but burgers and Chicken McNuggets, or perhaps McSweet 'n Sour™, McFried Rice, " and McLemon Chicken Nuggets" .

But contrary to doomsayers' dire predictions, McDonalds and KFC have not monopolized the fast food market, but helped create and expand it. As Pepsi (the perennial #2 of soft drinks) discovered, wherever Coke goes, the overall soft drink market expands, allowing Pepsi to make billions in Coke's wake. Likewise, rather than transforming the Celestial Kingdom into McDragon™, McDonalds has created new opportunities for domestic and foreign enterprises alike – and taught some valuable lessons on quality, cleanliness, and consistency.

So in closing…

KFC*hina?* Matthew has lived in China since he was six months old, so we make allowances for questions like the one he asked when we drove around America in 1995. "Dad, do they have Kentucky Fried Chicken in America?"

---

[5] The last straw: the last of many disappointments, frustrations or failures that lead one to finally give up hope, or to lose one's temper (derived from the proverb, "It's the last straw that breaks the camel's back". This reminds me of the ancient Chinese story of a man who killed his mule by loading too many sacks on its back—and then wondered which sack killed him, since they all weighed the same).

[6] In 1992, the elderly Stella Liebeck sued McDonald's after burning herself with hot coffee. She won $160,000 in compensation and 2.7 million USD in punitive damages. In 2001, Veronica Martin from Tennessee Sued McDonald's for $110,000 after burning her chin with a hot pickle.

[7] Only player on the field: only competitor.

[8] Demilitarized zone: an area in which military forces and combat is prohibited.

[9] Lin Duck (林家鸭庄): my favorite is this small restaurant across from Nanputuo Temple started by a Taiwanese family in 1988, the year I came to Xiamen. Both my sons prefer it over American fast food.

[10] Mom and pop: small family-owned businesses

要在美国，老太太就会控告麦当劳公司。然后，她和家人就可以什么都不做，高枕无忧地过上一辈子。麦当劳吸管也从此需要加印警告提示。吸管太小，没法印？那至少配个使用手册吧。

厦门麦当劳每天都有街边表演，每周还有“集齐全套” 塑料汉堡人，薯条人,塑料的史奴比玩偶，有吃有送，跟日本没有什么两样。在日本，孩子们都认为，巨无霸和寿司都是本土食品。如今，在厦门，麦当劳并不是唯一的洋快餐。在厦大，麦当劳和肯德基的快餐店相距不过百米。我经常看到，中国的麦当劳叔叔正想方设法把孩子们从肯德基的魔术师那里吸引过来。看起来，麦当劳叔叔更像日本能剧的明星！

想换口味的话，汉堡包和匹萨饼以及炸鸡都是不错的选择。在中国，生活中最令人满意的还是中国菜。花上相当于巨无霸汉堡一半的价钱，就可以吃到林家鸭庄的特色猪排炒饭，里面有米饭、蔬菜、茶叶蛋和肉。不过，这些老店在同麦当劳的竞争下显得步履艰难。如今，麦当劳的金色拱形标志几乎是无处不在。总有一天，来厦的观光客只能找到汉堡和鸡块，或者可能还有麦糖醋里脊 TM[11] 、麦炒饭 TM 和麦柠檬鸡块 TM 。

预言家的话虽然危言耸听，却没有应验。麦当劳和肯德基等洋快餐并没有垄断市场，而是帮助厦门创造并扩大了快餐市场。正如百事可乐（饮料业的老二）发现的那样，可口可乐去所到之处，软饮料市场就随之扩大。百事可乐尾随可口可乐，进账数十亿。同样的道理，麦当劳并没有把中国变成麦龙邦 TM，而是为中外企业提供了新的机会，并在质量、卫生和服务等方面提供了不少宝贵的经验。

总而言之……

♪中国肯德基

我们的马休六个月大的时候就来到中国。因此，我们能体谅他问的一些问题。比如说，1995 年我们全家开车环游美国的时候，他问道：“爸爸，美国有肯德基炸鸡吗？”

[11] TM：商标(当然只是在开玩笑，我为麦当劳食品编的名字不会是注册商标）。

Episode 31 Fuzhou Food

Buddha jumped the wall... when he saw the bill!

Introduction On today's episode of Magic Fujian, Dr. Bill explains to Joyce Liu why Americans say the best way to a man's heart is through his stomach—especially if it's Fuzhou food!

Dialogue—Buddha Jumps the Wall

Bill: You know, Joyce, in the supermarket I saw Buddha Jumps the Wall kits for only 25 Yuan!

Joyce: Impossible. It has to be fake, because I know the real Buddha jumps the wall costs 1000 Yuan for ten people.

Bill: Really? Well, the only thing nearer to my heart than my stomach is my wallet, so I'll eat the fake.

Fujian cuisine used to be low on the list of China's eight major cuisines until a chef from Fuzhou's famous Juchunyuan Hotel wowed Beijing culinary judges with three of his dishes. Ever since, people have flocked to Fuzhou to feast on Gaotang Haibang (which is Changle clams), Qishi She (a delicacy named after the tongue of an ancient beautiful maid!), and Hongzao Jirou (a chicken dish).

Buddha Jumps the Wall is Fuzhou's most famous dish—and the most expensive. Over 30 choice ingredients are stewed in an aged liquor, and served to ten or more people—at over 1000 Yuan a pot. I was told that ages ago, a fellow decided to keep various meats and vegetables from spoiling by stewing them for over a day. A monk was so entranced by the stew's aroma that even though he was a vegetarian he leaped a wall to get a bowl full.

Dialogue

Bill: Is all Fuzhou food so expensive?

Joyce: Not at all. Antai Lou, on 817 road, serves some of the best Fuzhou fast food and it is not expensive.

Bill: Really? Then let's check it out.

Joyce: Fine, as long as you pay the bill.

Bill: Again?

Antai Lou, on the second floor at the corner of August 17th Street and JinTai Rd., is always crowded—though increasingly local youth are flocking to Western fast food outlets and coffee bars instead.

I love Fuzhou's famous fish balls, which vary in taste, texture and elasticity depending on the ratio of meat to flour and the amount of shrimp.

第31集 饮食福州

导语

在今天的“老外看福建”节目里，潘维廉博士将向主持人刘银燕解释为什么美国人说女人如果想赢得男人的心就得给他做好吃的——当然了，如果做的是福州菜，那就更有效了。

现场

潘维廉：我在超市看到了用瓦罐装的佛跳墙。一小罐只要25块钱。

刘银燕：不可能吧。十人份的佛跳墙都要1000元。那些罐装的东西肯定是假的。

潘维廉：嗯，这个嘛，对我来说，钱包可比我的胃口更重要，所以我宁可要这些便宜的罐装佛跳墙。

解说

闽菜在中国八大菜系中的排名过去曾相对置后，后来福州著名的聚春园酒店的一位厨师以三道菜赢得了北京烹饪专家的好评。从那以后，人们开始涌入福州尽情享受高汤海蚌、西施舌以及红糟鸡肉。

佛跳墙是福州最有名的一道菜，同时也是最昂贵的。30多种精选原料用老酒来炖，供十个或者更多的人享用——一罐佛跳墙售价高达1000多元。

人们告诉我，在很久以前，有个福州人为了防止几种肉菜变质，就把这些东西放在一起炖了一整天。一个和尚闻到香味，垂涎欲滴，于是不顾清规戒律，跳过墙去，盛了满满一碗。

现场

潘维廉：是不是所有的福州菜都这么贵啊？

刘银燕：当然不是。八一七路的安泰楼有各种各样的福州风味小吃。

潘维廉：那我们去看一看吧！

刘银燕：好吧，只要是你买单就行。

解说

尽管越来越多的福州年轻人更喜欢上西式快餐店和咖啡馆，位于八一七路和津泰路交汇处的安泰楼还是一向热闹非凡。

我喜欢有名的福州鱼丸。它有各种口味，嫩滑可口，有弹性。做鱼丸需要一定比例的鱼肉、面粉和一定量的虾。

For a real treat, try the pounded pork shops in the "3 Wards 7 Streets" area. Like most Fujian people, Fuzhou folk argue that they have the best pounded pork in the province, if not China. But Fuzhou's pounded pork is 100% pig, no flour. I marveled how the pork pounder pounded away with his mallet for over ½ an hour without a break. He pounded the pork until it was so thin and white that I mistook it for the paper they wrap take-out in.

Pork Pounder

Locals say the best sample of take-out Fuzhou snacks is to be had at the award winning little shop just south of the tottering black pagoda. The shop has been in the family for 3 or 4 generations, and concocts all kinds of cakes and sweets that I can't begin to describe because we have nothing in America to compare them to! Well, almost! I bought a box of pumpkin pies. They were tasty but the glutinous little orange globes sprinkled with white sugar were not quite like the pies my mom made for Thanksgiving dinner back at home.

Fuzhou's cuisine is unique, but as people prosper they are demanding more variety, and now enjoy restaurants with cuisine from all over China—or the world. Sichuan food seems especially popular now. And there are many Western restaurants as well—though you never know what you'll get when you try Fuzhou Western Food.

B.B. Famous Fuzhou fast food shop

But whatever one's tastes—or lack of taste, as in my case—Fuzhou has something to offer. So while you're exploring Fuzhou, try some of the local delicacies.

如果你想美餐一顿的话，那就去三坊七巷的肉燕店吧。跟多数的福建人一样，福州人总觉得他们的肉燕即便不是全国最好，起码也是全省最棒的。福州的肉燕是纯粹用猪肉做成的，不加面粉。我很惊讶，这些做肉燕的怎么能够用木槌连捣一个半小时，中间不休息片刻。他们把猪肉捣到又白又薄为止，薄得我错把他们当作是他们包外卖的白纸了。

福州人说如果想尝尝可以外带的福州小吃，那你最好光临乌塔南边享有盛誉的一家小店。顺便说一句，乌塔摇摇欲坠，快赶上意大利比萨斜塔了。这家家族经营的小店已经传承了三四代人了。我不知道该怎么描述他们制作的各式糕点和甜品，因为在美国根本没有相类似的东西。嗯。差不多是这样。我买了一盒南瓜饼，挺好吃的。但是这些撒上白糖的粘粘的橘子形状的糕点跟我母亲在感恩节时做的馅饼可不太一样。

但是无论一个人的口味如何——或者干脆像我一样，没有什么特别的口味——福州总有些东西值得一试。所以当你游览福州的时候，一定别忘了尝尝当地的美味佳肴。

Episode 32 Intro to Wuyi Mountain

Introduction   Our old friend Dr Bill Brown is now working on his second edition of Magic Fujian. For this new book, Bill together with our reporter Deborah visited Wuyi Mountain at the beginning of this year. What did they find in the scenic wonderland? It's home of China's most exotic teas, the kingdom of snakes, and a biological wonderland!

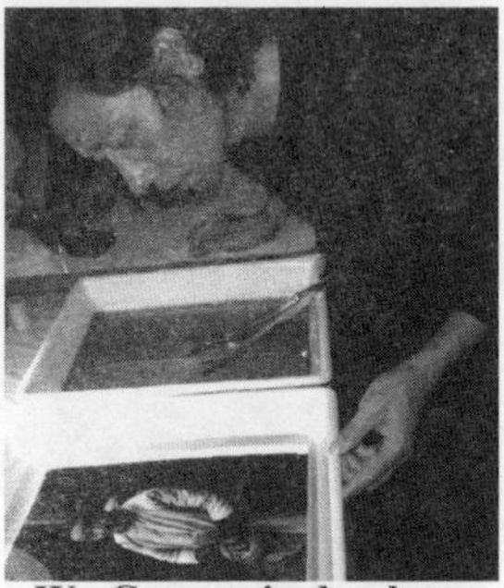

Wu Guangmin develops black and white photo

Dialogue

Bill: I heard that Zhuxi, the philosopher who started Neo-Confucianism lived here in Wuyi?

Deborah: Yes. And one of his favorite pastimes was to drink tea while bamboo rafting.

Bill: Really? Well, I have the water!

Wu Guangmin and wife

Wuyi was the cradle of the ancient Min kingdom, which gave us the earliest recorded history in Fujian. Wuyi is the only site in Fujian, and the 4th in China, that UN has accredited as Natural and Cultural World Heritage. Since the 1700s, Europeans have explored the region because of its amazing biological diversity, which probably rivals the Garden of Eden. And speaking of that garden—the great garden of Wuyi also has its serpents because it is the snake kingdom of the world. But the only way to learn about Wuyi's diversity is to find a good guide—and there are few who know Wuyi better than local photographer Wu Guangmin, who spends most his weekends traipsing around the countryside capturing on film the natural and historic beauty of his adopted home. But Guangmin is worried. He said that ancient China was rapidly disappearing, and like Babushka in Changting, Guangmin decided to capture Wuyi's marvelous cultural and historical heritage on film before it vanishes beneath the tide of modernization.

Philosopher Zhuxi   Wu Guangmin is not the only one who prizes Wuyi civilization. As far back as 1183, Zhu Xi, founder of Neo-Confucianism, set up an academy in Wuyi and began his teaching career. Zhuxi's works have dominated Asian cultures for centuries, much as the works of Socrates and Plato dominated Western philosophies. Even today, Zhu's descendents from home and abroad come to Wuyi to trace their ancestor's footsteps. In addition to Zhuxi, other ancient luminaries like the poet Liu Yong spent at least part of their life in Wuyi. Whether they lived in Wuyi during the start of their career or retired here, they left their marks in the form of priceless calligraphic inscriptions in the stones along the 9-bend stream. And even today, Wuyi has produced many distinguished national leaders.

第32集　武夷山简介

导语

欢迎收看系列报道“老外看福建”！从今天开始，我们将和厦门大学外教潘维廉博士一同，探寻福建的神奇魅力。首先，我们要到闻名中外的武夷山风景区去游览一番，那里出产中国最奇特的茶叶，同时也是蛇的王国和生态奇境。一起去看看吧。

解说

提到武夷山，大多数人会想到乘竹筏顺着九曲溪漂流而下，穿越诗情画意的山景。实际上，武夷山好玩的地方远不止这些。

现场

潘维廉：我听说理学家朱熹曾在武夷山生活过？
郑芬：没错。他最喜欢的一种休闲，就是在竹筏上边饮茶边漂流。
潘维廉：是吗！我也带了水！

解说

武夷山是古代闽越王国的发源地。福建最早有记录的历史就始于闽越王国。武夷山是福建省第一个、也是中国第四个被联合国授予“世界自然和文化遗产”称号的地方。武夷地区的生物多样性令人惊讶，足以和伊甸园媲美。早在18世纪，欧洲人就开始在这个地区探险。提到伊甸园，武夷山这座大园子也有蛇，它还有着“蛇的王国”的美称。要了解武夷山的生物多样性，一定要找一个好向导。当地摄影家吴光明对武夷山的了解几乎无人可比。他常在周末到山乡里四处搜寻，用胶片捕捉第二故乡武夷山的自然和历史美景。

不过吴光明也很担忧。他说，中国许多古老传统正在慢慢地消失，就像长汀的摄影师胡晓钢一样，吴光明决定，在武夷山那令人惊奇的文化和历史遗产还没有消失在现代文明的浪潮之前，把它们都一一用胶卷记录下来。好一个人文主义者！不过吴光明并不是重视武夷文明的第一人。早在1183年，后孔子主义的创始人朱熹就在武夷山建立了一个书院，开始了像苏格拉底和柏拉图那样的教书生涯。在中国乃至其他亚洲国家，朱熹的影响在漫长的历史年代里占据了统治地位。直到今天，遍布国内外的朱氏后裔还纷纷到武夷追寻他们祖先的足迹。除了朱熹，还有相当多的名人在武夷山生活过。其中包括宋朝时著名的婉约派词人柳永。你可以从他们留在九曲溪沿岸的手迹来判断他们是在武夷山发迹，还是退而隐居武夷。今天的武夷山同样接待了众多国内外名人。

In China, there is a saying that, "He who fails to climb the Great Wall can never be a man". Likewise, clever Fujianese claim: "A pity is he who has not seen Wuyi."

So it 's up to you—either hold a pity party[1] or visit the spectacular scenery of the Wuyi wonderland, with its sea of clouds enveloping Tianyou Peak, or the sublime beauty of the water curtain falls. Of course the favorite by far is the bamboo raft ride down the nine-bend stream. Throughout the 2 ½ hour journey the polemen recite poetry, stories, legends and folk tales nonstop while poling the boat down the meandering river.

Dialogue—Endless Names

Deborah: Did you know that over the past few thousand years local people have named every rock and hill?

Bill: Well, I think they're still naming them. When I was here last time, they pointed to a cliff like this and they said, "That's the Titanic!" Oh Jack!

Wuyi's landmark is Jade Maiden Peak. Locals say it resembles a beautiful maiden, with shrubs and trees for hair, standing gracefully. She gazes at her reflection in the water below, contemplating a bright future. Personally, she doesn't look like any maiden I've ever known, but regardless, I can appreciate her hopes for a bright future, because Wuyi has certainly had a bright past—at least 2,000 years of it!

Jade Maiden

[1] Pity Party: feel self-pity

The Titanic

中国有句老话叫作“不到长城非好汉”。聪明的福建人在后边加了一句：“不到武夷真遗憾。”

当然，你可以自己决定要遗憾到什么时候。武夷山是个人间仙境，拥有引人入胜的美景，比如天游峰顶的云海，以及美丽的水帘洞。但最让人钟情的莫过于乘竹筏沿九曲溪漂流了。艄公一边撑着竹筏，一面还滔滔不绝地向你介绍沿途的美景和相关的掌故。

现场

郑芬：你知道吗，几千年来，当地人给每一块岩石和山坡都起了名字？

潘维廉：他们现在还在这么做。我上次来的时候，他们指着一座这样形状的悬崖，说那叫“泰坦尼克”。哦！杰克！

解说

玉女峰是武夷山的标志。当地人说它像一位亭亭玉立的美少女，灌木丛和小树是她的头发。我个人认为这座山峰一点都不像我所认识的少女，不过我倒是很欣赏她对美好未来的憧憬。在我看来，武夷山的未来会很美，毕竟它已经拥有了了 2000 多年的美好历史。

FJTV Films Titanic?

Episode 33 Wuyi Mountain—Fujian's "Garden of Eden"

Introduction Welcome to today's episode of Magic Fujian as Xiamen University's Dr. Bill Brown and FJTV's Deborah take us to Garden of Eden—Wuyi Mountain!

Square Bamboo!

Wuyi Mountain has delighted both Chinese and foreign scientists for centuries with its endless biological diversity and scenic beauty, as well as its rich cultural and historic heritage. Over 200 years ago, Europeans explored the region, which is over 92% forested and home to plants and animals found nowhere else on earth. Wuyi has 2,466 higher plant species, 840 lower plant species, 475 vertebrate species, 100 species of animals, 300 species of birds, and 31 insect orders with 4,557 species!

Some of the unique plants include the strange four-sided black bamboo, which the famous Chinese poet Guo Moruo wrote a poem about. And some of the "unique" animals include snakes, ranging from king cobras to ten meter pythons. We were told that Wuyi is home to fully 2/3 of over 180 kinds of snakes.

Ancient Snake Carvings

Snake Kingdom No wonder Wuyi is considered a second Garden of Eden. And no wonder the ancient Min people worshipped serpents, and that even the character for Fujian is a serpent within a doorway! But worship or not, the locals' also crave snake –related products like snake wine, and snakeskin products—and they all appreciate the snake doctors!

Snake doctors don't necessarily work out of hospitals. In Xiamei, one of the well-preserved ancient villages, I was introduced to Master Wang, who inherited his family's ancient herbal cures for snake bites. Wang said that people bitten by cobras or bamboo vipers often lose an arm or a leg if they go to the hospital, but he has never yet lost either a patient or a limb.

第 33 集　武夷山:伊甸园福建版

♪导语

欢迎收看系列报道“老外看福建”。今天，厦门大学的潘维廉博士和我们的记者郑芬将带领我们游览福建版本的伊甸园——武夷山！

How many Wuyi snakes can you count?

♪解说

武夷山拥有丰富的生物资源、自然景观和历史文化遗产。数百年来，一直吸引着无数中外科学家。200 多年前，欧洲人就开始探索这一地区。武夷山的森林覆盖率达 92%，生长着世界上绝无仅有的许多珍稀动植物品种。武夷山拥有 2466 种高等植物，840 种低等植物，475 种脊椎动物，100 种哺乳动物，300 种鸟类，以及分属 31 目的 4557 种昆虫。其中还包括诸如黑皮方竹这样奇特的植物。关于这种方竹，中国著名诗人郭沫若曾写诗吟颂。武夷山还有一些奇特的动物，比如蛇。关于蛇，意大利著名诗人但丁也写过诗。

有人告诉我，中国的 180 多种蛇中，约三分之二产自武夷。武夷山完全称得上是伊甸园。古代闽越人崇拜毒蛇，甚至连汉字“闽”字也写成门里的一条蛇。尽管如此，依然阻挡不住当地人对与包括蛇酒在内的蛇制品以及蛇医的狂热追求。找蛇医，不一定非得上医院。在保存完好的古村落——下梅村，我认识了蛇医王师傅。王师傅继承了祖传的治蛇咬的草药方子。他说，被眼镜蛇或竹叶青咬了，如果送医院就医，肯定会丢胳膊少腿的。王师傅自己却从来没失手，让病人失望，或让他们失去什么。

Matt and friend

These self-taught grass roots snake doctors take care of human patients, but sick animals are not neglected either. In the nature preserve, locals set up a special facility to care for ill creatures—though my partner Deborah thought it was more like a zoo than a hospital.

Dialogue Animal Hospital

Bill: So how did this animal hospital get started?

Deborah: The locals find injured animals, and bring them here for treatment.

Bill: Well, after that last meal I don't feel so good. Maybe I should see the doctor myself!

He can *bear*ly reach the peanut!

Wuyi people have long taken pride in their natural heritage. In their eyes, every leaf, every stone, even every drop of water has magic power. Folk legend has it that a white-furred fox was fascinated by Zhuxi, transformed into a pretty girl, and served as his concubine for his entire lifetime. But what interests me most is that Zhuxi once raised a pen-tall monkey. The pet was said to be a considerate "scholar's aide." This monkey is thought to be extinct, but in 1996, Xinhua news agency reported the finding of a tiny 6 ounce monkey said to be the same kind that Zhuxi trained to prepare ink, pass brushes, and turn pages. The monkeys slept in brush pots and lived on nothing more than soybeans and peanuts—workers' exploitation, it seemed to me!

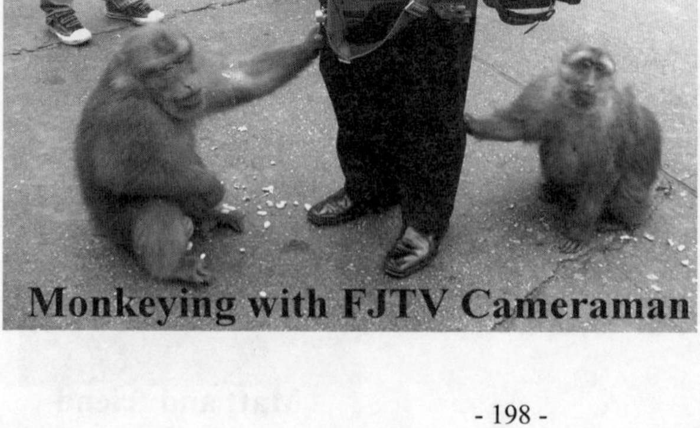

Monkeying with FJTV Cameraman

But Wuyi's modern monkeys aren't working for peanuts! When these large monkeys hear tourists coming, they swarm down from the mountainsides, and they don't work for a living making ink and passing brushes. They simply beg tourists for peanuts and fruit—and will grab the whole bag if you give them have a chance.

在武夷山，这些赤脚蛇医自学成才，治病救人。而动物生病也有人关照。武夷山建立了专门的动物医院。在我的搭档郑芬看来，这座医院倒更像是个动物园。

Snake Doctor Wang

♪现场

潘维廉：这个动物医院最初是怎样建成的呢？

郑芬：当地百姓发现受伤的动物，就把它们带到这里来治疗。

潘维廉：吃过饭后，我也感觉不怎么舒服。也许我该找个医生看看。

Snake Garden

♪解说

武夷山人民一直为他们的自然遗产而感到自豪。在他们看来，每一片叶子、每一块石头，甚至是每一滴水都拥有神奇的力量。传说有一只白毛狐狸因爱慕朱熹，变成一位美丽的姑娘，作了朱熹的侍女，一生服侍朱熹。不过，最让我感兴趣的是朱熹曾养过一只只有毛笔大小的小猕猴。据说，这只小猕猴还是服侍周到的“书童”呢。这种珍稀的小宠物一度已经绝种。不过 1996 年新华社报道说，当地又发现了大小只有 6 盎司的猴子。很可能就是当年朱熹收服后，用以研墨、递笔、换书页的“书猴”吧。传说它们睡在毛笔盒里，以黄豆或花生为食。在我看来，简直就是对劳苦大众的剥削的典型。不过它们的后字辈们可不是花生能打发的了，更不用说靠研墨递笔为生了。一听到游客的声音，猴子们成群结队地从半山腰蜂拥而下，向游客讨花生和果子吃。一有机会，它们就直接从游客手里抢！

Episode 34 The Origin of Min, Relic of the Han Town

Introduction Welcome to today's Episode of Magic Fujian, as Dr. Bill Brown of Xiamen University, and Deborah of FJTV, explore the ancient history and culture of Wuyi Mountain, the origin of the Min people.

Ruins of Min Palace

The Ancient Min King's Palace About 35 km south of Wuyi city lies the ancient foundation and the museum of the Min Kingdom, which over 2,000 years ago dominated Fujian. The 10,000 square meter foundation looks a little like part of a Mayan temple. One can guess how luxurious the temple must have been from the 10m by 5m bathing pool.

Dialogue—a Big Bathtub!

Bill: This is the bathtub? You're kidding. It looks like a swimming pool to me.

Deborah: But over there, beneath these glass casements you can see the original 2,000-year-old tiles.

Bill: Really? I'll take a look. 2,000 years, huh? I don't know. They look a lot like the modern tiles to me.

Deborah: But I don't think the modern tiles could survive 2,000 years!

Bill: Probably not. My bathroom tiles at home did not last 10 years.

The Min Kingdom Museum, just south of the ancient foundations, sheds light on the Min King. He was demoted to tribal head when the first Qin Emperor united China, but he got even by helping the Han defeat the Qin. In the 5th year of the Han dynasty, he was appointed King of the Minyue people—and this was the beginning of Fujian's recorded history! But the Min King's power went to his head.. He rebelled against the Han Emperor, and in 110 B.C. his palace was burned to the ground. All that is left today is the foundations, a 2,000-year-old well that still produces water—and odd stones with carvings of serpents, which were Min people's totem.

Dialogue

Deborah: You know this is part of the Min River?

Bill: Really? I read that this is the river that Marco Polo sailed down to reach Fuzhou. If that's so, it must have been a very small boat.

第 34 集　汉城，闽越发源地

导语

欢迎收看双语系列报道“老外看福建”。在今天的节目里，厦门大学的潘维廉博士和我们的记者郑芬将在福建人的发祥地武夷山探寻那里悠久的历史和文化。

解说

古老的闽越王国遗址和闽越博物馆位于武夷山市以南约 35 公里处。2000 多年前，福建处于闽越王国的统治之下。闽越王国宫殿遗址约一万平方米，看上去有点像玛雅神庙的一部分。宫殿里有一个 10 米×5 米大小的澡池。从这个澡池，人们不难想象这座宫殿当年是多么的富丽堂皇。

现场（看着古老的窗棂下的砖片）

潘维廉：你说这是个浴盆？开玩笑吧。我觉得它看起来像个游泳池。

郑芬：但是那边的那些玻璃下面，你可以看到有两千年历史的地砖。

潘维廉：是吗，我倒觉得它们更像现代的东西。

郑芬：我很怀疑现在的砖头是否经挡得住两千年的风风雨雨。

潘维廉:不可能.我们家浴室里的瓷砖甚至用不了十年。

解说（闽越王国博物馆）

坐落在宫殿遗址南面的闽越王国博物馆展示了闽越王国的由来。秦始皇统一中国后，闽王被贬为部落首领。后来，由于助汉灭秦有功，闽王于东汉五年被重新封为闽越王，开始了福建有历史的记录。不过后来闽越王权力膨胀，居然起兵反叛汉皇。公元前 110 年，闽越王被镇压下去，宫殿也被烧得片瓦无存。我们今天所能看到的,只有宫殿的地基、一口仍在涌水的千年古井和一些奇形怪状的石头。石头上面刻着蛇的图形，那是闽越人的图腾。

现场（武夷山自然保护区闽江源头）

郑芬：你知道吗？这里是闽江的一部分。

潘维廉:是吗？我在书上看到，马可·波罗就是坐船沿着这条河到福州的。要是这样的话，他坐的船肯定很小。

Ancient Ferry Crossing

With so glorious history, Wuyi people have good reason to be proud of their ancestral year. In Xiamei village, Mr. Zhao Shan Zhong proudly showed us his ancestral records which might prove that his veins runs the blood of Zhao Kuangyin, founder of the Song Dynasty. He exclaimed, "I am the 37th generation!" By comparison, many Americans cannot trace their ancestry even 5 generations!

Wheelbarrow Wisdom Peng Dehuai, one of the founders of People's Republic of China, once said, "CPC's victory was grassroots, using the Chinese one-wheelbarrow. In Wuyi, I could see why. The one-wheeled wheelbarrow is a perfect example of ancient Chinese' inventiveness and pragmatism. With only one wheel, they could easily navigate the narrow dikes between rice paddies, and with the load balanced evenly over the wheel, one did not have to lift—only guide. Even today, many American wheelbarrows are not as practical as those made in China over 1000 years ago! Chinese pragmatism, I suspect, is the primary reason that China has survived for over 5,000 years, and why China may still be around 5,000 years from now!

拥有如此辉煌的历史，武夷山人当然有理由为他们的祖先感到自豪。在下梅村，一位赵善忠先生非常自豪地向我们展示了他家的族谱。族谱证明，赵先生身上流淌的是大宋开国皇帝赵匡胤的鲜血。他说，“我是第37代！” 相比之下，很多美国人寻根问祖肯定超不过五代。

中华人民共和国的开国功臣之一彭德怀元帅曾经说过，中国共产党的胜利是人民群众用独轮车推出来的。在武夷山，我终于明白了这种可能性。当地的独轮车充分展示了古代中国人的创造性和实用主义。虽然只有一个轮子，独轮车却能轻松地行走在狭窄的田埂上，推车的人根本用不着向上使力来提，只管往前推就行了。即使在今天，美国很多地方的手推车还是不如中国人 1000 多年前创造的独轮车实用。中式实用主义！我想，正是因为有了这样的实用主义，中国才能历经 5000 多年长久不衰。正是因为有了这样的实用主义，再过 5000 年，中国还是中国！即使是 5000 年后，中国人很可能还在喝着让武夷山出名的饮料——茶！

Gucheng

Episode 35 Wuyi Tea—Soup for the Soul

House built of tea!

Introduction The word "tea" came from the Minnan word "dei," but when the Dutch first shipped tea from Macao to Europe, back in 1601, they called it "wooyee," because much tea originated in the Wuyi mountains.

Dialogue—The Tea Road

Bill: Have you heard of the Silk Road of the Sea?

Deborah: Of course. It was in Quanzhou, near where you live.

Bill: Well, Mr. Wu Guangmin told me that the Tea Road began right here in Wuyi Mountain, in Xiamei Town.

Deborah: Really?

Bill: Yes, hundreds of boats up and down this river.

Tea did not make it to Fujian until about 1,000 years ago, but since then, the innovative Fujianese have created 2 of the 6 major kinds of tea, and Wuyi is where the Fujian tea trade originated.

Dialogue—House of Tea

Deborah: So this family temple was built by Mr Zou 邹 during Qing Dynasty.

Bill: Where did he get so much money to build something like this?

Deborah: It all came from the tea selling.

Bill: Wow, so the house is made of tea? Is anybody home? Wei? Maybe ghosts?

I vowed I would never again take tea for granted! Mr. Zhao Shan Zhong (赵善忠), a proud 37th generation resident of Gucheng, recently opened a tea house in this home built in 1620, and he taught me the ancient art of Chinese tea brewing. Careful selection of water is crucial. The ancients were so skilled that they could tell, by taste, whether the water was from a spring, running river, or lake, and legend has it that some tea masters could actually pinpoint the specific province and source. Of course, much also depends upon how the tea is brewed, and few people brew it better than Wu Guangmin.

He excitedly brought out a panoply of tea paraphernalia—so many odd accessories that he reminded me of a Taoist mad scientist seeking the elixir of eternal life. But everything had a purpose—including the calligraphy brush, which he used to continually swab the surface of the steaming pot to preserve its temperature and the tea's flavor. He even told me how to drink the tea: eye the color, savor the aroma, then take a swallow and swish it noisily near the front of the mouth. I nearly choked trying to get the hang of that—and tea master Wu Guangmin did choke watching me!

第 35 集　武夷岩茶，心灵鸡汤

导语

“Tea”这个英文单词来自闽南语“Dei”。早在1601年，荷兰人第一次把茶叶从澳门运往欧洲时，他们把茶称为“Wooyee”，因为当初茶叶大多来自福建武夷山。

现场（下梅村，河边）

潘维廉：你听说过“海上丝绸之路”吗？
郑芬：当然听说过。它始于泉州，离你现在居住的厦门很近。
潘维廉：我从书上看到，中国的“茶叶之路”始于福建武夷山，就在下梅村。
郑芬：是吗？
潘维廉：不错。当年这里曾是千帆竞发的场景。

解说

茶是一直到距今千年以前才传入福建的。不过，聪明的福建人很快掌握了茶的艺术，创造出中国六大茶系中的两种。武夷山就是福建茶叶交易的发源地。在清朝鼎盛时期，商人挨家挨户收集茶叶，然后用船运走，结果发了大财。

现场

郑芬：建这座祠堂的是清朝一个姓邹的人。
潘维廉：他哪来那么多钱建这么大一座祠堂？
郑芬：做茶叶买卖挣来的。
潘维廉：啊，我琢磨着这房子是用茶叶造的。
（进门）有人在吗？或者有鬼在吗？

解说

这趟武夷行，让我再不敢小视茶叶了。赵善忠，就是那位自豪的赵匡胤的37代孙，最近在他那所建于1620年的古宅里开了家茶舍。他教了我几手品茶的方法。泡茶的水的质量是最关键的。据说古时候的大师们，单小啜一口，就能分辨出泡茶用的是泉水、河水还是用湖水。更有甚者，能直接点明茶叶出产地。当然，除了水，泡制的方法也很重要。没几个人能达到吴光明的泡茶水平。

看着他一脸兴奋地搬出一大套泡茶家伙，那样子让我想起了中国古时候那些修炼长生不老术的方士们。那些泡茶的家伙形状各异，每一样都有用处，包括一枝毛笔——吴光明用它来不停地拂拭水壶表面，以保持加热均匀，这样茶不会失去风味。他还教我怎样品茶：观其色，闻其味，啜一口，在唇齿间回吞。为了掌握这一技术，我差点呛着，而功夫茶大师吴光明真的呛了！——看我的尴尬相。

Big Red Robe But all the fuss of both preparation and drinking was well worth the effort, especially when Wu Guangmin served up a pot of that most precious of teas, Big Red Robe!

World's rarest tea--Big Red Robe

I asked what was the best tasting tea, and was told that the taste of all teas, including Big Red Robe, depends upon the growing conditions—the type of soil, mineral content, amount of rain, and the water. I'm told that Big Red Robe tastes flowery some years, and milky during others.

Dialogue—the World's Rarest Tea

Deborah: This is the rarest tea in the world.

Bill: What makes it so rare?

Deborah: Because all the Big Red Robe tea comes from these three bushes.

Bill: Really? No wonder its so expensive. I heard that last year in the 2002 Canton Tea Fair, they auctioned off 20 grams of this tea for 180,000 Yuan!

Deborah: 180,000 Yuan!

Bill: It's more than I make in a month! Maybe I should get a job planting tea.

Deborah: Yeah, good idea.

Wuyi is the holy of holies of tea because it offers the perfect climate, clean water, and the narrow valleys guarantee the perfect few amount of sunshine, and, according to the monks at least, spiritual enlightenment, via a cuppa tea.

Tao of Tea The abbot of a Wuyi monastery lectured me on how fine teas affect ones soul as well as ones palate. I was about to tell him that I could barely tell the difference between two Yuan tea and 2000 Yuan tea when he said, "Some people cannot tell the difference between good tea and bad tea." Before I could volunteer that I was one of those he added, "That's because those people have nothing within their souls!"

For once I remained silent! But I also wondered how the monk would fare if he had to distinguish between excellent coffees. Still, even with my impoverished palate, I've come to appreciate the taste and the feel of fine teas. And, better yet, even Western scientists nowadays are claiming that tea, especially green tea, is great for the body. Who knows? Tea may yet turn out to be a chief ingredient in the Taoists elixir of immortality! If so—I'll still be visiting Wuyi's wonderful mountains and sipping her fine teas from thimble-sized cups a few centuries from now!

不过，所有这些都是值得的——特别是当吴光明拿出了“大红袍”。我曾经请教过别人，最好的茶是什么茶，得到的答复是，所有的茶，包括大红袍在内，其风味因生长环境的不同而不同，土壤、矿物质、降雨量和水都有影响。大红袍有时喝起来有花香味，有时则有牛奶味。

现场（大红袍旁）

郑芬：大红袍是世界上最珍贵的茶叶。

潘维廉：为什么会这样珍贵呢？

郑芬：因为大红袍茶只有这三株。

潘维廉：所以，这茶叶才这样昂贵吧。我听说，在2002年广东茶博会上，20克大红袍拍出了18万元的天价！

郑芬：18万元！

潘维廉：比我一个月赚的还多。也许我该换个工作，改种茶叶。

郑芬：好主意！

解说

Tao of Tea

武夷山是茶生长的天堂。适宜的气候、纯净的水和幽兰的山谷，使得光照恰到好处。还有，用当地出家人的话来说，一股灵气！永乐寺的方丈教导我，好茶叶是怎样影响人的品味和灵魂。我正想告诉他我几乎分不出两块钱的茶叶和 2000 块钱的茶叶之间的区别时，他说，“有些人无法区分好茶叶和不好的茶叶”，我刚想坦白我就是那种人，他又接着说，“那是因为那些人的灵魂空无一物！”好半天，我没敢吭声。不过，我也想象不出如果要和尚们分辨咖啡的好坏时会是怎样。

尽管如此，我还是学会了鉴赏好茶的滋味和感觉了。更何况现在连西方科学家们都认为茶叶，尤其是绿茶，对身体是大有好处的。谁知道呢？茶叶也许还是道家长生不老药的主要成分呢！果真如此，从现在开始，我还是会常来游览武夷山的美景，并用顶针大小的杯子品尝武夷岩茶！

Episode 36 Introduction to Putian

Introduction Welcome to today's episode of Magic Fujian, as Xiamen University MBA Center's Dr. Bill Brown, and FJTV's Deborah take us to visit Putian, Minnan's northernmost city, one of China's leading fruit baskets, and the potential for becoming one of China's key coastal shipping centers.

Fujian's Four Great Women Of Fujian's four greatest women in ancient times, three were from Putian. They were Mazu, the sea goddess, Qian Siniang, the first to attempt to dam the Mulan River, and Jiang Caipin, the Emperor's concubine, also called the Plum Queen. Putian women have been famous for their courage and abilities since Qian Siniang tried to dam the Mulan River, the mother river of the Putian people.

Mulan Dam

Mulan Dam In 1064 A.D., just five years after Quanzhou built its marvelous Luoyang stone bridge, Lady Qian Siniang and Mr. Lin Chongshi tried to build a dam at the foot of Mulan Mountain. Lady Qian spent every penny she had to build this dam, but unfortunately, they chose the wrong site, and failed. In spite of her failure, Qian Siniang is revered for her courage and determination, and a Meizhou Island temple now has a large statue of Lady Qian sitting beside Mazu and holding a Chinese coin.

I too admire Lady Qian—though given that she lost everything, I would not seek her advice for investments!

Eleven years later, the Emperor sent Mr. Lihong to try again. He drew upon the lessons of his failed predecessors, but also sought the aid of a local monk, Fen Zhiri, and in eight years they completed the 219.3 meter dam, with 32 sluice gates.

The Mulan dam helped irrigate 32,000 acres of farmland, enabling Putian to feed its growing population, and from that time on Putian became a major city, as well as an international commercial hub, thanks to 30.9 kilometers of coastline.

Putian, settled in 568 A.D, lies only 72 miles from Taizhong, Taiwan, and is not only rich in history and traditions, but also a very modern city. Putian's long coastline has the potential for 150 10,000—ton deep water berths, roughly half of the deep water berths planned for the entire country! It also has a rich natural and cultural heritage, including the beauty of nine carp falls, and the traditions of Southern Shaolin Kung Fu.

第36集　莆田掠影

导语

欢迎收看双语系列报道“老外看福建”！在今天的节目中，厦门大学MBA 中心教授潘威廉博士和我们的记者郑芬将带我们去福建中部城市——莆田。莆田是中国的水果主产地之一，目前正致力于建设中国沿海的重要港口。

解说

远古时代，福建出了四位伟大女性，其中有三个来自莆田。她们分别是海上女神妈祖、与杨贵妃争宠的梅妃江采苹、古代大型水利工程木兰陂的始建者钱四娘。钱四娘是历史上第一位试图在莆田的母亲河——木兰溪上拦河筑坝的，莆田女子的勇气也从此闻名于世。

公元 1064 年，也就是著名的泉州洛阳桥建成 5 年之后，钱四娘和她的同乡林从世两人尝试着在木兰山脚修建河坝。为了修筑木兰陂，钱四娘倾尽家财。可惜的是，由于选址不当，钱、林两人的努力付诸东流。尽管如此，钱四娘的勇气与决心赢得了当地百姓的尊敬。湄州岛妈祖庙就将钱四娘塑像供奉在妈祖像旁。她的手里还拿着一枚中国钱币。

我很敬重钱四娘。不过，考虑到她理财失败的经历，我想我还是不求她保佑我财运亨通了。

11 年后，皇帝指派李宏在木兰河再试身手。李宏在僧人冯智日的协助下，总结先人教训，慎重选址，精心施工。经过 8 年的努力，终于建成了长 219.3 米，有 32 孔闸门的木兰陂。

木兰陂可以浇灌 20 万亩农田，足以哺育莆田日见增长的人口。莆田拥有 30.9 公里的海岸线。木兰陂建成后，莆田逐渐发展成福建中部重镇和重要的国际商贸中心。

莆田距台湾台中约115里，始建于公元568年，它不仅拥有悠久的历史与传统，市容市貌也颇为现代化。漫长的海岸线可以建造许多万吨级码头，吞吐能力在全中国也是屈指可数的。莆田的自然人文景观也很丰富，在这里你可以饱览九鲤湖的胜景，还可以领教正宗南少林的拳脚功夫。

Dialogue—Guanghua Temple

Bill: I hear that Guanghua Temple has a long history of printing Buddhist scriptures in China.

Deborah: That's true—but Guanghua deserves this privilege. As you can see from this column, it has a long history of translating and printing scriptures.

Guanghua Temple

The two granite columns in front of the temple's main building have ancient characters that shed light on not only the ancient translation of Buddhist scriptures from Hindu to Chinese, but also on the origins of the ancient Putian and Xianyou dialects.

Guanghua Temple, which was built in 558 A.D., is today one of Fujian's largest monasteries, with over 300 monks and students. They also have a pagoda that appears to be sinking, though in fact the ground around it is rising because of the surrounding hills' erosion.

No one contests Guanghua's claims to being an ancient source of sciptures, but Southern Shaolin Temple, which claims to be the origin of this unique martial art, has some stiff competition with Fuqing and Quanzhou.

Whether Southern Shaolin Kung Fu originated in Putian or not, the city certainly has a very ancient heritage of martial arts, and the temple has become a Mecca for martial arts enthusiasts and each year attracts delegations from all over the world.

Putian has many religious sites, but of course the most important one is Meizhou Island, birthplace of Mazu, goddess of the sea. We'll visit Mazu in the next episode of Magic Fujian.

♪现场

潘维廉：听说莆田广化寺是中国为数不多的几个授权能印行佛教经书的寺庙？

郑芬：是的。只有广化寺才能担此盛名！你看,从这根古石柱，就可以看到广化寺翻译与印刷经书的悠久历史。

Hi-tech Monk
(Guanghua Temple)

♪解说

广化寺大殿门口的这两根石柱上至今仍完好地保留着古代铭文。这些铭文不仅是研究早期梵文汉译的珍贵资料，也是考究莆田与仙游地区古方言的难得素材。

莆田广化寺建于公元558年，是福建省目前规模最大的寺庙之一。寺内有僧人和佛学弟子300多名。广化寺的释迦文佛塔塔身看上去似乎还在不停地下沉，实际上却是由于山体水土流失，致使四周地面上升而造成的错觉。

Still churning out books

广化寺是“中国古经书发源地”。对此，人们没有任何争议。然而，关于南少林的发祥地，莆田就遭遇了来自本省福清、泉州两座城市的强力挑战。不管正宗的南少林功夫是不是出于莆田，莆田的武术底蕴从古至今绵延深远。莆田南少林也因此成为武术迷的圣地，每年都有世界各地的武术爱好者不远千里前来拜师学艺。

当然，在莆田，还有许多与宗教信仰有关的名胜古迹，其中最重要的就是海上女神妈祖的湄州祖庙了。关于妈祖，我们将今后的节目中详细叙述。

Episode 37 Mazu—the Sea Goddess

Introduction Most know Mazu as the sea goddess, but not everyone knows she was ancient China's great feminist! So join us on today on Magic Fujian as Xiamen University MBA's Dr. Bill Brown, and FJTV's Deborah, take you to Meizhou Island, where Mazu was born over 1,000 years ago.

Dialogue—Silent Baby Mazu

Bill: So Mazu was a real person, right?

Deborah: Yes, when she died she was only 27, about the same age as I!

Bill: Really? And maybe you will be a goddess?

Deborah: I doubt it. I wasn't a silent baby!

Bill: Neither was I?

Mazu was called Mo because she was silent at birth. Who could have imagined that silent baby would, 1000 years later, be worshipped by an estimated 200 million Chinese worldwide.

By the age of eight, Mo could read and recite Buddhist scriptures, and by 12, she could read the mystical "blank book." It was said that those who could understand this book, which lacked both text and pictures,[1] would become deities. She began her career as a full-fledged[2] goddess after the age of 16, when Guanyin gave her a magical talisman that foretold the weather, and people's fortunes. The Trembling Stone in the square of Mazu temple trembled every time she performed a good deed. And after 11 years, and 1,999 good deeds, she announced that she was ready to depart this world. She stepped upon a cloud and soared into the heavens. And she's still flying high today—but on people's laps, in airplanes, as her followers take her idols back and forth between Meizhou Island and the rest of the planet.

Dialogue

Bill: So these nice little idols awaiting for their ceremony, right?

Deborah: Yes. A Meizhou granny is elected to hold the ceremony, and then these idols will be sent out to , Malaysia, Hong Kong, Taiwan, Singapore—

Bill: —and also to Vancouver and Los Angeles!

---

[1] A blank book? They must have done a lot of "reading between the lines!"

[2] Full-fledged: fully developed, full status, mature

第 37 集　海上女神妈祖

导语

大多数人都知道“海上女神”妈祖，但知道妈祖是古代中国杰出女性维权者的人并不太多。双语系列报道“老外看福建”今天将由厦大 MBA 中心的潘维廉博士和我们的记者郑芬带领大家去妈祖诞生地——福建莆田的湄州岛。

现场

潘维廉：历史上，妈祖确有其人，是吗？

郑芬：没错。妈祖仙逝时，年仅 27 岁，差不多就我这个年纪。

潘维廉：也许你也会成为一个女神？

郑芬：不可能。我出生时可一点都不沉默！

解说

妈祖姓林名默，据说是因为出生时不哭不闹而得名。没有人会想到，这个默默无闻的小孩，千年之后会拥有世界各地约 2 亿的信众。

林默天资聪慧，8 岁时能熟读经书，12 岁时已能读懂“无字天书”。据说能读懂天书的人，就会得道成仙。16 岁那年，林默遇观音，得到一件神奇的法宝，能预知天气，帮人卜卦。此后，林默便真正成为女神，救人济世。据说，妈祖每完成一件善事，妈祖广场上的心动石便会抖动一下。11 年后，林默完成了 1999 件善事，便“羽化升天”。直到如今，妈祖还飞翔在高空中呢——信徒们捧着她的塑像，坐着飞机来往于湄州岛和世界各地之间！

现场

潘维廉：这些都是准备开光的妈祖像吧？

郑芬：是的。就等岛上选出一位德高望重的老奶奶，来主持开光仪式。然后，这些妈祖像就被请到像新加坡、马来西亚、香港等地的妈祖分庙去。

潘维廉：甚至到加拿大的温哥华和美国的洛杉矶！

Step, belch, step, belch...

Over the past 1,000 years, people from humble fishermen to famous officials like General Shilang and Admiral Zhenghe credited safe journeys or success at war or business to Mazu's intervention.

Even today, Meizhou Island is visited by hundreds of thousands of Mazu devotees from all over the world, and especially from Taiwan, where 2/3 of the population worship Mazu. Mazu worship is one of the many close ties between Taiwanese and Fujian. Even the day we visited, we met two groups of Taiwanese worshippers. I wondered why one group of worshippers belched every few steps, and was told it was to expel unclean things from their body.

China's 5th International Mazu Cultural Festival, held in November, 2003, attracted tens of thousands of Mazu worshippers. They engaged in traditional religious ceremonies, as well as other activities.

Traces of Mazu worship can even be seen in Meizhou Islander's daily life. Some women still show their respect for Mazu by wearing the Mazu hair style, in which hair is coiled on the back of the head like a ship's sail.

In addition, virgins wear red trousers, in memory of Mazu's red pants. Wives wear trousers that are half red and half black, and widows' trousers are entirely black.

Our female Putian guide told us, with much pride, that in a sense, Mazu liberated Putian women, giving them equality with men. And as we saw in the Mazu temple, three goddesses are enthroned in the center, while the great men are standing on the sidelines! Even today, Putian women still have the upper hand; I just hope my wife doesn't follow their example.

Mazu Palace
Potala-on-the-Sea

♪解说

在过去的一千多年里，妈祖香客，上至诸如施琅将军和郑和这样的政府官员，下至普通渔民，都会把出海平安、生意成功、战场凯旋这样的盛举归功于妈祖的保佑。

如今，来自世界各地成千上万的妈祖信徒每年都要到莆田湄州岛妈祖祖庙进香，其中又以台湾香客居多。台湾三分之二的人口信奉妈祖，妈祖信仰也由此成为联系闽台两地的纽带。在湄州岛拍摄的当天，我们遇上了两拨来自台湾的香客。我搞不清楚他们为什么每上几步台阶就要大口吐气。旁人告诉我，他们是在借妈祖的神力“吐故纳新”。

Mazu Holy Water

2003 年 11 月，莆田湄州岛举行第五届中国妈祖文化旅游节，吸引了上万名的妈祖信徒。旅游节期间，除了传统的祭祖仪式外，还有其他各式各样的活动在岛上举行。

在湄州岛上，你还可以从居民的日常生活中发现妈祖信仰的痕迹。为了表达对妈祖的敬仰，有些妇女将头发梳成“妈祖头”，发髻高高盘在脑后，酷似渔船的风帆。此外，为了纪念妈祖终身未嫁，岛上的未婚女子都效仿妈祖穿红色的裤子。已婚女子是半红半黑的裤子，寡妇则是全黑的裤子。

Mazu “Boat” hairstyle

给我们做导游的莆田女子不无骄傲地告诉我们，在某种意义上，妈祖解放了莆田妇女，让她们享受到男女平等的待遇。看来的确如此！在妈祖庙内，我们看到，3 位女神高高端坐在大殿中央，而所有的男性神像则恭敬地立于大殿两侧。据说，现在莆田的家庭里仍然是女子做主。我希望我的妻子可别跟她们取经。

Episode 38 Putian—City of Lychee

Introduction Welcome to today's episode of Magic Fujian as Xiamen University's Dr. Bill Brown and FJTV's Deborah tell us about the Putian, one of China's richest fruit baskets, and home of one of Putian's famous ancient women, the fabled Cherry Queen.

Plum Queen

Plum Queen Jiang Caiping, the Plum Queen, was a Tang Dynasty beauty who rose from humble duck herder to imperial concubine. But life can be the pits even for a peach. Yang Yuhuang, one of China's legendary ancient beauties, was so jealous that she had Lady Jiang exiled to Shanyang palace, where she threw herself into a well, and died.

The Pukou Palace was erected in her honor in her native town of Jiangdong, and even today, millions enjoy Puxian Opera, which the legendary beauty is said to have created. Alas, the Plum Queen is gone—but today Putian has a veggie queen!

Veggie Queen On February 26, 2001, People's Daily told the story of Lin Shuiying, a 49-year-old woman whose family has farmed in Putian for many generations. Before the 1980s, she made ends meet by growing rice on 2 hectares of rented land, but when the rice market was saturated, ends no longer met. Fortunately, China's reform and opening up gave farmers freedom to choose their own crops and markets, and Ms. Lin chose to export vegetables! Ms. Lin rented 200 hectares near Aoshan village to grow tomatoes, peppers and eggplants, many of which are exported abroad, thanks to USD 60,000 invested in hydroponics. In 2000, she sold over 10,000 tons of produce to Russia alone. But Putian is most famous, both at home and abroad, for its fruit, and the city even has a fruit research institute!

Each year, Putian exports millions of dollars of fruits to countries all over the world. The fruit is shipped fresh, frozen, dried, canned, or bottled as juices, and the variety of fruits available staggers the imagination, but Putian's nickname of "Lychee City" suggests that the king of Putian fruit is the lychee, which is so popular that the trees have even been introduced to the United States and to S.E. Asian countries.

Lychee Lovers The famous modern poet, Guo Muoruo, wrote, "No place in Putian is without lychee trees." Grown mainly along the lower reaches of the Mulan River, Putian has over 20 varieties. Putian folk love lychees so much that they even stir-fry the fruit! Of course, the ultimate lychee lover was the imperial concubine whose demands led the emperor to set up a pony express from South China to the capital so she could get her favorite fruit fresh, daily! Which just proves that even Emperors were henpecked!

第38集　荔城莆田

Pukou Palace

导语

欢迎收看双语系列报道“老外看福建”。在今天的节目中，厦门大学的潘维廉博士和我们的记者郑芬将继续带我们游历莆田，这个中国最丰盛的果篮之一，同时也是中国古代传奇人物——唐朝梅妃的故里。

解说

梅妃原名江采苹，是唐朝的一大美人。她的前半生就是灰姑娘故事的翻版：从卑微的牧鸭姑娘变成唐明皇的宠妃。莆田一带流行的 “莆仙戏”据说与这位才貌双全的梅妃有关。不过，“自古红颜多薄命”。杨玉环入宫后，对梅妃心怀嫉妒，设计将梅妃贬入冷宫。“安史之乱”中，梅妃投井自尽。为了纪念梅妃，莆田江东村的父老乡亲为她修建了浦口宫。古时候的梅妃已经香消玉殒。但如今，莆田却出了个“蔬菜女皇”！

2001 年 2 月 26 日，《人民日报》刊发了关于莆田妇女林水英的报道。这位林姓妇女世代务农。20 世纪 80 年代前，她承包了 30 亩土地，种植粮食作物，勉强维持家庭生活。粮食市场饱和后，林家开始入不敷出。幸运的是，中国的改革开放给了农民自主权。他们可以自由选择自己想要种植的农作物。林水英选择了蔬菜，并做起了蔬菜出口生意！

林水英在鳌山村附近承包了 300 多亩土地，种植西红柿、胡椒和茄子。同时又贷款 6 万美元，引进无公害蔬菜营养液，产品大多销往海外市场。2000 年，仅出口俄罗斯的农产品就超过一万吨。莆田出名，靠的是水果，市里还专门有一个水果研究所提供技术支持。

莆田水果每年出口创汇都在几百万美元以上。这些水果通过保鲜、冷冻、烘干、罐装或瓶装，销往世界各地。莆田出产的水果品种之多，足以考验你的想像力。当然，莆田号称“荔城”，荔枝就是果中之王。荔枝很受欢迎，甚至连美国和东南亚国家都纷纷从莆田引种荔枝。

中国著名的现代诗人郭沫若曾写下“荔城无处不荔枝”的诗句。莆田荔枝有20多种，主要种植在木兰溪下游。当地人爱吃荔枝，甚至还把荔枝炒了吃！当然，说到吃荔枝，谁也比不上杨贵妃。“一骑红尘妃子笑，无人知是荔枝来。”可见，就连皇帝也难免会患上“妻管严”。

Dialogue—Lord of Lychee Trees

Deborah: This is the oldest lychee tree in Putian, over 1,000 years old!

Bill: Really? I heard that this is the tree that soldiers tried to cut down for firewood?

Deborah: Yes, and since then the lychees have all had a slash reminding us of the one branch that was cut off.

Bill: Well, Putian locals guarded this tree with their lives, but it doesn't look like anyone is caring for it now.

Over the past 1,000 years, this ancient tree, which was called "Song Jiaxiang (宋家乡), meaning "Song Dynasty Hometown," has witnessed Putian's development into one of China's major fruit producers.

But sadly, it is now neglected, surrounded by weeds and shadowed by a new high—rise. A worker said he had not seen anyone tend the tree in over a month. I hope the City of Fruit will give this historical treasure the care and respect it deserves—and erect a display so visitors can understand the role that this ancient tree has played.

现场

郑芬：这就是莆田最古老的荔枝树，有上千年的历史了。

潘维廉：就是那棵险些被乱兵砍去当柴火烧的荔枝树吗？

郑芬：不错。从此以后，这棵荔枝树上结出的果实都有一个凹道，酷似当年被砍的刀疤。

解说

千百年来，这棵名为“宋家乡”的荔枝树见证了莆田成为中国重要水果产地的历史。如今，它长在杂草丛中，被高楼所遮挡，没人管理，实在可惜。据公园里的一位工人说，最近一个多月，他没见到任何人来关心过这棵荔枝树。我希望“水果之乡”莆田能够珍惜并妥善保护这棵古老的荔枝树，并在这棵荔枝树旁立块牌子，让游人了解这棵荔枝树的来历。

Episode 39 Xianyou—Nine Carp Falls and Dream Praying

Introduction Have you ever dream prayed above nine flying carp? On today's episode of Magic Fujian, Xiamen University MBA's Dr. Bill Brown and FJTV's Deborah will show you how!

A Fishy Practice

Dialogue—Fishy[1] Practices

Bill: So why on earth would they hang a carp in a temple?

Deborah: Carps are everywhere in China, because they are symbols of good fortune.

Bill: Sounds fishy to me, but I'll take your word for it.

If carp symbolize good fortune, then Xianyou's Nine Carp Falls must be the luckiest place in Putian. And when you take the wonderful but winding mountain drive between Putian City and Xianyou, it is easy to understand why Chinese say that Fujian is 8 parts mountain, 1 part water and 1 part fields. The mountains, valleys and plains are a feast for the eyes—and for the ears as well, with a peaceful silence rarely found in the cities.

Xianyou's Nine-Carp Falls, which has captivated Chinese for over two millennia, gets its name from the tale of the nine Han Dynasty brothers who spent their lives developing pills of immortality and then flew to heaven on nine carps. Nine-Carp Falls cover ten kilometers, and the longest cascade is 100 meters. But our visit followed a long dry spell so the river bed was fairly dry. We were told that on weekends, officials release water from the dam upriver so tourists can enjoy the falls' beauty, rain or not.

Xianyou is also famous for caves, over 100 I'm told, though Chinese' idea of cave is different from ours. We think of caverns, whereas a Chinese cave might be a crack between two boulders, above which an ancient inscribed some saying like "Heavenly hole."

Dream Praying Prep

Dialogue—Dream Praying Culture

Bill: Is this where the monks sleep?"

Deborah: No, this is where the pilgrims do the dream prayer.

Bill: Dream praying?

Deborah: Yeah, want to try it?

Bill: Well, I've never heard of praying that way, but I'll try!

---

[1] Fishy: suspicious, unusual, odd

第 39 集　仙游：九鲤湖胜景与祈梦风俗

导语

你可曾试过在飞翔的九只鲤鱼背上边做梦边祈祷？在今天的双语系列报道“老外看福建”中，厦门大学 MBA 中心的潘维廉博士与我们的记者郑芬将给您做做示范。

现场

潘维廉：中国寺庙总喜欢在堂前挂只金属的鲤鱼，这究竟是为什么呢？
郑芬：因为在中国，鲤鱼是幸运的象征。所以，鲤鱼随处可见。
潘维廉：听起来怪怪的，不过还是权且听你的吧。

解说

如果鲤鱼象征幸运的话，那么仙游的九鲤湖应该是莆田最幸运的地方了。驱车从莆田市区前往仙游，沿途山路崎岖蜿蜒。福建“八山一水一分田”的说法也就不难理解了。险峰、峻岭和平地构成的无限风光令人大饱眼福，同时也大饱了“耳”福，因为山间的那种宁静是城市生活中很难找寻到的。

2000 多年来，仙游九鲤湖迷住了无数的中国人。九鲤湖名字的由来与汉朝九兄弟的传说有关。据说，九兄弟在九鲤湖修炼，得长生药，乘九尾鲤鱼升天而去。九鲤瀑布层层叠嶂，延绵十余里，最大的一幅瀑布落差上百米。可惜，我们造访时正值枯水期，河床干枯。导游告诉我们，要是周末，管理人员会从上游开闸放水。这样一来，不管是晴天还是雨天，游客都能观赏到瀑布奇观。

仙游的洞穴也颇有名。据说多达 100 来个。不过，中国人的洞穴含义与我们不同。我们所说的洞穴通常是指地质意义上的深洞。但在中国人眼里，两块巨石间的缝隙就是洞穴。上面通常都写上了“仙洞”之类的雅称。

现场

潘维廉：这是和尚们睡觉的地方吧？
郑芬：不，这是供香客祈梦的地方。想不想试一试？
潘维廉：我可从没在梦中做过祈祷，不妨一试！

According to Putian people, China's unique "dream praying culture" began over 2,000 years ago here in remote Xianyou. Each day, monks lay out straw mats, blankets and pillows in the "Dream Praying Temple" overlooking the Nine Carp Falls. Pilgrims then bed down in hopes that the local deities will give them guidance and answers to prayer in their dreams.

The temple at Nine Carp Falls is unusual in that it has both Buddhist and Taoist deities, so dream praying is not limited to one religion. In fact, we found that pilgrims to Meizhou Island also engage in dream-praying, in the hopes that Mazu will appear to them. Similar practices are also found among native Australians, Native Americans, and other peoples around the world.

Xianyou Woodcarving

Xianyou Woodwork Whether inspired by dreams or by the beautiful natural surroundings, Xianyou people are obviously an imaginative people, as is seen in their beautiful woodcarvings and handicrafts. Wooden carvings are found throughout Fujian, but Xianyou is unusual for the high percentage of people working as woodcarvers, as well as for the high quality of their work, which is recognized throughout Asia.

In the 1950s, Beijing used Fujian's Hui'an stonemasons to build Tiananmen. Likewise, when Taiwanese need master woodcarvers to renovate its temples, they seek master carvers from Xianyou.

Xianyou is heaven for woodcutters because of the vast forests surrounding the town. The locals also put their endless bamboo forests to good use. The ancients wrote that it is better to live without pork than without bamboo, which Chinese have found over 1,000 uses for. I marvel every time I see craftsman, using nothing but bare hands and a sharp curved blade, transform a common strip of bamboo into elegant tables, chairs, bookshelves, cups, bowls, garden rakes—even rocking chairs.

A bamboo craftsman proudly showed me his wares, and exclaimed, "This fits snugly inside another one—perfectly round. And durable too!" But like others, he lamented that people nowadays prefer plastic over bamboo, even though bamboo is cheap, durable, aesthetic, and, most importantly nowadays, all natural and biodegradable. Bamboo craftsman work long and hard, and make little for their efforts, so it is no wonder that few of their children follow in their footsteps.

I hope measures can be taken to preserve this unique Chinese art, as well as the many other unique crafts, customs and traditions unique to our province.

解说

莆田人告诉我们，中国独特的“祈梦文化”2000多年前就起源于仙游偏僻的九鲤湖。九鲤湖畔的祈梦殿内，和尚们每天都会备好草席、毛毯和枕头。香客们沉沉睡去，期盼神灵在睡梦中给他们解惑释疑。

九鲤湖的寺庙还有一个特别之处就是道佛合一。这也表明，祈梦就不止局限于某一种宗教。事实上，在湄州妈祖庙内，我们也发现有祈梦的做法，香客们希望在梦中妈祖会向他们显灵。类似的祈梦风俗在澳大利亚和北美的土著人以及世界其他地方也是常见的。

人杰地灵也罢，受梦境启发也罢，仙游人显然极其富有想像力。这可以从他们制作的木雕和各种手工艺品得到印证。在福建，木雕工艺随处可见，但仙游的与众不同之处在于，从事木雕的人口比例很高，而且手艺很好，闻名亚洲。

20世纪50年代，北京大修天安门时起用福建惠安的石匠。同样，台湾翻修妈祖庙，必定要到仙游找木匠大师。

仙游城乡四周森林密布，简直就是木雕艺人的理想天堂。仙游人也把当地丰富的竹林资源利用得淋漓尽致。中国古人曾说，“宁可无肉，不可一日无竹”。中国人迄今已经发现竹子的用途上千种。每回见到手工艺人单凭灵巧的两只手，辅以一片锋利的弧刀片，就能把普通的竹片变成桌子、椅子、书架、杯子、碗、耙子，甚至摇椅，我都感到惊奇不已。当然，竹子也是一道好菜——这倒不足为奇，因为在我看来，中国人几乎是无所不吃的！

Craftsman--a vanishing breed

一位竹匠自豪地向我展示他的手工艺品。他说，把一件竹器套入另外一件竹器，不会变形，而且结实耐用！不过，跟别的手艺人一样，这位竹匠也感叹道，竹子虽然便宜、耐用、美观，而且还很环保，但现代人却更喜欢用塑料制品。尽管辛苦劳作，可竹匠们的收入并不高。难怪很多手艺也就这么后继无人了。

我希望政府部门能够采取切实、有效的措施，保护福建这些特有的中国工艺以及其他许多福建独特的风俗习惯和文化传统。

Episode 40 Xiamen International School

Introduction In today's episode of Magic Fujian, Dr. Bill and Bobby Bao join up with Xiamen International School students and staff, who tomorrow will take the foreign children on a school field trip to the Hakka roundhouses.

Dialogue

Bobby: When you first came to China, what was the situation of education here?

Bill: Well, there was no quality international school like this until about 7 years ago, I think it was. The only choice that we had was to send our children to Chinese school. Chinese schools are good, but they weren't quite appropriate for our needs. And we still stuck it out, but a lot of people considered coming to Xiamen to do business here and to live here, and in the end they didn't come, because didn't have good schooling for their children. Foreign families, when they move here with their families, they want to make sure of two things: good education, good health care. It's very important.

Our #2 son Matthew is very outgoing, and after years of Chinese nursery school and kindergarten was thrilled about going to 1st grade. But Matt was the only foreign child in the school, and every child wanted to be his friend. As he cried one day, "There is only one of me and so many of them." After a few weeks, he was begging to stay home from school, so we used a correspondence program from an American school with 100 years experience at distance learning. But such programs take great discipline from both parents and students. That's why XIS was welcomed by the foreign community.

XIS Headmaster Rob Leivelee: We are a school that's six years young. It is a private school. It's a non-profit organization. But very, very astutely, in my opinion, municipal authorities here in Xiamen about eight years ago began a very serious study about what kind of assets should a city like Xiamen have in order to attract international Fortune 500-type companies. And one of the things their research showed quite clearly was the presence of an international school makes it much, much easier for a company to locate its headquarters or one of its main branches in its city.

第 40 集　厦门国际学校

导语

1997 年 9 月 8 日正式成立的厦门国际学校，是福建省首家由国家教育部批准的外籍人员子女学校。在 2003－2004 学年，学校的在册学生人数比上学年整整翻了一番。今天的系列报道“老外看福建”，让我们跟随厦门大学的潘维廉教授，一同到厦门国际学校去看一看。

现场

包东宇：您刚来中国的时候，这里的教育状况怎么样？

潘维廉：当时厦门还没有专业的国际学校，直到七年前还是这样。外国人只好把子女送到中文学校就学。中文学校虽好，但却不能完全满足我们的需要。我们一家是坚持了下来，不过好些准备来厦门经商和居住的外籍人士最后却没有来，因为他们找不到合适的学校让子女就学。外籍家庭在迁移的时候都会考虑两大条件：良好的教育和完备的医疗。这一点非常重要。

解说

我的次子马太性格外向，在中国的托儿所和幼儿园呆了几年之后，他对进入一年级感到很兴奋。可马太是学校里唯一的外国小孩，每个孩子都想跟他交朋友。有一天他终于受不了了，大叫道：“我只有一个人，而他们却有那么多人！”几个星期之后，他央求呆在家里不去上学，于是我们只好让他改读一所有着上百年远程教育经验的美国学校提供的函授课程。不过，上这样的函授课程，父母和学生都必须付出大量精力。正因为如此，厦门国际学校的出现受到了厦门外籍社群的欢迎。

现场

包东宇：我感兴趣的是，你为什么不把孩子送进中文学校读书。

潘维廉：其实，他们本来是想上中文学校的。可是一方面有语言障碍，全中文的教学难度较大，另一方面，中文学校的课业负担很重，那样他们就没有时间学习西方课程了，而这些课程对他们将来去美国读大学是很必要的。此外，作为学校里唯一的外国孩子压力也是很大的。因此，现在来到厦门的外籍家庭很幸运，他们可以把孩子送到国际学校读书。

采访（厦门国际学校校长若博·勒维力）

若博：我们的学校很年轻，只有六年的历史。它是一个私立学校，一个非盈利性的组织。厦门市有关部门大约在 8 年前进行了一项慎重的研究，研究的课题是，厦门应当具备怎样的硬件条件，才能吸引像《财富》500 强那样的跨国公司。研究得出的显著结论之一就是，拥有一所国际学校，对跨国公司在这里设立区域总部或者重要的分支机构非常有利。

Xiamen Kodak approached former Mayor Hong Yong Shi and asked him to help push through an international school for expatriate families, and the school was started in 1997. I don't know how many companies the school has influenced in coming to Xiamen, but I remember a representative of General Electric phoning me saying they were considering Xiamen, but wanted to first be sure Xiamen had a quality school for expat children.

XIS shared facilities with Xiamen Yingcai School for the first four years, and moved into its new, state of the art facility in August, 2002. And it has been one of the fastest growing schools in the area.

XIS Headmaster Rob: Last year at this time, for example, when I arrived as Xiamen International School's brand new headmaster, we had just over 120 students. By the time our academic year ended, we had almost 180 students. And then when we began this academic year, we had just under 200. We anticipate that before this year is completed by June, we'll probably have as many as 250 to 275 students. And within the next 3 to 5 years certainly, we'll have anywhere from 400 to 600 youngsters.

For Xiamen to truly be an international city, it must meet the needs of the international community, and quality education is fundamental. Now that XIS has quality facilities, and a fully accredited American—model curriculum, more companies are confident in sending foreign families to live here.

XIS offers a pre-K through grade 12 rigorous, American modeled curriculum and is fully accredited with the Western Association of Schools and Colleges. The International Baccalaureate Organization's Middle Years Program and Early Year's Program was introduced in the 2002-2003 school year with plans to introduce the Diploma Program as growth allows. At present, the school has twenty-five credentialed, expatriate teachers and administrators, and ten certified, native faculty members. According to the headmaster Dr. Rob Leveilee, the school will have to triple its size within the next 5 years to cope with the rapid growth.

Dialogue—XIS Students Get the "China Bug"[1]

Bill: The students that graduate from here from what I understand are really topnotch scholars, and they've gone into some of the best universities in America and other places. But one of the things I was happy to hear today is one of the students graduated, good students, and stayed in Xiamen for another year. He went to Xiamen University to study Chinese for a year before going back home. So I like that, it looks he has plans after college to come back to China.

Bobby: They want to develop their career here?

---

[1] Bug: contagious virus or illness (in this case, they're "addicted" to China)

♪解说——

厦门柯达公司向当时的厦门市长洪永世提出，希望市政府能够帮助建立一所外籍人员子弟学校。1997 年 9 月，学校正式成立。我不清楚这所学校曾经促使多少公司决定进驻厦门，不过我还记得，曾经有一位通用电器公司的代表给我打过电话，说他们正在考虑投资厦门，但首先要确认厦门是否拥有可供外籍员工子女就学的优秀学校。

在最初的四年中，厦门国际学校与厦门英才学校共用校舍和教学设施，2002 年 8 月，才正式迁入目前崭新漂亮的新校舍。现在，它是当地发展最迅速的学校之一。

♪采访（厦门国际学校校长勒维力博士）——

去年这个时候，当我来到厦门国际学校接任校长职位时（2002 年），我们只有 120 多名学生。一学年下来，我们学生的数量接近了 180。然后，新学期一开始，学校的在校生已经接近 200。我们预计，到六月份新学期结束时，我们的学生数量大致会在 250～275 名之间。预计在未来 3～5 年内，我们的学生人数肯定会达到 400～600。

♪解说——

厦门要真正成为一座国际性城市，就必须满足国际社群的需求，而优质的教育就是一项基本条件。正因为厦门国际学校拥有一流的教育设施和经过认证的美式课程体系，越来越多的跨国公司放心地把外籍员工家庭送到厦门。

厦门国际学校提供从学龄前开始直至 12 年级的完整的美式基础教育体系，并且已经获得西方院校联合会的全面认证。在 2002－2003 学年，学校已经采用了国际学位组织（International Baccalaureate Organization）的小学教纲和中学教纲，今后还计划引入证书课程。目前，学校拥有 25 名持有教师证书的外籍教师和行政管理人员，还聘任了 11 名资深的中国教师。校长勒维力博士介绍说，随着学校的快速发展，在五年之内，校园的面积要增长两倍才能满足需要。

♪现场——

潘维廉：据我所知，从这里毕业的学生大多进入了美国和世界各地的一流大学继续深造。今天我还听说了一件很令人高兴的事，据说有些优秀的毕业生毕业以后又在厦门多呆了一年。他们在回国之前，先到厦门大学学习一年的中文。看样子，他们在读完大学之后还要回到中国来。

包东宇：他们是想在这里发展自己的事业吧？

XIS Driver Wu Ci Wei(吴慈慰) and his Homemade Dragon

Bill: Well, I think anybody that lives in Xiamen for a year or two is going to get it in their blood, and have a heart for China. And I think the student is smart enough to see that the future is in China. My two boys plan on coming back, they are going to go back to America for college, but both say after college they are coming back to China.

Prior to coming to Xiamen, XIS Headmaster Dr. Rob Leveilee had enjoyed international administrative posts in the American International School of Australia, the International School of Beijing, and Shanghai American School. XIS is lucky to have him, because he chaired many accreditation teams and knows how to whip a school into shape.

One requirement for accreditation is that international schools help students understand their host country. XIS students are lucky in that regard. What country has a longer history or more cultural diversity than China?

To help students better appreciate China, XIS has taken students on various field trips around the province, and to athletic activities in other areas of China.

Dancing with Dragons

潘维廉：我想，每个在厦门住过一两年的人都会爱上这里，都会对中国怀有感情。这些学生能够看到中国未来发展的前景是很明智的。我的两个儿子都准备回美国上大学，他们都说，大学毕业后要回到中国来发展。

解说

在接任厦门国际学校校长之前，勒维力博士曾在澳大利亚美国国际学校、北京国际学校和上海美国学校担任过高级管理人员。他还曾经在秘鲁阿塔卡马沙漠的一所学校当过校长。在承担国际职务之前，勒维力博士曾在美国国内的马萨诸塞州和新罕布什尔州做过学校主管，并与新英格兰院校联合会关系密切。厦门国际学校能够拥有他是很幸运的，因为他知道应该如何打造一所优秀的学校。

要想通过国际认证，国际学校必须帮助他们的学生认识所在的国家。厦门国际学校的学生们很走运，有哪个国家比中国历史更悠久、文化更多样呢？

厦门国际学校经常组织学生到福建各地进行实地考察，还参加在其他省市举行的体育赛事，以帮助学生们更好地了解中国。

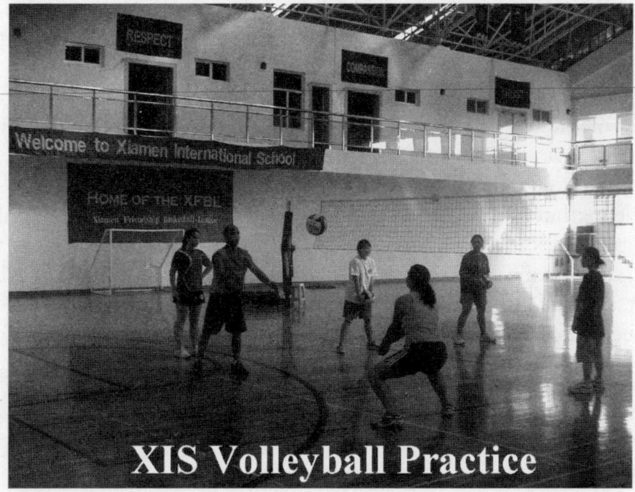

XIS Volleyball Practice

Supplementary Reading Five

These Are the Magi[1] (Gift-giving in China)

The Art of Chinese Gift-giving It is written that the wise men who brought gifts to the Christ child came from the East.[2] I suspect they meant China, because 1) you can't get any further East than China, and 2) Chinese have raised giving to an art form.

Our first Christmas in China, our elderly dean gave our two sons a toy electric car that set him back at least a week's wages. Two months later, on Chinese New Year, a teacher gave each of our sons a Hongbao (Red Envelope) stuffed with 100 rmb—a small fortune by that teacher's standards. Any doubts on the importance of gifts in China vanished when I read Lesson 38 in, "Modern Chinese Beginner's Course." The correct response to an impromptu invitation to a Chinese friend's home was, "But we haven't brought any gift."

Gift—giving rituals vary around China. Tibetans give a white silk scarf, while Hainan Islanders place a lei[3] of flowers over guests' shoulders. In Xiamen, the most common gifts are bags of fruit or packages of our local Oolong tea.

Xiamen folk avoid giving odd numbers of gifts. It must be two bottles of Chenggang medicinal wine, not one or three bottles, or 4 boxes of Tiekuanyin tea, never three or five. The gifts must be proffered respectfully with two hands, and accepted with two hands.

Americans have no qualms in giving an inexpensive gift or card to convey a sentiment because "it's the thought that counts."[4] But not in China, where face is everything, and a small or trifling gift may be worse than no gift at all. Conversely and perversely, the larger the gift, the more face for both parties. Over the years, our face has been lifted more times than Elizabeth Taylor's.[5]

---

[1] Magi: plural of magus (wise man, magician sorcerer; see note 18)

[2] Bible, Matthew 2:1-12;; the wise-men were probably astrologers from Persia or southern Arabia, both of which are east of Palestine, where Christ was born.

[3] Lei: Hawaiian word for a garland of woven flowers worn around the neck

[4] It's the thought that counts: the sentiment or feeling is more important than the cost

[5] Elizabeth Taylor: famous aging American actress rumored to have had numerous face-lifts

补充读物（五）

他们就是给耶稣送礼的东方智者
——中国人的送礼术

送礼的艺术

据载带礼物给耶稣的智者来自东方，我想他们指的是中国，原因有二：一是中国在最东边，二是中国人已将送礼变成一种艺术。

我们在中国的第一个圣诞节，我们的系主任送给我们两儿子一个玩具——电动汽车，至少花了他一星期的工资。两个月后，春节时，有位老师给我们的儿子每人一个红包，每个100元——这对他而言是一笔不小的财富。当我学了“现代汉语入门”第38课，我意识到送礼的重要性，心中所有的疑虑顿时一扫而光。若有人突然间邀请你去朋友家做客，你应该说：“我们没带礼物。”

送礼的方式各地有所不同。藏民送白色的哈达，海南人给客人脖子上戴花环。在厦门，最常见的礼物是水果或当地盛产的乌龙茶。

厦门人送礼忌单数。应送两瓶沉缸药酒，而不能一瓶或三瓶；四盒铁观音，不可以三盒或五盒。送礼时应毕恭毕敬两手捧着礼物，收礼时双手接受礼物。

美国人在送不贵重的礼物或送贺卡表达某种情感时则没有考虑方式，他们认为最重要的是一份心意。但在中国却不是这样，面子是最重要的，一份微不足道的小礼物还不如不送。礼物越大，双方的面子就越大。这些年来，中国人给我们面子的次数比伊莉莎白泰勒还多。

Anxi villagers bring get-well gifts
(4 hours by bus, with a live chicken!)

Guests have materialized on our threadbare[6] astroturf welcome mat with 50 bananas, or 30 pounds of roasted Longyan peanuts, or 15 pounds of freshly caught fish, or 4 dozen freshly fried home-made spring rolls. We've protested, futilely, that 50 pounds of bananas will rot before we can finish them off. In the end, we either go on banana binges[7] or make a quick pilgrimage to a Chinese colleague's home with a second-hand gift of bananas, tea, dried mushrooms or fresh fish. They probably pass them off too, but somewhere down the line some soul has to heave 50 pounds of bananas down the hatch.

Where's the Beef?[8] We had some knotty experiences until we learned the ropes[9] of Chinese gift giving. Shortly after we moved into Chinese professor's housing, Susan baked chocolate cake, which at that time few Xiamen folk had tried. She gave our neighbor a couple of slices to sample, and the astonished granny thanked her profusely and shut her door slowly, politely. Next morning, bright and early, she rapped on our door, and thrust a plate full of beef in Sue's face. She said, "For you," and beat a hasty retreat, ignoring Susan's protests.

"This is terrible, Bill," Sue said. "She should not have done that."

"This is great, Sue." I retorted. "Two pounds of beef costs a lot more than two slices of cake. Think how much we'll save on meat if we give cake to all our neighbors." Now I know why Marie Antoinette gave everyone cake.[10]

It is Cheaper to Give Than to Receive[11] Nowadays, we are more careful (though not paranoid!) with gift-giving, because it can be costly for all concerned. Those whom we give gifts feel compelled to reciprocate, whether they can afford it or not. But all things considered, I still think Chinese are the Magi—particularly where family and homeland are concerned.

Giving to the Motherland When overseas Chinese labored in abject poverty in the mines and fields of Africa and Colonial Asia, or to build American railroads, they invariably sent a large portion of their meager earnings home to family. It was these pittances, multiplied a million fold, that kept China afloat when we Westerners were bleeding her dry through the opium trade.

---

[6] Threadbare: worn out (by so many visitors showing up with 50 pounds of bananas)

[7] Binge: a period of uncontrolled, excessive eating or drinking

[8] Where's the beef?: American fast-food chain advertisements ridiculing competitors' burgers for having little beef.

[9] Ropes: specialized details or procedures (originated from sailors' 'learning the ropes' on sailing ships)

[10] Let them eat cake: usually attributed to Marie Antoinette, it was actually used by Rousseau when she was only ten years old.

[11] Cheaper to give than to receive: a variation of Jesus' saying quoted by Paul in the Bible, Acts 20:35

客人来我们家拜访时，他们总是提着50根香蕉，或30龙岩烤花生，或15磅鲜鱼，或 4 打自制的春卷出现在我们家门口的草垫上。我们推辞说，50 磅的香蕉还没来得及吃就烂了。但说什么也不奏效，最终，我们还是收下了，要不来个香蕉狂欢宴，就是赶紧又将香蕉、茶叶、香菇、鱼等转送给别人。他们很可能又送给别人，但是无论如何最终总得有人将50磅吞进肚里。

Taking Bananas to Teacher?

牛肉在哪里?

在我们知道中国人送礼的规矩前，我们有过几次尴尬的经历。我们刚搬进教授楼不久，苏珊烤巧克力饼，那时没几个厦门人尝过，做好后，苏珊送了几片给邻居，隔壁老太很吃惊，连声道谢，轻轻地很礼貌地关上门。第二天一大早，她就敲了我家的门，拿着一大盘牛肉到苏珊的脸前说，“给你”，然后就匆匆离开，不管苏珊乐意不乐意。

“好恐怖，比尔，”苏珊说，“她不应该这样。”

“这很棒，苏。”我说。“两磅牛肉可比两片饼干贵多了。想想如果我们给每个邻居送饼，那我们可以省多少肉钱！”

现在我终于明白为什么玛丽·安冬尼奥给每个人饼干。

送礼比收礼便宜

现在我们送礼时很小心，因为会让双方破费。我们一送礼，对方就觉得要回礼，不管是否能负担得起。不过，总的来说,我仍然认为,中国人就是带礼物给耶稣的东方智者,特别是提及他们的家族和祖国。

回报祖国

无论是在非洲和亚洲殖民地的矿井和田地里,还是在美国修建铁路，赤贫的中国人总是辛勤劳作，一点一滴赚取他们的血汗钱，尽管收入少得可怜，他们还是将大部分的收入寄回家。正是这些点点滴滴微薄的薪资汇集在一起，才使得中国得以度过鸦片贸易，不至于被西方列强榨干。

"Free for the foreign friend!" she said.

Some laborers became industrial magnates, like Tan Kah Kee, and donated millions to China. Even today, regardless of political persuasions, overseas Chinese continue to remit millions annually not only to their mainland relatives but to local governments to build schools, colleges, orphanages, and roads.

Chinese, rich and poor alike, are a generous people. A lowly mason who lives in a shack nearby gave me 5 pounds of freshly netted fish because he heard my in-laws were visiting from America. A disabled, retired campus laborer shows up occasionally with fresh greens from his garden, or new flowers for our yard. When word got around that I wanted a stone mill to grind wheat, several peasants headed to the rural stone quarries, and we were blessed with not one mill but three (never again will I take wheat for granite).

The mason, the disabled laborer, the peasants, sought nothing in return. They because we were friends—like the poor bicycle repairman who repeatedly insists, "It's a small thing. Pay me when you have a real problem to fix." The man's entire world is but a tiny, dusty shop only 8 feet wide and 4 feet deep. Greased bike chains and sprockets, rims and tires and tubes, bike seats and pedals hang from nails on the walls. His furniture consists of two bamboo stools, one for himself and one for customers, and a bamboo footstool that doubles as a table for his cheap tea set, which he sets up every time I stop by. He has spent more serving me tea than he will ever make from fixing my battered bicycle.

Chinese have always given sacrificially to family and their immediate community, but charity beyond that was rare, for it was seen as depriving family and local community of scarce resources. But times are better now, and Beijing is seeking to widen the scope of giving.

Half a dozen programs encourage wealthier urbanites to help their less fortunate and far more numerous comrades in the countryside. Every year, "Project Hope" (希望工程) allows millions of urban Chinese to help fund poor rural children's education. And "Helping Hand" pairs up city kids and country kids, who write to each other and exchange gifts.

有些劳工最终变成工业巨头并捐了大笔的钱，如陈嘉庚。即便到了现在，海外中国人仍不停地往中国寄钱，不仅给亲戚，还给当地政府修建大中小学校、孤儿院和道路。

中国人，无论贫富，都很大方。有个泥瓦匠，住在破烂的小屋里，听说我岳父母一家从美国来看我，马上送了我5斤新鲜的鱼。厦大的一位老工人，已退休，身有残疾，时不时往我家送他自己种的蔬菜和鲜花。一听说我想要一个石磨，好几个农民跑到乡下采石场，结果我们有了3个而不是1个石磨。从此,我再也不敢想当然,把麦子当作花岗岩了。

泥瓦匠，残废的工人，农民从未想过回报。他们送我东西因为我们是朋友——正如一位穷自行车修理工，坚持说："这是小事。你的车有大问题时再付我钱"。他的世界很小，只不过是一个仅有8尺宽4尺深的小店。满是油污的自行车链条、链轮齿、车轮、轮胎、作艺、脚踏板挂在墙上，家具只有两张竹凳和一个竹脚凳，竹凳一张他自己用，另外一张给客人；脚凳又被他当作茶几使用，每次我路过，他便摆上廉价的茶具，招呼我喝茶。

他招待我喝茶花的钱比帮我修理那破烂不堪的自行车赚的钱还多。

过去人总是对家庭和家族很慷慨，对外却较少给予资助，否则会被视为剥夺了家庭和其所在社区本来就很贫乏的资源。现在情况已有所好转，中央政府正在寻求路子做大慈善事业。

中国开展了好几个项目鼓励较富裕的城市居民帮助成千上万更为不幸、更为贫穷的乡下人。每年，希望工程能让数百万的中国人资助贫穷乡村儿童上学，让城市儿童与乡村儿童结对子，相互写信和交换礼物。

Episode 41 Nanjing's Hakka Roundhouses

Introduction In today's episode of Magic Fujian, Dr. Bill Brown and Bobby join Xiamen International School on a field trip to the Hakka Roundhouses in southern Fujian's Nanjing County.

Dialogue—The Pentagon & Roundhouses

Bobby: Dr. Brown, I heard that the Pentagon was pretty upset when they saw the first satellite photos of the Hakka Roundhouses.

Bill: Why was that?

Bobby: Because they thought they were missile silos!

Bill: Hah-hah, well, they would. Well I don't know about the military, but tourists sure like these roundhouses.

Bobby: The Hakka roundhouses are becoming a very hot tourist destination now.

Bill: Yeah, very popular, in China and the rest of the world, actually, [these] earthen houses.

Fuxing Castle

Nanjing has over 1700 square earthen houses and almost 400 round ones. It would take a lifetime to visit them all, so I've narrowed my itinerary down to a few favorites. But my favorite roundhouse is Prosperity Castle (Fuxing Lou) in Nanjing's Chizhou Village. Fuxing Lou is home to 4 generations, just over 200 people, ranging from babies to octogenarians.

Fuxing Lou was built in 1963 by the Xiao (肖) Clan. I asked how much it cost to build it and the man said, "Nothing! The wood and earth were all local, and the labor was our own. But we could not build a house like this nowadays because the trees are protected."

I told the Fuxing residents that I knew the true reason that roundhouses are round—to keep wives from getting their husbands in a corner. They laughed and said, "That's probably true!"

Each floor has a different purpose. The first floor is for cooking and working, and the central courtyard is sometimes used to dry grain. Grains are stored on the second floor, and grandparents live there. Younger people live on the upper 3 or 4 floors. They've sure designed these roundhouses well, but I think they forgot one thing. They need a basketball court in the center.

第41集　南靖客家土楼

导语

正在申报“世界文化遗产”的福建土楼主要包括永定、南靖、漳浦等地的土楼，其中南靖县是土楼建筑数量最多、保存最为完好的地区之一。系列报道“老外看福建”，今天让我们随潘维廉教授和厦门国际学校的师生一同到南靖土楼去走一走。

现场

包东宇：我听说五角大楼当初曾经对客家土楼的卫星照片大感震惊！

潘维廉：为什么？

包东宇：因为他们认为那是导弹基地！

潘维廉：哈哈，难怪！我不知道土楼会有什么军事用途，不过我知道，土楼确实很受游客的喜爱。

包东宇：客家土楼现在已经成了旅游热点之一。

潘维廉：是啊，土楼已经名扬世界了。

解说

南靖县有1700多座方土楼和400多座圆土楼。如果要全都参观一遍，恐怕一辈子的时间都不够用，所以我通常都把参观线路锁定在几座自己喜欢的土楼。我最喜欢的一座就是南靖书洋乡赤洲村的福兴楼。福兴楼里四代同堂，生活着200多人，既有吃奶的婴儿也有八十老妪。

福兴楼1963年由肖姓族人建成。我曾经问他们建楼花了多少钱。他们说，一分钱也没花，泥土和木料都是就地取材，肖家人自己出的劳力。可是现在不让随便砍树了，所以再建土楼就很难了。我曾经跟福兴楼的居民们开玩笑说，我知道土楼建成圆形的真正用意，是为了避免妻子把丈夫逼到墙角。他们都被逗笑了。

土楼里每一层的功能都有所不同。一楼是烹调和劳动的地方，中央的天井可以用作晒谷场。谷物储存在二楼，老人们也住在二楼，年轻人则住在三楼以上。我觉得土楼设计得相当完美，就是有一点没有考虑到：他们应该在土楼中央留个篮球场。

Dialogue [looking at dried vegetable in the courtyard]

Bill: Tea? Soup?

Student: Yeah, it's for soup.

Bill: So, you guys like this?

Student: What's this?

Bill: Bamboo shoot? In Changting in the west of the province, the very west, they sell this dry bamboo shoot. It's very famous. I said to the lady in the store, this was the best hotel there, She said, "This is great quality, export!" I said, "But you know, this is bamboo shoots, ands it says 'Mushrooms." You need to change it." She said, "It doesn't matter. Any idiot can see its bamboo shoots!"

No Basketball Court?

The Hakka's round earthen fortresses are one of the most unique types of architecture on the planet. For one thing, they are quakeproof, fire-resistant, and extremely durable. Ten are over 600 years old, and one is 1200 years old. Because they are built with local earth, wood and bamboo, they are not only inexpensive but also very aesthetic, blending into the environment rather than clashing with it. The thick walled houses keep warm in winter and cool in summer, and block outside noises. Occupants of roundhouses say the homes have a coziness not found in any other kind of house. It reminds me of J.R.R. Tolkien's hobbits, who loved their earthen caves. "It was a hobbit hole, and that means comfort." There is probably no home more comfortable or cozy than an earthen home.

Earthen architecture is used all over the world now, because it has so many advantages—especially when made with new techniques that make it more durable, strong and waterproof. Even my home of California has earthen architecture, because the adobe houses of the Southwest are earthen homes.

Earthen architecture is gaining popularity worldwide because it is so environmentally friendly. Builders don't have to waste energy on transporting materials, and upkeep is minimal. In addition, rammed earth is not only recyclable but also uses only 1/700th the energy necessary to fire bricks!

Because of its many advantages, earthen architecture is now used around the world for everything from simple homes to luxurious mansions, large hospitals, universities, churches and cathedrals, hotels—even holiday resorts. The 4 Star Kooralbyn Hotel Resort in Queensland, Australia was designed entirely with earthen buildings.

现场

潘维廉：这用来泡茶？还是煮汤？

学生：煮汤的吧。

潘维廉：你们认识这个吗？

学生：这是什么？

潘维廉：是竹笋吧。在福建最西部的长汀，这种笋干在当地很有名。在当地最好的宾馆里，一位女售货员对我说，这个质量很好，是出口产品。我对她说，这是笋干，可包装上写的却是香菇啊，你们应该改一改。她说，没关系，傻瓜都知道这是笋干。

学生：（大笑）哦，你在取笑我们！

解说

客家土楼是世界上最为独特的建筑形式之一。它们不但防震、防火，还很耐用。有十座土楼历史在600年以上，有一座甚至已经有1200岁了。因为土楼都是利用当地的粘土、木材和竹子等材料建成的，所以不但成本低廉，还兼具美感，能够跟周围的环境融为一体。厚重的土墙让土楼冬暖夏凉，还能隔绝外界的喧嚣。土楼人家认为，土楼里的那种安逸是别处无法比拟的。这让我想起托肯恩笔下住在泥土洞穴里的哈比人。“那是个哈比人的洞穴，也就是说很舒服。”也许，再没有比土房子更舒适安逸的住房了。

生土建筑目前在世界各地仍然得到广泛应用，因为它具备了诸多优点，尤其是一些新技术让它更加防水、更加坚固耐用。我的家乡加利福尼亚也有生土建筑，加州西南部的土砖住房就是土质建筑。

因为具有环保的特点，生土建筑在世界范围内都受到推崇。建筑者不需要为运送建筑材料耗费大量能源，而且维护费用也可以降到最低。此外，墙体使用的夯土不但可以循环使用，能耗更只是烧砖的七百分之一。

正因为生土建筑具备这么多的优点，所以世界各地都可以见到它们的影子，从简单的民房到豪华的大厦、医院、大学、教堂、旅馆，应有尽有，甚至还有度假村。澳大利亚昆士兰州四星级的库伦滨度假农庄就完全是用生土建成的。

Episode 42 Yongding Roundhouses

Introduction On today's episode of Magic Fujian, join Dr. Bill and Bobby Bao as they explore why and how the Hakka built their earthen fortresses—an architectural style so unique that China has applied for them to be listed under UNESCO World Heritage Status.

The Hakka earthen fortresses are one of the world's most unique forms of architecture, and so fascinating that I've visited these unusual dwellings at least 30 times, often taking a van load of foreign visitors, or of my Chinese MBA students, since many are from other provinces and have never had the opportunity to visit Yongding. In the past, I always took my guests to roundhouses that are still inhabited so they can experience Hakka life, and I left the so-called official sites for tourists—but since my last visit to Yongding I've decided that the stunning new Hakka cultural village is a mustsee on any earthen house itinerary!

Round W.C.

Dialogue—Hakka Cultural Village

Bill: I am really amazed. So much change since the last time I was here!

Bobby: The local government has spent a lot of time and money creating this Folk Cultural Village.

Bill: I notice they tore down all the modern buildings. They were real eyesores. But now, even the bathroom over there, the W.C. is like a roundhouse!

Bobby: And this is all part of the move to list the Hakka Earthen Houses as a World Cultural Heritage.

Bill: I hope they succeed.

This new Hakka theme park is one of the best laid out cultural attractions that I've seen in China, and includes not only several large earthen houses, but also an old Mazu temple, and two large, wooden waterwheels on the river. Even the tastefully designed tourist reception center reinforces rather than detracts from the overall theme. It's obvious that some professionals put a lot of thought into the park, with meticulous care given to everything from the roundhouse W.C.s to the rubbish bins carefully crafted to resemble tree stumps!

Across the nicely maintained lawn is a massive square earthen house that has only recently been renovated. I especially appreciated the beautiful woodwork on the railings and stairs.

第42集　永定土楼

导语

今年 6 月份，福建土楼申报世界文化遗产将进行表决，目前，土楼申报世遗的工作进展顺利，在厦门大学美籍教授潘维廉看来，经过精心整治的永定土楼景区是游客不可错过的绝佳景点。在今天的系列报道“老外看福建”中，我们就到闽西的永定县去看一看。

解说

客家土楼是世界上最为独特的民居建筑形式之一。我参观这些迷人的奇特建筑的次数不下 30 次。我来永定的时候，通常都是开着自己的面包车，里面载满了老外或者我的 MBA 学生，这些学生大多来自外省，从来没有机会见识土楼的风采。过去，我总是把客人带到那些还有村民居住的土楼中，让他们能够体验客家人的日常生活，至于那些所谓的“正式景点”，还是留给别的游客去看。不过，最近一次的永定之行让我改变了想法。我发觉，经过精心整治的永定客家土楼文化村绝对是任何土楼旅游线路都不能错过上佳景点。

现场

潘维廉：这里的变化真大，太让人吃惊了！

包东宇：为了搞好这个客家土楼民俗文化村，当地政府可花了不少的时间和财力。

潘维廉：我发现他们把所有和土楼景观不协调的现代建筑都拆掉了。现在这里就像一个客家土楼公园，连公厕都是土楼的外形！

包东宇：其实这些工作都是客家土楼申报“世遗”的步骤之一。

解说

这个崭新的客家主题公园是我在中国所见的规划最为完美的文化景观之一。这里不仅有数座风格各异的土楼，还有一座古老的妈祖庙，以及河边那两台巨大的木制水车，甚至连旅游接待中心也是别具匠心的设计，不但没有打破景观的和谐，还为整个景区增色不少。很显然，这个公园的建设中一定倾注了不少专家的心血，每个细节的处理都有周到的考虑，不但公厕具有土楼的风格，就连垃圾桶都巧妙地设计成树桩的形状。

穿过精心护养的草坪，你可以看到一座刚刚经过修葺的巨大方形土楼。我特别欣赏楼内走廊围栏和楼梯扶手上面优美的木雕。

As we toured the grand old building, a resident added to the atmosphere by playing traditional Chinese instruments, like the flute and the zither.

Hakka earthen houses come in every shape and size imaginable, including square, rectangular, triangular, pentagonal, and even octagonal. And in more remote areas, where Hakka had fewer neighbors, they even built one-storey dwellings that were only half-enclosed, and were nicknamed "cow-horn villages". But round earthen houses, like the imposing Zhencheng Lou, are the most popular with tourists.

Dialogue—Zhengcheng Lou

Bobby: You know, the Zhengcheng building is probably the most famous Hakka roundhouse.

Bill: Why, is it the oldest one?

Bobby: No, less than 100 years old. But it's the best preserved one, and is like a museum of Hakka Life.

Bill: Well, I like museums, so let's check it out. And who knows, maybe the tour guides are beautiful Hakka maidens!

Inside Zhengcheng Bldg.

The Zhencheng Earthen Castle was built in 1912 and has two concentric circles. The outer circle has 48 rooms on each of four floors, and the inner circle has 30 rooms on two floors. An ancestral hall with four massive granite pillars dominates the central courtyard, which is surrounded with rooms that once housed kitchens but are now souvenir shops offering books, miniature models of earthen houses, and local handicrafts.

At first glance, Hakka earthen architecture appears simple enough, but in fact the methods are quite sophisticated. The massive walls use "bones" of bamboo, which are then fleshed out with a mixture of earth, glutinous rice, and other materials. It's quite complicated, and as earthen architecture becomes increasingly popular around the globe, experts on earthen architecture are in great demand, and Yongding is becoming a Mecca not just for tourists but also for international architects. Scientists, of course, have been toying with new materials, technologies, and techniques, but many have come to the conclusion that, with earthen architecture at least, the old ways are the best.

Enthusiasts claim that earthen architecture produces the most practical, durable, aesthetic and comfortable of dwellings, but you judge for yourself! Spend a day in the Yongding Hakka Earthen House Cultural Center, where expert guides will show you how earthen houses are made, and what life is like in them. And after a hearty meal of Hakka cuisine, bed down for the night in a down-to-earth earthen hostel. Who knows? You might return home to build your own earthen home!

当我们走进土楼的时候，一位村民正在演奏笛子、古筝之类的中国传统乐器，为这座庞大的古老建筑增添了不少韵味。

客家土楼具有许多种外形和大小，除了圆形外，还有正方形、矩形、三角形、五角形，甚至还有八角形。在一些更为偏远、人烟稀少的地方，客家人还把土楼建成半圆形的平房，这种形式俗称为“牛角村”。不过，旅游者最为钟爱的还是圆形的土楼，雄伟壮观的振成楼就是个很好的例子。

现场

包东宇：振成楼恐怕是最有名的一座土楼了。

潘维廉：它是最古老的吗?

包东宇：不是，不过它是保存得最为完好的之一，就像一座客家风情博物馆。

潘维廉：哦，我很喜欢博物馆，我们这就进去瞧瞧吧。也许里面的导游是漂亮的客家妹子呢!

解说

振成楼始建于 1912 年，分为内外两环。外环四层，每层都有 48 个房间，而内环则有两层，每层各有 30 个房间。土楼中央的天井里有一座由四根巨大的花岗岩石柱支撑的祖祠，祠堂周围的房间原本是用来圈养鸡鸭的，如今都改成了纪念品商店，售卖旅游书籍、土楼模型和当地特产。

乍一看，客家土楼似乎很简单，其实这种建筑模式相当复杂。土楼厚重的外墙以竹片木条作为骨架，然后在粘土中加上糯米、红糖和其他材料，一起夯实。土楼的建筑过程相当繁复，其中蕴含着许多先进的建筑工艺，而在世界范围内，生土建筑一直经久不衰，于是永定不但成了游人关注的焦点，更成为世界各地建筑师朝圣的圣地。当然，建筑专家们总是致力于新材料、新技术和新工艺的研究。不过，至少在生土建筑方面，他们大多都得出了相同的结论：老方法还是最好的。

行家们声称以生土建筑作为住宅最为实用，不仅舒适，而且经久耐用，美观大方。不过，你最好还是自己体验一下！花一天时间到永定客家土楼文化中心，那里的讲解员会详尽地给你解释土楼是如何建成的，土楼里的生活又是什么样的。在饱餐一顿客家家常菜之后，你可以找一家最具乡土气息的土楼住上一宿。说不准，改天你要回家去自己建土楼了！

Episode 43 The South China Tigers of Meihua Mountain

Introduction The South China Tiger is one of the most endangered species in the world. Less than 100 of the tiger are living wild and in the zoos. On today's episode of Magic Fujian, We follow Xiamen University's Dr. Bill Brown to visit the rare South China tigers of Meihua Mountain!

West Fujian's Meihua Mountain (梅花山) Nature Reserve is a wonderland of waterfalls, rolling wooded hills, strange peaks, and breathtaking caverns, as well as home to almost 1500 kinds of plants and hundreds of varieties of reptiles, birds, and animals, including 40 endangered species like leopards and black bears. But its most beloved resident is the rare South China tiger.

Dialogue—Tigers Make a Comeback

Bobby: You know, the South China Tiger is considered as the ancestor of all tigers!

Bill: It's too bad they're almost extinct. Even into the 1930's they lived in Xiamen. Now the only place they're probably living is here and in zoos.

Bobby: Well, the tiger preservation program will help them to have a comeback.

Bill: I hope so! They've already had two tigers born here!

South China Tigers used to be so widespread that in the early 20th century an American found one in her backyard on Gulangyu Islet! Unfortunately, over recent decades tigers almost vanished as they were slaughtered for their pelts, bones, claws, and organs. Fortunately, in August 2000, West Fujian's Longyan City launched a $17.6 million USD tiger protection project that may be the key to the tiger's survival.

Dialogue—Tiger Cubs Born

Bill: On July 2001, Zhongzhong and Qiuqiu were born here, and since then four more tiger cubs have been born.

Bobby: Yes. We hope that by the year 2010, the population will reach 100.

Bill: Well, it has doubled from six to twelve already, so they're doing pretty good. What do they use? Maybe Viagra for tigers?

Bobby: Hah, I don't know. But they have already invested over $17 million US Dollars.

Bill: So they are pretty determined.

第 43 集　梅花山华南虎

导语

华南虎是中国特有的虎种，现存数量不足 100 只，甚至比大熊猫还要珍稀。近年来，位于龙岩梅花山的华南虎繁育研究所攻克了原野式环境中散养华南虎成功繁殖的难题，为华南虎保护带来希望。系列报道“老外看福建”今天带您同潘维廉教授一起，到梅花山中国虎园去领略“兽中之王”的雄风。

解说

福建西部的梅花山自然保护区内山峦耸峙，层林叠翠，山中到处是流泉飞瀑和奇峰怪洞。这里生长着 1500 多种植物和数百种昆虫和鸟兽，其中包括 40 多种濒危物种，如金钱豹和黑熊等等。不过这里最有名的居民要数珍稀的华南虎了。

现场

包东宇：据说华南虎是最原始的虎种。

潘维廉：可惜它们已经到了绝种的边缘。过去厦门岛上就有野生华南虎，可现在恐怕只有这里有了。

包东宇：梅花山的华南虎保护项目也许能帮助它们重振雄风。

潘维廉：但愿如此！他们已经在这里繁育了几只小老虎。

解说

20 世纪早期，华南虎曾经遍布江南各地。鼓浪屿上的一位美国人就曾在自家的后花园里发现过一只！不幸的是，在最近的几十年间，华南虎几乎销声匿迹了。然而值得庆幸的是，2000 年 8 月，闽西的龙岩市正式启动了一个总投资达 1760 万美元的华南虎繁育野化项目，这对华南虎的保护至关重要。

现场

潘维廉：2001 年 7 月，中中和秋秋在这里诞生，此后，又有几只虎崽相继出生。

包东宇：没错，按照规划，到 2010 年，这里的老虎将达到 100 只。

潘维廉：是吧？现在中国虎园的老虎数量已经翻了一番，看来他们为老虎研究出了特效药？

包东宇：这我可不知道。不过，他们已经为这个项目投资了几千万元！

潘维廉：看来他们是铁了心的。

Been in the catnip?

Very Big House Cats I was astonished at the sheer size of South China Tigers, which can reach up to 400 pounds and over 8 foot in length. Even the cubs born only two years ago were gigantic! And even though they looked like over grown house cats, and yawned contentedly just inches away from me, behind the wire fence, an angry snarl reminded me that these are indeed very wild creatures! It also reminded me of the delicate predicament for tiger preservationists.

Since Zhongzhong and Qiuqiu's births in 2001, four more cubs have been born, giving the preserve a population of 12 tigers. At that rate, they may well reach their goal of 100 tigers by 2010. But tigers need to roam, and though man is a danger to tigers, tigers are also quite a danger to man. I have a Chinese friend whose aunt was killed by a South China Tiger only 40 years ago—and not very far from Xiamen! Needless to say, my friend is not overly keen on tiger preservation. Hopefully Fujian authorities will find a way to insure the survival of both tigers and people!

Gutian Congress After leaving Meihua Mountain, we passed through the neighboring Gutian Town, where we saw tour buses and cars parked in front of what looked like an old farmhouse. I was curious what made it so special.

Dialogue—A Single Spark

Bobby: This former primary school was where Mao Zedong helped preside over the Gutian Congress in 1929.

Bill: Wasn't West Fujian also where the Long March started?

Bobby: Yes, one of the starts. Bill, do you know the famous sentence that Mao Zedong wrote while he was in Western Fujian?

Bill: Yeah! He wrote "A single spark can start a prairie fire!"

Bobby: You are right!

In Dec. 1929, the Fourth Troop of the Red Army held its conference in this elementary school, which was originally built in 1848 as the Liao family's ancestral hall. The sign above the school reads, "The Eternal Radiant/Glory of the Gutian Conference." Nearby is the Gutian Congress Exhibition Hall, which is Fujian's largest revolutionary museum. Built in 1974, it has over 7,303 historical relics.

I rented a revolutionary uniform from a couple outside the school, and posed for photos as I waved the flag back and forth. But even as I played at being solider, I thought of the real soldiers who fought and died here only decades ago to bring about the New China that nowadays we pretty much take for granted. We should never forget that had it not been for their sacrifices, Chinese would have suffered a fate worse than that meted out to tigers.

解说

华南虎的体型惊人，它们可以长到 300 多斤重，两米多长。只有两岁大的幼虎就已经身形庞大！虽说它们看上去就像长得过大的家猫，还在铁丝网那边离我只有几英寸远的地方慵懒地打着呵欠，可一个突如其来的咆哮提醒我，它们其实是很有野性的动物。同时我也意识到，保护老虎可能还会遇到另外一个困境。

从 2001 年开始，有 6 只幼虎在虎园里出生，目前中国虎园的老虎数量已经超过 10 只。按照这个繁殖速度，2010 年虎园的“虎口”达到 100 只应该没有问题。不过，老虎要有自己的生存空间，虽说人对老虎是个威胁，老虎对人也是不小的威胁。就在 40 年前，我一个中国朋友的姨妈就在离厦门不远的地方被老虎咬死了。不用说，我这个朋友对保护老虎可不会过分热心。希望有关部门能够找到一个让人虎和谐共存的两全之策。

从梅花山上下来后，我们途径附近的古田镇。我看见一座老房子附近停了不少旅游巴士和小汽车，原来那就是著名的古田会议旧址。

现场

包东宇：过去这里曾是一所小学。1929 年，毛泽东就在这里主持召开了著名的古田会议。

潘维廉：闽西是红军长征的起点，对吧？

包东宇：没错，是长征出发地之一。

包东宇：潘教授，你知道毛泽东曾在这里写下的那句名言吗？

潘维廉：当然知道。是“星星之火，可以燎原”嘛！

解说

1929 年 12 月，红军第四军在上杭古田的这所小学里召开大会，这所小学原先是廖氏宗祠，始建于 1848 年。古田会议旧址背后的山坡上竖着一排大字——“古田会议永放光芒”。不远处的古田会议纪念馆是福建省最大的革命历史博物馆。纪念馆成立于 1974 年，里面陈列着 7300 多件文物。

在古田会议旧址外面，我向一对夫妇租了一套红军军服，然后摇动红旗摆姿势照相。在扮成红军战士的时候，我想到了那些几十年前在这里为了新中国而战斗过的先烈们。我们永远都不应该忘记，没有他们的流血牺牲，也许中国人民还会在虎口中生活更久。

Episode 44 Liancheng's Guanzai Mountain

Introduction Join us on today's episode of Magic Fujian as FJTV's Bobby Bao and Xiamen University's Dr. Bill Brown explore the natural beauty of Liancheng.

Ancient Fujian's Information Technology! Longyan, in the West of Fujian, is famous both for its historical and cultural sites as well as natural attractions. Longyan is considered the birthplace of the Chinese revolution. And almost 1000 years ago, it was a center of the earliest revolution in information technology!

Liancheng's Sibao was one of ancient China's four famous printing centers, thanks to the wide availability of camphor forests for printing blocks, endless bamboo reserves for paper making, palm fibers and animal furs for brushes, and pine trees, which were burned to provide the soot for making ink. By the late 1700s, over 100 families, fully 60% of some villages' populations, produced and sold books that were well acclaimed throughout China.

Longyan's poets, philosophers and statesmen probably got their inspiration from the area's unparalleled natural beauty. Longyan has such attractions as Longkong Caverns, which has a grand hall that can hold 1,000 people, and Fushi Town's 10,000 square meter subterranean lake. But of all Longyan's sites, the most famous by far is the beautiful Guanzai Mountain region in Liancheng, a 123 sq. k. natural preserve that got its name because one peak resembles an ancient Chinese kings' hat.

Dialogue—Guanzai's Surrealistic[1] Scenery

Bobby: Guanzai Mountain has attracted philosophers and artists for many centuries.

Bill: It's no wonder. The mountains and lake look like something lifted right out of a Chinese painting. I used to think the ancient artists were drunk when they painted like this. But it's real. Of course, maybe they were drunk anyway.

I used to think the ancient Chinese landscape artists were either drunk or high on something other than altitude, but Guanzai's mountains really do resemble Chinese paintings. No wonder that for 1,000 years, the serenity of Guanzai Mountain drew scholars and leaders seeking solitude and inspiration. And today, Guanzai draws boatloads of tourists.

---

[1] Surrealistic: having an odd, dreamlike, unreal quality

第 44 集　连城冠豸山

导语

刚刚扩建完工的福建连城冠豸山机场将于今年 3 月份正式开航，这将大大增加连城及周边地区旅游客源市场的半径。在今天的系列报道“老外看福建”，我们和厦门大学的潘维廉教授一起，来认识闽西连城的神奇山水。

解说

福建西部的龙岩不仅古迹众多，而且风景秀丽。闽西被称为中国革命的摇篮，而在数百年前，这里还是早期“信息革命”的一个中心。

连城的四堡是中国古代四大雕版印刷业中心之一。附近丰富的樟木可供制作印刷雕版，满山的竹林则是造纸的原料。棕榈丝和兽毛可以制成毛笔，而松木燃烧后产生的煤烟则被用来制墨。到 18 世纪后期，当地经营书坊的人家多达上百家，有些村子从事印刷的人口占到 60%。四堡印刷的书籍畅销全国各地。

古往今来，闽西的神奇山水引发了无数文人墨客和政治家的激情与灵感。龙岩新罗区有龙硿洞，洞内最大的大厅可以容纳上千人。永定县抚市镇的仙湖洞也有个上万平方米的地下大厅。不过，龙岩的各大景区中，要数连城的冠豸山名声最响了。冠豸山风景区面积 123 平方公里，因为一座山峰形似古代的獬豸冠而得名。

现场

包东宇：千百年来，冠豸山吸引了许多文人和艺术家。

潘维廉：一点儿也不奇怪。这里美丽的湖光山色仿佛就是一幅中国水墨山水画卷。

解说

我曾经认为中国古代的画家在作画时，不是喝醉了酒，就是有些晕晕乎乎，不过看到冠豸山的时候，我真的觉得那就是一幅水墨画。难怪上千年来，冠豸山能够吸引众多文人和官员前来寻求宁静与灵感。而今天的冠豸山更是游客纷至沓来。

Dialogue—A Mountain of Calligraphy

Bill: You Chinese like climbing the mountains, but I'm lazy. I'll take the boat any day.

Bobby: From the boat you can enjoy some scenery, but you can't see the famous calligraphy.

Bill: Every place has calligraphy!

Bobby: Not like Guangzai Mountain. It has over 100 calligraphy pieces by famous ancient people like Ji Xiaolan and Lin Zexu.

Bill: Lin Zexu? Oh I met him…in a movie when I played the bad guy!

"Root of Life"
(Their name for it-- --not mine!)

The 5 km boat tour of Shimen Lake winds past mountains blanketed in unusual plants and flowers, and home to rare birds and animals. Every rock, hill and cave has a name, of course. My host pointed out the Elephant Playing in Water, or Crazy Monk Weaving a Hat. Some of Guanzai's fantastical peaks and caves so closely resemble human anatomical extremities that they should be off limits to minors. A vertical 60m stone column that locals call "The Root of Life could be the logo for Chinese Viagra!

Songfeng Pavilion, halfway up the endless steps of Lotus Peak, was set amongst cliffhanging pines, flaming red wild azaleas, and aromatic orchids. Vendors sold snacks, drinks, and local handicrafts.

Like virtually every other mountain resort, Guanzai has its 'Crack in the Sky,' as well as a site where yet another deceased Tang Dynasty Taoist concocted immortality pills. But the area has plenty of coffin makers so either the Taoist never figured it out or he kept the secret to himself.

Dialogue—Putting Liancheng on the Map[2]

Bobby: The new Liancheng airport will be a big boost for tourism.

Bill: And not just the airport. There's also the train and the new highway. The first time I drove here from Xiamen took over 10 hours. Soon it will be only 4 hours!

Bobby: Then you can come here every weekend.

Bill: Nah, maybe once a month is okay!

Thanks to the rapidly evolving infrastructure, Guanzai Mountain tourism is booming. And visitors who come during Chinese New Year enjoy an added bonus—the unique Hakka celebrations, such as the world's longest dragon dance, or the Zougushi on Lantern Festival, when children in make-up and traditional costumes are hoisted high on poles and paraded throughout the streets. And if they visit Changting, just an hour West, they can watch Hakka men engage in contests of strength to win the hearts of beautiful Hakka maidens!

---

[2] Put something on the map: popularize it, or make it more accessible

♪现场

潘维廉：中国人都爱爬山，可是我比较懒，喜欢坐船。

包东宇：坐船是可以欣赏到一些风景，不过那样就看不到那些著名的摩崖石刻了。

潘维廉：摩崖石刻我见得多了。

包东宇：冠豸山的可不一样。这里有上百幅古代名人的书法石刻，其中包括纪晓岚和林则徐的作品。

♪解说

石门湖 5 公里的水上游程在披满奇花异草的山峰之间迂回，那里还藏着各种珍禽异兽。当然，每块岩石、每座山峰和每个洞穴都有名字。导游把“双象戏水”、“和尚戴帽”等景点一一指给我看。冠豸山有些奇特的石峰和洞穴跟人体的某些部位非常相似，应当被列为儿童不宜的景点。有一根高达 60 米、垂直耸立的石柱叫作“生命之根”，把它当作中国伟哥的标志倒挺不错。

上莲花峰的半路上有个松风亭，就矗立在缘绝壁而生的松树、火红的杜鹃和芬芳的兰花从中。亭中还有小贩兜售零食、饮料和当地手工艺品。

就像其他的名山一样，冠豸山也有个“一线天”，同样，还有个唐代术士调炼仙丹的地方。我看到附近有不少制作棺材的店家，看来，要么是那道士炼丹失败，要么就是他的秘方失传。

♪现场

包东宇：新扩建的连城机场将大大推动当地旅游。

潘维廉：还有铁路和高速公路。我第一次从厦门开车来冠豸山花了十多个小时，以后恐怕只要四个小时就够了。

包东宇：那你每个周末都可以来了。

潘维廉：每个月来一回好了。

♪解说

随着基础设施的不断完善，冠豸山的旅游越来越红火。如果是在春节期间，游客还可以欣赏到独具特色的客家传统民俗，比如姑田“游大龙”号称世界最长的龙灯，还有元宵节的“走古事”，小男孩身着古装，面画油彩，站在轿顶，由人们抬着在乡间巡游。连城往西一小时车程就是长汀，在那里你还会看到客家汉子为赢得客家妹子的芳心而进行的角力比赛。

Episode 45 Changting—the Little Red Shanghai

Introduction On today's episode of Magic Fujian, FJTV's Bobby Bao and Xiamen University MBA Center's Dr. Bill Brown visit Changting, Fujian's "Little Red Shanghai!"

China's Most Beautiful Mountain Town The famous writer Rewi Alley once wrote that China's two most beautiful small cities were Hunan's Fenghuang and Fujian's Changting, and after visiting Changting I had to agree with him!

Changting is famous for many reasons. For one, it is the Hakka Homeland, and straddles the Ting River, which is the mother river of the Hakka. This 285 km river flows from the Dragon Gate, 31 km outside Changting, past Changting's enchanting Tang Dynasty city walls, all the way to Shantou, on the coast of Guangdong province. In 1929, Mao Zedong wrote, "Red banners leap the Ting River!" Of course, back then the Ting was a raging torrent. Today it's so small I could leap it myself.

Thanks to men like Mao Zedong and Zhou Enlai, who stayed in Changting, the city is also nicknamed "Cradle of the Revolution," and was a starting point of the Long March, hence the nickname "Little Red Shanghai." And if Hakka and revolutionary history are not enough, Changting is also renowned for its Hakka cuisine, which has won national awards. So even though at first glance Changting may appear to be an ordinary little mountain town, it has become one of my favorite places in Fujian. But in Changting, as elsewhere, it helps to have a local share the stories and legends that bring the place to life—and the man who breathed life into Changting was the local photographer, Babushka.

Dialogue–Babushka's Priceless Photos

Bill: Almost all of the Changting photos in my books *Amoy Magic* and *Fujian Adventure* were given to me by Babushka.

Bobby: So many! How much did he charge?

Bill: Not a penny. He said he was happy to help people understand Changting.

Bobby: Well, it's a good thing. You couldn't afford photos like these. They are priceless.

Changting's Babushka

Hu Xiaogang is called Babushka because when he came to Changting from Harbin as a child, he had blond hair, like a Russian. And this Chinese Cossack[1] is quite a character, full of laughter and love of life. He also had a great love for his wife and daughter, whom he proudly introduced to me—though I suspect he is like me—henpecked. He said that when his wife is angry, he follows the husband's time-honored recourse: he flees. He said it always works because by the time he returns she has forgotten why she's angry!

[1] Cossack: people of southern Russia and neighboring Asian countries, formerly famous as cavalrymen.

第45集　长汀：红色小上海

导语

去年的12月26日，是伟人毛泽东110周年诞辰纪念日。随着纪念活动的持续，闽西革命老区再次成为人们关注的焦点。在今天的系列报道“老外看福建”中，厦门大学的潘维廉教授对长汀这个曾经被称作“红色小上海”的闽西古城，产生了浓厚的兴趣。

解说

新西兰作家路易·艾黎曾经写到，中国有两个最美丽的小城，一个是湖南的凤凰，另一个是福建的长汀。在访问了长汀之后，我不由得对此深表赞同！

长汀出名的原因很多，其中一条就是这里是客家人的祖居地，客家母亲河汀江贯穿整个县城。全长285公里的汀江发源于长汀城外31公里处的龙门，从长汀城雄伟的唐代古城墙下蜿蜒流过，然后一路奔流到广东沿海的汕头。1929年，毛泽东写下了这样的诗句：“红旗跃过汀江，直下龙岩上杭。”当然，那时候汀江还是水流湍急，如今正值枯水季节，我自己就可以跃过汀江。

正因为毛泽东、周恩来等革命前辈曾经在长汀战斗、生活过，所以这座小城又被称作“中国革命的摇篮”。长汀是当年红军万里长征的出发地之一，还是中央苏区重要的生产基地，于是她又有了一个“红色小上海”的别称。如果说客家历史和革命故事还不足以说明问题的话，长汀的美食也是名声在外，长汀的客家名菜曾经多次获得国家级奖项。因此，虽说乍一看长汀跟任何普通的山区小城没有什么两样，然而我却越发地喜欢起这个地方来了。跟在其他地方一样，找个本地人分享一下当地的掌故是很有好处的，而这个让长汀在我印象中鲜活起来的人就是当地的摄影师胡晓钢。

现场

潘维廉：在我写的《魅力厦门》和《魅力福建》两本书中，几乎所有有关长汀的图片都是胡晓钢提供的。

包东宇：这么多！那他收了多少钱？

潘维廉：分文未收。他说，他很乐意帮助更多的人了解长汀。

包东宇：这可是件大好事啊。再说，你也付不起这些照片的价钱——它们可都是无价之宝。

解说

胡晓钢被当地人叫作“巴布什卡”，这是因为他小时候从哈尔滨来到长汀，当时他发色金黄，就像个俄国人。胡晓钢有着哥萨克人爽朗的性格，他热爱生活，成天都面带笑容。他对妻子和女儿也是宠爱有加，还自豪地把她们介绍给我——不过我怀疑他跟我一样，都是“妻管严”。他告诉我，当他妻子生气的时候，他就跑得远远的，据说这是丈夫们千百年来摸索出来的绝招。胡晓钢说这一招屡试不爽，因为每次他回到家里的时候，妻子已经忘记了自己为什么要生气。

Personally, I cannot imagine anyone being angry with Babushka for long. He was a delightful guide, and excited to show me every nook and corner of his beloved Changting. First stop, of course, was the Hakka Museum.

Dialogue—Hakka Museum

Bobby: The Hakka Museum gives a great overview of Hakka culture.

Bill: Isn't it also a museum of the revolution?

Bobby: Yes. And it is the former site of the Fujian Soviet government in the 1930s.

Bill: Oh I see. And this gives an introductions here.

Hakka Museum

The site of the Hakka museum was once the place holding official examinations in the ancient times. The history of the architecture could be told from the wooden windows, the stone lion, and even the two trees in the courtyard date back over 1200 years to the Tang Dynasty!

Dialogue

Bobby: You can see the museum is divided into two parts. This side is revolutionary history, and this side is Hakka culture.

Bill: So let's begin with the Hakka culture, coz I remember the Hakka guide is very pretty.

Bobby: Really?

Bill: [We see the Hakka guide] Hi! …What did I tell you!

The extensive Hakka Museum offers valuable insights into the history and culture of the Hakka people. I particularly enjoyed the wall-mounted photographs, many of which were taken by Babushka. The museum also had a broad display of Hakka farm equipment, clothing, furniture, musical instruments—virtually every aspect of Hakka life, including insights on such unique marriage customs as "walking the sieve," where brides step across the threshold onto two rice sieves painted with Taoist symbols. These sieves filter out the bad luck, leaving only the good.

I was especially intrigued by the model of the Hakka village, which I learned was in Tufang, only an hour away, and we were fortunate to be able to visit it the following day.

After visiting the Hakka exhibits on the left, we toured the revolutionary side of the museum, and visited the rooms in back in which the Fujian Soviet government was held, and also where a young martyr was kept before his execution. After seeing what an important role this little town played in pre-Revolutionary history, it was easy to see why it used to be called "Little Red Shanghai." But Little Red Shanghai's importance goes back long before the revolution. In fact, right across the street are lanes that date back well over 1,000 years to the Tang Dynasty, when Changting administered the entire area we now know as the Hakka Homeland.

依我看来，我实在想不出有人会跟胡晓钢长时间闹矛盾。他是个令人愉快的向导，总是不厌其烦地向我介绍他心爱的长汀的每个角落。我们的第一站自然就是客家博物馆。

♪现场

包东宇：长汀客家博物馆对客家文化有全面的展示。
潘维廉：这里同时还是一个革命历史博物馆，对吧？
包东宇：没错。上个世纪30年代，这里曾经是福建省苏维埃政府。
潘维廉：是吗？哦，这里有详细的介绍呢！

♪解说

客家博物馆的所在地又叫“汀州试院”，也就是古时候举行科举考试的地方。从那深褐色的木窗和古朴的石狮子可以看出，这个建筑物的年代已经非常久远，仅仅是院子里那两棵参天古柏就可以追溯到1200多年前的唐代。

♪现场

包东宇：客家博物馆分成两个部分，左边是客家文化展示，右边是革命史部分。
潘维廉：那我们先从客家文化看起吧，说不定还能碰见漂亮的客家妹子导游呢！
包东宇：好啊。
潘维廉：嗨！你好……看，我没说错吧？

♪解说

客家博物馆里的展品包罗万象，让人大开眼界，从这里可以很好地认识客家人的历史和文化。我特别喜欢那满墙的图片，里面有许多都是胡晓钢的作品。展厅里还陈列着不少客家人传统的农具、衣饰、家具和乐器，展示了客家人生活的方方面面，其中就有对“过米筛”这一独特婚俗的介绍。“过米筛”就是让新娘在迈进门槛的时候踏上两张贴着道符的筛子，寓示着筛去晦气，留下好运。

展厅里一个客家村落的模型引起了我的强烈兴趣。令我高兴的是，听说这个村落就在距离县城仅有一个小时路程的涂坊乡，我们第二天就可以亲自去看看。

看完左侧展厅的客家文化展示，我们又参观了右侧的革命历史展厅，还拜访了正面的福建省苏维埃政府旧址，在那里，我们还见到了方志敏烈士英勇就义前被关押的房间。了解了这个小城在中国革命史中的重要地位之后，我们就不难理解为什么它会被称为“红色小上海”。然而，“红色小上海”的重要地位实际上远在革命战争年代之前就已经确立了。客家博物馆的街对面就是一片有着上千年历史的唐代古老街巷，当时的汀州，管辖着如今被称为“客家祖地”的整个闽西地区。

Episode 46　Ancient Hakka Changting

Introduction　On today's episode of Magic Fujian, FJTV's Bobby Bao and Xiamen University MBA's Dr. Bill Brown explore the ancient Hakka Homeland of Changting.

Western Fujian's Changting is famous as Little Red Shanghai, but its importance dates back long before the 19th century to the Tang Dynasty, and walking the narrow, cobblestone streets behind the South Gate is like walking back in time 1,000 years.

Changting joined the Chinese Empire during the Han Dynasty, around 2,000 years ago, and the little mountain town is today an archaeological treasure trove, with such treasures as the Tang Dynasty Sanyuan Gate Tower, the 1,000-year-old Confucian temple, and the beautiful Tang Dynasty city wall that flanks the Ting River.

Dialogue

Bobby: It's hard to believe that this area is over 1,000 years old!

Bill: Are any of the buildings that old?

Bobby: No, only a few centuries. But they give a good understanding of the ancient life.

Bill: Well maybe we can visit some of the houses.

Bobby: Of course!

Tang Dynasty Gate

Open Doors　I felt embarrassed as Babushka waltzed right into the local's homes unannounced, without so much as a knock at the door!　Babushka shrugged and said, "If the door isn't locked, we're welcome!"　And sure enough, we were invariably met not with surprise but with "You've come.　Have some tea!"

These ancient homes are like museums, with their intricate stone and wooden carvings and classical architecture.　The courtyards are filled with potted plants, and tools and equipment probably the same as their ancestors used 1,000 years ago, but they work as well as ever, so why reinvent the wheel?!

We learned fascinating things about Hakka culture and customs.　For example, Hakka never bound their women's feet because the women were expected to be hearty enough to work the fields while the entrepreneurial men were away seeking their fortunes.　The robust Hakka women also were known to take up arms and fight off bandits!　Americans say that behind every great man is a strong woman, and that appears especially true about the Hakka.　They have long respected their women, as you can see from the giant statue of the Hakka Mother, which was erected in 1995 to symbolize the Ting River.

But though they did not bind women's feet, the Hakka had other customs that modern girls would not care for.

第46集 长汀：客家首府

导语

去年10月份，第十八届世界客属恳亲大会在河南郑州举行，再次引起人们对客家这一汉民族优秀民系的高度关注。龙岩市的长汀县古称汀州，自古就被誉为闽西客家首府。在今天的系列报道“老外看福建”中，我们和潘维廉博士一起去探询古汀州的客家风情。

解说

闽西的长汀有着“红色小上海”的别称，然而，长汀的重要地位早在遥远的唐代就已经确立了。走在南大街那卵石铺成的狭小街道上，仿佛时光倒流了一千年。

长汀的历史最早可以追溯到两千年前的汉朝。现在，这座山区小城仍然保留了许多珍贵的古迹，比如唐代的三元阁城楼、千年古文庙，以及汀江河畔那雄伟的唐代古城墙。

现场

包东宇：这片街区已经有上千年的历史了！
潘维廉：这些建筑的历史也有那么久吗？
包东宇：它们只有几百年历史，但也能很好的展示古代的生活图景。
潘维廉：或许我们可以找一两间古宅参观一下。

解说

当胡晓钢径直推门进入一户人家的时候，我还觉得有些冒昧，因为他连门都没敲一下！胡晓钢耸了耸肩说：“如果门没锁，就说明我们是受欢迎的。”果然如他所说，我们每到一家，主人都一点不觉得意外，还热情地说：“来了，喝茶！”

这些老房子简直就像博物馆，古典的雕梁画栋精美之极，漂亮的石雕也随处可见，庭院里满是盆栽的花木，各种传统的用具估计还是沿用千年不变的样式，而且还依然那么实用。

我们还了解到一些令人惊奇的客家风俗。例如，客家妇女从不裹小脚，因为客家男子在外闯荡打拼的时候，需要妇女在家全心料理田地。干练的客家女子还以能够操起武器击退土匪而闻名。美国人常说，一个成功的男人背后必定有一位坚强的女人，这句话对客家人来说特别恰当。客家人对妇女一向很尊重，1995年时长汀立起了一座客家母亲像，作为客家母亲河汀江的象征。

虽说客家妇女不绑小脚，不过，还是有些传统习俗对现代的女子来说是接受不了的。

For example, young girls were kept hidden away in a small upstairs room until they were married. Of course, given the legendary beauty of Hakka maidens, I can understand the concern. Still, I wondered what it would be like to be a Hakka maiden spending year after year in that small loft with nothing to look at but roof tiles.

Now repaired!

Dialogue

Bill: You know, the last time I was here, these beams had fallen down completely. Fortunately, the local government spent 3,000 Yuan repairing them.

Bobby: It's good to see they're protecting their ancient heritage.

Many of the ancient homes are in poor repair, but it costs a lot of time and money to keep them up, and Changting is still a relatively poor area. Last time I was here, a resident stopped me when I photographed a fallen beam, but Babushka chided him, "How will the government know of the need if you don't take photographs?" The man said, "That's right. Here—photograph it from this angle!" And, happily, the government did indeed invest money to repair this beautiful old house.

Hakka are famous for many things, but perhaps most of all for being entrepreneurs. The "guest people" have never feared cutting apron strings and heading abroad to seek, and usually find, their fortunes. But those that remain behind are equally entrepreneurial. Almost every home I visited had people engaged in small handicrafts—making tin cooking utensils, or small paper parasols, or matchboxes. And the streets were lined with folk, young and old, selling the famous Hakka snacks, or handmade wooden brushes, or repairing umbrellas and shoes. An industrious people, it's no wonder that they have made a name for themselves the world over. But of all their crafts, I most enjoyed the woodworking.

Dialogue—Changting Woodcarvers

Bobby: Changting is very famous for its wood carvings.

Bill: Yes, Babushka told me that temples from all over S.E. China, from Hong Kong, Macao, Taiwan, come here to get their idols carved.

One master wood carver told me that he enjoyed his craft, which was as much a hobby as a job. But he also lamented that his children had left town to seek their fortunes in other careers. "Woodcarving is a lot of work, for little pay," he said. "You have to love the work, not the money!" Unfortunately, this is increasingly true of many traditional Chinese crafts, like bamboo work, handmade paper, or wooden puppets. Hopefully, China will find ways to preserve these exquisite but vanishing arts.

比如，过去客家女子在出嫁之前，要一直深藏在阁楼上的闺房不许外出。当然，客家妹子以秀美闻名，我可以理解那种殷切的爱护。不过，我还是很难想象客家女子在闺阁中的生活，年复一年面对的只是一片屋瓦，日子该有多难熬。

♪现场 ——

潘维廉：上次我来的时候，这些屋梁已经倒下来了。听说当地政府花了3000元钱来维修它们。

包东宇：这些文化遗产能够得到保护真是件大好事啊。

♪解说 ——

长汀有不少明清古宅已经年久失修，要使它们保持原貌必须花费大量的时间和金钱，而长汀仍然是个经济相对落后的地区。上次来的时候，我正要给一处倒塌的屋梁拍照，一位居民就上前来阻止。胡晓钢责备他说："不让拍照的话，政府怎么会知道这里需要维修呢！"那个人说："没错啊，要拍就从这个角度拍！"令人欣慰的是，当地政府真的花钱维修了这座老房子。

客家人有着许多优良传统，其中最有名的就是勤劳和勇敢。这些"客人"向来敢于到海外闯荡，而且不少都功成名就。而留在家乡的人们同样勤勉能干。几乎我造访的每户人家都有人操着手工活计，不是打锡的，就是造洋纸伞的，或者粘火柴盒的。小街两侧的老老少少，有卖客家小吃的，有制作木刷的，还有修伞的、修鞋的，不一而足。真是勤劳的人民，难怪客家人在全世界都享有盛名。而在所有的手艺当中，我最喜欢的就是木雕。

♪现场 ——

包东宇：长汀的木雕很有名气。

潘维廉：是啊，胡晓钢说，东南亚各地以及港、澳、台等地的寺庙中，都有长汀雕刻的神像。

♪解说 ——

一位木匠师傅告诉我说，他喜欢这门手艺，这是一项工作，更是一个爱好。不过他也不无遗憾地说，他的子女都到外地从事其他工作去了。他说："木雕很花功夫，收入却很少。因此你爱的必须是工作，而不是钱。"很遗憾，许多中国的传统工艺都面临着相同的境遇，比如竹编、手工造纸，还有木偶雕刻。希望中国能够找到更好的方法来保护和发展这些濒临失传、弥足珍贵的手工艺。

Episode 47 Changting's Unusual Religious Sites

Introduction On today's episode of Magic Fujian, FJTV's Bobby Bao and Xiamen University MBA's Dr. Bill Brown visit Changting's unique religious sites, and also sample the heavenly Hakka cuisine.

Web-free Confucius

Like most ancient Chinese cities, Changting has plenty of temples, but Changting is unique in the sheer diversity of religions, as well as the unique stories behind some of the temples. Take the 900-year-old Confucian temple, for example, which has an exact duplicate in Taiwan.

Dialogue—Confucian Temple's Secret

Bobby: Bill, you know they claim this Confucian temple has not had spider webs in about 900 years!

Bill: You're kidding! I'll have to find the secret of this and put it on our "web"[1] site!

Another unusual site is the Changting mountain which has a Buddhist temple at the base and a Taoist temple at the top. Babushka exclaimed, "Rare indeed when Buddhists and Taoists eat from the same plate!"

To the south of town, local Buddhist are building the sprawling Southern Meditation Temple, which last I heard would cost over 50 million Yuan. Each building has its own Buddha, including one carved of pure white jade.

Dialogue—Fantastic Fengshui

Bill: Wow, it looks like they level an entire mountain to build this place!

Bobby: They did! And surrounded by mountains, it has great fengshui.

Bill: This is certainly a gigantic complex.

Bobby: Yes, and when it's finished, it will be the largest nunnery in Fujian.

Miss Mazu's Boudoir[2] I was also surprised to learn that Changting has a very large Mazu temple. In back of the temple is an ornate, exquisitely furnished apartment for the young sea goddess. The temple's caretakers even serve up a fine meal for her several times a day.

---

[1] Web site: spiders spin "webs"; the internet is also called the "web."

[2] Boudoir: woman's bedroom or private dressing room (from the French bouder, meaning *to sulk*)

第 47 集 长汀：独特的宗教胜迹

♪导语

在今天的系列报道“老外看福建”中，我们将和厦门大学的潘维廉教授一同参观长汀的几处宗教胜迹。

♪解说

像中国大多数的古城一样，长汀城里也有很多寺庙。长汀的独特之处在于，这里的宗教场所种类繁多，不少还带有生动的故事。就拿有着 900 多年历史的汀州文庙来说，在台湾也有一座跟它样式完全一致的文庙。

♪现场

包东宇：人们说 900 多年来这座孔庙里都没结过蜘蛛网。
潘维廉：真神奇，我要找出其中的奥秘，然后登到我们的网站上！

♪解说

长汀还有一座很独特的山，山脚下是佛寺，山顶上是道观。胡晓钢说，这里能看见和尚跟道士同桌吃饭的稀罕事。

在县城南郊，一座规模宏大的南禅寺正在兴建中，据说整个工程耗资超过 5000 万元人民币。南禅寺的三座大殿中都有菩萨，其中包括一座白玉佛像。

♪现场

潘维廉：看上去为了建这个寺庙，一座山头都被削平了。
包东宇：是啊，坐落在山坳里，风水挺不错的。
潘维廉：这座寺院挺大的吧？
包东宇：没错，等到全部建成，它将成为福建最大的尼众佛教寺庙。

♪解说

我还很吃惊地听说长汀也有一座很大的妈祖庙。汀州天后宫的后堂有一间布置得精致华丽的妈祖闺房。天后宫的管理人员每天都会送上一日三餐。

Miss Mazu's Boudoir

Dialogue—Sea Goddess on the River?

Bill: So why would Changting people, who are landlocked, worship a sea goddess Mazu?

Bobby: Because Changting people traveled by river, so they too wanted Mazu's protection.

Bill: Maybe so, but nowadays they travel by plane, train, bus—and the Mazu temple is bigger than ever!

Because Mazu is worshipped in Taiwan as well, the temple has helped forge bonds between mainland and Taiwanese Hakkas, who frequently send delegations to pay their respects at the Changting Mazu temple. This temple also serves as a gathering place for locals to hold various social activities.

Dialogue

Bill: This looks kind of like a stage to me.

Bobby: It is. Every year they hold several performances. People come from all over West Fujian and nearby Jiangxi.

Bill: Maybe we should give a performance!

A Revolutionary Church

A Revolutionary Protestant Church Just across the river from the Mazu Temple is a Protestant Church that played a very crucial role in Chinese history in the 1930s!

In 1908, the London Missionary Society opened Changting's Gospel Hospital and one of the foreign missionary doctors became famous for his support of the Communist party, and even delivered one of Mao's sons.

Dialogue–Protestant Church & Zhou Enlai

Bill: You know, the last time I was here, I learned that this Protestant church is very historical.

Bobby: Something to do with the Red Army, wasn't it?

Bill: Yeah, in fact, Zhou Enlai stayed here. I'll show you his room!

And for a time in the 1930s, the Protestant Church served as the residence of Zhou Enlai! During the 30s, Zhou Enlai and Mao Zedong probably considered themselves lucky to survive day-to-day, much less success in establishing a New China! It's easy to take modern China for granted, but a tour of these small rooms, with their plain wooden furniture, is sobering, and reminds us of the New China's humble origins only 70 years ago, and the almost insurmountable obstacles that Chinese had to overcome.

现场

潘维廉：住在山区的长汀人为什么也信仰妈祖呢？

包东宇：以前长汀人出行依靠汀江的航运，所以他们也寻求妈祖的庇护。

潘维廉：现在长汀人出行靠火车、汽车和飞机，可天后宫的香火还是更旺了！

解说

因为台湾人也信奉妈祖，所以汀州天后宫也是联系两岸客家同胞的一个纽带。台湾的客家人就经常组团前往长汀的天后宫进香。同时，这个天后宫还是当地人举行各种集会活动的场所。

现场

潘维廉：这好像是个戏台吧？

包东宇：没错。胡晓钢说他们每年都会举行几次庙会，整个闽西，还有临近的江西都有人过来看。

解说

天后宫的河对岸有一座基督教堂，在上个世纪 30 年代，那里曾经在中国历史上发挥过重要作用。

现场

潘维廉：上次我来这里时，听说这个基督教堂很有历史纪念意义。

包东宇：还是跟红军有关吧？

潘维廉：是的，周恩来曾经在这里住过。我带你去看他的房间。

解说

1908年，伦敦公会拨款在长汀建起了一个教会医院福音医院，后来，医院的院长傅连暲医生因为支持共产党和红军而闻名于世，他还为毛泽东的妻子贺子珍接生过一个儿子。在上个世纪30年代初，长汀基督教堂曾经是周恩来的住地。那个时期，毛泽东和周恩来还生活在动荡当中，时常要为自己的生命安全担忧。人们容易把当今中国的发展当成理所当然的事，不过，来到这些领导人的故居，看一看那些简单的木制家具和陈设，就会让人回想起仅仅在70年前，中国人民要克服多么大的艰难险阻，才能把新中国的萌芽培养长大。

Dialogue—Shaking the World

Bobby: You know, it is very moving to know what happened here.

Bill: I imagine that when they were meeting in the back of this old church, they never imagined that they would be changing the course of history!

This historic Protestant church was designated a Provincial Level Historic Preservation Site in 1960, but one of the most graphic reminders of Chinese struggles in the 1920s and 1930s lies neglected and unprotected in an abandoned farmhouse. Babushka discovered this revolutionary artwork, and showed it to us.

Zhou Enlai's Desk
(in Protestant Church)

The Revolution Began Here

♪现场

包东宇：当年这里发生的一切真是让人感动。

潘维廉：当他们在这座教堂后面会面的时候，大概没有想到中国的历史正在因为他们而改变吧！

Changting in the '30s

♪解说

这座古老的基督教堂在1960年被确定为福建省省级文物保护单位。不过，还有一些形象反映中国革命的文物被人们遗忘在一座废弃的农舍里，胡晓钢发现了这些革命艺术，他将带我们前去观看。

Painting in Hakka Museum

Episode 48 Tufang Village & Hakka Cuisine

Introduction On today's episode of Magic Fujian, FJTV's Bobby Bao and Xiamen University MBA's Dr. Bill Brown explore the Hakka village of Tufang—and find a revolutionary treasure!

The Road to Riches The last time I visited Tufang, the road was mud, but since then it had been nicely paved. Babushka said the Changting government encourages districts to build their own roads by reimbursing them for some expenses when they submit proof of completion. These kinds of activities are common not only all over Changting but in the rest of Fujian, and indeed all of China. To me, the Chinese' preoccupation with new roads and infrastructure is one of the best examples of their pragmatism. Rather than just doling out money to poor peasants, they build roads, which help end the age-old isolation and bring remote villages closer to markets and opportunities. It reminds me of an ancient Chinese proverb that warns it's better to teach a man to fish than to just give him a fish.

On the way to Tufang, Babushka showed us the abandoned farmhouse in which several years ago he discovered some priceless treasures that really should be moved to Changting's revolutionary museum.

Dialogue—Revolutionary Treasure

Bill: From looking at it you'd never guess that this old farmhouse has a priceless treasure!

Bobby: Like what? A goose that lays golden eggs?

Bill: Better yet! It has priceless revolutionary art work from the 1920s and 30s! Babushka discovered it and showed it to me! I hope it's still here.

When Babushka discovered the art in this farmhouse, he reported it to the authorities and urged them to move the panels to a safer place, because they are priceless! Unfortunately, no one heeded him, and the best work, which was a colored cartoon, had been destroyed since my last visit only a year ago.

Hidden Treasure

第48集　长汀：涂坊客家村落和客家美食

导语

在本期的系列报道“老外看福建”中，厦门大学的潘维廉博士将和记者包东宇一起，探访一个叫作涂坊的闽西客家村落，在那里，他们还找到了被人们遗忘的珍贵的红军壁画。

解说

上回我来涂坊的时候，乡间公路泥泞不堪，不过最近却铺成了平坦的水泥路。胡晓钢说，长汀县政府鼓励各乡镇自筹资金改造村道，只要各地按标准把路修好，财政就可以根据一定的比例提供补偿金。这种办法不仅在长汀很普遍，其实整个福建省，甚至全中国都在实行。对我来说，目前中国正在大力推行的道路和基础设施建设正是他们扎扎实实搞建设的最好例证。现在，中国人不再只是向贫困群众发放救济款，而是修路改善交通，帮助那些长年累月与世隔绝的偏远山村打开山门，找到脱贫致富的市场和机遇。这让我想起一个古老的中国谚语：“与其临渊羡鱼，不如退而结网。”

在前往涂坊的路上，胡晓钢带我们来到一座废弃的农家宅院。六七年前，他在这里发现了一些不可多得的文物，完全应该搬到长汀的革命历史博物馆里收藏起来。

现场

潘维廉：恐怕没有人会想到这座老旧的农舍里会藏着无价之宝！

包东宇：什么宝贝？会下金蛋的鹅吗？

潘维廉：比那还珍贵！是上个世纪二三十年代的革命艺术品！以前胡晓钢发现后带我来看过。

解说

Political Cartoons

胡晓钢六七年前在农舍里发现了这些红军的革命宣传画之后，曾经向有关部门报告，请他们把壁画保护起来，因为它们实在是难得一见的珍贵作品。遗憾的是，他的意见并没有引起重视。从我上次来看到现在才不过一年的时间，两面壁画中最精美的一幅彩色漫画已经被彻底毁坏。

Dialogue—Lost Treasure

Bill: Wow, last time I came here, there was one like that here—beautiful.

Bobby: Now it's in pieces.

Bill: If we don't take steps soon, that ones' going to receive the same fate—maybe just in months.

It looked like some farmer had thrown logs against the wall, and the fragile panel had fallen and broken to pieces. Such a loss, because this art, like Zhou Enlai's rooms behind the Changting Protestant church, throw great light upon a crucial period of China's history. Babushka and I are now redoubling our efforts to save the remaining panel, going so far as to pay for its relocation, but only time will tell if we are successful.

Tufang's Cow-Horn Hakka Village A few kilometers from the farmhouse we came to Tufang, which was the inspiration for the Hakka hamlet model in the Changting Hakka Museum.

Babushka in Tufang

Dialogue

Bobby: Bill, you notice that these Hakka fortresses are only 1 story high, not like Yongding's earthen houses that are 3 or 4 stories.

Bill: Yes, my teacher Babushka, he said that when the Hakkas moved here a long time ago, this area was less populated so they didn't need such strong defenses.

Some of the small fortresses are not even entirely enclosed, forming a half-circle. Locals call these "cows' horn" villages. We searched high and low for the best spot to film these unique dwellings, and finally discovered that the roof of a clinic offered the best vantage point. Then we wandered through the houses and courtyards, examining the traditional farming implements, and the Hakka way of life. And, of course, we were welcomed with "Have some tea!" Of course, I'd have preferred them saying "Have some lunch!" because Changting's Hakka cuisine is legendary, and fortunately, we did enjoy a hearty Hakka lunch before we left.

Dialogue—Heavenly Hetian Chicken

Bill: You know, one of my favorite things about Changting is the Hakka Cuisine.

Bobby: Well, knowing you, I'm not surprised. What's your favorite dish?

Bill: My favorite has to be Hetian chicken. No place makes it like here.

Bobby: Well, let me judge it for myself!

Bill: And dip it in this.

Bobby: Umh, really good!

Bill: It would be better if you dipped it in that!

♪现场

潘维廉：上次我们来的时候，这面墙板还在。
包东宇：可现在已经成了碎片。
潘维廉：如果不采取措施的话，可能过不了几个月时间，剩下的这一块也会遭遇相同的命运。

♪解说

现场看起来像是农户往墙边堆放木材时，隔墙上的壁板受了撞击，崩塌下来摔成了碎片。这真是惨痛的损失，因为，就跟长汀基督教堂后面周恩来曾经工作过的房间一样，这些红军壁画生动地反映了中国历史上一个关键而又特殊的时期。我和胡晓钢下决心加倍努力抢救仅剩的一幅壁画，甚至准备出资把它移放到博物馆中。不过，不知道我们还来不来得及做好这项工作。

经过这座农舍再走几公里就是涂坊，在这里我们看到了长汀客家博物馆中那个客家围屋模型的原型。

♪现场

包东宇：你看，这些小型客家土楼只有一层楼高，不像永定的土楼一般都是三四层楼高。
潘维廉：是啊，胡晓钢说，这是因为客家人搬迁到这里时，这一带人口还不多，所以没必要盖那么高的楼。

♪解说

有一些围屋甚至不是完整的一圈，只有半圆，当地人把这种房屋叫作“牛角村”。我们爬上爬下，想找一个最佳的地点拍摄这些围屋，最后发现一家诊所的楼上角度最好。然后，我们穿梭于一座围屋的房间、厅堂和天井之间，观察住户们使用的传统用具，想要多了解一些客家人的生活方式。不出意料的是，我们频频被邀请坐下来“喝口茶”。当然，我更情愿这些好客的主人请我们留下来“吃个饭”，因为长汀的客家菜是出名的美味。我们很走运，在离开长汀之前真的美餐了一顿。

♪现场

潘维廉：我最喜欢长汀的美食了。
包东宇：凭我对你的了解，这一点儿也不奇怪。你最喜欢的菜是什么？
潘维廉：当然是河田鸡。在长汀吃河田鸡那才叫正宗！
包东宇：那我还是自己来尝尝看！……嗯，真不错！
潘维廉：再蘸一点儿米酒姜汁味道就更好了。

The celebrated Hakka chef in the Changting Guesthouse gave us demonstrations, and made a dish I had never seen before: tofu Chinese dumplings! He sliced tofu very thin and used it as the wrapper! I was delighted, of course, because tofu and Chinese dumplings are two of my favorite foods, so to have them in one dish was heavenly.

Changting cuisine is so well regarded that books have been written about it, and I could spend days sampling such delights as BBQ beef with cilantro (xiangcai), braised pork ribs, and pork ball soup with sweet potato pasta—all washed down with the local wine called Red Army Cola. But I did have to draw the line at the popular Hakka dish, "Unicorn sticking its head out of a bag," which is simply puppy boiled in pig stomach. Canine cuisine is not on the top of my list!

After a hearty Hakka meal, we bid farewell to enchanting Changting, but I'll visit again soon because, as Rewi Alley wrote, it really is a beautiful little mountain town.

Supplementary Reading Six

Nights of the Round Table[1]

We spent our first New Year feast with our dean. Chinese rice wine and Tsingdao beer flowed like water, and we were urged to partake of the choicest delicacies—boiled seaworms embedded in a grayish round mold of cold jellyfish, giant platters of local crab, fish, shrimp, squid and octopus (my favorite, especially the suctions cups, which are chewy, rather like rubber grapes), red braised chicken, beef and peppers, pastries, soups, vegetables you've never dreamed of (like bitter melon and spinach roots), and of course the desserts: tiny individual egg custard pies, cakes stuffed with black beans, white fungus broth.

We were used to American dining, where the host lays all their cards on the table,[2] and we stuffed ourselves on the first 4 courses. We had no idea they had 16 more courses up their sleeves. By the 12th course I was stuffed to the gills.[3] By the 20th course, I never wanted to see Chinese food again in my life.

Chinese spend days shopping and preparing, and when they eat, they eat slowly (not like Americans who gulp their Thanksgiving turkey whole so they can retreat to the couch and the football game[4]). Chinese serve their painstakingly prepared dishes almost reverently, one at a time, placing them in the center of the Round Table.

---

[1] Nights of the round table: a play on "'knights' of the round table" (King Arthur's knights)

[2] Lay all cards on the table: to be completely open or candid, not hide anything (when playing poker).

[3] Stuffed to the gills: unable to eat anymore (as if stuffed with food all the way up to our necks).

[4] Football game: many Americans spend Thanksgiving afternoon watching football on TV. The Thanksgiving—football tradition began in 1876 when the Intercollegiate Football Association was formed and held its first championship game on Thanksgiving day. In 1893, the New York Herald declared that Thanksgiving was the official holiday for watching football. By the mid-1890s, over 5,000 football games were being held on Thanksgiving Day.

解说

长汀宾馆的大厨向我们展示了厨艺，他还现场制作了一道我从未见识过的菜式：豆腐饺。他用刀把一块豆腐片成薄片，当作饺子皮。这令我喜出望外，因为豆腐和饺子正好是我最喜欢的两种食品，这种“两位一体”的享受真是太棒了！

长汀美食名声显赫，甚至还有专门的菜谱。我愿意花上几天时间尝遍各色菜点，比如香菜烤肉、焖排骨、肉片兜汤等等，不少菜里面都加了当地的“红军可乐”——客家米酒。特别值得一提的是一道叫作“麒麟脱胎”的客家名菜，实际上就是把乳狗放在完整的猪肚里面炖熟。不过，狗肉并不是我的最爱。

在饱餐一顿客家盛宴之后，我们告别了迷人的长汀。正如路易·艾黎所说，长汀的确是座美丽的山城，我希望很快能机会再次造访。

补充读物（六）

圆桌之夜

我们来厦的第一个新年年夜饭是在系主任家吃的。席间，我们喝中国米酒和青岛啤酒就跟喝水似的。主人不断劝我们多吃些美味佳肴——土笋汤、大盘本地产螃蟹、鱼、虾、墨鱼、章鱼（我的最爱，尤其是章鱼头，很有韧性，咬起来像橡皮葡萄一样），红烧鸡块，青椒炒牛肉、酥皮甜饼、几道汤、你想象不出的蔬菜（像苦瓜和菠菜根），当然还有甜点：小小的蛋羹派、黑芝麻饼和白木耳汤。

我们以前习惯吃美国大餐，主人把菜都摆在桌上，头四道菜后我们就吃饱了。我们不知道他们居然后面还有16道菜。吃到第12道菜时，我已饱到动弹不得了。上第20道菜时，这辈子我再也不想看见中餐了。

中国人常常花好几天的时间采购和准备，而当吃饭时，他们就慢慢吃(不像美国人感恩节吃火鸡时是狼吞虎咽，以便饭后有更多时间躺在躺椅上看橄榄球赛）。中国人上菜时，很恭敬，每次只上一道精心准备的菜，放在圆桌的中央。

Chinese use round tables because they don't have individual servings or pass food. They serve the food on large "lazy Susans"[5] in the middle of the table and chopstick wielding diners dig right in. The hosts often fish out choice morsels of chicken for us, using the same chopsticks they've been eating with. Though we've not been sick from it yet, it makes us uneasy. And our hosts invariably interpret our hesitation as keqi' (ceremonial politeness) and stab us a few more crab legs, or chunks of beef or chicken.

It sounds distasteful, but it is done with great grace, and increasingly Chinese are familiar with foreigners' scruples, and set aside a set of chopsticks used solely for serving rice and cai.

Cai? Good question. When Matthew was five, he asked during a meal, "Daddy, how do you say cai in Chinese?"

"Cai is Chinese."

He looked confused, then said, "Oh. Then how do you say it in English?"

A Reverence for Rice Chinese have two main words for food – fan, for grains and rice, and cai, for vegetables and meat (just about everything but fan). Chinese revere rice, which is the focal point of ordinary meals. Rice three times a day still goes against my grain,[6] but I sure crave it at banquets, where just a spoonful of rice would help the jellied pig tendons go down. But bona fide banquets are allowed only those choice delicacies that stick to your wallet but not to your ribs.[7] It is all too common to go 18 rounds of fried fish lips, sauteed sow ears, jellied seaworms, deng deng, and return home famished from the feast.

But whether hosting a banquet or a simple lunch, Chinese are masters of etiquette, ceremony, and presentation, making dishes as much a feast for the eyes as for the stomach. Even common radishes and carrots are carved and laid out like phoenixes and dragons, and humble watermelons become dragon boats and pagodas.

Though Chinese are a race of convention and protocol, at the board[8] they let their hair down,[9] because the paramount purpose of Chinese dining is eating – and they are delightfully free from the bonds of etiquette that ensnare Western gastronomes.[10]

After 17 years of marriage, I still can't remember how to place the four spoons, 3 knives, and 4 forks, and in what order to use them. Even my dear mother-in-law has sought to exorcise her savage son-in-law's innate inelegance with such delicate dissuasions as, "Work from the outside to the inside, Bill."

Yes, but from which side of the outside, pray tell?

---

[5] Lazy Susan: revolving food tray, usually in the center of the table (for people too lazy to reach)

[6] Against the grain: unusual, not customary (refers to chopping wood against its "grain"—its direction of growth; also, rice is a "grain")

[7] Stick to the ribs: help one to feel full; if foods don't 'stick to your ribs,' you quickly become hungry again

[8] At the board: at the dining table (refers to old days when many tables were simply long boards)

[9] Let your hair down: relax, be informal (women "put their hair up" for formal occasions)

[10] Gastronome: lover of food

中国人用圆桌吃饭是因为他们不分餐或传递食物。他们用很大的容器装菜，上菜时放在桌子中央，夹菜的筷子直接伸进菜里头。主人常常会用他们自己夹菜的筷子夹些鸡块给我们。虽然我们对此不感到恶心，但使我们感到不舒服。主人对我们迟疑的样子总以为是客气，所以又会夹一些螃蟹腿或是大块牛肉或鸡肉给我们。

Shannon (age 2)

这听起来有点倒胃口，但却又做得很体面，而且中国人也越来越了解外国人的这种迟疑，故会在旁边放一双筷子专门吃饭夹cai用。

什么是Cai?

问得好。马太5岁时，有一次吃饭时他问我，“爸爸，中文‘菜’怎么说？”

Cai（菜）本身就是中文。

马太满脸迷惑。他接着问道，“那英语怎么说呢？”

中文里有许多词表示食物——fan（饭）表示谷物和米饭，cai（菜）表示蔬菜和肉（除fan以外的所有其他东西）。中国人很尊崇米饭，因为它是平常用餐的中心点。我一日三顿无法以米饭当主食，但在宴会上我一定会要一点米饭，哪怕一汤匙米饭也有助于咽下猪蹄筋。但在真正的宴会上，往往只允许点那些价值高但不能填饱肚子的佳肴。回到家里，依然饿着肚子。

Shannon (18) now eats Thanksgiving meal with chopsticks!

中国人一向循规蹈矩。但在饭桌上，他们却是毫无拘束，因为中国人吃饭的首要目的是吃——他们可以摆脱那些西方美食家的种种礼仪约束，欣然享受桌上的美食。

结婚17年了，我还是无法记住四把勺子、三把刀子和四把叉子的摆法以及使用顺序。连我亲爱的岳母大人都想方设法要纠正她这位粗鲁女婿的先天不雅行为，如以微妙的方式规劝我：“比尔，从外到内。”

遵命，可是从外面的那一侧开始呢？求您告诉我吧！

Dorothy Parker got it right when she wrote, "Those who have mastered etiquette, who are entirely, impeccably right, would seem to arrive at a point of exquisite dullness."

There is seldom exquisite dullness at a Chinese table. They don't use different pairs of chopsticks for meat and vegetables and desserts and rice or noodles. They wield but one pair, usually fashioned from humble bamboo, though more sophisticated Socialists are now opting for plastic, wooden or even bone chopsticks. And unused chopsticks may reside either side of the bowl -- though fishermen never place them across the top, lest their boat run aground, and no Chinese jams their chopsticks upright in the rice, for that resembles incense in the rice bowls sacrificed to demons and ancestors, and is a sure way to court[11] unwanted spiritual attention.

Wits and Half-Wits Chinese newspapers have reported that researchers suggest Chinese are more intelligent than us knife-and-fork-wielding barbarians because chopsticks require more dexterity. My response is that knife and fork take two hands, so we use both sides of the brain, whereas those who use but one hand use only half the brain – half their wit, in other words. But I too have begun to doubt our barbarian intelligence, given the panoply[12] of epicurean[13] protocol[14] beneath which we labor.

Consider the simple soupspoon. Sue forever intones, "Circular, Bill, away from you and up." Her dear mother adds, as if to a slow[15] child, "So you don't spill soup in your lap, Bill."

Chinese often don't even bother with soupspoons. It is proper, even expected, for one to eat the soup solids with chopsticks, hold the bowl to ones lips, and down the hatch[16] with the rest. Simple, and elegant.

But I suggest an innovation: "Chopstraws,™" or hollow chopsticks. Then one could suck the broth without slurping. Though don't follow the granny in McDonald's example and use them for piping hot soup.

---

[11] Court: attract, woo (young men court girls)

[12] Panoply: an impressive or broad array or display

[13] Epicurean: devoted to pursuing pleasure; fond of food and comfort

[14] Protocol: forms of etiquette and ceremony observed by dignitaries

[15] Slow: less than average intelligence or abilities

[16] Down the hatch: bottoms up (干杯!, ganbei!); guzzle, drink quickly (perhaps loudly)

多萝西·帕克曾写道："那些已掌握了礼节、举止得体、毫无瑕疵的人会给人一种接近极度呆板的印象。"她是对的。

在中国人的餐桌上很少有这种极度呆板的情况。他们不使用不同的筷子夹取肉和蔬菜以及甜品和米饭或面条。他们只挥动一双筷子，通常是简单的竹筷，尽管现在越来越多的高级社会主义者选择塑料的、木制的甚至是骨制的筷子。不使用的筷子可以放在碗的任何一侧。当然，渔民是决不会将筷子横在碗上的，因为他们担心船会搁浅。中国人也不会把筷子竖直插在米饭中，因为那样就像一支香插在祭祀神灵和祖先的饭碗中，必定会招致神灵的惩罚。

智者和愚人

中国报纸曾报道说，研究人员发现，中国人比我们这些使用刀叉的野蛮人更聪明，因为筷子的使用需要更高的灵敏度。我回应说，刀和叉要用两只手，所以，我们两边大脑都使用，而那些只使用一只手的人只用到一半大脑——换句话说，一半智力。不过，现在我自己也开始怀疑我们的野蛮智力，因为我们竟然要受全套美食家礼仪的约束。

至于简单的汤匙。苏珊常常以歌唱的声调说："环绕一圈，比尔，向外舀起。"她那亲爱的母亲又加上一句，"这样，就不会将汤洒在膝盖上，比尔"，好像对一个反应迟钝的小孩说话一样。

中国人甚至经常不用汤匙。如你所料，他们甚至可以用筷子吃汤里的固体，然后端起碗，靠着嘴唇，轻轻松松地将汤喝下。既简单，又不失优雅。不过，我建议创新一下：使用吸管或空心筷子。这样一来，就可以吸食肉汤，以免喝汤时发出响声。但是千万记住在麦当劳喝热饮的那位老奶奶的惨痛教训，别用吸管或空心筷子吸食滚烫的汤！

Episode 49 Introduction to Sanming

Introduction Welcome to today's episode of Magic Fujian as FJTV's Bobby Bao and Xiamen University's Dr. Bill Brown take us to Sanming, home to the Hakka people, and a scenic wonderland as beautiful below ground as above.

Western Fujian's Sanming is so remote, tucked away beyond rows of mountains and narrow valleys, that even the Japanese had a hard time reaching it during the wars. Locals say that before Sanming was designated a city in 1958, it was so small that farmers in the countryside could hear city people grinding soybeans to make doufu. It's hard to believe, given the size, and beauty, of Sanming city today! And building a city from scratch certainly had advantages, because it allowed planners to incorporate the latest urban development strategies to create a city that is both prosperous and clean.

Dialogue—Scenic and Sanitary Sanming

Bill: You know, for such an industrial place, Sanming certainly has a pretty clean environment.

Bobby: Yes, Sanming has been awarded national sanitary city, and even in the early 90s it is considered one of China's cleanest cities.

Bill: I can see why they'd keep the place clean. Living in Sanming is kind of like living in a natural park!

Bobby: That's true—and when it is lit up at night, it's like living in Disneyland!

Sanming people have long enjoyed their nights out of doors, and even more so now that the city's Night Lights light up the sky. The beautiful Shaxi River, which winds through the city, is lit up at night by festive billboards advertising products and some of Sanming's famous tourist sites, like Shaxian's sleeping Buddha. Lights festoon the bridges, and trees, and a radio tower on a hill lights the sky like a miniature Eiffel Tower.

The colorful Night Lights not only enliven the city but also encourage a healthful outdoor lifestyle—and use a lot less electricity than would be spent on air conditioning couch potatoes!

Dialogue—Burgeoning Hi-Tech

Bill: You know, Sanming is obviously very prosperous, but it's so remote! Where on earth doesall the money come from?

Bobby: In addition to tourism, Sanming has many major industries.

Bill: I'd imagine forestry is pretty big here, but what else brings in the money?

Bobby: Well, in spite of Sanming's remoteness, it is becoming a center of hi-technology.

Bill: Hi-tech? Here?

第49集　三明简介

♪导语

欢迎收看系列报道“老外看福建”节目。从今天开始，厦门大学的潘维廉博士和记者包东宇将带我们去三明，看看那里的客家祖地以及地底下和地面上一样美丽的人间仙境。

♪解说

三明隐藏于福建西部的深山峡谷之中，非常偏僻。二战期间，日本人妄图进犯三明，结果困难重重。当地人说，1958 年正式建市之前，三明只是一个无名的小镇，小得连田里的农夫都可以听到镇上磨豆腐的声音。看看现在三明市区的规模和美景，实在令人难以置信。当然，从零开始搞建设也有它的好处。这样一来，规划者就可以运用最新的城区发展规划，建设繁荣而又整洁的新城市。

♪现场（三明城区沙溪河畔）

潘维廉：对三明这样的工业城市来讲，这里的环境还是不错的。

包东宇：是的，三明曾经被授予国家卫生城市。早在 90 年代初，她就是中国最整洁的城市之一。

潘维廉：我现在终于明白，他们为什么要把城市搞得这么干净。住在三明简直就像住进了生态公园！

包东宇：没错！到了晚上，华灯齐放，这里简直就像迪斯尼乐园。

♪解说

长期以来，三明市民就喜欢夜里到户外去。实施夜景工程后，到户外去活动的人更多了。夜幕降临时，宣传三明产品和诸如沙县卧佛等著名旅游景点的户外广告牌亮起了彩灯，映红了流经三明市区美丽的沙溪河。桥头、树梢到处都闪烁着彩色的霓虹灯，山顶上的广播发射塔就像巴黎的埃菲尔铁塔一样闪闪发光。

五彩缤纷的夜景不仅使城市充满了生气，同时也激发市民走到户外，追求健康的生活方式。市民们的空调用电也明显减少了。

♪现场（沙县新城区小广场）

潘维廉：很显然，三明是很繁荣的，只是有一点偏僻。他们的财富是怎么积累的呢？

包东宇：除了旅游业，三明还有许多支柱产业。

潘维廉：我想，三明的林业应该比较发达。三明还有什么生财之道呢？

包东宇：嗯，尽管有点偏僻，三明正在成为福建的高科技产业中心之一。

潘维廉：高科技产业？三明？

Sanming's new Hi-tech Industrial Development Zone, Jinsha Park, is one of Fujian Province's 5 provincial level hi-tech parks, and is a joint project between Sanming city and Shaxian County. The city's remoteness would have made such a project unthinkable only ten years ago, but Sanming is no longer remote!

The city is building a new airport, and cargo ships carrying up to 300 tons can sail the Shaxi River right to Mawei Port on the coast. In addition, Shaxian is linked by rail and the new Fuzhou—Beijing highway will have 3 exits in Sanming.

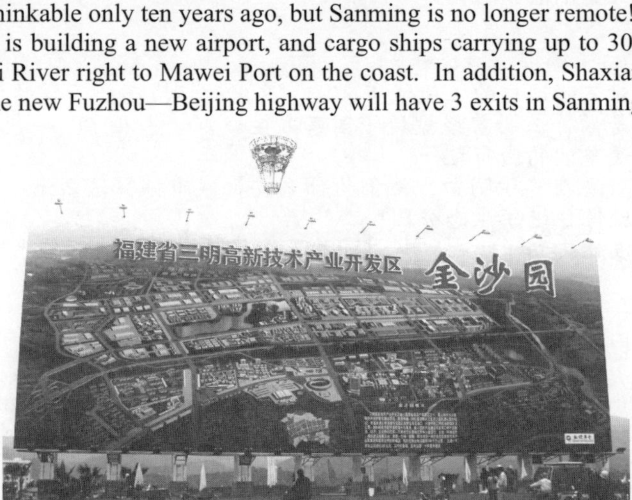

Jinsha (Gold Sands) Hi-tech Park

The 2 billion Yuan 18 sq. km. hi-tech park will focus on such fields as opto-mechanics, electronic integrity, new materials, and biological engineering.

Sanming people enjoy many unique cultural traditions, such as the "Shoulder opera," in which children perform opera standing on the shoulders of adults. I told a Sanming friend that if they used adults, they would not have to stand on people's shoulders to be seen—but he said I was missing the point. One thing is for sure. Sanming's "shoulder opera" stands head and shoulders above the competition!

♪解说

三明高新技术开发区金沙园是福建省五个省级高科技园区之一，由三明市和沙县共同投资兴建。要是早十年，这简直难以想像，因为当时三明还相当偏僻。现在可不一样了！三明正在兴建一个新机场，300 吨级的货船可从沙溪河直航福州马尾港。此外，三明还有铁路和 205 国道贯穿全境。新建的京福高速公路给沙县留下了三个出口。

投资 20 亿、占地 18 平方公里的三明高新技术产业开发区金沙园将优先发展光机电一体化、新型建材、生物工程等产业。

三明还拥有许多独特的文化传统。比如肩膀戏，就是让小孩子站在大人肩膀上表演的那种。我曾问一个三明朋友，为什么不直接用大人，这样演员就不用站在别人肩膀上表演了。他说我不懂肩膀戏的真谛。起码有一点我敢肯定，那就是：敢站在肩膀上演戏，沙县肩膀戏已经比别人技高一筹了。

Episode 50 Sanming—the Ancient Culture and Geshikao

Introduction In English, the phrase "animal, vegetable and mineral" covers everything, so with this in mind, Sanming has just about everything! This beautiful prefecture has some of Fujian's most ancient cultural and archaeological sites, unique natural wonder like the Geshikao forests, and the gem stone center of Mingxi. In today's episode of Magic Fujian Xiamen University's Dr. Bill Brown explored the ancient treasures, both natural and cultural, of Scenic Sanming.

On our way to Wanshouyan, site of stone-age Fujian settlers, we stayed in the delightful Hengkeng Hot Springs Holiday Village! It's off the beaten path, about 38 km south of Sanming City, but given its excellent amenities, and secluded location, nestled amongst bamboo and pine groves, I'm sure this 5 million Yuan 2.5 acre complex will become one of Sanming's hot tourist attractions. The hot springs, which flow from a depth of 117 meters and maintain a temperature of 48 degrees centigrade, puts out 350 tons daily of waters rich in such medicinal minerals as radon, radium, lithium, uranium, etc.

In addition to hot springs, the resort also boasts a large swimming pool, fishing ponds, ping pong tables, barbeque facilities, and well-appointed rooms, suits, and meeting rooms of all sizes. All in all, Hengkeng hot springs is a great place to stop off before going back in time 200,000 years in nearby Wanshouyan.

Dialogue—Prehistoric Sanming Settlers

Bill: Wow, I thought people had lived in Fujian for only 5 or 6,000 years.

Bobby: Only five years ago, Chinese experts thought the same thing. But the discovery of this cave suggests that people lived here 20,000 years ago.

Bill: 20,000 years! Wow—that was before my time!

Bobby: Before my time too!

Laowai or Laonei?

The relics were discovered when locals were mining for stone for concrete. In the oldest of the two caves, the 13 sq. meter Lingfeng cave灵峰洞, which is 37 meters up a cliff face, researchers discovered some 300 fragments of stone age implements. Various dating methods gave different results, but experts guess the average age at about 180,000 years.

The 350m^2 Chuanfan Cave 船帆洞, at the base of the cliff, gave up over 500 stone age artifacts. Scientists were excited by the discovery of a 150m^2 stone floor, with provisions for water drainage. It is the oldest and largest floor of its type in the world, and in fact, looked very much to me like the 2,000 year old Han Dynasty roads in Northwest Fujian!

第 50 集 万寿岩古文化遗址和格氏栲森林

导语

欢迎收看系列报道“老外看福建”。在今天的节目中，厦门大学的潘维廉博士和我们的记者包东宇将带领大家一起去看看三明的历史文化和名胜古迹。

解说

英文“动物、植物和矿物”这个短语意味着世间万物。按照这种说法，三明可是什么都不缺！这座美丽的城市境内拥有福建省最古老的人类文化考古遗迹，也有诸如格氏栲原始森林保护区这样独特的自然景观，还有中国第四大蓝宝石产地以及红宝石和其他宝石的供应地——明溪。

在前往福建旧石器时代古人类遗址——万寿岩的途中，我们非常愉快地在横坑温泉度假村作短暂停留。度假村位于三明市区以南约 38 公里的地方，有点偏僻。不过，由于设施齐全，隐居山野，四周松林、竹林环抱，我想这个投资 500 万、占地 2.5 英亩的度假村肯定会成为三明一个最热门的休闲旅游去处。这里的温泉源自地下 117 米深的地方，温度保持在摄氏 48 度，日出温泉 350 吨，富含氡、镭、锂和铀等对人体有益的矿物质。

除了温泉，度假村还配有游泳池、钓鱼池、乒乓球桌和烧烤工具，以及装修完善的标间、套间和大小不一的会议室。说实在的，在前往万寿岩回顾 20 万年前的历史之前，横坑温泉度假村是个稍作停留的好地方。

现场（万寿岩古人类遗迹）

潘维廉：过去我总以为，福建的历史顶多就是五六千年。

包东宇：就在 5 年前，专家们也是这么认为的。不过，1999 年 9 月，在万寿岩的这个洞穴里发现了 20 万年前人类活动的遗迹。

解说

据说这个洞穴遗址是当地企业开采石灰石时发现的。年代较为久远的洞穴叫灵峰洞，在万寿岩 37 米高的山崖当中，面积约 13 平方米。在这里，研究人员已经发现了 75 件旧石器时代的石器碎片。不同的年代测定方法得出的结论有所不同。不过，专家们估计，这些石器的平均历史应该在 18 万年左右。

船帆洞位于万寿岩的山脚下，面积 350 平方米，发掘出石器时代的史前文物 500 余件。在这里，考古学家发现了一处面积 150 平方米、设置了排水通道的人工石铺地面，这是迄今为止世界上面积最大、最为古老的人工石铺地面。在我看来，这些人工石铺地面颇像闽西北具有两千多年历史的汉朝古驿道。

Ancient cave dwelling (just a "hole in the wall")

While enthusiastic experts can write volumes on data extracted from a tiny fossilized bird bone, it's hard for novices like myself to envision what life was like so long ago in this isolated valley. Fortunately, the well-designed park has been laid out with sculptures that kindle even my feeble imagination! Statues of stone-age people going about daily tasks surround a small pond in the midst of the large, well-kept field facing the cliff. Bobby Bao posed for a photo, pretending he was skinning a deer with a sharp stone. Actually, he was quite adept with that stone, and I determined that if I ever made him angry, I'd make sure he did not have any stones at hand!

Chinquapin Natural Protection Region Not far from Wanshou Yan is the 1,158 hectare Chinquapin Natural Protection Region, which boasts the largest grove of this type of Chinquapin trees in China. This particular kind of tree was discovered by an Englishman in the 1930s, in neighboring Guangdong province.

In addition to this unique evergreen tree, the region is also home to a menagerie of such rare creatures as giant pythons (which reach 10 meters in length in Fujian!), black bears, clouded leopards, masked civets, silver pheasants, pangolins, which are a rare anteater, and over 2,000 kinds of insects and amphibians.

Dialogue

Bobby: Good place to relax!

Bill: Yeah—I've really enjoyed the 2 or 3 minutes here![1]

Chinquapin Park

This unique attraction already receives over 35,000 visitors a year, and the Sanyuan Forestry Bureau is now investing over 9 million Yuan in state-of-the-art facilities to further boost tourism.

Ancient cultures, rare plants and animals—Sanming has it all. But one of the biggest attractions for me, given that I've collected minerals and crystals since I was six-years-old, is the gem center of Mingxi, which is only an hour West.

[1] 2 or 3 minutes: it was a great place to relax, but our filming schedule was so tight we just rushed in, filmed, and rushed out; at least we got to enjoy the hot springs the night before!

Prehistoric KFC?

从小小的一片鸟骨化石析取的数据，热情似火的考古专家就可以写出许多宏篇大作。但是，对于像我这样的菜鸟，简直难以想象那么久远的过去，在这个与世隔绝的山谷里，人类生活会是怎样的模样。幸运的是，万寿岩山下的园地里摆放的各种雕塑激发了我原本贫弱的想像力。在万寿岩正前方是一大片养护得很好的草地，石器时代的古人类在当中一个小池塘的四周忙碌着。我的搭档摆出一个姿势，装着用锋利的石器剥鹿皮。他手拿石块居然相当老练。我发誓，假如我惹他生气的话，要先确定他手里没有拿着石头！

距离万寿岩不远的地方就是格氏栲森林，这个自然保护区占地 1158 公顷，是中国面积最大的一片格氏栲原始森林。这种栲树是上个世纪 30 年代英国人格端米在与福建相邻的广东省发现的，并以他的名字命名。

♪现场 ——

包东宇：感觉真不错！

潘维廉：空气好。在这里呆上两三分钟真是一种享受啊……

包东宇：是啊，好，享受完该上路了！

A really deep past!

♪解说 ——

除了格氏栲这种常绿树外，保护区还是蟒蛇、黑熊、云豹、果子狸、银雉、穿山甲以及两千多种昆虫和爬行动物的栖息地。格氏栲自然保护区目前每年接待 35000 千多名游客。三元区林业局还将投入 900 多万元资金，建设一流的基础设施，进一步发展这里的森林生态旅游。

古老的历史文化，珍稀的动植物，三明市应有尽有。不过，因为我从六岁起就开始收集各种矿石和水晶，因此对我来说，最有吸引力的还是市区以西一个小时车程的宝石城——明溪。

Episode 51 Ancient Shaxian

Introduction On today's episode of Magic Fujian, FJTV's Bobby Bao and Xiamen University's Dr. Bill Brown unravel 1600 years of Shaxian history!

Dialogue—1600 Years of Shaxian History!

Bill: You know, most Chinese cities have only one temple god, so why does Shaxian have two?

Bobby: Because the county seat used to be in Guxian, and when it moved to Shaxian they built a second temple for a new god.

Bill: Really? So Shaxian must be pretty old then?

Bobby: Actually, Shaxian is nearly 1600 years old! In fact, Sanming city's location used to be part of Shaxian.

City God Temple

The Guxian City God Temple was built over 600 years ago, and was city headquarters until a Yamen was built in 884. The city god temple moved to the present position in 1737, the 9th year of Emperor Qianlong during the Qing Dynasty, and is the best preserved city god Temple in Fujian today, right down to the ancient stone statues of animals and guards lining both sides of the courtyard.

Just west of the temple is the Xing Guo Temple, built in 882 during the reign of the Tang Dynasty emperor Zhonghe, and in memory of the patriot and local hero, Prime Minister Li Gang.

Li Gang's Message from Heaven Li Gang was an imperial official who lived from 1083 to 1114. When he urged the Emperor to strengthen the defenses against possible attacks by northern nomads, the impotent ruler demoted Li Gang to Shaxian tax officer. While in Shaxian he lived in Xing Guo Temple, enjoyed and help name Shaxian's "8 scenic spots," associated with men of letters, and wrote many great poems. But he eventually returned to power—six years after a message straight from heaven!

A heavenly messenger was supposed to have told Li Gang a cryptic riddle:

"Qing zhuoli, kang qumi, na shijie, zai guanghui."

The first part was a play on words, adding li to qing to create jing, and subtracting mi米 from kang糠 to create kang 康(rice husk for animals). The result, jingkang, 靖, referred to the year of a new emperor, and so the message meant "At that time (Jingkang), glory will return (Li Gang will be restored to power). And sure enough, six years later a new emperor came into power, and Li Gang returned

第51集 沙县访古

Shaxian City God Temple

导语

在今天的“老外看福建”节目中，厦门大学的潘维廉博士和记者包东宇将带我们一同探寻沙县的千年历史。

现场

潘维廉：中国大多数的城市只有一座城隍庙，为什么沙县却有两座呢？

包东宇：因为以前沙县县城在古县。后来，县城搬到新址。沙县人再建了一座城隍庙。

潘维廉：那么，沙县的历史应该是非常悠久喽？

包东宇：没错！到了 2005 年，沙县建县就 1600 年了。事实上，三明市区过去还是沙县的一部分。

解说

古县在唐武德三年之前一直是沙县旧县治所在地。公元 884 年，沙县衙门迁往沙溪水北凤岗山，也就是现在沙县人民政府所在地——凤岗镇。现在的沙县城关城隍庙建于清乾隆九年，是福建省保存最为完整的一座城隍庙。

从城隍庙稍微向西，就到了兴国寺。兴国寺建于唐中和二年。南宋名臣李纲因上书议论朝政被贬沙县任管库，入住兴国寺。李纲在沙县期间，与文人墨客畅游沙县山水名胜，为“沙阳八景”命名。传说，李纲曾遇定光佛，并得偈语。偈语说：“青着立，糠去米，那时节，再光辉。”其实，这只是一种文字游戏。给“青”字加上“立”字旁，然后再把“糠”字的“米”字旁去掉，就变成了靖康——南宋新皇帝赵桓！也就是说，到了靖康皇帝登基，李纲就会重掌大权。传说归传说，李纲果然在谪居沙县7年后复出。兴国寺也由此名声大振。

to favor and became Prime Minister. Whether true or not, this legend did add an air of mystery to Li Gang's political life, and the Xing Guo Temple has been famous ever since.

In 1934, General Peng Dehuai led the Red Army to liberate Shaxian and made the Xing Guo Temple his headquarters, and this temple has become one of the revolutionary Meccas for the Shaxian people. Also in Shaxian, you will find China's largest reclining Buddha in memory of Ligang's heavenly messenger!

Dialogue—China's Largest Reclining Buddha

Bobby: Do you know why they built China's largest sleeping Buddha in such a remote place?

Bill: Of course. So the city noise wouldn't wake him up.

Bobby: Good guess. But wrong. It was in this area the heavenly messenger told Li Gang there would be a new emperor and he would return to power.

Bill: Oh, and it was after that he became Prime Minister, right?

Bobby: That's right.

Bill: So, you think he would give me a promotion too?

Bobby: Hope so!

The original 20m Buddha was destroyed during the Cultural Revolution, so during a 16-month period from 1992-94, a new reclining Buddha, China's largest at 38 meters long, 10 meters wide and 11 meters high, was carved on Taojin Mountain. Taojin Mountain is heavily forested and covered with thousand-year-old sago cycas and bay trees.

Shaxian is also famous for its many crafts, including woodcarving and paper cutting, which we saw demonstrated in Luo Congyan Ancestral Temple. Luo Congyan, which was first built in 1314 A.D., has Fujian's oldest ancestral records for the Luo clan, and receives visitors from all over China who wish to update or correct their Luo clan records. Fascinating, of course, but what mesmerized me was the paper cutting demonstration held right in front of the temple.

Little papercutting student

A Cut Above[1] I marveled as the 74-year-old Ms. Deng Yinji, Shaxian's "Queen of Paper Cutting", deftly wielded scissors to rapidly transform squares of red paper into animals, birds, or beautiful Chinese maidens. And she is passing on her craft to dozens of children.

[1] "A cut above": above average; excellent

1934 年，彭德怀将军率领中国工农红军东方军红三军团解放沙县，司令部也驻扎在兴国寺，兴国寺又成为革命史迹。

在沙县，你还可以看到给李纲偈语的定光佛睡像。据说，这是中国目前最大的卧佛。

现场

包东宇：老潘，沙县人把中国最大的卧佛造在清静的淘金山上。你知道这是为什么吗?

潘维廉：当然知道！这样的话，城市的喧嚣就不会打扰卧佛的睡眠。

包东宇：猜得不错！但没猜对！是因为定光佛在这里遇见李纲并告诉他复出为相的偈语。

潘维廉：李纲后来真的做上宰相了吧?

包东宇：没错。

潘维廉：我真想知道，卧佛会不会也提携提携我！

解说

淘金山原来有一座 8 米长的定光佛睡像，后来被毁。1992 年 11 月，沙县人民重雕定光佛睡像，历时 16 个月方告功成。卧佛长 38 米，宽 10 米，高 11 米，国内精雕卧佛无有出其右者，堪称华夏第一。淘金山景区林木茂盛，还拥有全国罕见的连片生长的野生千年铁树群及宋桂花树。

沙县的手工艺也非常出名。我们在罗从彦纪念馆观赏了在那里展示的木雕和剪纸。罗从彦纪念馆，原称豫章贤祠，始建于元代至正元年（公元 1341 年），坐落于沙县城关西门外，坐北朝南，是后人为祭祀罗从彦而建的。馆内收藏着福建罗氏最完整的族谱，中国各地的罗氏后裔每年都要前来查阅或续写族谱。

你看，74 岁的邓银姬老大娘她手持剪刀，飞快地把四方形的红纸变成各种各样的鸟兽和漂亮的中国少女。简直把我看呆了！眼下，邓大娘正在把她的剪纸手艺传给后人。

Dialogue–Paper Cutting Kids

Bill: This is amazing. My boys would have never had the patience to do this when they were this small.

Bobby: Yes, it's amazing. Some people learn paper cutting at 5 to 6 years old.

Bill: How long do you think it takes to make one of these?

Bobby: A simple one like this takes only a few minutes, but I will show you one that has taken over one year!

[Bill says to a child] "Hi, can I keep this?"

[Bill examines Zhou Jianbo's 10,000 butterflies and asks] "He just uses these little scissors?"

Bobby: And every one is different!

Granny Deng's a "cut up"!

Mr. Zhou Jianbo's 10,000 butterflies will easily beat the Guinness World Record, but Shaxian folks' have demonstrated prowess in so many other areas as well. Shaxian is also famous for unique traditions like the famous Shaxian Shoulder Opera.

Dialogue—Shaxian Shoulder Opera

Bill: So this is the 100-year-old Shaxian Shoulder Opera?

Bobby: Yes, the only one of its kind in China. And you can also say it's a kind of show of live puppets, but the children are the puppets.

Bill: However you look at it, you have to say that Shaxian Shoulder Opera is head and shoulders above the competition!

Shaxian Shoulder Opera, which began in the Qing Dynasty about 100 years ago, is unique in China, and has one major advantage: it can be performed anywhere, anytime, because no stage is ever needed! Audiences are spellbound watching the tiny actors perform upon adults' shoulders. Locals most enjoy Shaxian Shoulder Opera during traditional Chinese festivals, and it is catching on elsewhere as well. When Hong Kong and Macao returned to China in 1997 and 1999 respectively, the Shoulder Opera troupe was asked to perform at the ceremonies, and in 2001, this unique art won a gold medal in the 5th China Folk Art Festival in Hubei.

Shaxian's traditions and crafts seem endless, but the city's greatest claim to fame is, of course, is its legendary Shaxian cuisine.

♪现场

潘维廉：我家两个小鬼这么大的时候可没这耐心来学做剪纸。

包东宇：是吗？这剪纸真令人叫绝。有些小孩五六岁就开始学了。

潘维廉：剪这么一张要花多长时间？

包东宇：像这样简单点的，几分钟就够了。不过，有个作品已经花了一年功夫。看，这里有 2400 只不同形状的蝴蝶。这不，周建波先生正向一万只冲刺呢！

潘维廉：哇，就用这样一把小剪刀？

♪解说

剪一万只蝴蝶，周建坡先生不费吹灰之力就可以打破吉尼斯世界纪录。事实上，沙县的民俗文化还展示在其他许多方面。比如说，沙县的肩膀戏也很有名。

♪现场

潘维廉：这就是拥有百年历史的沙县肩膀戏？

包东宇：没错！沙县肩膀戏是中国独一无二的民间表演艺术。小孩站在大人肩膀上表演，这简直就是小孩木偶秀！

潘维廉：没错！敢在肩膀上演戏，沙县肩膀戏的确比别人高一筹。

♪解说

沙县肩膀戏始创于 100 多年前的清朝末年，是中国绝无仅有的戏种。这个戏种的最大优点是随时随地可以演出，无须搭建舞台。每逢传统节日，肩膀戏的表演是最受老百姓欢迎的节目之一。1997 年和 1999 年，沙县肩膀戏分别应邀前往香港、澳门参加庆典活动的演出。2001 年，沙县肩膀戏以其独特的艺术形式，在第五届中国民间艺术节上荣获金奖。

沙县的传统文化异彩纷呈。不过，最让沙县出名的当属沙县小吃。

Episode 52 Shaxian—Fujian's Gourmet City!

Introduction Join us on today's episode of Magic Fujian as FJTV's Bobby Bao and Xiamen University's Dr. Bill Brown learn why Shaxian cuisine is taking China by storm—and catching on abroad as well!

Locals said that over 1100 years ago, folks moved to Shaxian from all over China, and each people group brought with them their unique cuisines. Over the centuries, the more extreme styles mellowed, and eventually Shaxian developed a cuisine that is not only very diverse but also tame enough that most people can appreciate it. Sanming Foreign Affair's Mr. Hong said, "If people want hot, sweet, sour, salty or bitter, they just dunk their food in the right sauce. Everyone is free to eat as they wish. Democratic dining!"

People from all over China and Southeast Asia reveled in Democratic Dining in December 2003, when Shaxian held its annual Shaxian Snack Folk Cultural Festival. Top entertainment artists performed on the large stage at the hi-tech park, and the city held a parade down the pedestrian plaza. Streets and squares were thronged with visitors examining Shaxian's local specialties and handicrafts. But the drawing card , of course, was the food!

Dialogue–Shaxian Snacks

Bill: So these little things are appetizers, right?

Bobby: No, these are the main courses.

Bill: You're kidding! If these are the main courses, I'm going home hungry tonight.

Bobby: I doubt even you will walk away from a Shaxian table hungry—because they have over 160 kinds of these little foods!

Bill: You're kidding! Then, I'd better eat slowly.

Bobby: Yeah, have a good try!

With over 160 snacks to sample, Shaxian locals recommend that visitors plan on at least a week to sample a couple dozen a day! I only tasted a fraction of those dishes offered, but each was heavenly. I enjoyed mushrooms, taro, and tofu served in many ways. My absolute favorite was the dumplings, especially the Xiao Mai Wan, though the four most famous dishes are Shaomai烧麦, Bianrou扁肉, Yubao 芋包, and Baoxin DoufuWan 包心豆腐.

第52集　沙县：福建美食城

导语

沙县小吃在福建省可以说是无人不知，在中国的其他地方也发展得红红火火，甚至还在向海外拓展。在今天的“老外看福建”中，我们来了解一下沙县的小吃产业。

解说

沙县人告诉我，一千多年来，商业繁荣的沙县人来人往，带来了各自的饮食习惯。数百年来，他们创造了独具特色的沙县小吃，品种丰富，口味适中。无论你想吃辣的，甜的，酸的，咸的，或者苦的，只要往调味盘里沾一下，问题全部解决。爱吃什么点什么，非常民主！

2003 年 12 月 8 日，沙县举行第七届小吃文化节。来自中国各地和东南亚地区的宾客聚集沙县，尽享沙县小吃的民主吃法。金沙园标准厂房内的大型舞台上，群星闪烁；步行街上的文艺踩街热闹非凡。街道、广场，人山人海，大家都在尽情地选购沙县的土特产品和手工艺品。当然，最引人注目的还是沙县小吃。

现场

潘维廉：这么说，这些小吃算是开胃小菜？

包东宇：你弄错了。这些菜就是沙县小吃的主食。

潘维廉：如果说这些小菜就算主食的话，那么今天晚上我肯定得吃不饱。

包东宇：沙县小吃有一百多种，我不相信你会饿着离开饭桌！

潘维廉：你没开玩笑吧？这么说，我得慢慢地品尝品尝。

包东宇：没错。好好尝尝吧！

解说

沙县小吃有 160 多个品种。当地人告诉我，要吃个遍，必须腾出一周，每天品尝 10 来种！我只尝过十来种，样样鲜美。我喜欢用蘑菇、芋头和豆腐做成的沙县小吃，最爱吃的是烧麦，接下来就是扁肉、芋包子和包心豆腐丸。

Shaxian's festive Snack Street makes it a cinch for even illiterate Laowai to order. Just point at the photos, eat, and pay. And happily, Shaxian cuisine is both tasty and inexpensive—though low prices haven't stopped many Shaxian folk from making fortunes, as I learned when I visited the home of Shaxian's legendary cuisine, Xiamao Town.

Of Xiamao Town's 30,000 residents, over 14,000 are doing business elsewhere! I'd have never believed little snack shops could bring in so much money until I visited the home of Mr. Luo Bing Jian罗秉建. Just ten years ago, he set out with 10,000 Yuan of borrowed money. Today, he has a 4-story 300,000 Yuan home with the money from shops in Fuzhou, Xiamen and Shenzhen. He modestly said, "It was only a few Yuan here, a few Yuan there. But of course, it all adds up!" He pointed to his house and said, "The metal came from noodles. The bricks came from pounded pork!"

Thanks to organizations like the Shaxian Snack Association (Shaxian Xiaochi Tongye Hui), Mr. Luo's prosperity is no exception in Xiamao Town. The streets are lined with beautiful new homes, and while this is still a country town, the shops offer fashions and electronics found only in coastal cities a mere five years ago. A local official said the best change has been in people's attitudes. "The poor just had more children, which made them poorer," he said. "People are better off now, and are happy to have only one child—and there is less crime and violence today as well. Lives are changing in everyway."

Lao Pantou Leads by Example Shaxian's entrepreneurial people are obviously not afraid to exert a little elbow-grease, as I saw when we visited Lao Pantou's Foodstuff's Factory. The General Manager himself was at the front gate in suit, tie and rubber boots, scrubbing down the driveway with

with a broom and water hose. He paused from his work to greet us, but then excused himself and went right back to work. Obviously he's heard the phrase "Lead by example!"

Lao Pantou is only one of many Shaxian firms producing such quality foodstuffs as Shaxian chili sauce, peanut butter, soy sauce, bean sauce, MSG, cooking utensils—and they're incorporating not only the latest but the greenest techniques.

Environmentally—Minded MSG Factory I was amazed at the comprehensiveness of an MSG factory's environmental measures. First season rice is used to produce glucose, from which is derived the acid to make MSG. First stage waste is converted to animal feed, and the wastewater is processed to create fertilizer. Nothing wasted—and the environment remains unharmed. A manager said, "We are in the upper reaches of the Min River, so environmental protection is paramount."

Shaxian's preoccupation with preservation of its environment obviously hasn't hampered Shaxian's economic success.

热闹的沙县小吃街对不识汉字的比尔来说简直就是天堂。食客只需按图索骥，点菜吃饭，掏腰包。还有更令人开心的是，沙县小吃味美价廉。当然，价廉并不意味着沙县人赚不到钱，发不了财。在走访沙县小吃重镇——夏茂之后，我对沙县小吃和沙县人的美食有了进一步的认识。

夏茂镇人口三万，外出做小吃的农民却多达一万四千人。在走进罗秉建先生的家门之前，我无论如何也不相信，小小的沙县小吃店会给沙县赚回这么多的钞票。十年前，罗先生外出经营沙县小吃时，兜里揣着向别人借来的一万元钱。如今，用在福州、厦门和深圳小吃店里赚来的钱，罗先生盖起了一栋价值 30 万元的四层洋房。对此，罗先生只是淡淡地说，这里赚几块，那里抓一把。加起来就厉害啦！“面条是钢筋，扁肉是砖头”，罗先生指着自家的房子对我说。

在夏茂，像罗先生这样富裕的农民大有人在。镇里、街上，新建的楼房鳞次栉比。这其中，像沙县小吃同业公会这样的组织机构功不可没。当地的一位政府官员说，最大的变化是人们思想观念的转变。他告诉我，“以前，农民越穷越生，越生越穷。现在好多了。老百姓已经乐于接受独生子女政策。违法犯罪行为减少了，人民的生活发生了翻天覆地的变化。”

Lead by example at Lao Pantou

沙县人精明能干，同时又能吃苦耐劳。这在老潘头食品厂得到了很好的印证。走近食品厂，我们看到总经理身着西装、领带，脚穿雨鞋，手持扫把、水龙，正在冲洗工厂门口的车道。看到我们来访，他稍停片刻，跟我们打完招呼，然后又马上埋头苦干去了。很显然，这位总经理深知：榜样的力量是无限的。

在沙县，像老潘头这样的食品厂还有很多。它们主要生产沙县小吃所需要的辣椒酱、花生酱、酱油、味精和各种各样的厨房用具。在生产过程中，这些工厂非常重视采用最新的环保技术。沙县味精厂就是很好的一个例子。他们用早米生产出葡萄糖，再从中提炼谷氨酸制造味精。废弃物加工成饲料，废水制成化肥。变废为宝，既不浪费，又很环保。正如厂里的一位经理所说，我们的工厂地处闽江上游，环境保护至关重要。

显然，环境保护并没有影响沙县经济发展。

With Shaxian's unparalleled natural and human resources, and its painstaking care of both, it's no wonder that Shaxian is again becoming the industrial, economic, cultural, communications, and transportation hub of central Fujian!

In the year 2003, the Shaxian county government has set up a goal to build Shaxian into an industrial and trading city with good ecological environment. Shaxian County has carefully planned its industrial development and infrastructure construction along the highway. The county also plans to build a framework for green industry and urban trade within 5 years, and fulfill the goal by 2015. And the population and the area of the downtown will be doubled. By then, Shaxian will surely have become one of the best business and living environments in North-west Fujian.

Dialogue—Pedestrian Plaza

Bobby: Wah! I've never imagined that Shaxian would be this lively at night!

Bill: Yeah, I think this is just as "renao" as Shanghai's Nanjing Road, though a lot more festive, I think.

Bobby: hum!

Shaxian pulsates with vitality. By day, young and old alike frolic on the rides and boats of the Sand 'n Sun Amusement Park (Shayang Leyuan), the largest city park amongst Minbei's county level cities. By night, the beautiful new pedestrian plaza is more colorful and exciting than even Shanghai's famed Nanjing Street.

In 15 years in China, I've never seen a place or people so obviously excited about both their present and their future. Of course, their eagerness to embrace the future is in part because of the almost 1600 years of tradition, culture and innovation already under their belt! Shaxian is indeed a magical place with a great past, and an even greater future.

丰富的自然资源和优越的地理位置，沙县成为福建中部工业、经济、文化、通讯和交通中心指日可待。

2003 年，沙县县委、县政府提出了“建设绿色工贸城市”的构想。他们开始沿着国道和高速公路两侧进行工贸发展规划和基础设施建设。根据绿色工贸城市的构想，沙县提出自己的奋斗目标，也就是：在近五年，在绿色工贸城建设方面，要初步形成一个框架。计划到 2015 年，要建成绿色工贸城的雏形。整个城区的人口、面积都要比现在翻一番。届时，沙县将成为闽西北重要的物流集散地和最佳的人口居住地。

现场（沙县步行街夜景）——

包东宇：哇！真没想到沙县夜景会这么漂亮。

潘维廉：是啊，简直可以和上海的南京路相媲美，而且节日气氛更浓！

包东宇：没错。

解说——

沙县活力四射。白天，老老少少或骑车兜风，或到闽中地区最大的县级公园——沙阳乐园游玩。到了夜晚，新建成的步行街简直和上海的南京路一样热闹，而且多姿多彩。

在中国生活 15 年，沙县是我走过的最为神奇的地方，沙县人是我见过的最为热情的人民。他们对自己的历史充满了自豪，对未来充满了自信。当然，这种自信或多或少跟沙县 1600 年的历史传统和创新意识是分不开的。

沙县，这片神奇的土地，拥有辉煌的历史。沙县的明天更美好。

A young Shaxian father
Proud and prosperous

Episode 53 Mingxi—the Gem Capital of Fujian

Baskets of Gems

Introduction Join us on today's episode of Magic Fujian as Bobby Bao and Dr. Bill Brown explore Fujian's gem capital, Mingxi!

Dialogue—Captivated by Crystals

Bobby: This is nice!

Bill: Pyrite crystal.

Bobby: So you must really like gems and crystals!

Bill: I sure do. I've been collecting them since I was six or seven years old! When I drove around China in 1994, I loaded up Toy Ota with several hundred pounds.

Bobby: Do you have crystals from Fujian as well?

Bill: Yes of course. I have several beautiful ones. Fujian produces beautiful crystals, and Sanming has Mingxi!

Bobby: Really?!

I had no idea that Fujian was a treasure trove of gems and crystals until an Anxi farmer dug one from his field, phoned me, and said, "Professor Pan, I have a rock for you!" It was a ten pound crystal! And later, our entire family enjoyed a Saturday outing to Zhangzhou, where we dug over a dozen beautiful quartz crystals from the red clay of a friend's farm. But if I was happy then, I was in hog heaven [very happy!] when I discovered that Sanming's Mingxi is one of the gem capitals of China! Since then I've visited the city 3 times!

Dialogue—Red Treasure

Bill: You know, Mingxi is one of my favorite places in Fujian.

Bobby: Knowing you, it must be the food—like their famous red mushrooms.

Bill: Well, got the color right, but I'm talking about rubies, not mushrooms. One of my hobbies is collecting gemstones and crystals, and Mingxi Produces rubies.

Bobby: Oh? Mingxi is also the 4th largest producer of sapphires. They dig them right out of the river bed.

Bill: Really? Well I have a spoon. And so after we visit this jewelry center I'm going to start digging.

第53集　宝石之都明溪县

导语

欢迎收看系列报道“老外看福建”。今天，厦门大学的潘维廉博士和我们的记者包东宇将带大家去见识一下福建的宝石之都——明溪。

现场（潘维廉家中）

包东宇：看来你相当喜欢宝石和水晶！

潘维廉：我从六岁就开始收集宝石和水晶。1994 年，我们全家驾车环游中国，我们的“疯甜”车满载而归，里面装了好几百磅的水晶石。

包东宇：这里面有没有福建的水晶？

潘维廉：当然有。福建出产的水晶很美。三明的明溪还是中国的蓝宝石四大产地之一呢。

解说

在安溪的一位农民从地里挖出水晶石之前，我还不知道福建是宝石和水晶的宝库。这位农民朋友打电话告诉我：“潘教授，我有块石头要给你！”一块十磅重的水晶石！后来，我们全家周末到漳州玩，又从朋友的农田里挖出了十几块漂亮的石英石。如果用开心来形容我当时的心情的话，那么当我得知三明的明溪是中国四大蓝宝石产地之一时，我简直高兴坏了。为了宝石，我专门去了三趟明溪！

现场

潘维廉：老外很少有知道明溪的，但那却是我最喜欢的地方之一。

包东宇：我知道，肯定又是吃的，明溪的红菇就很有名。

潘维廉：嗯，颜色倒是给你猜中了。我六岁就开始收集宝石和矿石，而明溪是红宝石的产地！

Mingxi treasure chest

包东宇：是吗？我知道明溪是中国蓝宝石的第四大产地。他们就从河床里挖宝石。

潘维廉：真的吗？我手头上恰好带着铲子。到了宝石之都，我可要开挖了！

4th-Largest Gem Field Mingxi, the fourth largest gem-producing area in China, has 20 different kinds of gemstones, including my all time favorite, amethyst. The 800 square kilometer gem-bed has produced over 1 billion grams of gems! In 1992, income from gems amounted to only 500,000 Yuan or so. Thanks to government encouragement and seed money, by 2001,the 20-plus gem firms brought in a revenue of over 6 million Yuan, and Mingxi's future is crystal clear!

Actually, there were over 50 firms in 1993, but many went under. As one gem producer told me, "It was hard getting orders for gems from overseas buyers. We were unknown, and buyers at international fairs simply said, "We can get the same thing from other countries." Then the Mingxi government stepped in, encouraging folks to not just sell raw crystals by the pound but to innovate and add value. Mingxi began crafting elegant jewelry from not only local gems but also stones imported from all over China. Today, Mingxi gem artisans are developing a name for themselves, both at home and abroad! As another Mingxi gem expert told me, "People can buy stones anywhere, but for quality work, we do it better, faster, and to any specifications that they can dream up!"

Dialogue—Cutting-Edge Gem Tech

Bill: You know, with all these gems, Mingxi must be famous for jewelry.
Bobby: Not just for jewelry. They also use gems to make swords and knives!
Bill: That's a sharp idea. Must be some pretty cutting edge technology!

Mingxi Swordsmith

After visiting several gem producers, we stopped by at a factory that produces breathtakingly beautiful swords and knives, and inlays them with beautiful gems. I bought one that reminded me of an elf's knife used in Tolkien's "Lord of the Rings!" And these aren't just ornamental pieces, but finely crafted. I watched them hammer and hone a blade until it was not only sharp as a razor but as supple as a cane whip!

For years I've taught my MBA students that to survive in today's increasingly competitive global markets, we can't just sell commodities by the ton, like a peasant farmer. We have to innovate, and add value. And Mingxi jewelry and gem-inlaid weaponry are excellent examples of how to do it! The rest of China could learn some lessons from this little gem of a town!

解说

作为中国第四大宝石产地，明溪出产包括我最喜欢的紫水晶在内的 20 多种宝石。明溪蓝宝石的分布面积约有 800 平方公里，储量在一亿克拉以上。1992 年，明溪宝石业的产值仅仅 50 万元。由于政府鼓励，加上来钱快，2001 年明溪 20 多家珠宝企业的纳税超过 600 万元。明溪的未来光辉灿烂！

事实上，1993 年时，明溪的珠宝企业曾一度达到 50 多家，后来许多都倒闭了。一位企业家告诉我："我们当时没有什么知名度，很难从外国客户手中拿到订单。参加国际珠宝展的买家经常说，'我们可以从别的国家买到同样的货。'" 这时候，明溪县政府站了出来，鼓励宝石生产企业进行创新，增加附加值，而不只是按重量出卖原石。于是，明溪开始利用本地和来自中国各地的宝石生产精美的珠宝产品。如今，明溪的珠宝艺人已经在国内外珠宝行业赢得了声誉。明溪的一位宝石专家告诉我："到处都可以买到宝石。只是在加工方面，我们做得更快、更好，花色品种随他们定！"

现场（刀剑厂门市）

潘维廉：有这么多的宝石，明溪的珠宝首饰应该很出名吧。

包东宇：明溪出名的不仅仅是珠宝首饰，他们还有用宝石镶嵌的刀剑！

潘维廉：够犀利！这恐怕要数高精尖技术了！

解说

看过几家珠宝企业，我们在一家刀剑厂稍作停留。这家宝剑厂生产的宝剑和宝刀有漂亮的宝石镶嵌，简直精美绝伦。我买了一把，就像《指环王》里矮人族用的那种宝刀。这些刀剑做工精致，绝对不是做装饰用的花架子。我看着他们又锤又磨，直至把剑做得利如剃刀，软若藤鞭！

多年来，我一直教导我的MBA学生：要想在当今竞争日趋激烈的全球市场生存，我们就不能像农民那样仅仅批量贩卖原材料。我们应该创新，增加附加值。明溪的珠宝厂和刀剑厂就是很好的案例。他们的做法值得中国其他地方的企业学习。

Episode 54 Shibi—Hakka Homeland

Introduction Welcome to today's episode of Magic Fujian, as FJTV's Bobby Bao and Xiamen University MBA's Dr. Bill Brown visit Shibi, the Hakka Homeland!

The Hakka people, who are known around the world as successful entrepreneurs, have over 1,000 years of innovativeness under their belt! Hakka means "Guest people", and over a millennium ago they fled the wars and famines of central China's plains to find a new life in Southeast China. The perpetual new kids on the block, the "Guest People" spent a lot of time being run off until they found the natural fortress of Shibi, which is a deep basin with flat fields surrounded by rings of mountains. And according to experts, the basins and mountains also create what is some of the best fengshui on the planet. So when the Hakka found Shibi, the guest people were home at last! And each year, tens of thousands of Hakka return from all over China, and indeed all over the world, to Shibi to pay tribute to their esteemed ancestors in the great Hakka ancestral hall.

Dialogue—Hakka Ancestral Temple

Bill: So this is an ancient Hakka ancestral temple, huh?

Bobby: No, actually it is quite new!

Bill: New? Then why on earth every year do Hakka come from all over the world to this remote place?

Bobby: Because the real ancestral temples are too scattered and even more remote!

Hakka Ancestral Temple

Hakka ancestral temples are spread all over Fujian, some of them in extremely remote and inaccessible areas. So in 1995 the government donated land and part of the 6 million Yuan needed to build a central Hakka Ancestral Hall in Shibi. Each year, on holidays like October 16th, Hakka from all over the world return here to pay their respects. They fly great yellow flags at the front of clan processions that march up the 500-meter stone road to the Hall, where the great doors are thrown wide open only on these festivals. Once inside, they locate their ancient ancestors with modern technology!

第 54 集　客家祖地宁化石壁

♪ 导语 ———

欢迎收看系列报道“老外看福建”。今天，厦门大学的潘维廉教授和我们的记者包东宇将带大家到客家祖地——宁化石壁去看一看。

♪ 解说 ———

客家人敢创业、善经营是举世公认的。千百年来，他们一直秉承着勇于创新的精神。“客家”的意思就是“做客的人家”。一千多年前，客家先民为了逃避中原的战乱和饥荒，开始向中国东南部迁徙，寻求新的生活环境。作为这个地区的外来者，客家人长期以来居无定所。后来，终于找到了宁化这个天然堡垒。这里群山环绕，谷深地平，被专家们确认为世上风水最好的地方之一。因此，客家人就开始在石壁安家落户繁衍生息。来自世界各地成千上万的客家乡亲每年都会聚集到石壁客家公祠，祭拜祖先。

♪ 现场 ———

潘维廉：这就是古代的客家公祠？

包东宇：不，这是新建的。

潘维廉：那为什么世界各地的客家人每年都要到这里祭拜呢？

包东宇：因为客家人的祖祠太分散了，而且大多都很偏僻！

Hakka Ancestral Temple (Shibi)

♪ 解说 ———

客家各姓氏的祖祠散布在福建各地，有些祖祠非常偏僻，交通极为不便。因此，1995 年，政府部门划拨了土地和建祠所需 600 万元资金的一部分，在福建宁化兴建了石壁客家公祠。每逢诸如 10 月 16 日这样的节日，来自世界各地的客家乡亲都会聚集在宁化石壁，谒祖寻根。祭祀队伍排成长龙，高举着黄色祭旗，沿着 500 米长的石板路，鱼贯进入客家公祠。只有在重要的节日，祖祠才会正门大开。进入祖祠，他们就会利用现代技术，找找祖先的牌位。

Dialogue—Laowai Lack Ancestors?

Bobby: Every clan has its own ancestral tablet. See—push the button by your name, down here, and it lights up!

Bill: Does it have my Chinese name, Pan?

Bobby: Of course—yours is on that side.

Bill: Last time I was here, one of the Chinese found out that my real name wasn't Pan. He said, "You don't have any ancestors!"

Push-button Geneology

By Chinese standards, maybe I don't have ancestors! Like many Americans, I can trace my ancestry back only 3 or 4 generations. I know my grandfather was Norwegian and my grandmother Apache Indian, and beyond that I've no idea, and though I'm curious, it's not really very important to me. But some Chinese can trace their ancestry back dozens of generations, and travel far and near to update and verify the accuracy of their ancestral records!

While Chinese in general put great stock in keeping ancestral records, Hakka have an additional motive. While many people think Hakka are a minority, they are in fact Han Chinese, and fiercely proud of it. And so they keep ancestral records dating back centuries to prove their Han identity.

The stairs to the left of the ancestral Hall lead to a second floor museum on Hakka culture and customs. Hakka ingenuity was evident in the old wooden machines used for making burlap cloth, the ingenious water conveyor belt, and the peerless one-wheeled wheelbarrows. I marvel each time I see these ancient machines, many of which were invented 2,000 years ago, and some of which the West was not able to duplicate until as late as the 19th century! In fact, the agricultural revolution that allowed the industrial revolution was only possible because Dutch traders borrowed ancient Chinese agricultural machinery and farming techniques. It's a good thing we don't have to pay royalties!

Given Hakka ingenuity and innovativeness, it's no wonder that today the guest people are highly successful not only in China but throughout the rest of the world as well.

Dialogue—Where's the Real Hakka Home?

Bill: You know, I'm a little bit confused—as usual! If Shibi claims to be the Hakka Homeland, and Changting claims to be the Hakka Homeland, which is true?

Bobby: Both are true! And in ancient times, Shibi was under Changting's jurisdiction.

Bill: Well, in that case to better understand Hakka people I think we should visit Changting as well.

♪现场

包东宇：每个姓氏都有自己的祖先牌位。根据你的姓氏，按下开关，老祖宗牌位的灯就亮了起来。看，包姓在这里！

潘维廉：能不能帮我找找？我姓潘。

包东宇：没问题。在这！

潘维廉：我上次来的时候，有人发现我不是真正的潘氏后裔，感到很惊讶。于是，就对我说："你没有祖先！"

♪解说

按照中国人的标准，或许我是没有祖先！跟许多美国人一样，我的祖宗只能追溯到我前面的三四代。我知道，我的祖父是挪威人，祖母是阿帕契族的印第安人。再往前，我就搞不清楚了。尽管我很想知道，但是这对我来说已经不是很重要了。相比之下，一些中国人寻根问祖甚至可以追溯到几百年之遥，而且还会不远万里四处查考，修订和续写族谱。

中国人一般都会为保存和修订族谱而感到自豪。客家人修谱还有另外一个目的。那是因为许多人都把客家人当作少数民族。事实上，他们也是汉族同胞，并且特别引以为豪。因此，他们保存几百年的族谱，可以证明他们的汉族身份。

客家公祠左侧的楼梯直通二楼的客家民俗博物馆。从古老的木制麻布纺织机、精致的水车到独轮手推车，都印证了客家人的聪明才智。这些古老的机械大多发明于两千多年前，其中有一些直到 19 世纪西方人才学会制造和使用。这不能不让我感到惊奇！事实上，正是因为荷兰人借鉴了中国的农业机械和耕作技术，才使得西方工业革命之前的农业革命成为可能。幸好我们不必为此向中国人缴纳专利费！

Ancient Hakka Ingenuity

正是因为客家人具有这样的聪明才智和开拓精神，所以就不难理解为什么他们在全中国乃至世界各地都很成功。

♪现场

潘维廉：我有点搞糊涂了，石壁和长汀都说自己是客家祖地，那到底哪个才是真的？

包东宇：都是！因为在古代，宁化石壁也归汀州府管辖。

潘维廉：这么说，要想充分了解客家人，我们还应该去趟长汀！

Episode 55 Taining—Ming Dynasty House and Gold Lake

Introduction On today's episode of Magic Fujian, FJTV's Bobby Bao and Xiamen University MBA's Dr. Bill Brown take us to the scenic and historic town of Taining!

Ming Dynasty Home Taining's well preserved Ming Dynasty architecture was a totally unexpected delight for me. The buildings are in excellent shape, thanks to overseas Chinese, Mr. Huang Shuang'an, who donated 600,000 Yuan in 1992 to restore the site. Over 6,000 meters have been completed, and eventually the museum will comprise over 10,000 meters.

Dialogue—Ming Dynasty Residents!

Bill: Walking around this ancient village is kind of like walking back in time.

Bobby: Actually, this 6,000 square meter area is not a village. It is the house of a Ming Dynasty minister!

Bill: You're kidding! A 6,000 square meter house? That's about 600 times bigger than my Xiada apartment! I wish I could meet the people who lived here.

Bobby: Some are still walking around. Let me introduce you.

Bill: As long as they're not ghosts!

I wasn't sure if I was touring the Ming Dynasty or Disneyland when I saw half a dozen rooms crowded with life-sized animated wax figures. A one Yuan coin in the wood boxes' slot brings them to life, with lots of action, and lots of loud!

In one room, a peachy Ming Dynasty maiden served peach-shaped steamed buns to 3 mechanical men drinking tea. Next door, two girls pedaled away at a crank-operated wooden mallet while a third stirred sticky rice in a giant wooden tub. In yet another room, mechanical youth did the Dragon dance, each boy shouldering a board on which was a balanced lantern. Very nicely done!

第55集　泰宁：尚书第与大金湖

导语

欢迎收看系列报道“老外看福建”。今天，厦门大学的潘维廉博士和我们的记者包东宇将带我们去看看泰宁的尚书第和金湖。

解说

泰宁的明代民居建筑——尚书第保存得十分完好，这完全出乎我的意料。1992 年，闽籍侨胞黄双安先生捐资 60 万元，用于修复泰宁尚书第，这才使得尚书第恢复原貌。目前已经修复的面积有 6000 多平方米，最终修复的规模将超过 1 万平方米。

现场

潘维廉：走进这个明朝古村，就像走进了历史。

包东宇：实际上，这 6000 平方米的明朝建筑不是一个村落，而是明朝一位尚书的府第。

潘维廉：哇！6000 平方米，比我厦大的套房大了整整 60 倍！可惜就是遇不到在这里住过的人。

包东宇：附近肯定找得着。我来找找看。

潘维廉：好吧，只要不是幽灵就行！

解说

当我看到尚书第的好几个房间里都满是真人大小的人物蜡像时，我真怀疑自己是不是到了明朝或者迪斯尼乐园。往蜡像旁边的木盒里扔一枚硬币，蜡像便随着乐曲活动起来，动静还挺大。在一个房间里，有一组蜡像是三个男人在喝茶、吃寿桃包的场景，旁边还有一位脸颊粉红的丫鬟伺候着。另外一个房间里，两名少女脚踩木棰，还有一个少女则站在旁边翻动大木臼里的糯米团。还有一个房间展示的是会转圈的桥灯，每个蜡像男子都是肩扛木板，上面放着灯笼。做得实在棒极了。

Ming Dynasty Theater Next door to the Ming Dynasty house is a theater, which each evening hosts performances of the local opera, which has received acclaim all over Fujian, and the rest of China as well. We enjoyed watching the girls, bundled up against the cold, practice one of their dances. A pity we could not stay for the performance that night!

Golden Lake During the Song Dynasty, about 820,000 people moved to Taining, in part because it was one of Fujian's few stretches of flat land, and in part because it produced gold. Eventually the gold petered out, and gold creek was dammed to produce gold lake. But today, the beautiful gold lake is bringing in another kind of gold!

Dialogue—A New Source of Gold

Bobby: Bill, did you know that the great Golden Lake shares the same mountain range as the Wuyi Mountains?

Bill: If that is so, then Taining must have the same rich biological diversity that has made Wuyi mountain famous worldwide.

Bobby: Yeah, it's a pity that Taining gets fewer tourists because it's so remote.

Bill: It's remote, but once the Fuzhou to Beijing highway is opened up, Gold Lake is going to bring in a new kind of gold. Tourism!

Over 50,000 tourists a year visit Gold Lake. They come to fish, or parasail, or relax on the 15 km boat cruise, which winds along the 99 bends and 88 shoals past stunning cave-studded red cliffs and green mountains that are so beautiful that a brochure claims, "The sky is humiliated by the mountains."

A Taining man said, "We have everything Wuyi does! They just have better publicity!" But that will change! A "Golden Lake Tourist Train" from Fuzhou to Shaowu is under construction, and on October 1st, 2004, the Fuzhou—Taining highway will open, cutting the drive to 3 hours and making it easier for people to enjoy Taining's scenery—below ground as well as above!

尚书第隔壁的金湖风情演艺馆几乎每天都上演当地的地方戏。泰宁的梅林戏很有名，不仅在福建，在中国各地都深受好评。我们饶有兴趣地看了一会儿剧团演员们在寒风中排练舞蹈，可惜时间紧迫，我们晚上不能留下来看她们表演。

宋朝的时候，约有 82 万人移居泰宁，原因之一是泰宁是福建少有的平地之一，另一个原因则是这里发现了黄金。现在黄金采完了，但是政府在河上拦起大坝，修建了金湖。如今，美丽的金湖给泰宁带来了另外一种黄金。

♪现场 ——

包东宇：你知道吗？金湖地区和武夷山同属一个山脉。

潘维廉：生物多样性让武夷山驰名中外。泰宁应该也有一份吧！

包东宇：可惜泰宁太偏僻了，游客还来得不多。

潘维廉：这就是说，新建的高速公路一旦通车，金湖就会产出另外一种黄金——旅游！

♪解说 ——

目前，金湖每年接待游客 5 万多人次。他们到金湖垂钓、驾滑翔伞，或者干脆就在游船上放松心情。15 公里的上清溪漂流途中有 99 道弯，88 个浅滩，景色优美，正如一本宣传册上所言“丹山碧水羞天穹”。

On Golden Lake

有一位泰宁人对我说：“武夷山有的，我们都有！只是他们宣传做得比我们好。” 福州至邵武的旅游专列开通后，前往泰宁的游客人数有望继续攀升。京福速公路建成通车后，游客从福州到金湖只要三个小时。那时候，到泰宁上天入地欣赏美景可就方便多了。

Dialogue—Yuhua Cave

Subterranean Lake

Bobby: Yuhua Cave is one of the reasons Sanming is as beautiful below ground as above.

Bill: Really? I also heard it was one of the 4 most famous ancient caverns in China.

Bobby: Actually, it was considered number two, number one is Beijing's Shihua Cave.

Bill: Well, it's definitely #1 in Fujian, so why don't we crawl down there and find out why.

Xu Xiake
(Entrance to Yuhua Cave)

Xu Xiake, the great Ming Dynasty traveler who visited Taining in 1628, wrote that Fujian's two most impressive sites were 1, Wuyi Mountain, and 2, Yuhua Cave. And exploring these majestic caverns I could understand why! The vast caverns are spectacular, and many of the formations had uncanny resemblances to various animals. Of course, I was delighted when I discovered something my guides had never noticed—a stone that looked exactly like a monkey. Of course, it may help that I was born in the year of the monkey!

After the cave tour, our guide treated us to the delightful Hakka pounded tea. While some Hakka make it with meat and veggies, Jiangle pounded tea was made mainly from pounded sesame seeds, and was delightfully refreshing, especially when accompanied with the local roasted peanuts. But when I saw how much work it was to make the tea, I decided I'd stick with teabags!

现场

包东宇：人们都说，三明地下的景观和地上一样美，玉华洞就是一个代表。

潘维廉：没错。我还听说，玉华洞是中国四大名洞之一。

包东宇：事实上，玉华洞应该排名第二，排名第一的是北京石花洞。

潘维廉：那就算福建第一吧。我们进去看看。

解说

1628 年，中国明代伟大的旅行家徐霞客到过泰宁。他在游记中提到福建两处景观给他留下了深刻印象，一处是武夷山，接下来就是玉华洞。看过玉华洞，我终于体会到了其中的奥秘。这个巨大的溶洞实在壮观，洞里许多景观的形态极像各种各样的动物。我还兴奋地发现了一处新景观，那是一块连导游都以前都没注意到的酷似猴子的石头！当然，这跟我是猴年出生的也许有点关系。

Pounding Tea for F J Tea V!

从玉华洞出来，导游请我们喝客家擂茶。客家人一般用肉或者蔬菜做擂茶，而将乐擂茶的主要原料则是捣碎了的芝麻。擂茶配当地的烤花生，喝起来特别提神。不过，当我了解到制作擂茶的复杂过程之后，我决定还是继续喝我的袋泡茶。

Episode 56 Anxi—Tea Capital of China

Introduction On today's episode of Magic Fujian, FJTV's Bobby Bao and Xiamen University MBA Center's Dr. Bill Brown take us to the home of Oolong tea, Anxi!

Anxi has long been famous as one of China's major tea capitals, and home of the famous Oolong tea. Anxi tea has been enjoyed all over the world for several centuries, and has even has an effect on Western history!

Dialogue—How Anxi Helped Free America!

Bill: So, did you know that Anxi helped America get independence from the British?

Bobby: No way! How could that be?

Bill: America revolted against England by throwing tea into the sea during the Boston Tea Party—and that tea was right here from Anxi!

Bobby: So Anxi tea helped tee[1] off the British!

Anxi is probably the home of the elegant Minnan Tea Ceremony, with its tiny thimble-sized cups and elaborate procedures for choosing the best water and tea, and preparing the pot and cups. Many scholars even say that this beautiful ceremony is the origin of the Japanese tea ceremony.

Unfortunately, until the past decade, the very people who grew some of the world's finest teas were too poor to afford to drink them, and had to settle with brewing up herbs or even grass—but times have changed!

Dialogue—Anxi Attacks Poverty

Bobby: It's hard to believe that only ten years ago, Anxi was one of the poorest places in Fujian.

Bill: Really? It looks pretty wealthy now. What brought about the change?

Bobby: Anxi is among the top 100 counties in China economically, thanks to a strong anti-poverty program!

Bill: Looks like it worked.

Amoymagic.com

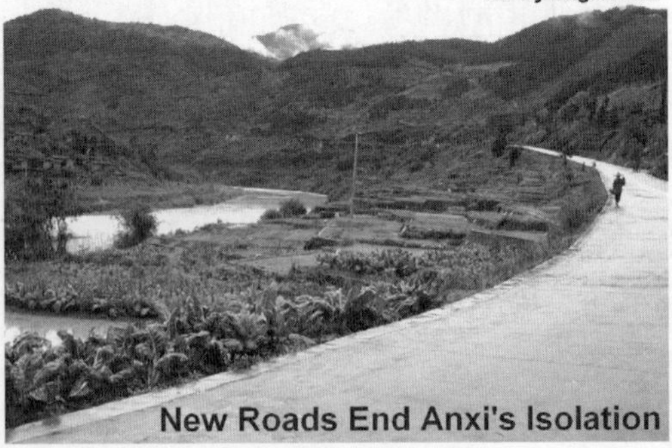

New Roads End Anxi's Isolation

[1] Tee off: make angry ("tee" sounds like "tea")

第56集　茶都安溪

导语

在今天的系列报道“老外看福建”中，我们跟随记者包东宇和厦门大学的潘维廉教授一起到乌龙茶的故乡安溪去走一走。

解说

安溪一向号称中国茶都，这里是著名的乌龙茶的故乡。几百年来，安溪茶享誉全世界，甚至对西方历史都产生过影响。

现场

潘维廉：你知道吗？安溪曾经帮助美国摆脱英国获得独立。

包东宇：不会吧！这怎么可能？

潘维廉：在波士顿倾茶事件中，美国人把茶叶倒进海里，以此表示对英国统治的反抗。而那些茶叶就来自安溪！

包东宇：原来是安溪茶把英美关系给“咔嚓”了！

解说

雅致的闽南茶艺也许就发源于安溪。茶道的程序复杂而细致，要用小如顶针的茶杯，选用最好的水和茶叶，喝茶前要仔细摆弄茶壶和茶杯。许多学者还认为日本的茶道就源自于这种优美的茶艺。

遗憾的是，直到十几年前，安溪人还饱受贫困折磨，他们不但没钱享受自己种出的好茶，甚至还有人住在茅草搭盖的棚屋里。不过现在情况已经大不相同了！

现场

包东宇：真是令人难以置信，就在十年前，安溪还是福建最穷的地方之一。

潘维廉：现在看来，这里已经相当富裕了。为什么变化那么快？

包东宇：安溪目前已经跻身中国经济百强县，这要归功于强有力的扶贫措施。

潘维廉：这些措施看来蛮有效的。

No Longer Isolated—or Poor. Over 700,000 Overseas Chinese claim Anxi as their home, but though many of them have prospered greatly abroad, those back at home in Anxi suffered great poverty, primarily because of its remote mountainous location. But new roads and highways are eliminating Anxi's age-old isolation. While the drive from Xiamen to Anxi took over 8 hours in the 1980s, it now takes only two! In addition, the government has given farmers seed money to scientifically improve traditional crops like tea, or to start new industries, such as mushrooms and edible fungus.

Longmen Township was selected as a "Science and Technology Anti-Poverty Demonstration Site," and after experts from the Fujian Academy of Agricultural Scientists helped improve agriculture and livestock practices, income grew 160% in only four years!

New Roads Help Anxi Prosper New roads and bridges have not only given Anxi farmers easier access to markets but also allowed tourists to more easily visit such famous Anxi sites as Nine Peaks Cliff Temple, Prime Minister Li Guangdi's former residence in Anxi's Hutou Township, and of course the beautiful Qingshui Temple.

Dialogue—Anxi's Potala Palace

Bill: This Qingshui Temple reminds me of Tibet's Potala Palace, the way it kind of clings to the mountainside here! Is it very old?

Bobby: It's almost 1000 years old, and it is considered a very holy place for Buddhists.

Bill: Especially for Taiwanese Buddhists, I hear.

Bobby: That's true. And they have come here to light incense for over 100 Taiwanese temples.

When renovated in 1564, Qingshui Cliff Temple was home to over 70 monks and nuns. Today, the beautifully sprawling temple attracts over 600,000 visitors annually, and I can see why. But for me, the biggest attraction is the incredible scenery, and the massive trees. An ancient camphor tree is so large it takes half a dozen people holding hands to reach around it. The ancient sentinel is called "Facing North" because when the tree heard that the good general Yue Fei (岳飞) had been murdered by a treacherous official, the tree held out all its branches to the north to express its sorrow.

Whether tea, trade or tourism, Anxi is once again prospering—and so is its once-glamorous neighbor to the north, Dehua, which in Marco Polo's day produced the white Chinese porcelain prized the world over.

♪解说

安溪号称拥有 70 多万海外乡亲，他们当中不少人都成就显赫，然而安溪本地的乡亲却长期忍受着贫困的煎熬，这主要是因为安溪地处偏远的深山。现在，新修的大小道路正在逐步消除安溪长期与世隔绝的状态。上个世纪 80 年代，开车从厦门到安溪要花八个小时以上，现在只要两个小时就够了！此外，政府还出资帮助农民改良茶叶等传统作物的品种，或者帮助他们从事香菇等食用菌的生产。

安溪龙门镇被确定为“科技扶贫示范点”。在福建省农科院的专家们进行了农业和畜禽生产扶持之后，当地农民的收入在四年内增长了 160%。

崭新的道路和桥梁不但拉近了安溪农民与市场的距离，同时也为游客出行提供了便利，安溪著名的景点有“凤山胜景”东岳寺、湖头镇的李光地故居，以及风光旖旎的清水岩风景区等等。

♪现场

潘维廉：清水岩让我想起西藏的布达拉宫，同样也是依山势而建，气势磅礴。它的历史很久了吧？

包东宇：差不多有一千年的历史了吧，这里是著名的佛家朝圣旅游胜地。

潘维廉：听说台湾的信众特别多是吧？

包东宇：没错。据说清水岩的香火传到了一百多座台湾的寺庙。

Qingshuiyan (Anxi)

♪解说

清水岩重修于 1564 年，这里常住着 70 多名僧众。这座气势恢宏的岩寺每年都吸引 60 多万中外游客前来游览。对我来说，这里神奇的风光和那些参天古树最有吸引力。有一棵粗壮的古樟树要六七个人才能环抱。这株古树被称为“枝枝超北”，传说是因为南宋名将岳飞被害的消息传来时，老树的枝叶全部向北伸展以表达哀悼。

因为有了茶叶和旅游，安溪正再次繁荣起来。而它北面的邻居德化也在重振昔日辉煌，德化出产的中国白瓷在马可·波罗时代就已经名扬世界。

Episode 57 Porcelain Capital of Dehua

Introduction Join us on today's episode as FJTV's Bobby Bao and Xiamen University's Dr. Bill Brown explore Dehua, one of ancient China's greatest producers of porcelain.

During Marco Polo's day, silk could fetch a king's ransom in Europe, but Chinese porcelain nearly bankrupted a few Western kingdoms! During a time when Europeans largely ate with their fingers, and used boards or pieces of hard bread for plates, Chinese enjoyed their celestial cuisine serves in bowls, saucers and platters of porcelain so fine that it was translucent, like egg shells, and rang like a bell when struck. Chinese porcelain exerted such a seductive appeal upon Westerners that the word "china" even became a euphemism for sex! European kings spent vast fortunes trying to discover the secret of porcelain production, and even went so far as to imprison alchemists until their either produced porcelain or died trying. Most died trying! But the answer lay right here in Dehua, one of China's 3 three great producers of porcelain.

Dialogue--Qudougong Ancient Kiln

Bobby: Have you ever seen an ancient dragon kiln like this.

Bill: Yeah, I have. Wuyi Mountain has two of them that have been pretty well preserved. But I kind of wonder, where'd they get the name dragon kiln?

Bobby: Well, it looks like a long dragon climbing the mountain.

Bill: That's true. And probably when it was fired up it smoked like a dragon too!

Since 1949, archaeologists have discovered over 180 ancient kilns, like the Qudougong kiln in Dehua. This kiln was discovered in 1976 on the southwest slopes of Mount Pozhai. The sheer scale of production during ancient times can be guessed at from the fact that scientists have recovered over 6,700 Song and Yuan dynasty relics from the kiln's 17 chambers. It's something to realize that on the slopes of this hill, craftsman produced the heavenly porcelain that intrigued European royalty for centuries! And when you understand the incredible complexity behind porcelain production, you can understand why it took Westerners several centuries to decipher its secrets, for porcelain making is as much science as art.

第57集　瓷都德化

导语——

在今天的系列报道“老外看福建”中，厦门大学的潘维廉教授将带我们前往中国的古瓷都之一——德化。

解说——

在马可·波罗时代的欧洲，如果国王被绑架，丝绸可以用作赎金，而中国瓷器更让一些小国耗尽国库储备。当欧洲人还普遍用手抓饭吃，把木板或者硬面包片当作盘子的时候，中国人已经在用陶瓷制成的碗碟享受美食了。这些精美的瓷器像卵壳一般透明，敲上去像铜铃般悦耳。中国瓷器对西方人的诱惑力达到了极致，“china”（瓷器）这个词甚至被用作“性感”的比喻。一些欧洲王室为研究瓷器的生产工艺花费了大笔财富。有的工匠甚至被监禁起来，直到制作出瓷器为止，可惜他们大多数到死也没造出来。而福建的德化就出产瓷器，并且还是中国古代三大陶瓷产地之一。

现场（屈斗宫古窑址）——

包东宇：你以前见过这样的龙窑吗？

潘维廉：见过，武夷山就有两座保护得很好的龙窑。可“龙窑”这个名字是怎么得来的呢？

包东宇：因为它们看上去就像一条龙趴在山坡上。

潘维廉：的确如此。如果把这些窑烧起来的话，恐怕也会像火龙一样会喷烟冒火吧。

解说——

1949年以后，考古工作者在德化发现了180多座古窑址，其中，屈斗宫古窑址是1976年在德化浔中镇破寨山西南坡发现的。古时候的生产规模仅从出土文物的数量就可见一斑。在一条长57米、共有17间窑室的窑基中，总共发掘出宋元时期的瓷器6793件。想象一下，就是在这样一个山坡上生产出来的瓷器，让欧洲的王室和贵族为之如痴如狂足足几个世纪。而当你了解了瓷器的生产过程是如何的繁复之后，你就会理解为什么西方人足足花了几百年来破解它的奥秘。制造瓷器不仅是一项技艺，更是一门艺术。

Porcelain is made with a pure white clay that we call kaolin in English, from the Chinese word gaolin. It is mixed with a feldspar mineral that forms a glassy glaze, and fired at a high temperature. The amounts and proportions must be exact, and the product must be fired at the perfect temperature for the exact amount of time. Wouldbe Europeans pottery makers tried literally thousands of combinations over the centuries before they got it down. Even then, European porcelain was made with a so-called soft paste, so it was not as fine and durable as Chinese pottery, which dominated global porcelain markets until a couple centuries ago.

Dialogue—Dehua Pottery Museum

Bill: You know, Bobby, I've been to Dehua 5 times and this is the first time that I'd ever heard that they have a porcelain museum!

Bobby: This museum has a quite extensive display of ancient porcelain.

Bill: And where are these things from?

Bobby: These are from the largest underwater archaeological discovery yet.

Bill: Oh, I heard about that. In 1999 they found over 350,000 pieces of pottery. I bet my wife could use some of these.

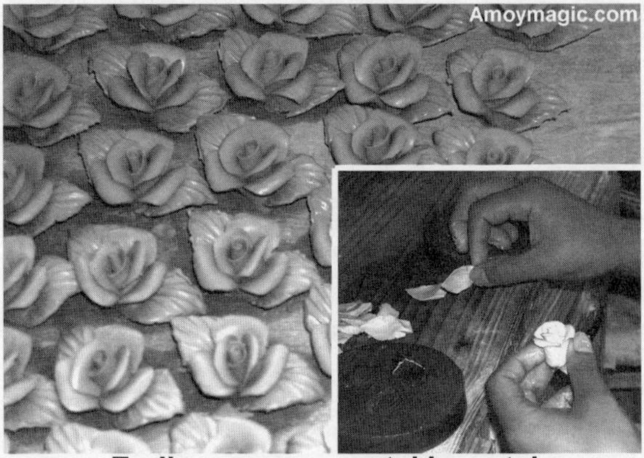

Endless roses -- petal by petal

As Europe perfected its own porcelain production, and the Ming closed China's doors to foreign trade, Dehua declined. But today, the ancient city is again on the fast track to become a leading producer of Chinese porcelain. Modern Dehua factories not only reproduce classic designs but also continue to innovate not only with form and color but materials and function. Nowadays, they can, and do, make just about anything to order, and ship their delicate wares all over the globe.

Dialogue—Porcelain Workshop

Bill: You know my wife would have a field day if these factories would sell her some of this porcelain.

Bobby: So she would love the Porcelain Street.

Bill: What's Porcelain Street? A street made of porcelain?

Bobby: Of course not! It's a street with lots of shops selling porcelain.

Bill: Well, let's visit it. But don't tell my wife about it or I'll have to ask Xiamen University for a pay raise!

瓷器的原料是一种叫“高岭土”的白色瓷土，英文中“kaolin”这个词就来自中文的“高岭”。在涂上一层用长石矿物制成的釉质之后，再用高温烧制。原料的配比必须精准，而烧制的温度和时间也要把握得非常精确。欧洲的陶瓷工匠在成功制作出瓷器之前，估计耗费了几百年的时间，尝试了数千种配方。而当时欧洲的瓷器依然还是一种“幼陶器”，不如中国瓷器精美和耐用，因此中国出产的瓷器直到两三百年前还主宰着国际市场。

♪**现场**（陶瓷博物馆）———

潘维廉：你知道吗，小包，我到过德化五次了，还是第一次听说这里有个陶瓷博物馆！

包东宇：这个博物馆展示了许多古瓷精品呢。

潘维廉：这些瓷器是从哪里来的?

包东宇：这些瓷器是从迄今为止最大的一次水下考古发现中打捞出来的。

潘维廉：哦，我听说过。1999 年，人们从一艘沉船中打捞出 35 万件销往东南亚的青花古瓷。我敢说我妻子也想弄两件使使。

♪**解说**———

当欧洲的陶瓷工艺正在不断改进的时候，中国的明朝朝廷关闭了对外贸易的大门，德化随之没落了。然而，今天这座古老的瓷都再次焕发了青春，成为中国陶瓷主产区之一。德化现代化的瓷厂不但生产传统的瓷器产品，还在不断开发新的花色品种，以及研究新材料和新功能。如今，他们能够根据订单生产各式各样的产品，精美的德化陶瓷已经远销世界各地。

♪**现场**（瓷雕作坊）———

潘维廉：我妻子如果看到工厂里的这些瓷器，她一定想好好地挑选一番。

包东宇：那她肯定会喜欢德化的陶瓷街。

潘维廉：什么，用陶瓷做成的街道吗?

包东宇：当然不是！那是一条布满瓷器商店的街道。

潘维廉：好，我们这就去看看吧。不过可别告诉我妻子，不然我就要请求厦门大学给我涨工资了。

Fortunately, Dehua porcelain is not only high quality but also reasonably priced, so when I've brought foreign visitors to Dehua, they've invariably left with boxes of delicate Dehua dinnerware, porcelain figurines, or elegant vases, in both traditional and modern styles. Luckily, I have a large van, but for those without wheels, Dehua shops are happy to ship their products to customers' homes, whether in China or abroad.

Monkeying Around

Dialogue—Bill Buys a Bird

Bill: This is the Xiamen symbol. I like it. Nice bird.

Bobby: The bird…or the …

Bill: The bird. I won't say the girl. My wife would kill me. I want to buy one of these but my wife won't let me…but she's not here—

Bobby: You can buy one.

Bill: So don't tell her. I'll buy one, and put it in my office.

解说

德化瓷器不仅质量好，价格也适中。我每次带外国客人来德化，他们都会大盒小盒地带走各种精美的德化瓷器，从餐具，瓷雕，到雅致的花瓶，有传统花色的，也有现代风格的。幸好我有一辆面包车，能装不少东西。不能亲自来德化也没关系，不论是在中国内地还是海外，德化的许多商家都乐意提供送货上门的服务。

现场

潘维廉：这个是厦门的标志！
包东宇：哦，白鹭女神雕像。
潘维廉：很漂亮，对吧？我喜欢。
包东宇：喜欢鸟呢，还是……？
潘维廉：当然是鸟儿，不是那个女孩！上次我就想买一个，可我妻子不让。这次她不在，我偷偷买一个放在办公室怎么样？
包东宇：赶紧啊！
……
潘维廉：这个好！（付款）谢谢！

Porcelain Street
Where budgets go to pot

Episode 58 A Yen[1] for Yongtai

Introduction On today's episode of Magic Fujian, FJTV's Bobby Bao and Xiamen University MBA Center's Dr. Bill Brown explore one of Fujian's most enchanting natural wonderlands—Yongtai.

It's hard to believe I never even heard of Yongtai until about 5 years ago [1999] because Chinese have known about this beautiful county for ages. It was first settled by very lucky Stone Age dwellers, and then made an official county in 766 A.D. While hundreds of thousands of Chinese visit Yongtai annually, few foreigners knew about it because it was so remote, secreted away behind rows of towering mountains—but no longer! Thanks to new roads, Yongtai's gorges, high meadows and countless waterfalls are now only an hour's drive west of Fuzhou. So when an American businessman in Fuzhou claimed Yongtai was so beautiful that he spent every weekend in it, we drove there the very next day—and have had a yen for Yongtai ever since.

Dialogue—Getting High[2] on Yongtai

Bobby: Bill, did you know that Yongtai has at least 77 peaks that exceed 1,000 meters?

Bill: I can believe it. And you know what I really like here is the rivers and waterfalls.

Bobby: I do too. And especially their unusual names.

Bill: Like what?

Bobby: Like "Runny Nose Waterfall."

Bill: Remind me not to swim in that one!"

Last October, my wife and I rented a bus and invited over 50 foreigners to spend a weekend at the White Horse Hostel. And they too were spellbound by Yongtai's beauty. They especially enjoyed the six monkeys that clamor down from the cliffs each morning, but the favorite by far was the mountain roller coaster!

---

[1] Yen: yearning; to long for, to wish for

[2] High: high elevation; intoxicated (as with drugs, alcohol, or "intoxicated with beauty")

第 58 集　喜欢永泰

导语

在今天的系列报道“老外看福建”中，我们将和厦门大学的潘维廉教授一同去体验永泰的迷人风光。

解说

说来惭愧，五年前我才第一次听说永泰这个地方，而我的许多中国朋友早就认识这个风景迷人的小城了。早在石器时代，这块土地上就有人类居住，到公元 766 年，永泰正式置县。每年都有数万名来自中国各地的游客前来游览，可认识永泰的老外却很少，因为它地处深山，非常偏僻。现在不同了，新修的公路直铺到景区，从福州市区驱车西行，只要个把小时就能到达，美丽的峡谷、高山草场和瀑布群全都近在眼前。因此，当一位在福州的美国商人朋友向我宣称，他每个周末都到永泰度假欣赏美景后，我们一家第二天就开车去玩，并从此迷上了永泰。

现场

包东宇：你知道吗？永泰有 77 座山峰的海拔在一千米以上。

潘维廉：我相信。永泰这里是一山更比一山高。不过我对溪流和瀑布更着迷。

包东宇：我也是。我觉得有的瀑布的名字特别有趣，比如“鼻涕瀑布”。

潘维廉：呃，记得提醒我千万别在那下面游泳！

解说

去年十月份，我和我妻子租了一辆大巴，邀上50多位外国朋友到永泰青云山白马山庄度周末。他们也都对永泰的美景非常着迷。他们特别喜欢每天早晨从山崖上下来嬉戏的那六只猴子，不过最痴迷的还是这里的“峡谷过山车”。

Dialogue—Mountain Roller Coaster

Bobby: The General Manager of the White Horse Villa said this truck ride is the tourist's favorite activity.

Bill: I can believe that. When we brought over 50 foreign guests here a couple months ago, they said this was their favorite thing. They said it's like a mountain roller coaster.

Bobby: Okay then, let's roll![3]

Yongtai Roller Coaster

We rode on the back of the hostel's tourist trucks, which careened for 3 km, up and down and around the narrow road that ascends the deep valley. When the road ended, we walked the remaining 2 km along beautifully maintained paths to the White Horse Falls, with a few pit stops to visit other smaller falls and scenic views.

White Horse Falls is so spectacular that an American, James Sheeron, has invested over 1 million Yuan on its development, and will put a few million more into creating a 4 star world-class resort nearby.

Yongtai's most famous waterfalls complex is probably Qingyuan Mountain, just half a kilometer or so north of White Horse Hostel. This beautiful scenic region is also a haven for wildlife such as unusual insects, birds, butterflies, and animals such as a raccoon-like creature I photographed recently. Of course, Qingyun has plenty of snakes as well, though fortunately, they're more afraid of us than we are of them!

Dialogue—A Hot[4] Destination

Bill: Bobby, you know, waterfalls and rivers are fine, but this is winter, and I'm cold!

Bobby: Not to worry! Yongtai is also famous for its hot springs!

Bill: Well, I'm going to go soak in one.

Bobby: Well, you're always getting in hot water anyway!

Bill: Yeah, especially with you around!

Of Yongtai's 13 hot springs, our family's favorite is the mammoth hot springs swimming pool beside the downtown Hot Springs Hotel. Year round the pool stays at 98 degrees, thanks to steaming water gushing from 400 feet below ground. A good hot soak is the perfect way to cap a long day of hiking through valleys and high mountain meadows.

---

[3] Let's roll: let's go

[4] Hot: popular ("WTO reform is a hot topic nowadays")

现场

包东宇：白马山庄的总经理说，游客们最爱坐这种观光小卡车了。

潘维廉：上次我带 50 个老外来玩儿的时候，他们也这么说。这种游览车才叫真正的“翻滚过山车”。

包东宇：噢，那我们就来翻滚一次吧！

解说

我们坐在观光小卡车的背后，在三公里长的狭窄水泥路上左冲右突、上下翻腾，一路往深深的峡谷里飞驰。到了山间公路的尽头，我们又沿着林荫小道步行两公里，这才来到白马瀑布，其间还停下来看了几处比较小的瀑布和峡谷景点。

白马瀑布景色壮美。美国人詹姆斯·希尔隆投资了一百多万元人民币开发这个景区，他还将投入数百万元在附近建设一座四星级的度假村。

永泰最著名的瀑布群恐怕要数青云山的青龙瀑布了。青龙瀑布景区距离白马山庄以北约一里路程。这个景色宜人的地区也是各种野生动物的天堂，珍禽异兽和奇特的昆虫数不胜数。当然，青云山还有多种蛇类出没，不过别担心，我们怕蛇，蛇更怕我们。

现场

潘维廉：这里的溪水和瀑布在夏天的时候特别漂亮，不过现在是冬天，我觉得好冷！

包东宇：别担心，永泰的温泉也很有名呢！

潘维廉：那我们去泡个热水澡吧。

包东宇：好吧，反正你也不怕开水烫！哈哈……

Yongtai Hot Springs Pool

解说

永泰有13处温泉，我们一家最喜欢的是城关温泉宾馆旁的那个温泉游泳池。温泉从地下400英尺深的地方不断喷涌而出，保证了游泳池的水温常年保持在40℃左右。好好泡个温泉澡，是在山岭之间徒步穿越一整天之后消除疲劳的最好方式。

Laowai Hike Beautiful Yongtai Valley

While Yongtai is most famous for natural beauty, it also has well over 100 historical and cultural relics. Two of the most popular attractions are the Yuan Dynasty Mo' Ai cliff inscriptions and the Fangguang Palace, which is a cliff-side Buddhist temple that reminds me somewhat of ancient Indian cliff dwellings in the Southwestern United States. Yongtai is also famous for many modern traditions—like Chinese martial arts.

The little city of Yongtai, I learned, has over 30 martial arts stadiums, and over 60,000 people practice the art! In addition, locals enjoy performances of Southern Chinese Opera, folk dances on stilts, dragon dances and lion dances, and even dragon boat races.

Today, Yongtai is attracting not just tourists but investors as well. The refurbished White Horse Villa, for example, is owned by an American, and over 30 foreign enterprises have gone into production in agricultural products, foodstuffs like candied fruits, clothing, tourism, etc. In addition, the county is rich in such resources as gold, silver, and copper.

With such vast reserves of lumber, it's not surprise that locals have developed a knack for producing and exporting beautiful wooden handicrafts—or beautiful bamboo and wicker ware like that at Ms. Song's factory, which exports 100% of its products.

Yongtai's no longer a secret, for either foreigners or Chinese. So now that the secret's out, give it a visit, and like me, you'll probably wish you could hang your hat there!

永泰不但以其自然美景远近闻名，这里还有着上百处文物古迹。最有名的两处古迹分别是元代的名山室摩崖石刻和方广岩胜景。方广岩是建于悬崖中央岩洞中的佛寺，这让我想起美国西南部悬崖上的印第安人古建筑。永泰还有不少优良传统，比如说武术就很出名。

我听说永泰这个小县城至少有 30 间武馆，有六万多人习武。此外，当地人还经常举办地方戏表演，逢年过节还有踩高跷、舞龙、舞狮以及龙舟赛等活动。

Shannon learns to fly!

今天的永泰不但游客纷至沓来，也越来越受到投资者的青睐。比如这崭新的白马山庄就是一位美商的产业，全县还有 30 多家外商投资企业已经投入运营，涉及农产品、食品、服装、旅游等多个领域。除此之外，永泰县金、银、铜等矿产的储量都很丰富，森林资源更是首屈一指。当地的木雕、竹器等手工艺品是热门的出口产品，像宋女士这家工厂生产的竹藤制品和草编工艺品就是 100% 出口。

如今，对老外或者老内来说，永泰都已经不再神秘。既然如此，那何不到此一游呢？你一定会像我一样流连忘返的。

Episode 59　Fuzhou's Colonial Architecture

Introduction　On today's episode of Magic Fujian, join FJTV's Bobby Bao and Xiamen University's Dr. Bill Brown as they explore Fuzhou's 19th and 20th century Western colonial architecture—and how it is being used today!

In the mid 1800s, many of the majestic Yankee tea clippers that sailed between China and New York, San Francisco, and London, set sail from the exotic port of Fuzhou—or Foochow, as foreigners called it. Their port of departure was Pagoda Anchorage, which lies at the mouth of the Min River, and was the first place of residence for Western consular officers. But it was a lonely post, and several actually went crazy! So their governments requested permission for foreigners to move into the city of Fuzhou itself.

Dialogue—Foreign Devil Neighbors

Bobby: I don't think Fuzhou people were thrilled with having Laowai as neighbors.

Bill: But it was kind of understandable. It was bad enough having opium forced on them at gunpoint, without having drug traffickers living side-by-side with them.

Bobby: Of course, not all foreigners sold opium.

Bill: Yeah, but those who didn't did not do very much to stop those that did. Otherwise, the drug trade would not have lasted for a whole century.

After much cajoling[1] and pressure, Fuzhou officials finally gave in, and chose Nantai Island to become the foreign settlement. Chinese didn't care to live there anyway because they thought it was haunted. But Foreign Devils and Chinese ghosts evidently got along well because foreigners prospered on Cangshan, which was eventually graced with mansions, churches, a rotary club, and consulates for many countries, including Britain, Spain, France, America, etc.

On the hill behind the former U.S. consulate, beside where the British consulate once stood, is the former Rotary Club, though it is hard to imagine the now dilapidated building was once the setting for high society.

Dialogue—Bygone Era

Bill: This beautiful building here used to be the Rotary Club, and right next to it over here was the British consulate. It was a magnificent building, but it was torn down to build this retirement center for PLA officers.

Bobby: That's true, but there are still many beautiful examples of Western architecture scattered around Fuzhou. Let me show you some.

Bill: Ok. Then we should start with the U.S. consulate, since I'm an American.

---

[1] Cajoling: urging repeatedly, often with flattery; wheedling; pleading, (almost "begging")

第 59 集　福州：殖民时代的老建筑

导语

Former British Consulate

在今天的系列报道“老外看福建”中，厦门大学的潘维廉教授将和我们的记者包东宇一起，探访福州仓山的西方殖民时代建筑，看一看它们今天被人们利用的情况。

解说

19 世纪中叶，许多庞大的运茶帆船往来于中国和纽约、旧金山、伦敦这些地方，它们起始的港口就是福州。当时福州被外国人称为“Foochow”，船只出发的港口就位于闽江口的马尾罗星塔下。这里还是西方国家领事官员最早的驻扎地。不过当时马尾太过冷清，一些外国官员实在受不了，因此这些国家就提出允许外国人住进福州市区。

现场（马尾罗星塔公园）

包东宇：我觉得福州人对跟老外做邻居并不感到很兴奋。

潘维廉：这也难怪。本来在枪口之下接受鸦片贸易就已经很糟糕了，再跟毒品贩子做邻居就更难为他们了。

包东宇：当然，并不是所有外国人都贩卖鸦片。

潘维廉：没错。不过那些不卖鸦片的也并没有阻止那些卖的。不然的话，鸦片贸易也不会持续整整一个世纪。

解说

在一番威逼利诱之下，清政府的官员妥协了，他们把南台岛指定为外国人居住区。中国居民似乎对此并不在乎，因为据说那里本来就闹鬼。不过看起来“外国鬼子”跟中国鬼魂相处得还不错，因为住在仓山的外国人越来越多，仓山也出现了许多漂亮的洋楼、教堂，还有一个“扶轮社”，以及美国、意大利、荷兰等十多个国家的领事馆。

在旧美国领事馆后面的山顶上，从前的扶轮社大楼曾经跟英国领事馆相邻而立，可这个一度名流云集的建筑如今已经显得相当破败。

现场（前扶轮社大楼前）

潘维廉：这就是以前的扶轮国际社，那边是前英国领事馆的馆址，以前那座建筑非常精美，可惜后来被拆掉，改成了现在的省军区干休所。

包东宇：是啊，不过现在福州还保存着不少漂亮的西方建筑。我带你去看看。

潘维廉：好啊。我是美国人，先去看看以前的美国领事馆怎么样？

Bobby: Good idea. And maybe you can check out a book or two, because now it's a library!

Bill: Maybe I'll get educated yet.

The former U.S. consulate is indeed now a library—in a nursing school. And it appeared the students are nursing hopes of visiting America.

Trinity College One of the most beautiful places used to be the Fuzhou Trinity College, which was modeled after the original in Dublin, Ireland, but most of its old buildings are torn down and replaced by a modern school. All that is left standing is the Irish church bell. But just across the bell is the former Russian consulate, which was recently renovated, thanks to donations by locals. And to the north of the Russian consulate is a large old brick church, though it is now being used to store paint. But up the hill, there is also a beautiful stone church storing nothing but quietness.

Dialogue—The Old Stone Church

Bill: You know, this stone church I think is one of the most beautiful examples of western architecture in all of China. It looks like it was transplanted right out of Ireland. But it has deteriorated a lot just in the past year.

Bobby: The sign out front says it's a protected cultural relic, but I don't think it's a church now.

Bill: No, it's a printing press for the army now. And I doubt they're printing bibles!

The stone church's belfry was damaged during the Cultural Revolution, but now that the building is a historical site, I hope to see it restored to its former beauty someday. Just down the hill from the stone church is the former Anglo-Chinese school, from which graduated many Chinese politicians, intellectuals, academicians, and scientists. The church has been beautifully restored—though now it's a gymnasium.

The former Hua Nan School for Women is also an imposing structure. It was used as a cheap hotel until the 1990s, but today it is being put to good use as the Fujian Normal University's Institute of Geography.

The Westerners who a century ago built these magnificent structures would have never imagined the uses to which they were eventually put! But I appreciate the irony of the fate of the French consulate. Which just goes to show what I've suspected all along—that the Chinese' greatest virtue is patience!

包东宇：好主意。你还可以在那里找两本书看看，因为它现在是一间图书馆！

潘维廉：看来我还能在那里学点儿东西。

♪解说

以前的美国领事馆现在果然是一个图书馆，就在福州卫生学校里。福州三一学院是建筑物最精美的地方之一。这个学校是按照爱尔兰的都柏林三一学院建造的，现在叫福州外国语学校，可如今，大多数老建筑已经被拆除，换成了现代化的校舍。唯一剩下的原始建筑就是这座爱尔兰式的钟楼。离钟楼不远的地方是原来的俄国领事馆。多亏有校友的捐款，这座房子最近刚刚翻新了一遍。俄国领事馆北边不远有一座挺大的老式红砖教堂，不过现在已经被用来存放油漆和涂料。在山顶上还有一座漂亮的石头教堂，现在空置着。

Former Trinity Tower

♪现场（石头教堂）

潘维廉：我觉得这个石头教堂是中国最漂亮的外国建筑之一，看上去就像是直接从爱尔兰搬过来的。

包东宇：外面的石碑上说这是一处文物保护单位，不过这里现在好像已经不是教堂了。

潘维廉：这是现在是一家印刷厂，不过，我想他们不印圣经吧。

♪解说

这座教堂的钟楼在“文革”期间被毁坏了，不过既然这是文物保护单位，我希望有一天它能恢复原貌。从石头教堂往山坡下走一小段路就是英华外语学校，这里曾经培养了许多有名的官员、文人、院士和科学家。校园里有一座修整一新的教堂，不过它现在其实是一间体育馆。

以前的华南女子学院里也有一座宏伟的建筑。直到上个世纪 90 年代那里还是一个小招待所，现在成了福建师范大学的地理科学学院。

一个世纪以前建造这些宏伟建筑的西方人绝对想象不到它们今天的命运。原法国领事馆的变迁就很有趣。1884 年，法国舰队发动突然袭击，摧毁了停泊在马尾的福建水师。而一个多世纪后的今天，法国领事馆成了中国海军的一处营地！这也印证了一个我一直以来的观点——中国人特别有耐心！

Episode 60 The Fujian of the Future!

Introduction Over recent weeks we've explored the Fujian of the past and present. Today, Xiamen University's Dr. Bill Brown, together with FJTV's Bobby Bao, venture into the Fujian of the Future!

Fujian is China's most fascinating province, with endless mountains harboring unparalleled biological diversity and natural wonders, and long isolated villages with unique customs and traditions, as well as China's largest number of dialects. But most importantly to an MBA professor like myself, Fujianese have for over 2,000 years been an entrepreneurial and adventurous people—and their future promises to be even greater than their past!

Dialogue—Strategic Fujian

Bobby: Bill, why do you think Fujian has such a great future?

Bill: Well, I think Fujian is very strategic geographically, politically, and economically.

Bobby: Now you sound like you're teaching MBA!

Bill: For the past 15 years, Fujianese have taught me a lot more than I taught them.

Bobby: Really? Then it's a good thing they didn't charge you tuition!

Shaxian High Schoolers Learn Rocketry

Fujian is geographically strategic because she lies halfway between Hong Kong and Shanghai, and faces Taiwan province, and Fujian has some of the planet's best natural deep water harbors. A century ago, Sun Yat-sen envisioned an "Oriental Mega-Port" in Xiamen, but Fujian has the potential for half a dozen such ports up and down the entire coast!

Fujian is also politically strategic because she is home to most Overseas Chinese, who are China's ambassadors to the world. In addition, Fujian faces Taiwan Province, and ¾ of Taiwanese are from Fujian! In the mid 1970s, I thought I was "protecting" Taiwan when I served there for two years in the US Air Force. Now I understand that Taiwan's future peace and prosperity hinges on peaceful reunification with the mainland because, after all, both sides are one family.

第60集 未来福建

导语

一个月来，在系列报道“老外看福建”中，我们浏览了福建的历史和今天，在今天的最后一期节目中，厦门大学的潘维廉教授将和我们一起展望福建的未来。

解说

福建是中国最迷人的省份之一，连绵不绝的大山中蕴藏着无与伦比的生物多样性和自然奇观，深藏在山谷里的村落保留着独特的民俗传统，以及中国最多样的方言语种。对于我这样一个 MBA 教授来说，比山海奇观更为重要的是，福建人两千多年来一直秉承着勤劳创业的精神。福建的未来一定比过去更加辉煌。

现场（闽江江畔）

包东宇：你为什么对福建的未来那么有信心呢？

潘维廉：因为无论从地理、人文还是经济角度来看，福建都具有重要的战略地位。

包东宇：你听起来就像在上 MBA 课程！

潘维廉：实际上，这 15 年来，我从福建人身上学到的东西比我传授的要丰富得多。

包东宇：是吗？没向你收学费就不错了！

解说

福建的地理位置重要，这是因为她介于香港和上海之间，与台湾隔海相望，并且拥有一些世界上最好的天然深水良港。上个世纪之初，孙中山就曾经设想，在厦门建设一个“东方超级大港”，其实，在整个福建沿海，完全有条件建设好几个这样的大型港口。

福建在人文上也有重大影响，这是因为她是遍布世界各地的海外华侨最大的祖籍地之一。此外，在海峡对岸的台湾，有四分之三的人口祖籍在福建。上个世纪70年代中期，当我在台湾的美国空军基地服役的时候，我以为自己是在“保护”台湾。现在我才明白，台湾未来的和平与繁荣，关键在于与大陆的和平统一，毕竟，两岸本来就是一家人。

Dialogue—Fujian Provincial Sci-tech Hall

Bobby: How do you think Fujian will most influence China's future?

Bill: I think the greatest influence will be cultural.

Bobby: But Fujian is not really considered a great social or cultural center.

Bill: On the contrary—the Fujianese have long been known for their unique ability to balance both commerce and culture and education!

Fuzhou not only began China's maritime industry over 2000 years ago, but also has China's first public library. And like their ancestors, modern Fujianese are keen entrepreneurs who maintain balance culturally, spiritually—and even physically!

From his college years, when he wrote a paper on physical education, Mao Zedong emphasized that health is fundamental to wealth. Unfortunately, as Chinese become wealthier, too many are becoming like Westerners, who are too busy to eat properly or to exercise, and are now dying of diseases unknown to so-called poor folks! While wealth is fine, as the old saying goes, "You can't take it with you!" Too many Chinese will follow America's poor example unless they heed people like Xiamen's Zhang Ke, who is known as Ray to foreign friends.

Dialogue—At a Xiamen Health Club

Bill: Most people think its' kind of strange that Ray gave up a career in international business to become a personal fitness trainer!

Bobby: Doesn't seem like there is much of a future in this.

Bill: Well, that's what I said, but Ray said that, you know, he's making his own future, because this is a new field in China.

Bobby: Yes, and an important field in China. Even Chairman Mao emphasized healthy bodies as well as healthy minds.

Zhangke (Ray)

Zhang Ke dismayed friends and relatives by becoming a personal fitness trainer after graduating from Fuzhou University, but he said, "University wasn't wasted. It gave me the foundation to develop my personal philosophy of training, and of life."

Over the years, Ray has adapted what he's learned from Chinese and foreign experts to develop his own personal training techniques and philosophy. While his ideas have yet to catch on, he notes that Americans also took a long time to fully appreciate fitness training, and he expects that as Chinese get wealthier—and fatter!—they too will have to face what Mao Zedong said all along—that health is the foundation of wealth.

Fujianese are also expanding their intellects and horizons by embracing future technology with a passion, as I saw when I toured Xiamen's Cyber-Mart's Digital Family's Home. But in many ways, this futuristic home already exists.

现场（福建省科技馆外）———

包东宇：你认为福建对未来中国的影响主要体现在哪里？

潘维廉：福建最大的贡献也许在文化方面。

包东宇：可福建好像并不是一个影响力很大的文化中心啊。

潘维廉：恰恰相反——勤勉的福建人一向以善于协调经商与文教而闻名。

解说 ———

福州不仅是中国近代造船业的发祥地，还拥有中国最早的公共图书馆之一。和他们先辈一样，现代的福建人在艰苦创业的同时，也非常重视文化熏陶、精神修养，乃至体育锻炼。

毛泽东早年在湖南第一师范学校读书的时候，曾经写过一篇《体育之研究》的论文，强调健康的体魄是强国富民的根本。遗憾的是，随着中国一步步走向富裕，许多国人都变得像当年的西方人一样，因为太过忙碌而忽视了合理的饮食和锻炼，从而患上了这样那样的所谓“富贵病”。赚钱当然没错，不过老话讲得好：“生不带来死不带去。”现在有太多的中国人正在模仿美国人的坏榜样，幸好，像厦门的张柯这样的健身爱好者也越来越多了，外国朋友都管张柯叫“Ray”。

现场（厦门健身俱乐部）———

潘维廉：不少人都不理解，为什么张柯放弃了所学的国际贸易专业，改行当起了私人健身教练。

包东宇：你不觉得这也很有前瞻性么？

潘维廉：没错。张柯说，健身在中国还是新事物，他要为自己开创一片新天地。

包东宇：是啊，毛主席他老人家早就教导我们要锻炼身体，增强体质……

解说 ———

张柯当年从福州大学国际贸易专业毕业后当起了健身教练，他的家人和朋友对此都很失望。不过张柯却说：“大学的时光并没有浪费，我正是在大学中为自己的训练理论和未来的人生打下了基础。”

几年下来，张柯把他从中外健身专家那里学到的知识融会贯通，逐渐形成了自己的训练体系和技巧。他的观念对许多人来说还有些超前，毕竟，美国人也是花了很长一段时间才逐渐接受健身训练的。张柯说，等到中国人更富裕一些的时候，肥胖问题肯定会越发突出，大家就会对毛主席“身体是革命本钱”的教导更有切身体会了。

而当我前往厦门赛博数码广场参加数字家庭的演示活动时，我又发现，福建人正在以极大的热情，迎接未来科技带来的新天地。其实在很多方面，这个虚拟的未来家庭已经在现实生活中得到了体现。

My, how things have changed since we arrived in Xiamen in 1988—when we not only did not have computers but also often lacked electricity as well! Back then, my first telephone cost 4,500 Yuan and a 3 year wait! Today, in many areas of technology, Chinese are ahead of the West!

Affordable services meant my Chinese students had cell phones before they were common in America, even in business circles. The same goes for internet, which is costly in America, but can be accessed anywhere in China, even without an internet account, simply by dialing 16300. When I shared this fact with some Americans, one said, "America should be learning from China!"

Dialogue—in a Computer Classroom

Bobby: Sounds like Fujian has an exciting future. But is there any trend you regret?

Bill: There's one thing I really regret, and that is the rest of the world understands China a lot less than China understands the world—and we Fujianese aren't doing enough to remedy this.

While information technology has opened Chinese' eyes to the world, the rest of the planet has failed to use that same technology to better understand China. No wonder some people think China has changed little since the Cultural Revolution, or misunderstand the Taiwan issue. These misunderstandings have resulted both from misinformation abroad and from the lack of adequate information from China. Fortunately, things are improving.

Chinese articles and TV programming are improving in both quantity and quality, and each year, hundreds of thousands of foreign tourists leave China with opened eyes, minds, and hearts. But much still needs to be done—especially in Fujian. Of the tens of thousands of foreign books on China, only a handful are about Fujian, and the typical foreigner has no idea if Fujian lies next to Taiwan or Tibet! It's up to us Fujianese to remedy this. That's why I've spent much time and money writing articles, and books like *Amoy Magic*, *Mystic Quanzhou*, and the *Fujian Adventure*. And that's why I feel so thankful, and honored, to have been allowed to help with FJTV's *Magic Fujian*! I hope this program helps people to truly see the Magic of my adopted home, Fujian!

Dialogue—Lots of Homework!

Bobby: Nice lesson, Professor Bill. Anything else?

Bill: Oh, no—not for now. Class Dismissed. But you have plenty of homework!

Bobby: I thought homework ended when I graduated from university?

Bill: We're never finished learning or teaching—at least not in this life!

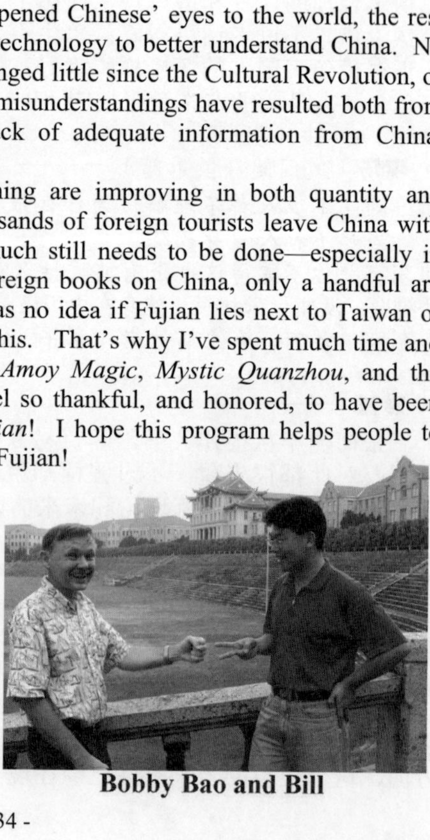

Bobby Bao and Bill

天哪，跟 1988 年我们刚来厦门的时候相比，变化可真大！要知道，当时我们非但没有电脑，甚至还经常缺电。那个时候，我们家花了 4500 元钱才装上第一部电话，而且还等了三年！现在，在不少技术领域，中国已经领先于西方了。

我的学生们很早就用上了便宜的手机服务，当时甚至在美国的商业圈内手机都还没有普及。互联网服务也是这样，美国的网络费用很高，然而在中国，无论你身在何处，就算没有网络账户，只要用电话拨叫 16300 就可以上网。当我把这种情况告诉一些美国朋友的时候，一个朋友说："看来美国要向中国学习了！"

♪**现场**（电脑教室）——

包东宇：听起来福建的未来很不错。那你觉得有没有不足的地方呢？

潘维廉：我只有一个遗憾，那就是世界了解中国的程度，要远远低于中国认识世界的程度，而我们福建人为消除这种隔阂所做的工作还很不够。

♪**解说**——

正当现代资讯科技大大开阔中国人眼界的时候，世界的其他地方却没能充分运用同样的方式来更好地理解中国。正因为如此，还有不少人认为"文革"之后中国没有多少改变，或者对台湾问题存在误解。这些误解的产生，一方面是由于海外舆论的误导，另一方面则是因为缺乏来自中国的正确信息。可喜的是，情况正在得到改善。

中国的报刊和电视节目越来越丰富，质量也在不断提高。每年还有成千上万的外国游客来到中国，增长了见识，更新了观念。不过，需要做的工作还很多，对福建来说尤其如此。在数以万计有关中国的外文书籍中，只有屈指可数的几种是介绍福建的。一般的外国人甚至不知道福建是与台湾相邻，还是在西藏旁边。我们福建人正是要改变这种状况。正因为如此，我才花费大量的时间和财力撰写文章，出版像《魅力厦门》、《魅力泉州》和《魅力福建》这样的书籍。也正因为如此，我很高兴能参与福建电视台"老外看福建"系列报道的拍摄，并深感荣幸！我希望这个节目能够对人们领略我的第二故乡福建的魅力有所帮助！

♪**现场**——

包东宇：您给我上了一课，潘教授。还有吗？

潘维廉：先说到这儿，可以下课了。不过有很多家庭作业要做！

包东宇：我还以为大学毕业以后就可以不用再做作业了呢！

潘维廉：学无止境啊——至少我们这辈子不能停止学习或者传授！

图书在版编目(CIP)数据

老外看福建/(美)潘维廉著;潘文功等译. —厦门:厦门大学出版社,2005.5(2019.2 重印)
(魅力·老潘)
ISBN 978-7-5615-2377-7

Ⅰ.①老… Ⅱ.①潘…②潘… Ⅲ.①福建省—概况—英文
Ⅳ.①K925.73

中国版本图书馆 CIP 数据核字(2005)第 042737 号

出 版 人 郑文礼
责任编辑 施高翔

出版发行 厦门大学出版社
社　　址 厦门市软件园二期望海路 39 号
邮政编码 361008
总 编 办 0592-2182177 0592-2181406(传真)
营销中心 0592-2184458 0592-2181365
网　　址 http://www.xmupress.com
邮　　箱 xmup@xmupress.com
印　　刷 厦门集大印刷厂

开本 880 mm×1 230 mm 1/32
印张 11
插页 6
字数 380 千字
版次 2005 年 6 月第 1 版
印次 2019 年 2 月第 2 次印刷
定价 30.00 元

本书如有印装质量问题请直接寄承印厂调换

厦门大学出版社
微信二维码

厦门大学出版社
微博二维码